WHAT THE NATION REALLY NEEDS TO KNOW

What the Nation Really Needs to Know

The JNU Nationalism Lectures

Edited by
Rohit Azad, Janaki Nair,
Mohinder Singh, Mallarika Sinha Roy

on behalf of
Jawaharlal Nehru University
Teachers' Association

HarperCollins *Publishers* India

First published in India in 2016 by
HarperCollins *Publishers* India
HarperCollins *Publishers* India, Cyber City, Building 10-A, Gurugram, Haryana – 122002, India
www.harpercollins.co.in

1 2 3 4 5 6 7 8 9 10

P-ISBN: 978-93-5264-025-6
E-ISBN: 978-93-5264-026-3

Typeset in 10.5/13.5 Adobe Caslon Pro and 11.5/14.3 Kruti Dev 010
By Saanvi Graphics Noida

Printed and bound at
Repro India Ltd.

HarperCollins *Publishers*, Macken House, 39/40 Mayor Street Upper, Dublin 1, D01 C9W8, Ireland

Contents

Acknowledgements

ON 12 FEBRUARY 2016, THE ELECTED president of the Jawaharlal Nehru University Students' Union (JNUSU), Kanhaiya Kumar, was picked up by the police from the campus. The arrest of two more students followed. During the three weeks that the arrested students, including Kanhaiya Kumar, remained in jail before securing bail, the JNUSU president, teachers and media persons faced physical attacks and intimidation at the court premises, even in the presence of the police.

All this was perpetuated in the name of 'nationalism'. Some television channels and print media aroused passions by pronouncing judgments against students, faculty and even branded the university as 'anti-national'. With law enforcement agencies remaining mute spectators, teachers were assaulted in different parts of the country by those who had reduced nationalism to sloganeering and to the exclusion of many groups on the basis of identity. The JNU Teachers' Association (JNUTA) resisted this orchestrated assault on the university and the very idea of critical and independent thinking. The campaign to 'Save JNU' was led and supported by JNU alumni that included many eminent politicians, bureaucrats, police officers, journalists, writers and intellectuals in India and abroad. Hundreds of academicians and institutions from within and outside the country sent letters of support to JNUTA and organized protests in their campuses in defence of free speech and liberal values.

With each passing day, more and more citizens came out to 'Stand with JNU' to defend the 'freedom of expression' and 'autonomy of academic institutions'. These two became the rallying points for the protest movement that continues in one or another form.

The protest in JNU was also unique in the way it went beyond rallies, dharnas and hunger strikes. It demonstrated a strong cultural and intellectual component. The JNUTA decided to organize lectures on various perspectives on nationalism and on different meanings of freedom to defend the heterogeneous intellectual tradition that is today under threat. Hundreds of students and teachers from different disciplines gathered in the evening at the protest site, called Freedom Square, to listen to scientists, philosophers and social scientists speaking on issues of nationalism, academic autonomy and freedom of speech.

The credit for sustaining the protests and organizing different activities including the lecture series goes to the teacher colleagues who were always ready to volunteer for any activity that was planned. The JNUTA was successful in carrying forward most of its decisions during this period due to the untiring efforts of its executive committee members and other teachers who stood by the association during a very critical juncture. Their participation in each and every event went into the making of this strong protest movement.

Prof. Janaki Nair, Dr Rohit Azad, Dr Rajarshi Dasgupta, Dr Joy Pachuau, Dr Mohinder Singh and Dr Mallarika Sinha Roy were part of the team that organized the 'Nationalism Lecture Series' and deserve special mention. We would like to thank Samim Asgor Ali, Gayatri Balusha, K. Fayaz Ahmad and Sorit Gupto (*Down to Earth*) for the images. A word of thanks to Rahel Philipose for her work in transcribing the lectures. And Kartikey Singh of Jamia Millia Islamia for the 'Rose Fist' on the spine, painted as part of a mural on the JNU Administration Building during the hunger strike. Dr Nupur Chowdhury, Dr Navaneetha Mokkil, Dr Veena Hariharan, Dr Urmimala Sarkar, Prof. Ranjani Mazumdar, Prof. Shukla Sawant, and Prof. Bishnupriya Dutt helped in various ways to bring this book together. A heartfelt thanks to all those who have contributed their time and effort in turning these lectures into a publishable form. We would also like to place on record our special thanks to HarperCollins for having come forward to publish the book. Through this, we hope to reach a wider audience and make this effort really worthwhile.

Ajay Patnaik
President, JNUTA

Bikramaditya K. Choudhary
Secretary, JNUTA

Introduction: A Teach-in for a JNU Spring[1]

Janaki Nair

IN FEBRUARY 2016, ONE OF INDIA'S foremost public universities, Jawaharlal Nehru University, became the site of a series of events which posed a serious challenge to collective institutional life as we had known it. It also led to a most impressive and sustained period of student–teacher solidarity in defence of the public research university as a crucial space of dissent and debate.

Many signs of a concerted attack on public educational institutions were blowing in the wind from all corners of the country for at least six months previously: from Indian Institute of Technology (IIT), Chennai; Film and Television Institute of India (FTII), Pune; Jadavpur University, Kolkata; Allahabad University, Uttar Pradesh; and in the sudden end to non-NET fellowships by the University Grants Commission (UGC). Spirited and creative responses and protests followed: the 'Occupy UGC!' movement and the 139-day strike at FTII met with partial success. A most chilling tragedy that occurred at Hyderabad Central University on 17 January 2016 became the tipping point: Rohith Vemula's desperate suicide brought to the forefront the contradictory achievements of the public university in ensuring the 'politics of presence', in this case, of Dalit students. It also shone the light on the massive failures of higher educational institutions in making provisions to enable and sustain first-generation, seriously underprivileged, students. But the heart-breaking eloquence of the suicide note stunned India into a recognition of injustice, and rallied them to the demand for equality.

On 12 February 2016, Jawaharlal Nehru University Students' Union (JNUSU) president, Kanhaiya Kumar, was arrested under Section 124A of the Indian Penal Code on charges of sedition, and similar charges were imposed on other JNU students for their organization of, and participation in, an evening of poetry, speeches, talks and song on campus on 9 February 2016 related to the execution of Afzal Guru in 2013. The event, for which permission was withdrawn at the last minute, became contentious due to allegations – as yet unattributed to the specific students concerned – of two controversial slogans that were raised at the meeting. The quick and inflammatory role of the televisual and social media, the significantly mendacious political interventions, and the disproportionate energies expended in Parliament, soon called the loyalties of the entire teaching and student body at JNU into question. Indeed, there was an unprovoked physical attack by some lawyers on JNU teachers who were present in the courtroom at Patiala House where Kanhaiya Kumar was to be produced for his first hearing on 15 February 2016, and highly publicized physical attacks by some lawyers on Kanhaiya Kumar himself within the court premises followed.

The JNU Teachers' Association (JNUTA) took a principled position against the violence that was unleashed, and what they believed was an unfair, unprecedented and unduly harsh treatment of student activists, by the state, by many sections of the media, and by the JNU administration.

Why a Teach-In?

Who or what is 'anti-national'?

Soon after 9 February 2016, the country was turned into a choric chamber in which the accusation of 'anti-nationalism' was repeatedly echoed, a pejorative attribute which attached itself to the whole JNU community. It produced great political and intellectual disquiet among the JNU community of students and teachers. But an extraordinarily creative repertoire of protests – talks, music, theatre, artwork, photographs, cartoons – organized by the JNUSU, swiftly followed. They transformed the grand steps and adjoining spaces in front of JNU's Administrative Block into a 'Freedom Square'. The JNUTA's decision to stand with the cause of democratic thinking and justice added to the energetic creativity that was already on display.

The JNUTA began a dignified answer to the shrill public campaign by turning the accusation into a question to be seriously addressed. The teach-in, entitled 'What the Nation Really Needs to Know: India, the Nation and Nationalism', was conceived. The lectures, which began on 17 February 2016, were focused on the meanings, histories and experience of nationalism, and its unresolved dilemmas, both within and beyond India. The teach-in was initially to last a week; the response was so enthusiastic that it was extended to two weeks, and finally ended only a month later on 17 March 2016. For two more weeks, an equally riveting series on 'Azadi – Many Meanings of Freedom' was organized at the same site.

The teach-in lectures, which usually began at 5 p.m., were originally intended for members of the JNU community, and were to be delivered principally by JNU teachers. In the end, many other teachers and public intellectuals from across Delhi and other parts of the country participated in and delivered lectures in the series. The series soon gained unanticipated audiences across India and in international forums. Reports and translations of the lectures in many Indian languages, the live-streaming of some of the teach-ins, and the discussions and collective viewings of the teach-ins in other parts of the country and the world made for a reach that echoed well beyond the Freedom Square in JNU, the space of this intellectual and political occupation.

Twenty-four lectures were delivered in this series, which was attended by hundreds of JNU teachers and students as well as a large section of the general public. It was entirely appropriate that some of the lectures were in Hindi, the language best understood locally. The lectures were not only a public demonstration of what JNU teachers did best, i.e., lecture, but also decisively proved that the potentially most dangerous activity that happens at public universities like JNU is *thinking*. The JNUSU and the JNUTA collectively demonstrated a commitment to a culture of learning and intellectual engagement. On display to the people of this nation, and the world at large, was not just the historic unity of teachers and students. The lectures also became an important demonstration of the crucial role played by the university in helping people to connect data, rethink information, and indeed, respond to misinformation in this age of digital information glut. Above all, the teach-in demonstrated that we at JNU value debate, discussion and dissent, in the best spirit of the freedom of speech, while equally demonstrating the importance of cordial, civil and respectful ways of listening, as part of our commitment to the right to be heard.

In spite of the politically charged atmosphere, and the frequent public rallies in which JNU teachers and students participated, there was the committed return of a steady audience to the Freedom Square for each lecture. Also, the format itself allowed for a brief question-answer session, in which members of the audience engaged with speakers.

Although courses and lectures on nationalism, both Indian and non-Indian, have been taught in many departments of JNU over the last forty years, the nationalism lectures pioneered not only new ways of thinking about anti-colonial and postcolonial nationalisms, but about the possible future of nationalisms as well. We realized that we needed a thick, not a thin, description of nationalisms; a complex and unruly, not a simple, history; and a robustly academic, not a politically facile, definition of the term that was haunting our public life.

We realized that we cannot leave it to the political scientists or historians alone, but must invite perspectives from economics, law, literature, science and the creative arts. We did not always succeed: there were glaring silences and absences – the sciences, the creative and the performing arts, for instance, were too poorly represented. We are chastened by our failure to include themes and speakers from the north-east, from among the minority communities of India, or from those who specialized in the visual media. We had a very limited representation of those speaking for the new nationalism and patriotism, by which all Indians are now being judged, and too little discussion of the virulent communalist and divisive legacies to which we are heir. Did the inaugural moment of the JNU struggle, Afzal Guru and the Kashmir issue, retreat into the background? Was the somewhat muted engagement with the Dalit struggle at Hyderabad Central University also not a sign of failure?

Despite many such shortcomings, JNUTA's teach-in had an extraordinary resonance and electrifying effect within India and beyond. Students and general audiences as far apart as Jadavpur University, Kolkata (West Bengal), Mahatma Gandhi University, Kottayam

(Kerala), Solapur University (Maharashtra), Kannada University, Hampi (Karnataka), MS University, Baroda (Gujarat) and University of Göettingen (Germany) organized protests, lectures and events, as well as collective viewing sessions of the lectures in a fine testimony to its success. Sometimes, the screening of the 'JNU Nationalism Lectures', as they began to be called, invited the wrath of university authorities in parts of India. That JNU authorities did not prohibit or overtly interrupt the student protests and teachers' actions, which were played out before the JNU community and the national media at Freedom Square, is the finest tribute to the traditions of dissent and debate that had been nurtured in JNU since its inception.

Why the Book?

If the nationalism lectures were as successful as mentioned above, why bother with the book? Today, more than ever before, people all over India want to know the roots of the dark neo-nationalism that has filled our public spaces, the repressive, majoritarian version that rules our lives. We need to know why so many young people have talked, in public, on the social media, of 'their blood boiling' when they see a particular face or hear a particular slogan – or indeed do not hear other kinds of slogans. We need to know whether nationalism always carried the seeds of this darkness, or whether it is some distorted vision of what is essentially a good thing. We need to know our histories, with all their silences, convolutions and contradictions, rather than the triumphalist account of nationhood that we are currently being force-fed. We need to acknowledge, as many of our speakers emphasized, the challenges posed by both history and geography to the possibility of a homogenous nation.

The book, therefore, adheres to the oral form of the teach-in as closely as possible. It follows a diarized form, respecting the order in which the lectures were delivered. It attempts to bring to the reader the textures of that ephemeral moment, replete with its pauses, interruptions, disruptions and simply the challenge of engaging an open-air audience of up to 2,000 people. Although nearly all speakers have made minor changes to their scripts to render them more coherent, in nearly all cases, the flavour of the original oral version has been retained.

This introduction does not review current debates on nationalism, or critically assess the contributions of each speaker to the large and sophisticated body of work that exists on the theories and practice of Indian and other nationalisms. It does not stake claim to originality; it serves the much more modest purpose of locating the teach-in within the context of new and immediate political concerns. It flags the urgently felt compulsion of many speakers to privilege certain questions over others, and underscores the emphases that most speakers placed on the urgency of upholding constitutional democracy in this time of crisis. It picks out recurring themes, historical figures and questions as an indication of the unexpected, even unplanned, focus that the very varied lectures began to take. It is inevitable, therefore, that an introduction such as this will be uneven in its discussion of the individual lectures that are included in this volume.

An Intellectual Occupation

The teach-in began on 17 February 2016 with the talk by Gopal Guru in which he asked, and answered, the question, 'What is the nation?' (herein 'Taking Indian Nationalism Seriously'). Is the nation the same thing as the state? Or indeed the same thing as the government? Why is it important to remind ourselves of these differences? Guru spoke of a more affirmative nationalism, of a possible nation that was located in an 'argumentative' rather than in an 'emotional' collectivity, rooted in that document that defines us in more than one way, the Indian Constitution. The reminder of the Constitution and its guarantees, as well as the law and its limits, was of course central to many of the nationalism lectures. Was not the public outcry against the archaic Section 124A in our penal code also against the ways in which it had been used against opponents of the government, or even of a party? Lawrence Liang in his lecture 'Dissent and Law' [herein 'A Gadfly Jurisprudence of Dissent'], therefore, reminded us not only of the painstaking victories that have been won by those committed to democracy, especially after independence, within and beyond courts, but of the ways in which the postcolonial Indian state has found it convenient to hold on to this controversial section as a legal weapon. Historical developments themselves serve as a warning against too much reliance on the law as saviour.

Indeed, following Guru, it was an obvious question to ask: when did the nation historically become yoked to the state? The nation state, that specific political form that is a product of nationalism, is, as many speakers emphasized, a relatively recent historical development. It is the result of creations/ideologies, and, we should add, mythologies. As Achin Vanaik reminded us, in his lecture 'The Power of Nationalism' (herein, 'Nationalism: Its Power and Limits'), even the date we normally associate with the rise of nations, the Treaty of Westphalia of 1648, may be misplaced; it is only in the nineteenth century that the non-absolutist, independent nation state really took shape.

When Vanaik asked 'Is nationalism a good thing, a bad thing or both?' he posed no rhetorical question. The lectures provided different answers to this fundamental problem. Some argued for distinguishing between good and bad nationalisms: in 'What it Means to be National' (herein 'Two Concepts of Nationalism'), Prabhat Patnaik, for instance, spoke of the road to fascism taken by the rise and growth of European nationalism. It looked for an enemy within, was imperialist from the start, and sought a kind of power that was aimed at enhancing national wealth, often by a process of aggrandizement. He distinguished it from a more inclusive nationalism, of the anti-colonial Indian kind, one that anticipated, early on, the importance of democracy and universal suffrage. In 'Anti-National Policies of NDA' (herein 'On Anti-National Economics'), Jayati Ghosh chose to apply the idea of 'anti-national' to the policies of post-independence governments, and the economic policies in particular, which could have devastating effects on people's lives. The guarantees that are ensured by the Constitution are rendered meaningless when substantive citizenship, which assures access to, say, education and health, is adversely affected, as it had been in the past few decades.

By turning away from these ideological and material roots, Jairus Banaji, in his lecture, 'The Political Culture of Fascism', pointed to the much less discussed dangers of a nationalism which drew equally on deep psychological structures to bring forth the fearsome, exclusive and threatening visage of fascism, as in Germany under Nazi rule. In the emphasis that he placed on gender relations and family forms, and on styles of authority which were incubated in the family itself, which could explain the collective desire for the imposition of order,

Banaji attempted a rational account, as it were, of what appears to us as 'irrational' mass behaviour.

Apart from the attractions of dealing with the mass face of political movements, and their sometimes dark wellsprings, many speakers revisited the lives and labours of important Indian thinkers. The man who is everywhere memorialized, though not always respected or admired, M.K. Gandhi, was quite naturally foregrounded in several lectures. Tanika Sarkar's 'Gandhi's Nation' not only recalled the Mahatma's finest hours, during the last and bloody years of colonialism's withdrawal, in the aftermath of the riots in Noakhali and Calcutta, but also his silences, his confusions and contradictions. Similarly, in his lecture, entitled 'Gandhi ka Akhri Thikana', Apoorvanand drew a fine portrait of this frail hero, making a conceptual distinction between rashtra on the one hand and watan and desh, on the other. Apoorvanand usefully pointed out that the ideas and the modes of protest represented by the JNU students' and teachers' protests laid more legitimate claim to the legacy of Gandhian politics than all the official claimants. Both lectures revealed Gandhi's uncertainties about nationalism, and his contradictory stances on many important questions, such as untouchability, women, or on representation itself.

Makarand Paranjape in his 'India's Uncivil Wars? Tagore, Gandhi ... JNU ... and What's "Left" of the Nation' brought the two great men into posthumous dialogue. Both Paranjape and Ranabir Chakravarti in 'A Take on Tagore's Nationalism' (herein 'Tagore's take on "the Self-Love of the Nation"') challenged any narrow readings of Tagore's stand on whether nationalism could be good or bad. Both reflected on his well-known stand against nationalism, while simultaneously underscoring the importance of understanding Tagore's critique of nationalism in the context of his anti-imperialism. As Chakravarti pointed out, Tagore's preference for the term 'swadesh' rather than 'rashtriyavad' or 'jaativad' re-centred ideas of nationalism. Tagore's remarkable metaphorical observation, which likened the great disconnect between the aeroplane in take-off and earth (rendering the little people increasingly indistinguishable and therefore easier to exterminate), referenced Arjuna's soaring away from the earth, distancing himself perforce from the battleground, as advised by the Gita.

Why were questions of uncertainty, silence, inconsistency, as exemplified by, say, Gandhi or Tagore, Periyar or Ambedkar, so crucial to the ways in which different speakers problematized nationalism? Especially at this moment, many felt the imperative to denaturalize nationalism, reiterate that nations and nationalism are not god-given, pre-existing formations. Nationalisms produce nations. There is no essence which is contained in religion, language or ethnicity, since nations since the nineteenth century have arisen from a wide range of histories.

Indeed, all nations need history, like the body needs oxygen: 'A nation without a past,' as E.J. Hobsbawm once reminded us, 'is a contradiction in terms'.[2] Indian nationalism was no exception to this rule of history-making, and historical myth-making. Nationalism chooses and picks from the past, as happened, and continues to happen, in India. But the part or section of history that is chosen is itself a self-conscious and deliberate act of imagination, myth-making, and, if necessary, invention. Within our own history, what is emphasized and what is de-emphasized? Romila Thapar in 'The Nation and History 1' (herein 'The Past as Seen in Ideologies Claiming to be Nationalist') and Harbans Mukhia in 'The Nation and History 2' (herein 'Reinstituting the Colonial History of Medieval India') discussed why the period of early India has become a much more important resource for Indian nationalism than either medieval or even modern history. Moreover, as Thapar pointed out, there was no history as such of a unified Indian territory prior to colonial rule, therefore, much of the interpretation of the common Indian past as rooted in two 'antagonistic' religions is derived from colonial historians. Yet, neither are religions always antagonistic, nor are cultures so isolated and independent, and Mukhia's discussion of the Indian medieval period drew attention to these rich complexities.

Where there are regions with fewer claims to a knowledge of the past, such history may even need to be invented. Among the countries of Africa, for instance, as Ari Sitas pointed out to us in his talk entitled 'South Africa Meets India,' where arbitrary geographical boundaries were created in the late nineteenth century, a history appropriate to nation-building had to be invented. Each emergent nation, or even those with older histories, singles out elements, irons out complexities and asserts a version of history in order to build a single, usable past.

National movements such as the Indian one were, however, equally engaged in the imagining of new futures. Even before the Indian national movement took on its mass form during the Swadeshi movement, Mridula Mukherjee said in 'Civil Liberties and Indian Nationalism', a civil rights movement took root. From the time of Surendranath Banerjee, sentenced for contempt of court in 1883, to Tilak (1908) and Gandhi (1922), who were tried under the dreaded Section 124A, those who continue to fight against the unjust use of state power have a long heritage of simultaneously building civil rights.

But does all anti-imperialism produce the same kind of nationalism? Is it enough to point to the shared anti-imperialism of Gandhi and Savarkar, or Savarkar and Bhagat Singh, without simultaneously pointing to the diametrically opposed ideas of the nation that they each held dear?[3] Moreover, as many others pointed out, even during the period of anti-colonial nationalism, there was no consensus about whether nationalism was an unequivocally good ideology. We are getting to know now, as research in this university itself increasingly demonstrates, that there were many Rabindranaths, in different languages, regions and above all among different castes.

No surprise, therefore, that several speakers questioned the verities of nationalist history, and asked whether Indian nationalism was indeed as inclusive as we have usually been taught. Did the Indian people as a whole rally around opposition to British rule in exactly the same way? Different regions of India, as many of the speakers revealed, generated alternative understandings of colonialism, and therefore as many approaches to anti-colonial nationalism. The Kannada writer and Jnanpith award winner K.V. Puttappa (Kuvempu) once said that he would still have been swilling cow dung in the Brahmin's house or living like a pig if it had not been for the opportunities offered by British rule.[4] Yet no one could accuse him of any less love of country.

As both G. Arunima and A. Mangai showed us, Tamil nationalism, which developed on the twin bases of a passion for the tongue and a critique of Brahminism, was at an angle to the nationalism of other parts of India. Southern and western India's engagements with the monstrous antagonisms of caste revealed other kinds of approaches to the national question. At the same time, despite its radical alterity, Arunima ('The

Nation and Its Regions: How Does it all Add Up?') noted that language never became the rallying cry in Kerala. These are histories – which have left their indelible mark on the contemporary – that will only with difficulty be brushed aside in the attempt to forge the neo-nation.

In short, India today is not the space of benign *diversity*, resembling the colours of the rainbow, but hierarchized, multiple *differences*, which are of varying kinds and intensities. Some of them intersect, some of the differences remain divergent, but all of them must be acknowledged before being addressed. For instance, Mangai, speaking of Tamils as 'default anti-nationals', provided a critical review of language- and caste-based sub-nationalism while 'Exploring Tamil Nationalism Historically' (herein 'One Hundred Years of Tamil Nationalism'). Yet, we must also ask, how has the once potentially destabilizing sub-nationalism of the Tamils today been 'normalized'?

This returns us to the twinning of nation to the state form: do all nations need to become states? A country like India, which is undeniably multilingual, multi-ethnic, multi-religious, and not least, multi-gastronomic, has one of the most fragmented social bodies in the world. We are uniquely divided in South Asia, across all religions, on the basis of caste. And there are, as we were continually reminded, discrepant histories of nationalism even within this nation state called India. There are political and territorial issues at stake, as much as there are affective ones, as both B.S. Butola's talk 'Crisis of Nationalism' (herein 'Crisis of Indian Nationalism') and G. Arunima reminded us. Territories are historicized and histories territorialized: Butola focussed on a geographical extremity, India's north-east, to make his point about the dangers of one single story being the idea of India. The single story that is being forged is not merely a territorial one, but one that disavows deep and divisive differences, such as caste, in the name of 'unity in diversity'. Therefore, Anand Kumar's talk entitled 'Nationalism and National Unity in India' (herein 'Nation-building in India and Its Contemporary Challenges') felt compelled to address the new call to unity, when he reminded listeners that the RSS–BJP's model of nation-building was drawn, ironically, from the nineteenth-century European formula of the culturally (and linguistically) homogenous nation. Do we, as he pointed out, have the capacity to build a nation based on religious plurality, caste difference, gender equality and regional disparity? Is India uniquely poised to make such a conceptualization of the nation possible, and if so, through which institutional form?

Posing these difficult questions itself invites the charge of being 'anti-national'. So fragile are the bases on which nation states are founded that once they are created or born, the work of nationalism is far from over. It is relentless activity requiring constant reminders and renewals, in short it is, in Nivedita Menon's quotation, 'a daily plebiscite'. Her lecture entitled 'Rashtra: Ek Rozana Raishumari' (herein 'Rashtravad Banaam Janvad') emphasized that nothing about nationalism can be taken for granted, that building nationalist sentiments is a task from which there can be no rest: it is an act of daily construction and reconstruction. Yet to point out that continuous claims of unity by the Indian state may not be shared by those inhabiting regions which have long experienced and encountered a very different face of the state cannot in itself be seen as an act of disloyalty. If the act of nation-building is a relentless task, we could equally say that there is no rest from our task, as responsible intellectuals, of uncovering the specific historical conditions and circumstances under which nations are born. This may require us to remember both the heroic and the tragic consequences of nationalism throughout history.

All nations sustain themselves on symbols such as the slogan, and the flag, and the museum, and the map, and the census, to constantly remind people of the nation to which they belong. But the slogan, the flag, the map, or the census are clearly not enough, and could become the source of new divisions and hierarchies. During the JNU struggle, retired army personnel met the administration to propose not only flying the flag on the campus but rolling in a tank in order to 'instil' nationalism. (As JNUSU Vice President Shehla Rashid then pointed out, if loyalty to the nation flourished at the mere sight of a gun, there should have been no problem in Kashmir at all!) It is perhaps necessary, therefore, to remember the man who understood and interpreted Section 124A and its pernicious intent. As Lawrence Liang cites in his lecture, Gandhi said, 'Affection cannot be manufactured or regulated by law. One should be free to give full expression to their disaffection unless it incites violence' (p. 108 of this book).

Should we therefore build up a richer idea of difference, and the constitutional guarantees that protect such difference, as the basis for imagining the future of our republic? Badri Narayan's talk on contemporary politics in Uttar Pradesh, 'Dalits and Hindutva Agenda' (herein 'Rashtravad ki Kalpana: Smriti, Mithak aur Ugra Hindutva'), was a sobering reminder, on the contrary, of the 'unifying' strategy of the Hindutvawadis. By reworking Dalit myths and narratives to present them in anti-Muslim garb, Dalits in UP are being brought into the fold of Hindu nationalism. Therefore, the question of who is responsible for the oppressions of Dalits, and how that historical wound should be redressed in the present day, receives a disturbing resolution in the hands of Hindutvawadis.

A very different note on difference was struck by Satyajit Rath, the biologist, who spoke on 'Biological Perspectives on Diversity and Unity' [herein 'Vividhata aur Ekta ka Vaigyanik Pehlu']. What happens when we ask the usual question about 'unity and diversity', this time about biological organisms and their integrity? As he asked, with examples from the history of science, and of the human body in particular: are there some instructive lessons to be learnt from the 'diversity', even 'antagonism', which goes into the making of the healthy body? Is difference vital to survival itself? Rather than drawing any simplistic socio-biological implications of such reasoning, the audience was presented with a very illuminating way of thinking about the positive values of difference.

Therefore, producing a future that guarantees equity and justice, and one that cherishes rather than decries difference, is much more challenging than mere 'desh bhakti' based on sloganeering, as Satish Deshpande reminded us. In his talk entitled 'Vishwadristhti, Vishwavidyalaya aur Rashtra', Deshpande drew attention to the university as a space that nurtured thinking, the only space where some modicum of equality could be practised and realized among students coming from unequal and heterogeneous backgrounds. Yet there are two important, patently contradictory features of the public university. We cannot deny that a university like JNU produces people who join the power elite that eventually governs the nation, while at one and the same time remaining a space which articulates resistance to state power.

Within and beyond universities, there are constant oppositions to the idea of the nation even after it has been born, which states must challenge, suppress or defeat in order for a singular, majoritarian nationalism to take its place. If territory is the space around which so much militarized assertion takes place, the question of language, or rather the conquest of language, the violence of bringing people to share the same tongue, is a crucial aspect of nationalism. Historians like Eugene Weber have shown us that French people became united only at the end of the First World War, when universal schooling finally subjugated all the local dialects and patois to make one recognizable language called French.[5] In India, as the lectures by Ayesha Kidwai entitled 'Languages or Mother Tongues? India's Linguistic Diversity' and Nivedita Menon revealed, the recognition of some languages as official languages (Kidwai), and the language of instruction in our schools (Menon), has led to the dwindling of many others. Sometimes, languages die as they are consolidated within one hegemonic language, such as Hindi. These processes often radically alienate the people who do not emotionally or linguistically identify with such hegemonic languages. Many such little deaths – in language policies, in textbooks, in public celebrations – occur in the process of forging national unity.

What then are the possible futures of a nationalism that is equitable and just? Here again, there was striking consensus about the promise of the Constitution. A common refrain of the lectures was the normative nationalism of the Constitution, which, in a region marked by foundational differences, can and must be the possible unifier. Everyone should defend it precisely because it alone upholds and defends the idea of difference, while creating a community of equals, a set of rights which cannot be violated by a nationalism based on an essence or a spirit. Commenting on television on the judgment of the Delhi High Court, which granted Kanhaiya Kumar bail, Fali Nariman usefully reminded us that it is the Constitution that guarantees the freedom of speech, rather than the soldiers who may indeed defend territorial boundaries. That these are two incommensurate registers must be recognized. And this is as good a moment as any to recall Tagore: '… it is my conviction that my countrymen will gain truly their India by fighting against that education which teaches them that a country is greater than the ideals of humanity.'[6]

It was entirely appropriate that the teach-in concluded with the talk by Suvir Kaul, 'At the Limits of Postcolonial Nationalisms' which was a personal–political reflection on the troubled history of Kashmir. What are the chances, he asked, of shaking off the colonial legacy, both in terms of the legal provisions, the dreaded Section 124A, which were at the heart of the JNU troubles, but also the militarized nationalism that is taking the place of celebrated and more democratic anti-colonial struggles? How, except by insisting on continued dialogue, by declaring an openness to more than one possible answer to the questions we ask? The 'flash point' of February 2016 on which JNU stumbled, he pointed out, opened up important lines of questioning, a search that has no easy answers. Yet the university, above all, can and should continue to be the space of critique as well as of alternative imaginings.

JNU and the Imagination of the Public University

Has JNU forfeited its role of posing uncomfortable questions to the nation at large because it may have remained silent on some issues in the past? In contrast to the strongly deprecatory account of JNU's alleged left sectarianism, as in Paranjape's lecture, was the attention given to the richly contradictory achievements of the university in Deshpande's talk. The walls of JNU themselves, lest we forget, are testimony to the rich variety of contending student associations and perspectives. So too is the intellectual culture reflected in JNU's course structure. It cannot, after all, be mere coincidence that a wide range of full-time politicians have had their formative years in JNU.

If anything, the four-month-long struggle at JNU, of which the lecture series on nationalism was a part, was a public staging of the university's achievements. We have demonstrated to the country and the world that there is a possibility of creating a community that is relatively equal, inclusive, based, however incompletely, on ideas of equality and justice for castes, genders, sexualities and, above all, thoughts and ideas. Without putting too fine a point on the university's uniqueness, the mingling of red and blue (symbolizing the colours of the left and the Dalit–Bahujan movements) throughout the protests, was a step towards a new and difficult unity. Nor does that tell the whole story, because as we all know, feminists were a very active part of these protests as well, remaining unrepresented by any one colour.

The teach-in strove to articulate a new civility, and indeed a new aesthetic, at a time when the darkest of human passions was on display in unbearably virulent and disruptive forms. Not just JNU but HCU, FTII, Allahabad, Jadavapur and all the locations that were inflamed in early 2016, must urgently marshal their achievements. As the idea of the university itself is under challenge, as we are being asked to turn it from an *institution* into a *mechanism*, producing bits of human capital, we need to preserve and extend these all-important achievements, and review our failures. As we will have to counter the charge, now articulated with renewed vigour, of being 'intellectual terrorists', we would do well to insist on the continued virtue of risky, and even disturbing, thinking, of which the teach-in was just one striking example. This will be in keeping with our commitment to principle, rather than to the state, or to power, as many in this series have pointed out.

This book, therefore, is both an archive of that historic moment, and a tribute to the effort, in all parts of the country, that succeeded in refocusing attention on the university as the appropriate space for sustaining serious, well-historicized thought. Through the teach-in, the JNUTA also demonstrated the obligation of university teachers to engage, with passionate detachment, some of the ideas that move people to action. We at JNUTA sincerely hope that we will continue to be, to use Lawrence Liang's felicitous term, the 'swarm of gadflies' speaking truth to power.

*

Notes/References/Bibliography

1. The teach-in was organized by a collective which included Rohit Azad, Rajarshi Dasgupta, Joy Pachuau, Mohinder Singh, Mallarika Sinha-Roy and myself. I would like to take this chance to emphasize the collective effort that has also brought this book to completion. Countless members of the Teachers' Association – too numerous to name – provided support, assistance, advice, and above all encouragement to make this book possible. Many of our colleagues volunteered to deliver lectures, but, regrettably, we were unable to include all of them, given the constraints of time. I would like to thank the editorial collective, Neeladri Bhattacharya, Ayesha Kidwai, Udaya Kumar and Pradip K. Datta for their close and critical readings of this introduction.

2. E.J. Hobsbawm, 1996, 2012 (rpt), 'Ethnicity and Nationalism in Europe Today' in *Mapping the Nation*, ed. Gopal Balakrishnan, London and New York: Verso Books, pp. 255-66, esp. p. 255.
3. A recent nuanced comparison of Gandhi and Savarkar, and the reasons why we may have to bear the collective responsibility for the rise of Narendra Modi, is in U.R. Ananthamurthy's *Hindutva athava Hind Swaraj?*, Bengaluru: Abhinava, 2014, published shortly after his death.
4. D. Javare Gowda, 2004, 'Rashtra Kavi Sandarshana' in *Kuvempu Samagra Gadhe*, Volume 2, Bengaluru: Rashtra Kavi Pratishtana, p. 854.
5. Eugen Weber, 1979, *Peasants into Frenchmen: The Modernization of Rural France, 1870-1914*, Stanford: Stanford University Press.
6. Sisir Kumar Das, ed., 1996, *Nationalism (1917): English Writings of Rabindranath Tagore*, Vol. II, Delhi, p. 456, as cited in Sabyasachi Bhattacharya, 'Antinomies of Nationalism and Rabindranath Tagore', *Economic and Political Weekly*, Vol. LI, No. 6, 6 February 2016, pp. 39-45, esp. pp. 41-2.

Picture credit: Samim Asgor Ali

Taking Indian Nationalism Seriously

Gopal Guru

(17 FEBRUARY 2016)

LET ME BEGIN THIS ESSAY WITH a reference to an analogy of a proverbial peasant and a live charcoal. A peasant, during the winter seasons, keeps a charcoal simmering in a heap of dead ash, only to be taken out as and when he requires it to light his chileem (a small smoking pipe). Nationalism, when viewed from the point of view of social and political forces with strong right-wing orientation, tends to acquire the essence of a live charcoal, as these forces also keep it simmering at the bottom of the consciousness of a section of people. These forces also summon this raw consciousness of nationalism into communal mobilization with far greater degree of intense expression. These forces tend to use nationalism as and when they require it. The use and abuse of nationalism depends on an inability of these forces to manage the legitimacy crisis they face in their project to gain support from the masses. Thus, a contingent articulation of nationalism is very often intended to perform a subversive function of creating divisions among the people by fanning hostilities between them.

Considered from this point of view, it is possible to argue that nationalism, like live charcoal, also has an instrumental value. In this particular understanding, nationalism, thus, retains its source of destructive fire in a sedimented form. But it seldom succeeds in extinguishing the fire in the belly of a hungry people who ironically are an embodiment of such a consciousness. We shall discuss this point in some detail in the following section; however, let us acknowledge that in contemporary times, some of the right-wing political forces in India seem to be using nationalism to mobilize people's emotions to push their particular ideological project. These political parties, however, hide this particular ideological interest by discursively elevating the meaning of nationalism from being instrumental to being sacred. Once it is couched in a sacred language it becomes easy for such forces to monopolize it by way of seeking insulation of critical voices from engaging with the entity called nation.

As we have seen in the recent controversy that surrounded JNU, the right-wing forces used nationalism as a moral weapon to morph the expression of the critical voices. Such a position which the right-wing parties tend to acquire through self-authorized claim over nationalism acquires strength from a skewed and flawed conception of moral duty. One can very well explain this skewed nature of moral duty by citing a well-known phrase that is used for putting nationalism on the high moral ground. It goes like this: 'Do not think what the nation does for you but think what you can do for the nation.' To put it differently, you have a duty to protect the honour of the nation, but the reverse is never the case in the sense that these political forces never raise the point as to what moral duty the nation has towards a large section of tormented humanity. The question, 'what can the nation do for you?' is completely ruled out in this skewed notion of public morality. To put it differently, other moral concerns are subordinated to the dominant notion of moral duty to nation. The recent controversy that was created in the name of nationalism in JNU had this intention of subordinating other moral ethical questions to a skewed morality, which turned JNU into a haven of deshdrohis (anti-nationals). It indicates that the nation has been used by certain parties to tarnish the image of JNU; to destroy the international reputation that it enjoys. Going back to the analogy of the peasant, he uses the little blowpipe in order to give air to the fire in the charcoal. Interestingly, the right-wing parties use rumours, empty slogans, self-authorized assertions and even polemics as the little blowpipe to inflame people's emotions about nationalism. Obviously, such parties do not take the risk of summoning a set of arguments in order to aid their understanding of nationalism. This, in their calculation, will go against both their intention as well as pose a challenge to their epistemic capacity to produce better argument. Hence they find it easy to flare up the emotions of nationalism that are mired in deep-seated prejudices.

The political forces with right-wing orientation, however, claim complete monopoly over the truth of nationalism, and for them the truth is an external enemy who resides across the border. Such forces latch on to a self-serving notion of the truth of nationalism. And for retaining their hold on such a truth, they indulge in a thorough and constant construction of the other which becomes easy and comes in handy as it has an instant charge in flaring up emotions. One could see such charged emotions of nationalism among the self-styled landowners of Munirka, a locality in the JNU neighbourhood, and also in far-off places. For such right-wing forces, truth of nationalism, thus, is given, in fact buried in sedimented subconsciousness. Since it is given, it does not have to be discovered or accessed through the theoretical analysis of either normative or concrete content of nationalism. Such a self-authorized claim over the truth of nationalism necessarily results in an unwarranted judgement, which then can be delivered at the gates of JNU. Remember, the self-fashioned nationalists, during the troubled times in JNU, were dashing at JNU gates and calling the JNU community anti-national. Unwarranted judgement necessarily assigns a kind of maltreatment to nationalism, which has both moral/ethical as well as theoretical dimensions to it.

The developments in and around JNU have compelled some of us to raise the following set of questions that we need to address particularly in the interest of the nation. First, if talk of the nation from a certain point of view is impossible, why should one talk about nationalism? If we leave the nation unattended, what implication does it have for engagement with right-wing conceptions of nationalism? Second, if at all one decides to talk of nationalism, in what language should one talk about nationalism? Third, if we separate the nation from the theory question or the moral question and send the discussion on holiday as the right-wing supporters of nationalism seem to be doing, what implications does it have for the social groups that exist on the margins and even outside the margins of the Indian nation?

Talking of Nationalism as a Social Need

The issue of nationalism remains continuously embattled because the ground on which nationalism has to be freely discussed and debated has already been captured, if not colonized, by the right-wing forces. They seem to have arrogated to themselves the moral authority to not only define what nationalism is but also to coerce people into accepting the self-fashioned definition of nationalism. We need to not only resist this unreasonable claim on nationalism but also offer much richer and deeper understandings of nationalism. Hence, it is our social need to question as to how one particular party can claim that its own understanding or take on nationalism defines a common good for the rest of the population. On what ground do such parties defend their claims as being inclusive, and that they are not influenced by narrow exclusivist interests?

Let me argue that we need to talk of the nation, not simply to wrest control of nation, nationalism and nation state, from the self-authorized claims made by the right-wing parties, but because we see the promise that the framework of nationalism offers for subaltern self-realization. This particular point requires more explanation that, however, cannot be offered here for the usual reason that I do not have space for it. Nevertheless, I have made some efforts to elaborate on this point in some details in the section on transformative role of nation state. Secondly, we cannot avoid discussion on nationalism, just because it has a flip side or it tends to be coercive in terms of extracting allegiance from those who for the right reasons are sceptical about its relationship with the well-being of the people. The state, which is using the nation for surrogacy purposes, has to be caught by its tail because we cannot catch it by its horns which have been knocked off by globalization. Finally, the nation provides a framework to evaluate the performance of the nation state. The nation is not something which is either a supernatural entity or has a superhuman image; in fact it is the standard by which one can measure the ethical, material standing of the state. In other words, nation offers us the analytical opportunity to decide on the ethical/moral stamina of the state. It offers us an opportunity to decide its normative stamina in terms of equality, justice, freedom and dignity. The dignity of the individual is coextensive with the dignity of the nation. It is in this sense that the nation state is the earthly expression of the nation.

We, in my opinion, do need to stake a claim on nation and nationalism. This is because, the nation not only offers standards by which we can measure the degree of (positive/negative) impact made by the state on the concrete life chances of common people, but it also entails, within its boundaries, the opportunity resources to be redistributed. To put it differently, in order to conserve and distribute resources for achieving the normative goal of equality, justice, freedom and dignity, we require the nation. The nation thus acquires a benign face through the active intervention of the state. The state has to play a transformative role in the material life of people that constitute the nation. Although the state is an earthly expression of the nation, caution has to be taken to disabuse the term 'earthly expression' from the problematic meaning that this dimension of nation carries in its ontology.

Limits of the Ontology of Nationalism

We need to offer a cool response backed by both morally cultivated reason as well as reason that is theoretically arrived at. We need to use morally cultivated reason so as to detect the fault line that is internal to nationalism that is externally defined in terms of the Line of Control (LOC). We have to develop this reason by pointing out the ontological inconsistency between the LOC and the internal fault line. They do not see the limits while they use ontological criteria to define the nation. We can point out these limits at two levels. The right-wing forces use extraterritorial loyalty as the negative criterion to define who is a nationalist. Thus, ontological association with 'Bhumi' or land (motherland) becomes an absolute criterion to define the nation. But they do not want to factor in the ontological reduction of the Dalits to spaces that continue to exist in this 'Bharatvarsha' for millions of years. Within this 'Bharatvarsha' or '*Parishkrut Bharat*' (sacred India) there continues to be a *Bahishkrut* India ('quarantined India'), to use Ambedkar's expression.[1] One can see this paradox in the right-wing imagination or formulation of India, its stand on territoriality as the core criterion of defining nation is backed by self-authorized assertion, while it completely lacks moral stamina to critically reflect on the predicament of '*Bahishkrut*

Bharat' or quarantined India. It is quite sensitive over the LOC but fails to demonstrate the same degree of sensitivity over the need to remove the internal fault line (untouchability) that is in contradiction with the LOC. The connection with the nation is not ontological as it puts undue premium on the territorial conception of nation. To put it differently, this imagination gives prominence and validity to binaries between insider/outsider and territorial/extraterritorial.

In fact, the logic of such construction would turn itself against those who are using the ontological basis to imagine India as a nation. There are sections which are using the criterion of original inhabitants of India to argue that Aryans, the top of the twice-born castes have come to India from outside. They are the outsiders. This counter-use of their ontological premises radically undercuts the moral significance of those who are using the LOC argument as the core criterion for imagining nation. For example, the Dalits and the Adivasis or Mulnivasis (original inhabitants) have been making this argument that the Aryans are outsiders. However, there are limits to the ontological claim on nationalism. This is because it is India that is offered as a creative context within which every person living in India has discovered his/her intrinsic worth as a sentient being. Hence, we need to move away from ontology and take recourse to the epistemology of the nation. It is here that we need to empower our argument by using a robust category of explanation. It is in this sense that we have the special responsibility to take the argument forward by liberating it from the constraining sphere of ontology. Without this take on understating nationalism, we will not be able to arrest the speed of propaganda that seeks to construct the members of minorities as the dangerous other by using the ontological roots. A self-authorized claim on nationalism acquires a coercive force that then is deployed to question somebody's existence in the land of India. Many people are asked to leave India on account of their lack of a commitment to national fidelity. There is growing stigmatization. The inclusive nation then is turned into its ontological fragmentation. In order to understand the internal inconsistency that is present in the right-wing, self-authorized discourse on nationalism, one therefore requires moral stamina to cultivate reasons that are so necessary for self-realization of these two levels of inconsistency. One requires this mode to reason out with those who refuse to accept limits on their attempts to put ontological premium on nationalism.

From Ontology to Epistemology of Nationalism

We, who have gathered at the Freedom Square in JNU, are here to assign credence to nationalism in terms of both theoretical as well as ethical/moral significance. We believe in a deliberative, dialogical process rather than the didactic which is based on preaching emotional narratives of nationalism. We sincerely believe that the nation and arguments are very closely tied to each other, and therefore we have to offer a very deep theoretical response to the idea of the nation. The nation has to be imagined, as far as I can understand, in terms of the promises the nation is making and aspirations it is offering to the people.

Within the epistemic framework, offering reasons forms a part of the theoretical inquiry. A reason has to be rooted in conditions that give rise to the very debate and discussion on nationalism, which, however, does not find its justification in the conditions that normally give rise to such a debate. Debates, particularly on nationalism, necessarily occur normally in two mutually exclusive conditions, which either appear to be tantalizing or acquire a tragic side. On the tantalizing side of nationalism one, thus, talks of the glory or the pride of nationalism when some defence forces achieve military victory or some sportspersons either collectively or individually achieve victory in nationally important sports such as hockey or cricket. Thus, to talk of nationalism, one requires reasons that are rooted in these conditions. However, debates over nationalism necessitated by the defence concern ultimately have a tragic side to it. Conditions that provide reasons, however, are not naturally given; on the contrary, they are created from the context where they do not exist. They are either created due to the expansive design of the powerful nations or they are created by the ruling party whose particular interest overrides the national interest. We did notice this design in the recent agitation against JNU. Thus, external threat or internal threat that is so serious would need us to take on board the question of nationalism. The question that one needs to raise is: did we, in the recent context of JNU, have such conditions that necessitated a debate on the question of nationalism? Answering this question in either way would help us to produce only the rhetorical response to those who have only skin-deep interest in such a question. In fact, what is important here is to establish a theoretically as well as ethically substantive relationship with such a question. Rhetorical responses tend to be ad hoc and strategically useful. Keeping in view this particular priority, it has to be argued here that one need not wait for the appropriate conditions but must debate nationalism almost on an everyday basis both in the classroom situation and, more importantly, in the larger public sphere.

State as the Earthly Expression of Nationalism

The essence of the nation is the self-realization of its people, while physical progress and protection of physical boundaries are part of its existential dimension. In the Hegelian sense, the state is an earthly expression of the nation.

The state, in order to realize the normative content of nation, has to make some actual space for the principle of equality. Interestingly, much against the usual anti-Western rhetoric of the postcolonial as well as the 'swadeshi' supporters, we have the principle of equality present in the radical symbolism of Ashok Chakra from Buddhism.

If you look at the idea of chakra – Ashok Chakra on our Tiranga, tricolour flag – this is one kind of radical symbolism that the nation has incorporated in its own imagination. What is this radical symbolism that has been a part of our nationalist imagination in the Ashok Chakra? The Ashok Chakra is constitutive of inner blades that ensure coherence to dynamism. Dynamism finds its transformative meaning in the rotation principle. Rotation principle would then suggest radical reconfiguration of spheres of life pushing up those who are at the bottom of the opportunity structures that exist in different spheres. There are two ways to achieve this rotation: one through the constitutional provision and the other through the moral stamina to vacate the top for those who have never been to the top. Is it not explained in the hermeneutic understanding of Ashok Chakra? Yes it is! The way you look at the chakra, every blade in the chakra has to go up and come down in its rotation – what powerful symbolism we have got in terms of this chakra. And if you really interpret it in terms of its hermeneutic capacities, you'll find that the nation has to be reformed, it has to be made radical in terms of changing rigid/

hierarchical spaces into a liberating space. Radical rotation principle would turn rigid places into freely flowing spaces. In the sense that some people are scavengers here, there are sanitary workers, they should change radically. This radical rotation, if practised sincerely by the state, would annihilate the class of free riders, which Marx, Jyotirao Phule, Gandhi and Ambedkar deeply detested. And we need to insist on the necessity that the state puts in ceaseless but sincere efforts to make sure that this chakra acquires this dynamism. We as young scholars of this university have to ask this political class how sincerely and to what extent they are actually putting the principle of radical rotation into practice. What kind of material support is the state making available so as to provide some push to this radical dynamism that is entailed in the Ashok Chakra? So the nation has to invest in some kind of egalitarianism. And that is there in our Indian Constitution and in our philosophy of Buddhism.

What Should the State Do?

The state should not become more important than the nation. The state, particularly its existence, i.e., government, has to take precautions so that it does not subordinate the nation to its narrow interest. In the present context of JNU, it was very clear that the state was overriding the essence of nation. It tried to become more important than the nation. Let us then take a couple of illustrations to underline the role of the state in becoming an earthly expression of the nation.

We require explanatory insight to locate the areas where the tension between nation and state is becoming much more problematic to the extent that the latter is trying to become more powerful than the nation. This is happening despite the fact that the force of neo-liberalism has knocked off the horns that the welfare state arguably possessed before 1991. The state, rather than the common people, is defining the meaning of nation and soliciting people's support to this particular meaning of nation by disciplining them through splashing sedition charges against them. It is important, therefore, to free the nation from the unreasonable and hence undesirable grip of the state.

So am I suggesting that we should really go for the recovery of nation. In case one goes, which one should for such a recovery of nation, one will have to fight all the residual liabilities of caste and gender injustice. Following from the Indian Constitution, the state has to take the lead in eliminating these residual liabilities. However, the state is facing the challenge in terms of removing these liabilities that are entrenched in the institutional life of the nation. In fact, one could find the overlap of boundaries between the caste-based civil society and modern bureaucracy. This mixture is threatening to defeat the justice principle that provides normative content to a very transformative imagination of nation. The use of nationalism to defeat the principle of justice was very obvious in Rohith Vemula's case. In fact, the lack of efficiency in delivering what was due to Rohith has led not just to the denial of justice but much more importantly, it created a deep sense of nothingness in his life. I still remember Rohith Vemula's poem and particularly its last two or three lines. These lines, in my opinion, are the most profound in nature. They are the reflection on the failure of nation to fill the void in a common Dalit life with promises fulfilled. In fact, it is the state that is failing the nation. As we have seen in the earlier sections, it is not the state but the nation that provides normative standards for the state so that the latter could give concrete expression to universal principles of justice, equality and dignity. Rohith's poem sends us a tragic reminder about the nation. According to this poem, if a nation is creating a void, an emptiness in your life, what kind of nation am I living in? What is that void, that emptiness in Rohith Vemula? That he was known as having a star on his caste certificate. The students and the officials on the Hyderabad campus knew Rohith with a star that was put against his caste background. His intellectual identity was bracketed not with the star in the sky (a modernist symbolism) but with the star indicating his caste (traditionalist symbols). And he, for the right reasons, was fed up with this social production of a star on the caste certificate.[2] And, therefore, his last poem suggests that he wanted to join the galaxy of stars in the sky. In fact, his academic career had the brightness of the star in the sky. A nation that fails to remove the star that is the marker of somebody's caste background lives with its grotesque image as *Bahishkrut Bharat*. Tragedy, in case of Rohith, becomes the condition for the articulation of nationalism. Rohith's powerful imagination of a star in the sky indicates a void that is created by the failing state.

Which is why I think the role of the state and its bureaucracy has to be to respond to the Dalit aspirations that necessarily coincide with nation. It is at this point one could locate the tension between state and nation. On the positive side it should eliminate the paradox on which any nation, including the Indian nation, stands. The paradox is pretty obvious. Whatever the nation promises at the time of its birth, it subsequently fails to deliver it in favour of those who, unlike the NRIs, cannot desert the nation. The state has to make the internal dimension of nation seamless by removing the internal fault lines.

*

Notes/References/Bibliography

1. Writings and Speeches of Babasaheb Ambedkar in *Bahishkrut Bharat* (Marathi), 1979, Education Department, Government of Maharashtra, Bombay.
2. In Hyderabad Central University, the administration does not mention the caste of students. Instead, it codifies caste into stars: Scheduled Caste is one star and Scheduled Tribes, two stars.

Picture credit: Samim Asgor Ali

South Africa Meets India

Ari Sitas

(19 FEBRUARY 2016)

I AM HONOURED TO BE HERE because you have shown an incredible self-restraint. It's amazing what you have achieved in the last week. But my role here is as a teacher and I'm going to start my talk by saying: in the history of colonialism there emerged a family of anti-colonial movements that sought national independence and national liberation. In the course of the twentieth century you were the first to achieve Independence and South Africa was the last in that family to achieve enfranchisement in 1994.

The problem is that we are intricately interconnected. You sent 'that' lawyer in a dark suit to Durban in the late nineteenth century – you sent him as Mohandas and we sent him back to you as Mahatma. He was the first to start using the word Congress there in 1894. There was the formation of the Indian Congress there. And then, after the intransigence of the colonial powers, African leaders started calling themselves the South African Native Congress and formed the African National Congress in 1912.

So this idea of Congress somehow goes down the years, and in a sense because of the large Indian community in South Africa, because of the history of indenture, because indenture came to replace slave labour, because of the millions by-now Indians in South Africa – the story of

India has always been close to us. I have spent twenty-seven years of my teaching life in Durban and I have followed India very closely.

Nationalism starts in the colonies from two sources, I'd say. The first one is of an idea of a response. It's a response to colonial powers that says: hey, we also come from a long way back and you can't treat us like this – collectively or individually. It's this response – no, nah, nada, ca, stop it! All national movements start from that response – enough, we don't want it! And then of course colonial powers have been so crazy at drawing boundaries on maps and using rulers to just divide territories that borders do not correspond to prior histories.

And in Africa in the 1880s, they all sat together in Berlin and they divided Africa up and they colonized it up to this or that predetermined line. So in a sense it has to become, not only a 'stop it', a 'no' response, but it also has to be the work of the imagination. How do we bring all these people together who are being brought together by colonial rule in their differences, in their complexities, in their cultures, in their religions, into a movement now that will create the new.

So in other words, the anti-colonial movements are a response, but also a kind of work of the imagination: to imagine the 'as not yet', that future, whatever we call it – 'azadi', freedom, 'inkululeko', something like that. And then the hard work of the imagination starts.

But if we want to understand this work of imagination, we have to seriously study the history of how European powers started foraging up and down the coastline, and you know what foraging is. In the beginning it's, 'Hey, I want your shoes, nice shoes, can I have your shoes please,' and they start grabbing, taking, bartering, trading, and this foraging in a sense then moves towards settlement. 'Okay, I'll sit next to you, better take off your shoes, I like your shoes.' So settlement starts, and settlement starts creating these initial conditions of the Other!

All of a sudden, you are the Other in a place where you were standing yesterday. All of a sudden you are the Other in the place where you were born. And can you imagine, looking for India the wrong way across the Atlantic and calling all those people, those Others – Indians. A simple generic term – didn't matter where they came from, what their qualities were and so on, they were all 'Indians'. And then they got John Wayne in the movies to shoot them. Sorry, that was a nasty aside!

From settlement starts this Othering, and starts the process of colonization. During the period of white settlement, it was necessary to have your people there, because you needed the slave trade, you needed the trade in ivory, and in gold. You had to settle some people there and of course countries were overpopulating in the north and some settlers started coming in droves, but by no means was it colonization proper. It was the beginning of land grabs and expropriation.

We did share with you the British East India Company, and you didn't have the 'joy' of having the Dutch East India Company all over your place. All of a sudden, the process of colonization started in earnest and that process created the sense of governance, the sense of rules, the sense of regulation, the inclusions and exclusions, the classifications and the codes of what needs to be done for these Others – you, me and so on – to be Othered and to be made to admire the civilizational mission that was imposed on us.

Only a deep study of these processes of colonization will allow us to understand why these nationalisms in the colony differ from nationalisms in other places that have not been colonized. Of course the British had a horrid time in India, poor chaps, but they managed through the British East India Company to assume total control of the subcontinent. They had to get a sense of this difference – classify people, measure their heads, put them away, and so on until they had a sense of control and mastery. They admitted that India was diverse and complex and their elites, such as the Nizams, enjoyed a lot and were gobsmacked about their wealth, and they enjoyed particularly their diamonds and gold, the British did, they enjoyed things shiny very much. And to the misfortune of Africa, southern Africa, diamonds and gold were in abundance.

The story of colonization, of real control, for the southern African nations starts with the so-called discovery of diamonds and then, afterwards, the so-called discovery of gold. And there you see a rush of all kinds of people trying to benefit from this situation – you see tensions escalating between the Boers (the Dutch) and the Britons, you see the emergence of people like Cecil John Rhodes. I'm sure you've heard about the Rhodes Must Fall movements this year.

Cecil John Rhodes takes control of the diamond fields and establishes systems and then moves onto the goldfields and before you know it, after the Boer War, where the Britons fight the Boers and they come together and decide – let's have a Union of South Africa and let's decide on the rules of the Union – and they decide to exclude the black majority, 75 per cent of the population, from that Union of South Africa.

So it is very important to understand in terms of the South African story, this process of colonization: the discovery of gold, the creation of labour forces to dig that gold, the creation of a migrant labour system to dig out that gold and to see the Union of South Africa emerging as a state and the majority to be excluded. It was a quick process.

In 1874, you put all blacks, whom you have called natives, in reserves – that was 13 per cent of the land. Natives then have to be tribes, they can't be polities or nations, they have to be tribes ruled by customary rules and therefore they have to have their homeland. That's where they have to go.

In 1886, you create the pass laws: no Native can move out of the reserves without having a pass; if you do, oops! You go to jail, and why? To regulate the labour system to dig out the gold. You needed the labour, but you needed to exclude at the same time. That happens in 1886 and of course they find out that the Zulu people and the Xhosa people are not really interested in digging gold 3 kilometres underground.

So you create the poll tax in 1906 which compels every household to pay taxes in cash and therefore somebody has to work. And so by 1906, you have a regular stream of labour, by 1913 you have the Land Act that demarcates what is private property for whites and what is reserved land for blacks, and whoever is in the way – off to the reserves; and by 1923 you have the Urban Area Act that says nobody can be here who is black, in the city by right, only by exemption. You have all kinds of exemptions for some people to be in the cities, but never permanently: nine-year leases, ninety-nine-year leases, and so on, but the majority is supposed to be tribal and in the reserves.

So, that is in a sense how the story starts and then to cap it all, in 1924, you have the Industrial Conciliation Act that defines Africans as non-employees and therefore, even if they organize trade unions and movements, they won't be recognized. There is no compulsion to recognize them. So, Native Rule, the creation of the Native in southern Africa was all about that.

At the same time, what I'm also trying to say is that through the classification of the Natives in general, but also the tribes in particular you could impose indirect rule. And they did it because they said they learnt their lesson. Mr Lugard learned his lesson in India, and therefore he wouldn't repeat the mistakes that he did in India. Therefore you need this regulated and regular system of control – so there you have Native Rule. But then you have other problems because you have to separate all kinds of other colours. You take all those people who were liberated as slaves by them because the slave trade was abolished, people that came from Malabar, Malaysia, Indonesia, East Africa, and were working on the vineyards and so on of the Cape. You got all those people who were the descendants of the people who were either children of love between the races or children of rape between the races – all of those people were grouped under the category 'Coloured' and were separated.

But then because Mr Gandhi was making too much noise and Indians were not wanting to be repatriated and there were lots of movements there, they constructed the category 'Indian' as a separate category. And since then we have had this separation of colours with different administrations between the colour groups, or race groups.

I said before – it also involved a response from the natives and it involved the work of an imagination as well. Why did the first people, let's say the parents of Mandela to make the story more tangible, why did they say no? No native description for us – but African? Why did they insist on 'Africanity'?

It was the work of students in those days. If you were clever in the colonies, you were sent to London, or the Tuskegee College in the US, or to Paris even, or Lisbon if you were from the Portuguese colonies, and there you met all kinds of other people. They were all from the African continent, or the African diaspora who grew up under the same conditions as you – speaking the same colonial languages, meeting on the way a lot of the African American people and ideas about Africa – the imagination of wanting to return home because slaves were homogenized, no matter where they came from, they were moulded together as slaves, they had to develop a new consciousness, as African Americans, in the long term and reject other derogatory terms in between.

And they were all dreaming of a liberated Africa in those spaces, and out of these encounters this idea of pan-Africanism emerged and everyone went back to their colonial worlds, and back to the Union of South Africa, and decided that 'we are an African People's movement'. And that's how African National Congress as opposed to a Natives' Congress was born – at once, the work of defying colonialism and of imagining a collective identity.

Another feature that movements in India and those in South Africa shared was that they were not just any kind of nationalism. You do indeed have varieties of nationalisms. They were movements that promised the most difficult of promises: a search for a balance between freedom and equality. There are movements that have it slightly easier – you want to restore an ancient past, where you want to restore feudal relations, and movements that bring back the king and bring back the queen, and bring back their horses, and bring back their elephants, and their giraffes and so on, and you yearn for a restoration of the past.

And there are movements that want to have this search for a balance, but nobody is getting it quite right, this balance between freedom and equality. But at least the movement promised it and that's what makes them different from other movements in the colonial world. So if that point is understood, the generation of the parents of Mandela bequeathed to the next generation an idea of African freedom, 'inkululeko' in the local languages, the kind of promise that would revalue the past but promise to create a better future.

Mobilization followed mobilization and the Second World War came and the white government promised, if you come and fight, we will give you your freedom and they went and fought and they didn't get their freedom; and nationalism started becoming a little more strident and militant.

At the same time, Afrikaner nationalism was on the rise too (of the white descendants of the Dutch settlers) and demanded stricter separation of the races, and for whites to keep and tighten control of the country. They kicked Jan Smuts out in 1948, and apartheid as we have come to know it was born. Apartheid did not invent racism and racial domination, but perfected it.

Of course, this created new waves of militant opposition in the black majority. This opposition created two currents by the late 1950s. On the one hand there were the people who supported the Freedom Charter that brought together the African National Congress – the Natal and the Transvaal Indian Congresses, the Coloured People's Congresses and the Congress of Democrats among whites. And so, all the Congress traditions adopted the Freedom Charter that argued that South Africa belongs to all who live in it and therefore it was non-racial. We don't have time today to discuss exactly what the Freedom Charter involved. On the other hand, there was the pan-Africanist movement that didn't like it and said, 'Africa is for the Africans.'

These movements started getting more and more militant – there were anti-pass campaigns, there were strikes, there were demonstrations and then there was a state crackdown from hell and people were arrested, were detained, were tried, were sent to prison, people fled, went into exile. Mandela and others then decided to go the Bhagat Singh way – pick up arms. And he was arrested, and we know the story – twenty-seven years in jail. So his generation having been bequeathed this idea of African nationalism started making it into a militant African nationalism that aimed for revolution and transformation.

After the crackdown came years of seeming quietude, until the late 1960s. Passions in the black majority were simmering and boiling and new challenges started emerging, and you see the emergence then, of my generation, not Mandela's generation, but my generation. You see in quick succession versions of a Black Consciousness movement, a revival of the Charterist movement in the United Democratic Front, of women's movements, of all kinds of movements starting with civil disobedience all over again. In that ferment, we witnessed one of the most militant trade union movements ever seen in recent history. So these township, labour, youth and women's struggles coalesce into major confrontations by the 1980s with the apartheid regime and it gets into a situation where civil war is started in certain areas and the bloodshed starts and you know – you think when you're in there that there is no hope – that you're caught in a vicious circle of violence where neither the state can suppress the opposition nor can the opposition shake the state out of its power.

The interesting thing, though, is that the ability to shake the state came from a highly organized working class because once you are deeply organized on the shop floor and you control 80 per cent of the shop floors and you have democratic shop steward and factory structures, and the state removes that leadership, you elect the next one and then the bosses start getting pissed off if you take too many workers away from the shop floor. All this energy comes to a head in 1989 with another state of emergency declared (you heard the word emergency, if it comes about it is serious), you knew it from earlier days and people get picked up and you don't know what's happening to people and they disappear and so on. The Truth and Reconciliation Commission ended with listing people who disappeared in the 1980s and early 1990s.

Anyway, you are stuck in 1989 and you think there is no way forward and then starts a defiance campaign again and all of a sudden Mandela is released and change starts happening. But we don't have time tonight to talk about what the implications of these nationalisms are once a negotiated settlement is reached.

And we have been constantly asking: what does it mean? This balance between equality and freedom. Could it be reached? In our case, there were three compromises and a promise, before democracy could be reached.

The three compromises – first was about land. Land will not be considered for restitution for the period before 1910, the formation of the Union of South Africa. This was a major concession, because the mines and also the colonized land could not be returned to the communities that lost them. Secondly, it was a compromise where governments, managements and labour formed a tripartite arrangement so that they can talk to each other instead of fighting each other. And the third was a compromise between traditional authorities – chiefs, kings and so on in the countryside and urban modernists that you would keep the customary areas under customary rule. Finally, the promise was a reconstruction and development programme that would bring about equality.

There was no problem on the freedom front – the constitution that came about was about total freedom. At the moment I can say anything I like but that doesn't mean my neighbours won't break my back. But at least I won't get any formal sanction.

So, South Africa, this latest postcolonial society, is still searching for the ways in which growing inequality in the world can be redressed or addressed. But the tensions are many and new movements are coming up and it's complicated. All I'm trying to say is that looking at India from afar we saw India also as the laboratory for the national question – your national question. We read extensively – Tagore, Gandhi, Bhagat Singh. We learnt about Nehru, EMS and Ambedkar, we learnt all about these tensions, saw India struggling to find itself in terms of its promise of creating a better society that balances freedom and equality and you've got your Constitution and we've got ours – they are very problematic.

But I hope that JNU is the custodian of this national question and that's why it was created, and still keeps such a tradition of thinking alive. We expect you to look at us, to look at our problems – what we write, what we achieve, what we fail at, we have got the genius, some say, to dream big and the diabolical kind of idiocy in destroying every dream the next day. So you can learn and unlearn things from us. But we are in this process of trying to make this promise real. And the new generation – our children, Mandela's grandchildren, are exploding in anger in South Africa – there are students' movements rising and trade unions breaking up, new trade union formations are being created, but it's all a search, of trying to make the promise real in this arbitrary geographic space; to give it a meaning, to give it a purpose, to redress gender imbalances, to redress voice imbalances, to redress value imbalances and to achieve a better society that looks after its people.

Freedom is not a constitution, or the day it is declared, it's a long process and all of us, each one of us removing ... removing the constraints that keep us unfree. We don't want all of us to be the same, we want to help each other remove those constraints provided that equity comes with it. The legacy of anti-colonial nationalisms weighs heavily in our hearts and minds. We have said a No, we have imagined a We, we have promised the 'as not yet'. It is your generation's turn to deny, affirm and dream.

So I thank you for your generosity, I thank you for your ears, I'll be around for this semester, if you want further encounters with our story. I thank you.

*

Notes/References/Bibliography

Magubane, Ben (ed.), 2004, *The Road to Democracy in South Africa*, Vol. 1, 1960–1970, Cape Town: Zebra

Masilela, Ntongela, 2012, *The Historical Figures of the New African Movement*, Volume 1, Trenton, NJ: Africa World Press

Simons, Jack and Ray Simons, 1969, *Class and Colour in South Africa*, Harmondsworth: Penguin

Sitas, Ari, 2010, *The Mandela Decade: Labour, Culture and Society in Post-Apartheid South Africa*, Pretoria: University of South Africa Press

Wolpe, Harold, 1990, *Race, Class and the Apartheid State*, Trenton, NJ: Africa World Press

Picture credit: Samim Asgor Ali

The Nation and Its Regions: How Does it All Add Up?

G. Arunima

(20 FEBRUARY 2016)

I ACTUALLY THOUGHT A LOT ABOUT what I wanted to say to you today, and I decided that the way to address the 'national question' as it is unfolding in front of us would be for us to think instead about the region. Now, before I start thinking together with you about the region, and why I thought this might be a more productive way to enter the question that we are engaging right now, I do want to make a few prefatory remarks about my own position vis-à-vis some of the kinds of issues we are engaging at the moment. At the outset, I must say that I come from a time and a generation where my own imagination was structured by all kinds of ideas and inspirations that presented the possibility of a critique, or at least alternatives, to the 'nation'. Of these, I'd place Tagore and his famous poem 'Where the mind is without fear' as one of my earliest motivations, which as you know speaks very eloquently and beautifully about a future for an entire humanity that is not broken up by the 'small walls of domesticity'.[1] A second source was the Workers' International, which actually dreamt of an international world order which would be completely different, and where workers' unity would actually be what would define the ways in which we thought about ourselves – thereby rejecting once again the small domestic walls of the nation.[2] And finally, John Lennon and the influence of his song '*Imagine*'.[3] So I must say that I was fortunate to grow up at a time when people were not wedded to reiterating a desperate, violent and intense passion for the nation. I put myself down as someone who is nation agnostic – I'm an Indian because my parents are Indians and I have a passport that tells me that is what I am. Yet I have never felt the need to wake up every morning and start swearing my allegiance to the country. I must also add that I find the present moment of 'nation worship' reprehensible and frightening, and I oppose intensely the attempts to muzzle dissenting voices in the name of upholding the nation.

So, what are the kinds of questions that came to my mind when faced with this issue of thinking about the nation? I must start this lecture by saying that as primarily a student of history, one of the things I'm always struck by is the fact that the nation is quite a recent social form. Two or two-and-a-half centuries are not such a long period of time, and certainly, students of history will bear me out on that. Those of you who are history aficionados will also realize that if you were to study histories of what are known as 'ancient societies' or 'feudalism' – those 'forms' also spread across several centuries. Yet it is only the nation that demands that one constantly speak about oneself in relation to the nation, and that too in certain kinds of ways. Now, there are two or three kinds of issues that I think are significant before we get on to question of the region. One – I think it is important to remember the fact that while there are political and territorial issues at stake when we speak about the nation, these are also bound up in affective issues. And it is the coming together, in not very predictable ways, of the political, the territorial and the affective, in the kinds of thinking, writing and politics of different groups of people that often creates a conflictual environment in relation to the nation. In a way, the extreme anger, passion and indeed bellicose behaviour that we see today is because there is nothing 'natural' or inherent about the nation. It is, in fact, an unwieldy form that is an uncomfortable sum of its differences. The second is a point that Ari had made yesterday and I want to reiterate in a slightly different way. Which is that when we think about the histories of nations, it is always told in the form of what one might consider to be its 'birthing story'. We know that the stories coming from an anti-colonial context is quite different from the master narratives that we have from Europe. This is important because if you think about nationalism along the lines of ideas about black consciousness or Marxism, these are written and thought about very differently in the colonies than in the European context.[4] I'm not saying that these are hermetically sealed, or that they are not internally differentiated in those regions or in ours, but I think that there is something about the production of ideologies in different ways in different political contexts and histories that we do need to think about.

Now that's what made me think about how to address this question about the nation. I want us to think about two phrases that certainly every Indian knows. One is 'We the People' and the other 'Unity in Diversity'. I want us to think about both of these because what I want to talk about today is the way in which one can have an imagination of a nation, via its people, and pose a question about what that would mean. And alongside, about what the question of diversity actually forces us to think about. Is it simply pluralism, or differences of culture; the fact that I speak Malayalam alongside Hindi (when I'm forced to), for instance, or the fact that there are actually structural, material, cultural, political, differences in the country? So I want us to think about the idea of difference, not just diversity. This is because difference is a more productive political concept to think about, and permits me to keep the idea of 'people' in mind when speaking about it. And here I want to say, using the title of a very beautiful piece by the Nigerian writer Chimamanda Adichie, 'The Danger of a Single Story' – and for me that's a moving title and also speaks to the kinds of issues we are discussing here – that the single story is something that we must be very wary of. So, what are these different kinds of stories, the stories that will not add up, the stories that we want to keep alive in our minds, the stories that frighten and disturb us, as indeed the ones that strengthen us, and fuel our dreams? So let us keep these differences, and the idea of difference, alive and integral to the ways in which dreams and desires are supposedly made.

One of my interests today is to speak of the manner in which the region is imagined, and this is not simply to reference the famous phrase of Ben Anderson: 'The nation as an imagined community', coined from the title of a famous book of his.[5] I would suggest that there are actually different rhythms and imaginations from regions which are very productive for us to think with. A large part of my work is on Kerala, which is an exceedingly marginal region within the story of the nation. However, before I begin my discussion I want to give you two examples – one facetious, and the other serious – about my own personal encounter with the idea of the region. The facetious example first. For years I taught at a south Delhi college called Lady Shri Ram College (LSR). One day I went into the canteen of this college to eat lunch and looked at its menu. I found, to my great amusement, that LSR's canteen board differentiated categorically between what it called 'Indian' dishes and what it considered to be 'south Indian'. And I thought, okay, that is interesting, this is one kind of way in which we think about our difference, that is through our food habits, though of course I was delighted by the way 'south India' was demarcated as quite separate from 'India'. More significantly, there is something about the manner in which difference gets imprinted in our minds. We feel we are different, we are made to feel different, and there are ways in which differences get articulated in each of these instances and encounters, producing affects that are important to think with.

Now, the second, more serious reflection is about my encounter with belonging to an academically 'invisible' region. In the mid-1980s, I was an MA student here at the Centre for Historical Studies (CHS) and I, with great happiness, would say that the reason I continue in academia is because of that MA. So, my identification with JNU comes mainly from that moment in my personal association with this institution, though of course I've been teaching here now for more than a decade. Now, when I used to sit in modern Indian history classes in CHS, I was often left wondering why it was that I never studied anything about Kerala. This, I must say, was a pressing question for me. So other than feeling 'different', growing up in a city like Delhi, there was also the fact that even the best classes did not teach anything about regions that many of us came from. 'Modern India' seemed like a sum of UP and Bengal, with some Punjab thrown in for good measure! It is unsurprising, then, that many, even in academic contexts, would have felt excluded, and certainly would not have been particularly 'nation' identified.

So, how does one actually think about this thing called the region: Do you think about it as a geographical unit? Do you think about a region because contiguous regions, like Tamil Nadu and Kerala, or

Tamil Nadu, Kerala, Karnataka, and Andhra, co-produce a region? Or, are we speaking about political and social structures, and differences in kinship patterns? Is the region an idea? Or is it an identification? Is it something that's attributed? For instance, people saying, 'Oh! You are a south Indian, I'm not a south Indian'. Even as all of these are important, what I want to speak about are the manners in which the rhythms of regions produce different kinds of articulations. So I will address very briefly a few issues that come up in Tamil Nadu and in Kerala and think about how they actually contribute to a way of imagining the region. Here, I am most interested in the kinds of ways in which the regional gets inscribed in an understanding of identities. While I am not directly speaking to the question of identities here, much of what I have to say will have a bearing on that. Having said which, I also wish to flag right at the outset that thinking about the region also means engaging with its internal differentiation. This is because, in the spirit of Adichie's 'The Danger of a Single Story', it is important to constantly remember what is at stake. In other words, keeping the question of difference alive is essential for not merely the story of the nation but also for that of the region. So it's not merely the problem of one story, but that of constantly maintaining caution against the tendency of folding everything into a hegemonic narrative. And one of the dominant narratives in India's 'nation story' is to see it within a framing of the freedom struggle and the national movement. Therefore, introducing the differential histories from the region in relation to this single story of the nation is to say that engaging these variegated imaginations is not simply necessary, but that this engagement might actually make it possible for us, at this political moment, to rethink the nation in far more capacious ways for the future.

Now, if you think about Tamil Nadu, there are two kinds of analytics that become relevant, and reflect the manner in which debates there were shaped in recent times. One is the question of language and its affective relationship to the Tamil people. The other is the question of caste. Significantly, both these were deeply intertwined in the first half of the twentieth century. If, on the other hand, you think about Kerala, the language question does come up but is not produced affectively as in the Tamil case. Also, in Kerala we find an articulation of the future of the region (in the early twentieth century) as one that needed to engage the inequities of class differences and power. However, there is also an imagination of Kerala that comes from not necessarily the late nineteenth and early twentieth centuries, but from a much longer regional imagination. This situates it within the wider geography of the Indian Ocean – as there would be no Kerala had there not been that wider geography – with its population that's a mixed bag of Christians, Muslims, Jews and Hindus, belonging to different castes. The question is: why is Kerala populated in this manner? Why are all these people collectively considered to be Malayali today? And that can only be understood if you push the story back to at least the sixteenth century, if not earlier, and you think about waves of people who came there from different parts of the world. And unless and until one tries to understand Kerala within this Indian Ocean geography, from West Asia and the Arab world on the west, to China on the east, with South-East Asia thrown in, there is no way in which you can make any sense of Kerala.[6] I will come back to that point later, time permitting, as I want to focus more on how certain kinds of political imaginations, in the Tamil and the Kerala context, are different and why that's a productive thing for us to think with. Suffice it to say here that it is essential to understand the longue durée of the histories of regional subjectivities as these are often lost, or obscured, by the grand narrative of the nation.

Let us begin by looking in slightly greater detail at the Tamil context. As many here may know, E.V. Ramasamy Naicker, also known as Periyar, brought together between the late 1920s and the '30s and again during the 1960s at least three or four different kinds of questions – that of self-respect, anti-Brahminism, the politics and modes of raising the caste question, which included a deep understanding of gender inequality and engaged directly with the need for the abolition of caste. Now, it is a fact that if you actually think about the Periyar-led movement and compare that to the contemporary DMK, you find that much has changed. This is the reason I was saying earlier that it is extremely important to bear in mind that neither regions nor politics are static, and that the changes may indicate a great rupture with the earlier project of reimagining the regional self. Thinkers, and especially political thinkers like Periyar, were imagining what it meant to be free, and what the conditions of this freedom might be (unfortunately, a large part of the Periyar archive is yet to be translated, so we are left with a much more diminished body of writing, or dependence on scholars who have worked on him). However, even from one of the pithy, beautiful things that he said – 'Is the Brahman rule Swaraj for the Parayas (the untouchables), is the cat's rule Swaraj for the rat, is the landlord's rule Swaraj for the peasants, is the rule of the propertied Swaraj for the labourers'[7] – it is clear that his was a very interesting and important critique of the idea of Swaraj. What Periyar was asking was who would be a part of this Swaraj, this 'self ruling' nation? This is asking the 'people' question, this is asking the question about difference, this is asking the political question about an ideal that you imagine you are working towards. If Swaraj is the ideal, who will be a member of that ideal? Who will be a member of that Swaraj when it is to come? This is the question that Periyar is forcing us to ask.

As some of you might know, from the 1940s through to the 1960s there was, starting with Periyar, and later by Annadurai, a demand for a separate Dravidasthan, which was variously known as Dravidanad or Dravidadesham too. In 1954 in fact, Annadurai expanded this notion and said that Kerala and Karnataka could also be part of this political unit of Dravidanad.[8] This generated enormous discussions, though what I find most interesting were the mottos that Annadurai and others were raising, which included ones like 'divide on the basis of language, unite on the basis of race'. So the Dravida movement was invoking the idea of a separate space of 'south India', based on racial difference, and this was understood as Dravidanad. The invitation was to rethink Swaraj – which would not have included many, particularly the underprivileged, in the Dravida regions. Of course when we look at the manners in which the Dravidian question gets articulated later, we see that the radical sharpness and difference of imagining 'south India' on grounds of race and caste difference gets recast as a language question.

The 1960s, as those of you who know a little about Tamil history will know, witnessed a series of suicides, which reformulated Tamil Nadu's difference with the nation as one founded on language. One of the slogans of that time, emblazoned in the dramatic phrase *'Udal Mannukku Uyir Tamilukku'* ('body to earth and life for Tamil'), expressed quite clearly what Sumathi Ramaswamy calls the 'passions of the tongue',[9] and speaks of the centrality of the affective while thinking the political. In other words, you identify so much with the language that your political identification, your affective or emotional identification is actually with language.

Now it is interesting that when the language question came up in Kerala, right across the border from Tamil Nadu, in the late nineteenth century, it was articulated quite differently. This was a period when Kerala witnessed a lot of debate about Malayalam language. This is clear from the magazines of the period which had long discussions on the idea of bhasha, language, and these included all manners of issues from form, style and speech to questions of standardization, creation of literary canons, and the need for good grammars and dictionaries. One of the people who wrote enormously on this issue, even though we know little about him, was a man called C.D. David, whose take on the language question was quite at variance with the more literary aspects of this issue.[10] He was concerned, amongst other matters, with the way in which people must speak about their relationship to Malayalam. And, in what I consider to be quite an extraordinary move, he characterized it as *samudaya swatta* – or 'community wealth'. I believe that this is very interesting – this idea of language as shared, as common property, as something that everybody has equal access to. Equally, I must add that there is something really interesting about thinking about language as common property, or resource, rather than collapsing it into the more available idea of passionate identification. This is at great variance from the almost life-consuming investment in language that has been one of the grounds for huge amounts of warfare in this country, and the subcontinent itself, the best example of which is the Hindi vs Urdu battle.

The Kerala example of thinking Malayalam gives us a very different mode of engagement with what is now considered a primordial relationship between 'a people' and 'their tongue'. Now, other than C.D. David who wrote a lot and we don't know much about, I do want to make a point here that when we think about the histories of languages, it is worth remembering that the people who were central to this enterprise were not necessarily established scholars or litterateurs. In the Kerala context, the people who were most significant in the making, and the popularizing of a demotic prose, were people like Kandathil Varghese Mappila, the journalist who set up *Malayala Manorama*. Other than Varghese Mappila, Murkoth Kumaran, a Thiya[11] intellectual, was one of the most significant figures in the late nineteenth and early twentieth centuries who engaged the language question consistently. So, if you actually think about the figures responsible for making Malayalam demotic, and available, it was not a savarna, or an upper-caste, enterprise at all. Large numbers of the key figures were avarna, like Murkoth Kumaran, avarna Christian, like C.D. David, or involved a significant presence of Syrian Christians like Varghese Mappila. Indeed, it is precisely because of this that Malayalam could have been conceptualized as a shared community resource – an idea which I believe needs to be revived as it has enormously enabling possibilities.

Another kind of 'regional rhythm' I would like us to consider here is the Kerala matrilineal story. Now one may well ask why this is significant or relevant for us today, or what we may learn from it. In the mid-nineteenth century – and this is something that most people do not take much notice of but I think is worth reiterating – almost 50 per cent of Kerala's population, across class, religious community and caste was matrilineal. This essentially meant that the inheritance was in the women's line, that children's primary affiliation was with their mothers, and that kinship was defined in the mother's line. Now, this really important statistic, and configuration, become relevant when one assumes all of India to have an extremely homogeneous notion of family, attendant rights and structures, and patriarchy itself. So what we can take away from the matrilineal story, I think, is the different manners in which rights for women were historically articulated. And this is not simply rights over property, but also rights of sexuality and indeed autonomy. This difference of matrilineal women, which was abolished by the Kerala state legislature in 1976, survives in other ways. For instance, the modes of self-articulation of Malayali women, their relationships with their matrikin, or the natal household, speaks not only about a memory of other kinds of filiation but also suggests a reason for their continued identification with their natal contexts.

I would suggest that there is something significant about thinking of the cultural questions at stake while thinking of subjectivities of this kind. As we can see these do not boil down to simply quantifiable data. Indeed the history of greater autonomy, rights or control over sexuality for Malayali women – which have steadily been eroded through a combination of statist interventions and other misogynist trajectories – provides a different dimension to the way in which one may wish to read the idea of region (in this case Kerala). I would also suggest that the changing landscape of diminishing rights of Malayali women was in part a result of Kerala's 'mainstreaming', and becoming 'national' (in this instance, the abolition of matriliny), amongst other things. I believe there are serious questions here which we are yet to begin to address.[12]

Finally, what I want to speak about here very briefly is a last issue in relation to the Kerala/Tamil Nadu difference. Earlier in this lecture I had spoken about how ideas of equality and freedom in twentieth-century Tamil Nadu are articulated in the language of caste power, its eradication, and by situating it within an idea of language-centric autonomy. Kerala, on the contrary, addresses this, in the same period, in the idiom of class war, and an abolition of class power. Here I want us to think about two significant figures of the early twentieth century who were central to this theorization. One was Krishna Pillai, one of the founders of the Kerala Communist Party, who wrote in 1934 that the whole world belonged to 'one caste', which was 'the human caste'. I think that is an interesting kind of way of imagining the region question as it actually did away with both the regional and the national, and introduced the unmarked 'human' as the agent of political change. In 1934, in his essay 'Fascism and Communism', Krishna Pillai wrote: 'The capitalists would be destroyed and the rule of the country will be passed into the hands of *Daridra Narayan*.'[13] Now, the language of that time notwithstanding, I think it is important to acknowledge the fact that here is a communist ideologue who is not only openly addressing the question of fascism and thinking about communism as an alternative, but was also thinking about the manner in which class power, the power of the working class (referred to here as the Daridra Narayan) would be the agency for political change. This humanized the poor and the workers; it also enabled them to be cast in the role of political transformers. It is important to remember that these are imaginations of equality which are not subsumed within an imagination of Swaraj or a monolithic notion of the nation. Indeed, if we go back to 'The Danger of a Single Story' and think only about the freedom struggle and nationalism in very narrow ways, these are the stories that almost always get left out. Similarly, if we think about a 1948 text written by the Malayali Marxist ideologue, E.M.S. Namboodiripad, '*Keralam, Malayalikalude Mathrubhumi*' or 'Kerala – The Malayali Motherland', one can see a return of the region, albeit envisaged differently. Of course the book does not go on to exactly outline a simple story of regional alterity; in fact, it is very much within a Marxist mode of production argument about change, detailing how these would ultimately happen while thinking about the overthrow of feudal landlordism and the rightful place of the working classes within this process. Yet I think the title is very significant, and one should not undermine the importance of this. One, the idea of a Kerala as the 'motherland', or 'nation', of the Malayalis is not only marking the difference of the region, it is more significantly separating itself from the nation. Secondly, I would think that the use of the phrase *Keralam Malayalikalude Mathrubhoomi* is significant at a time when you have, across the corner (in Tamil Nadu), people speaking about Dravidanad. If read against the Dravidanad imagination, it also signals an internal rupture within the region itself, marking 'south India' very differently. It strikes me that this speaks to both the internal tensions regarding the DMK's imagination of the region, and to the strategies by which the Malayali communists were extricating themselves from within that. For instance, they may have feared – though one needs to research this further – a larger Tamil hegemony, despite statements to the contrary by Annadurai and others saying that Karnataka and Kerala would actually be autonomous within Dravidanad. However, as this is the first time I, or anyone else, have read 'south India' in this fashion, I would add that many of the above thoughts are speculative at present, and would need to be developed further with research and analysis.

So these have been, in principle, the main sets of thoughts that I wanted to place before us today. Yet what can we finally take away from some of these reflections? Let us return briefly to two of the issues that I started with – one, the question of commitment to the people, and second, the need to underscore the question of difference, when thinking of 'the people'. I think we do need to take difference seriously because one of the most frightening issues that we are faced with every day is the attempts to homogenize; this is not simply a worry about making all of us the same, which is impossible, but because politically, homogenization poses great dangers. Difference in that sense, vis-à-vis its cultural, social or material iterations, is not only about pluralism but also about political and social power differences. Therefore, unless we address the question of difference frontally, we will not be able to think about equality and social change. I want to end this lecture with one last concern – which is the issue of violence. So even though our regional imagination shows us that there were other rhythms, other imaginations, other ways of thinking about selfhood and subjectivity, I must also say that we have different articulations of violence from these sites that need to be addressed seriously. It is important to actually engage the fact that romanticizing deterritorialization faces us with difficulties, not the least of which is that this might end up mimicking certain kinds of structures of power, and enactments of violence, that we reject about the nation.

For me, a politics of alterity from the inherited commitments to the nation is rejecting this cult of violence. One part of my critique of violence derives from one of the German philosophers whom I love – Walter Benjamin. To simplify Benjamin's critique of violence in one sentence – there is no good or bad violence.[14] We need to think about it in a very different kind of a way where we do not end up saying that my violence is good and yours is not. And when I hear slogans of violence from whichever side, I am deeply disheartened, because the other part of my critique is shaped by questions the women's movement has consistently raised in this regard. For me, to think about feminism and politics, is also to fight for a just world where there is no violence – be it gender, caste, statist, or against any minority. The move away from the dominant narrative of the nation, founded as it is on the silencing, and rendering invisible, of difference, dissent and heterodoxies, is also a commitment to politics that is not merely non-, but actually anti-violence.

So I think I will leave you all with this thought. Thank you very much – you have been wonderful. Long live JNU.

*

Notes/References/Bibliography

1. Published in 1910, and English translation in 1912.
2. The Fourth, or Workers' International was born out of the Trotskyite critique of the 'bureaucratic centralism' of Stalinism that was seen as destroying the proletarian, or worker-centric, imagination of the 1917 October revolution in Russia. The hope was to struggle against imperialism and deploy proletarian energies towards a revolution that would destroy the capitalist world order.
3. '*Imagine*' was released as a single in 1975. It had a new release in 1980, shortly after Lennon's death when it became UK's #1, and gained an unprecedented international circulation.
4. Frantz Fanon, 1963, *Wretched of the Earth*, New York: Grove Press; Walter D. Mignolo and Arturo Escobar (eds), 2010, *Globalization and the Decolonial Option*, London and New York: Routledge.
5. Benedict Anderson, 2006, *Imagined Communities: Reflections on the Origin and Spread of Nationalism*, Verso: London and New York, Revised edition.
6. G. Arunima, 2006, 'Who is a Malayali Anyway? Language, Community and Identity in precolonial Kerala', in Satish Saberwal and Mushirul Hasan (eds), *Assertive Religious Identities in India*, Delhi: Manohar.
7. Swaraj, or self-rule, was the foundational condition of imagining the nation. Such a critique questioned the swa, or the self, in self-rule. Periyar's reference is from *Viduthalai*, Vol. 19, No. 1, 1948, quoted in 'Fuzzy and Neutrosophic Analysis of Periyar's Views on Untouchability', W.B. Vasantha Kandasamy, Florentin Smarandache, K. Kandasamy, November 2005, https://arxiv.org/pdf/math/0511559.pdf, p. 246, accessed on 15 February 2016. This contains extensive translated excerpts from Periyar's speeches and writings.
8. Eugene F. Irschick, 1969, *Politics and Social Conflict in South India: The Non-Brahman Movement and Tamil Separatism, 1916-1929*, Berkeley: University of California.
9. Sumathi Ramaswamy, 1997, *Passions of the Tongue: Language Devotion in Tamil Nadu*, 1891-1970, Berkeley: University of California.
10. See for instance, C. D. David's essays on 'Kerala Bhashaposhini Sabha' [Kerala Language Development Society], *Vidyavinodini*, Book 3, No. 10, 1892; or 'Malayalabhasha' [Malayalam Language], *Vidyavinodini*, Book 2, no. 12, 1892.

11. Thiyas are an avarna caste, which would today be seen as part of the larger OBC consolidation.
12. G. Arunima, 2003, *'There Comes Papa': Colonialism and the Transformation of Matriliny in Kerala, Malabar, c. 1850-1940*, Hyderabad: Orient Longman.
13. Krishna Pillai, 1934, 'Fasciasvum Communisavum' in *Mathrubhumi.*
14. Walter Benjamin, 2004, 'The Critique of Violence' in Marcus Bullock and Michael W. Jennings (eds), *Walter Benjamin: Selected Writings*, Vol. 1, Cambridge: Belknap Press.

Picture credit: Samim Asgor Ali

Languages or Mother Tongues?: India's Linguistic Diversity

Ayesha Kidwai

(21 FEBRUARY 2016)

TODAY IS INTERNATIONAL MOTHER LANGUAGE DAY. First celebrated by the United Nations in 1999, it was formally adopted as a day to be celebrated across the world in 2009. This year's theme is the importance of mother tongue education. In a university campus which is facing sustained attack and great travails and great resistance, it is important to remember why this day was chosen. This has to do with events in our neighbouring country of Bangladesh, then East Pakistan, a tragic series of events that arose because of the suppression of the Bangla language in the newly born Pakistani nation.

On 21 February 1952, which is known in Bangladesh and in West Bengal as *Ekushe*, in response to a call for a demonstration in Dhaka University, students gathered by the thousands at the university gates (quite like what is happening in JNU these days). The demonstration was called to honour the Bangla language, and to protest the government proposal that Bangla should be written in the Perso-Arabic script. Police arrested several students, despite the intervention of the vice chancellor (a better one than ours) and university professors. The protests spread, and later in the day, outside the East Bengal Legislative Assembly, five students were shot dead in police firing.

In today's *The Hindu*, this story has been retold by Ashis Dutta. He reminds us of the relevance that this story has for us today in India, as *Ekushe* is 'about the voice of the marginalized', and a recognition that India's 'teeming diversity' renders each of us a 'minority' in some way or the other.[1]

It is particularly fitting that we remember *Ekushe* in the locale that we are in today, a site where the rights of people have been asserted over the obedience demanded by national governments. And today we do so to honour our mother tongues and the promises that the Indian Constitution makes to linguistic minorities and their mother tongues and for a nation that is above all multilingual.[2] Some of these promises are:

- Article 29 enshrines a commitment to the maintenance of India's linguistic diversity: 'Any section of the citizens residing in the territory of India or any part thereof having a distinct language, script or culture of its own shall have the right to conserve the same.'
- Article 30 guarantees minorities the right to develop and propagate these languages (and their speakers) through managing and running educational institutions.
- Article 350A provides for instruction in their own mother tongues at the primary stage of education to children belonging to the linguistic minorities: 'It shall be the endeavour of every State, and of every local authority within the State, to provide adequate facilities for instruction in the mother tongue at the primary stage of education to children belonging to linguistic minority groups; and the President may issue such directions to any State as he considers necessary or proper for securing the provision of such facilities.'
- Articles 345 and 120 promote multilingual governance. Article 345 leaves a State free, through its legislature, to adopt Hindi or any language used in its territory as its official language(s). Article 120 permits member(s) to use his/her mother tongue in the Indian Parliament.

In a very real way, and tragically so, the story of the Indian nation in the year 2016 is a story of an overall failure to realize the promises we made to ourselves in the Constitution, as many mother tongues spoken in the Indian subcontinent are either in danger of completely vanishing or are spoken less and less. We do not even know how many mother tongues are spoken in India today, as the policy of successive Indian governments has actually been directed at finding ways *not* to implement constitutional guarantees.

The Census of India has since the 1970s emerged as the main instrument through which the mother tongues of the people are systematically underrepresented. The need for such underrepresentation arose, in the main, because of the 1961 census, which was the last time the number of mother tongues the Indian people laid claim to was revealed. The number there was 1,652, and one can only imagine the panic that must have set in at this number: if this figure was to be maintained, the government would have to commit vast resources to implement the constitutional guarantee for mother tongue education at the primary level. Rather than incurring this expenditure, successive governments have taken the easy way out by employing a methodology that masks the linguistic diversity of India, and reduces the number and importance of mother tongues. Though census enumerators still ask citizens about the languages they speak – and are mandated to record the answers without editorializing them – it is what the census does to them afterwards that radically reduces the number of mother tongues spoken by the people of India.

In every census, the people of India return far more language names than are actually recorded. For example, in the 1991 census, they returned 10,400 language names, and in the 2001 census, 6,661 names. The census' rationalization reduces the language names returned to names of 'probable languages', using the colonial *Linguistic Survey of India* (1894–1928) and other publications, as well as the experiences of earlier censuses. In 1991, this resulted in 1,576 probable languages, whereas in 2001, this yielded 1,635. This difference in figures should be enough to make us wonder at the methodology employed for rationalization (which is not revealed), but things actually get worse, as being a 'probable language' is no longer enough to be a 'mother tongue'.

In order to be a 'mother tongue', a probable language needs to be classified. Using the same resources as those employed for rationalization, the census further classifies probable languages into mother tongues (again, the principles of classification are kept secret). In 2001, this process yielded 234 mother tongues, i.e., 14.3 per cent of probable languages, and in 1991, the number was 216, i.e., 13.7 per cent of probable languages.

To be a mother tongue is not the endpoint for the census, however, which continues its mission of managing India's linguistic diversity. Mother tongues are further classified into Languages (with a capital L), i.e., those mother tongues it recognizes and accords prestige to. In 1991, the census found 122 Languages in the Indian nation, and in 2001, it found 114. In other words, on an average 7.3 per cent of probable languages end up as Languages that the Indian government gives patronage and official encouragement to.

In this progression from language name to probable language to mother tongue to Language, there are many elisions of distinct cultures and their languages. The first step of rationalization is something that all censuses must do, as often, people just give the names of their caste, region or village (this is not unusual, as one's language is rarely named by the self, it is usually the Other). Quite expectedly, the census must rationalize such responses, and pare them down. However, it is when the census classifies languages that the most injustice and insult is generated.

Perhaps the most detrimental strategy is the decision that if less than 10,000 speakers return a language name, it is not to be named as a distinct mother tongue. This is in particular cruel to Adivasi and other linguistic minorities, whose populations might be quite small. We have personally encountered students from the North-East and tribal areas whose distinct language is spoken just in their village, and numbers of speakers have been stable between 800 and 1,200. So this is one way to deny us the promise of our Constitution, as by not naming them, we are writing them out of our nation. These languages will never be taught in school, no one will create varnamalas (alphabet books) or grammar books for them, more and more of their speakers will stop speaking them out of shame, or at least they will be made to feel that their language has no value. From what we know, there are a large number of such languages that do not get named and therefore counted – somewhere near a thousand of them.

But this strategy gets rid of only about a thousand mother tongues, and does not trick the constitutional promise enough. To pare down the number of mother tongues further, the strategy of grouping many languages under one language is employed. It is this strategy that has led to the popular but incorrect belief that Hindi is widely spoken across India and is our national language.[3] From the 2001 census we learn that more than fifty languages, including Chhattisgarhi, Bhojpuri and Garhwali, are grouped under the Language 'Hindi'. This makes a mockery of the answers that the Indian people have given the census – by naming the languages they speak, 33,099,497 Bhojpuri, 13,260,186 Chhattisgarhi, and 2,267,314 Garhwali speakers were telling the government that their language is *not* Hindi, but the artefact of the census ensures that their acts of linguistic identity do not undermine Hindi's claim to prestige and power. And Hindi itself is not redefined in the process either, as a language of a continuum amongst the people. In fact, the census data on languages can hardly be relied upon at all, as it is notoriously sensitive to political manipulation by respondents. The case of Sanskrit is particularly amusing, as the language registered a decadal growth of 714.54 per cent between 1981 and 1991, with the 6,106 speakers of the language as a mother tongue rising to 49,736 in number by 1991. Given that the census requires mother tongue identification to be determined by birth to a mother who speaks the same language, this suggests a sharp spike in the fertility of the few thousand Sanskrit-speaking mothers. Assuming (quite unreasonably) that half the 6,106 speakers of the language in 1981 were women, each woman would have had to give birth to roughly fourteen children in that decade! (The following decade saw an equally alarming slump, by the way, as Sanskrit speakers declined by 71.54 per cent to a number of 14,135.)[4]

The Census of India's language data, as an instance of language policy, thus creates a social tension between languages and produces a society that is hostile to the survival and maintenance of languages spoken by smaller and disadvantaged groups. However, the census is not the only means by which inequality between languages has been created. It is a matter of great shame for this nation that not every language in India has a script. There are many points of comparisons in which we might feel better off than the Soviet Union, but this is one place where we're not. Because in the Soviet Union, which had thousands of languages, every language was given a script by 1925, but here in 2016 there is no way to write the many languages of India.

Why is preserving minority languages important? The death of a language is the loss of much more than a means of expression. Globally, language attrition and death has become a matter of great concern, particularly as the world hurtles headlong along the path of criminal development by which more and more people are displaced or made to leave their homes and lands. Well-meaning arguments tend to be phrased in utilitarian terms such as preservation is essential because language is the medium of 'indigenous knowledge systems' that record, for example, the medicinal uses of flora and fauna, the sources and use of important minerals, etc. However, if the need to maintain languages is to be justified in terms of preserving the knowledge embodied in them, there must be a corresponding assurance that the right to use and propagate this knowledge rests with the community. If the preservation of language is to be argued for in terms of facilitating (capitalist) exploitation of natural resources, it isn't much of an argument at all.

In my view – and this is one shared by a large number of linguists – the best argument for the preservation of minority languages is one that foregrounds the importance of language in our understanding of what it is to be human. There are many ways to do linguistics, including the one that many of you are most familiar with (the politics of language, its discursive properties and its role in the creation of social meanings), but what I am referring to is a perspective on language first articulated by Noam Chomsky.

In this way of approaching language, every language that exists in any individual instantiates a specific version of the general human linguistic ability. This is a knowledge that has nothing to do with nationalities, nothing to do with nations, nothing to do with elective groupings, nothing to do with caste, gender, and religion – as we learn more and more about this knowledge, we find that Santali has more in common with French and Spanish than Hindi, and Malayalam may share many properties of Korean and Japanese. This uniquely human ability is a domain-specific knowledge distinct from other cognitive abilities, and is equally available across the species to enable the human mind to express itself, to externalize thought as it were. As a consequence, every language (whether the government gives it a script or grammar or not) tells us something about what it means to be human. In this view, the loss of any one language is the loss of a means of understanding this unique human ability; and a society that enables every individual to maintain her/his language preserves the possibility of our understanding the human mind. Our Constitution envisions a language policy that would have realized such a society one day, but our nation has never trodden the path envisioned for it.

The university is the natural place in which discussions and critiques about India's language policy must take place, precisely because it is in this space that we seek to advance human knowledge in an egalitarian and socially sensitive manner. What is at stake is not only the substantive equality of all citizens, but also the nature of scientific inquiry. For insisting on the university as a space of the freedom of thought and expression, we have been plunged into a terrible crisis, but I have no doubt that we shall overcome it, as we see ourselves as part of a great humanist tradition of inquiry that approaches even the smallest of languages with humility and is forever mindful of the human dignity of its speakers. For us, every language is equal and equally precious, and fundamentally undifferentiated in terms of value, even if it is labelled as classical or ancient.

Even as we take on the challenges posed by this crackdown on our university, we have much to change in the way we approach ours and others' languages. Every year, when fresh students come into the classroom, two groups behave quite differently. The larger of the two have a common response to teachers' queries about the languages they speak – they usually return the names of the more prestigious languages – Hindi, English, Bangla, Oriya, Malayalam, Tamil, Marathi, Punjabi, etc. – all languages with a capital L. By the time we are done with them (usually by the end of the first semester), I am happy to report, their real languages have made a showing, and they begin to identify themselves as speakers of Bajjika, Angika, Magahi, Sylheti, Santali, Kurux, Haryanvi, Kutchchi, etc., i.e., all languages that have been submerged under the capital L.

The second, and much smaller group of students is from the North-East, who never ever let the politics of the bigger languages of the region, including Hindi, elide the names of their languages. From this group, we often hear the names of languages for the first time, spoken by communities as small as 400-500. It is this refusal to let powerful languages determine how we characterize ourselves that we must learn from our friends from the North-East, and we must, on this day and every other day, speak our distinct languages and speak them with pride. For, in asserting India's linguistic pluralism inheres a powerful resistance to the fallacies of 'one language, one nation', a path that our Constitution very firmly directs us away from.

*

Notes/References/Bibliography

1. Ashis Dutta, 'The Language of Other People', *The Hindu*, 20 February 2016.
2. Contrary to popular perception, the Indian Constitution does *not* designate Hindi as the 'national Language'. Rather, it is the 'official' language of the Union (and English is the associate official language until Parliament rules otherwise).
3. There is no notion of a national language in the Constitution, whose eighth schedule lists twenty-two languages, with no capital L.
4. All data as provided by http://www.censusindia.gov.in/Census_Data_2001/Census_Data_Online/Language/Statement7.aspx, accessed on 17 February 2016.

Picture credit: K. Fayaz Ahmad

राष्ट्रवाद बनाम जनवाद

निवेदिता मेनन

(22 फरवरी 2016)

मोदी सरकार द्वारा विश्वविद्यालयों पर हुए हमलों से एक बड़ा लाभ यह हुआ है कि देश भर के कैम्पसों में एक नई एकजुटता दिख रही है, नयी स्फूर्ति, जो वामपंथी, अम्बेडकरवादी और नारीवादी ताकतों के बीच संवाद से उभर रही हैं।

लेक्चर शुरू करने से पहले मैं यह स्पष्ट कर दूँ कि आज मै हिन्दी में बोलूँगी – इसलिए नहीं कि हिन्दी राष्ट्रभाषा है, क्योंकि यह राष्ट्रभाषा नहीं, महज राज्यभाषा है। यह वो भाषा है, जिस में राज्य के अंगों और अफ़सरशाही के बीच वार्तालाप होता है। बल्कि मैं हिन्दी में बोलूँगी क्योंकि हिन्दी यहाँ की स्थानीय भाषाओं में से एक है, और हम सब के लिए अपनी मातृभाषा के आलावा एक अन्य भाषा भी जानना जरूरी होना चाहिए। ऐसा नहीं है कि मेरी हिन्दी बड़ी दुरुस्त है, ख़ासकर जेंडर के मामले में काफी डाँवाडोल है। इसलिए राष्ट्रवाद की बात को सबसे पहले भाषा से ही शुरू करना उचित होगा। कल प्रो. आइशा किदवई के लेक्चर के बाद किसी ने यह सवाल उठाया था कि एक राष्ट्र बनने के लिए क्या एक भाषा की जरूरत नहीं है? लेकिन असली सवाल यह है कि अगर राष्ट्र में एकता लाने के लिए एक भाषा होनी चाहिए, तो वह भाषा कौन–सी होगी? कौन–सी ज़ुबान होगी? कौन यह तय करेगा कि इस देश की भाषा या ज़ुबान कौन–सी होगी? होता क्या है कि जब भी निर्णय लिया जाता है कि एक देश के लिए किसी एक चीज़ की जरूरत है, चाहे वह भाषा हो, सिविल कोड हो या कुछ और, तब वो एक चीज़ ताकतवर तबकों की संस्कृति और रहन–सहन के तरीकों से उठाई जाती है। हमारे देश में जब किसी एक चीज़ को घोषित किया जाता है कि यह भारतीय है, तो वह ज़्यादातर सवर्ण तबकों की ही होती है और

उसमें भी हिन्दी–भाषी क्षेत्र की संस्कृति और मूल्यों को ही भारतीय माना जाता रहा है। उदाहरण के तौर पर अगर आप हिन्दू कोड बिल के दौरान हुई संसदीय बहस को देखें, तो बार–बार पायेंगे कि संसद सदस्य, जिनके नाम सुब्रमण्यम, श्रीनिवासन वगैरह हैं, यानि कि वे दक्षिण से हैं, या जो बंगाल के घोष आदि हैं, वे कहते हैं कि हमारे यहाँ लड़कियों की शादी के बाद लड़कियों के घर जाना या मिलना हमारे लिए वर्जित नहीं है। तब कोई श्रीवास्तव या अग्रवाल उठकर खड़ा हो जाता है (ये संसदीय बहस की बात है) और कहता है, यह आपके बंगाल में होता होगा, आपके तमिलनाडु में होता होगा, लेकिन यह भारतीय नहीं है क्योंकि हमारे यहाँ किसी ब्याही हुई लड़की के यहाँ हम पानी तक नहीं पीते।

इसी तरह हिन्दी को भी हमारी राष्ट्रभाषा कहलवाने के लिए काफी संवेदनाओं के साथ खेलना पड़ा है। कितने प्रतिशत लोग 2001 की जनगणना के दौरान बताते हैं कि हिन्दी उनकी मातृभाषा है? करीब 25 प्रतिशत लोग। अब इस 25 प्रतिशत को 41 प्रतिशत बनाया जाता है, करीब 50 अन्य भाषाओं को हिन्दी मानकर। इसमें भोजपुरी, ब्रज, अवधी, बुन्देली, जैसी जो भाषाएँ हैं, उनकी अपनी संस्कृति है, अपना साहित्य है, इनको हिन्दी के अन्तर्गत लाया गया है, यह दर्शाने के लिए कि ये स्वायत्त भाषाएँ नहीं हैं और भारत में 50 प्रतिशत लोग हिन्दी बोलते हैं। हम ये भी जानते हैं कि सरकारी हिन्दी का गठन राष्ट्रीय आन्दोलन के दौरान इन्हीं मध्यमवर्गीय सवर्ण तबकों ने किया था। हिन्दुस्तानी से उर्दू, फ़ारसी के शब्द निकाल कर बोल–चाल की हिन्दुस्तानी को साफ किया गया और सरहद के उस पार उर्दू को भी उसी तरह साफ किया गया। तो हम देखते हैं कि देश या राष्ट्र शुद्धता माँगता है हमसे, और शुद्धता के पैमाने या शुद्धता के मापदण्ड तय करते हैं वही ताकतवर तबके जिन की एक ख़ासियत यह भी है कि वे घोर पुरुषवादी होते हैं। जब ये तबके उस शुद्धता को परखने की बात करते हैं तो ज़ाहिर है, उस पैमाने पर कम ही लोग खरे उतर पाते हैं – हम सब अशुद्ध निकलेंगे।

घर में हम हिन्दी नहीं बोलते थे, मेरी मातृभाषा मलयालम है। हम फिल्मों से हिन्दी सीखते थे। लेकिन हिन्दी की क्लास में अगर मैंने मोहब्बत लिखा तो उसे काटकर प्रेम लिखा जाता था। अगर मैंने मुश्किल कहा तो उसको कठिन कर दिया जाता था। एक कठोर किस्म का संस्कृतकरण जो हिन्दी के साथ हुआ है वो भी एक वजह है कि हम जैसे लोग जिनकी मातृभाषा हिन्दी नहीं है, हम उस तरह से ठीक और शुद्ध हिन्दी नहीं बोल सकते। हिन्दी बोलने का हौसला मेरा तब बढ़ा जब मैं पोलिटिकल ऐक्टिविज़्म में उतरी, तब मैंने देखा कि बिहार और राजस्थान से भी कामरेड आते हैं, उनकी मातृभाषा भी हिन्दी है, लेकिन उनमें कोई झिझक नहीं है शब्दों के लिंग वगैरह के बारे में। वे हिन्दी वैसी ही बोलते हैं जैसी उनके यहाँ बोली जाती है। हिन्दी बोलने का साहस मुझे उन्हीं से मिला।

उन्नीसवीं सदी के एक इतिहासकार एर्नस्ट रेनान ने कहा था 'Nation is a Daily Plebiscite' यानी कि "राष्ट्र एक रोज़ाना रायशुमारी है"। इसका अर्थ है कि राष्ट्र कोई प्राकृतिक चीज़ नहीं है। राष्ट्र का एक इतिहास है। जब से धरती पे इंसान रहे हैं, तब से लोग तरह–तरह के समुदायों में साथ–साथ रहते रहे हैं। राष्ट्र उनमें से ही एक समुदाय है, जो एक ख़ास ऐतिहासिक क्षण में जन्म लेता है। यूरोप में 18वीं सदी के आखिर से और भारत में 19वीं सदी से राष्ट्र के गठन की प्रक्रिया शुरू होती है। हमारे यहाँ राष्ट्रीय आन्दोलन के दौरान साम्राज्यवाद के ख़िलाफ राष्ट्र के निर्माण के कई स्रोत रहे हैं, चाहे वो 'सेक्युलर नेहरूवादी' हों या 'हिन्दुत्ववादी' हों। इण्डिया नामक आईडिया का स्वरूप 19वीं सदी में उभर कर आता है, जब से यह कहा जाने लगा कि इण्डिया या भारत हज़ारों साल पुराना है।

जब साम्राज्यवाद को हटाकर देश को आज़ादी मिल जाती है, तब से यह माना जाने लगता है कि अब राष्ट्र के बारे में कोई सवाल उठाना बिल्कुल नाजायज़ है। राष्ट्रीय आन्दोलन के दौरान कई सारे प्रश्नों पर विवाद होता रहा, मसलन इण्डिया क्या है, भारतीय कौन है, अर्थव्यवस्था किस तरह की होनी चाहिए, वगैरह लेकिन 15 अगस्त 1947 की तारीख जब आ गयी, आज़ादी मिल गई, तो उसके बाद न्याय–अन्याय के बारे में सवाल उठाना, हमारी सम्पदाओं पर किसका हक़ हो, यह पूछना, या पर्यावरणीय स्थिरता को ले के कोई भी सवाल उठाना, अचानक एण्टी–नेशनल यानी देशद्रोह करार किया जाने लगा। यह राष्ट्र–राज्य का एक बहुत ही महत्वपूर्ण खेल है। इसके बाद आप सवाल नहीं उठायेंगे और इसके बाद यदि आप सवाल उठाते हैं तो आप देशद्रोही हैं। इसलिये राजद्रोह या सेडीशन का कानून मौजूद है, सेक्शन 124ए, जिसके अन्तर्गत हमारे दोस्तों को एण्टी नेशनल कहा जा रहा है। ऐसा पहली बार नहीं हो रहा है। राजद्रोह का चार्ज पहले भी उन पत्रकारों पर और देशभर में कई लोगों पर लगा है, जिन्होंने सरकार की आलोचना की है। स्वतंत्र भारत की सरकारों को इस उपनिवेशवादी कानून को बिल्कुल भी बदलने की कभी कोई ज़रूरत नहीं महसूस हुई। इस कानून में से कुछ शब्द निकाले गये जो कि स्वतंत्र भारत के सन्दर्भ में अप्रासंगिक लगे, जैसे कि 'हर मेजेस्टी', 'क्राउन रिप्रेजेन्टेटिव', 'ब्रिटिश इण्डिया', 'ब्रिटिश बर्मा' बस! बस यही शब्द निकाले गये। 150 साल पुराना ये वही कानून है जिसके बूते पर एक साम्राज्यवादी सरकार ने इस देश को चलाया था। उसी कानून के जरिये अब एक तथाकथित स्वायत्त, स्वतंत्र राष्ट्र इस देश को चला रहा है। बिल्कुल सतही या 'कॉस्मेटिक' परिवर्तन हुए हैं उस साम्राज्यवादी कानून में।

जब हम कहते हैं कि राष्ट्र एक 'रोज़ाना रायशुमारी' है, हम क्या कर रहे हैं? हम जनतंत्र को ज़्यादा प्राथमिकता दे रहे हैं। हम कह रहे हैं कि सबसे बड़ा मूल्य है, जनतंत्र। जनतंत्र एक प्रक्रिया है जो जारी रहती है, चलती रहती है और वो कभी

ख़त्म नहीं होती। जब आपको लगेगा कि सभी तबके इसमें आ गये हैं, तभी एक नयी 'पहचान' खड़ी हो जायेगी यह दावा करते हुए कि आपने हमारे बारे में नहीं सोचा। तरह–तरह की चुनौतियाँ आयेंगी। जनतंत्रीकरण एक हमेशा आगे बढ़ती प्रक्रिया है, जबकि राष्ट्र–राज्य एक ऐसी संस्था है जिसको समझा जाता है कि वो बन चुकी है, उसकी प्रक्रिया खत्म हो चुकी है। जैसे कि वो एक तरह से जम गया है भारत राष्ट्र है, अब इसके बारे में कोई सवाल नहीं उठाया जायेगा। इसीलिए हमारे कई जाने–माने लेखक और चिन्तक, जो साम्राज्यवाद के ख़िलाफ खड़े हुए, जैसे टैगोर से लेकर गाँधी, अम्बेडकर, पेरियार तक, सभी ने राष्ट्रवाद और राष्ट्र–राज्य को शक की नज़र से देखा।

टैगोर ने कहा, 'the nation should not become all powerful at the cost of a higher social life'. अम्बेडकर 'साइमन कमीशन' से मिलकर आये, जबकि बाकी सारे राष्ट्रवादी 'साइमन कमीशन' का बहिष्कार कर रहे थे। अम्बेडकर को पता था कि इस उभरते हुए राष्ट्र–राज्य में जो भी प्रभावशाली तबके हैं, जो ब्राह्मणवादी तत्व हैं, वही राष्ट्र को अपने हित में कर लेंगे। अम्बेडकर समझते थे कि अगर 'साइमन कमीशन' से दलितों और पिछड़ी जातियों को कुछ सहारा मिले तो उन्हें उनसे मिलने के लिए तैयार होना चाहिए। इसी को लेकर अरुण शौरी ने अम्बेडकर को एण्टी–नेशनल कहा। क्या सम्मान मिल रहा है हम को, जे. एन. यू. को, कि हमें वो उपाधि दी जा रही है जो बाबासाहेब अम्बेडकर को मिली! पेरियार ने भी राष्ट्रवाद को शक की नज़र से देखा था। वे भी यही समझते थे कि यह एक प्रक्रिया है जिसे कभी ख़त्म नहीं होना चाहिए। इस पर सवाल उठेंगे और सामाजिक परिवर्तन होता रहेगा।

सावित्री बाई फुले ने पुणे में सब से पहला स्त्री शिक्षा का स्कूल खोला था। उसमें ग्यारह साल की एक दलित छात्रा मुक्ताबाई पढ़ती थीं। 1855 में मराठी पत्रिका *ज्ञानोदय* में उनका लिखा हुआ एक रोचक पैसेज सुना रही हूँ:

"पहले, गोखले, आप्टे, त्रिम्काजी ये सारे ब्राह्मण नाम हैं, अपने घर में चूहों को मार कर अपनी बहादुरी दिखाने वाले, बिना वजह हम पर अत्याचार करते थे, गर्भवती महिलाओं को भी नहीं छोड़ते थे। ये सब अब बन्द हो गया। पेशवों के जमाने में महार और मांग दलित जाति, लोगों का शोषण आम बात थी, अब वो नहीं होता। किलों और महलों की नींव डालते वक़्त दलितों का मनुष्य–बलिदान जैसी कुरीति अब नहीं रही। अब हमारे लोग आबाद हैं। पहले, अगर महार और मांग अच्छे कपड़े पहनते, तो ब्राह्मण कहते कि उनका ही हक़ बनता है ढंग के कपड़े पहनने का, और इस जुर्रत के लिए दलितों को सज़ा देते, पेड़ों से बाँध कर पीटते। पर अब, ब्रिटिश शासन में, जिसके पास पैसे हैं, वो अच्छे कपड़े खरीद के पहन सकते हैं।"

मुक्ताबाई की समझ में, दरअसल, ब्रिटिश शासन के रहने से ब्राह्मणवाद को बहुत बड़ी चोट पहुँची। उनको कोई भी हिचकिचाहट नहीं है यह कहने में कि अब, ब्रिटिश के रहने से, ब्राह्मणवाद पर प्रहार हुआ है, देश आगे बढ़ा है।

संक्षेप में, मेरे कहने का मतलब है कि राष्ट्रविरोधी होने की हमारी बहुत गौरवशाली परम्परा है!

राष्ट्र–राज्य और जनतंत्र में एक गहरा अन्तर्विरोध है और यह अन्तर्विरोध अधिक गहरा होता जा रहा है क्योंकि जैसे–जैसे लोग जनवादी आवाजें उठाते हैं, उनको राष्ट्र–राज्य राष्ट्रहित के नाम पे कुचलने की कोशिश करता है। राष्ट्रहित सिर्फ एक एलीट तबके के नज़रिए से समझा जाता है। ज़ाहिर है, कि कोई भी सवाल उठायेगा तो उस पर राष्ट्रद्रोही होने का लेबल लगाया जायेगा।

अब मैं तीन कहानियाँ सुनाऊँगी। इनसे ये समझ सकते हैं कि राष्ट्र वास्तव में कितना नाज़ुक है। हमें लगता है कि राष्ट्र–राज्य बहुत ही मज़बूत चीज़ है। लेकिन अगर इतना ही मज़बूत होता तो दो लड़कों या पाँच लड़कों ने कोई नारा लगाया भी होता तो इस तरह नहीं डरता। उस बात को हवा में उड़ा देता जैसे मक्खी को उड़ाते हैं। 26 जनवरी को राजपथ पर जो हम हथियारों की परेड देखते हैं, वो ही है साक्षात राष्ट्र–राज्य! और इतना डर कि चार लड़कों ने कोई स्लोगन उठाया और राष्ट्र–राज्य हिल गया? तो ज़ाहिर है राष्ट्र–राज्य इतना मज़बूत नहीं है जितना हम समझते हैं। उस मज़बूती को बनाये रखने के लिए उनको हर टैंक, हर बन्दूक, हर कानून की ज़रूरत पड़ती है।

पहली कहानी सादिया की है। एक पाकिस्तानी लड़की जो हमारी दोस्त बन गयी, दिल्ली में रह रही थी, ओडिसी नृत्य सीखने के लिए। ज़ाहिर है पाकिस्तान में, वहाँ के जो देशभक्त हैं, वे सादिया को बहुत बड़ा देशद्रोही समझते होंगे, क्योंकि वह भारत आकर ओडिसी सीख रही थी। सादिया के घर में जो औरत काम करती थी, उसे कभी समझ में नहीं आया कि सादिया कहाँ से है। वह कभी–कभी सादिया से पूछती थी – 'दीदी आप कहाँ से हैं?' तो सादिया कहती थी – 'पाकिस्तान से।' उसे जब बात समझ में नहीं आयी, तो सादिया कहती थी कि मैं यहाँ से नहीं हूँ, मैं और एक देश से हूँ। तब वो औरत पूछती थी, 'यहाँ मतलब? आप दिल्ली से नहीं हैं?' सादिया कहती कि मैं हिन्दुस्तान से ही नहीं हूँ। लेकिन इस औरत को कभी समझ में नहीं आता था कि पाकिस्तान–हिन्दुस्तान हैं क्या चीज़! कि भारत 'हमारा' देश है और सरहद पार एक दुश्मन देश भी है!

इससे हम क्या समझ सकते हैं? ये औरत घरेलू काम करके अपना गुज़ारा कर रही थी। ज़ाहिर है वह ज़्यादा पढ़ी–लिखी नहीं थी। उसे समझ में ही नहीं आ रहा था कि ये भारत या हिन्दुस्तान क्या है, हिन्दुस्तान से न होने का मतलब क्या है। यानी, ये चीज़ कोई प्राकृतिक ज्ञान नहीं है, जैसे कि बच्चा पैदा होते ही माँ से दूध

पीना जानता है, वैसे ही वह राष्ट्र को फ़ौरन पहचान जाता हो। हमें हर चीज़ सीखनी पड़ती है। आख़िर हमें मर्द और औरत बनना भी हर रोज़ सीखना–सिखाना पड़ता है। जेंडर भी एक रोज़ाना रायशुमारी है। खैर।

जब हमें हर दिन सीखना पड़ता है कि कैसे मर्द बन के रहें, कैसे औरत बनके रहें, जब इतनी प्राकृतिक चीज़ हमें सीखनी पड़ती है, तो ज़ाहिर है कि राष्ट्रवाद भी सीखना पड़ता है। इसीलिए बेनेडिक्ट एण्डर्सन ने राष्ट्र को 'इमैजिंड कम्युनिटी' कहा है। उनका मतलब यह नहीं था कि राष्ट्र महज़ काल्पनिक कम्युनिटी है, यह असली नहीं है। उनका मतलब यह था कि इसका गठन करना पड़ता है। कल्पना में लाकर इसका गठन करना पड़ता है। इस गठन में तरह–तरह की आशाएँ होंगी। तरह–तरह की उम्मीदें होंगी। तरह–तरह की माँगे होंगी। अगर हम इन सभी चीज़ों को साथ लेकर नहीं चलते तो राष्ट्र का गठन नहीं होगा। लेकिन जितने लोगों को इसके अन्दर शामिल करने की कोशिश रहती है, उतनी ही कोशिश लोगों को बाहर रखने की होती है। कोई भी राष्ट्र–राज्य नहीं कहता कि सारी दुनिया के लोग इस देश के नागरिक हैं। इसीलिए ही टैगोर को राष्ट्र पर सन्देह था।

तो लीजिये दूसरी कहानी। मैं दिल्ली विश्वविद्यालय के छात्रों के बीच एक बहस के दौरान की गई टिप्पणी की बात करती हूँ। वे हैरानी में कह रहे थे कि नागा विद्यार्थी जब दिल्ली आते हैं, तो कहते हैं इण्डिया जा रहे हैं। वे नागालैंड को भारत का भाग नहीं मानते हैं। मुद्दा क्या है? कि हम नागालैंड को इण्डिया का भाग मानते हैं मगर वो लोग अपने आप को इण्डियन नहीं मानते। ग़ौर कीजिये, कि 'हम' और 'इण्डिया' में सम्मिश्रण हो रहा है। दिल्ली के कुछ विद्यार्थी 'हम' कह सकते हैं ये मानते हुए कि वे इण्डिया की आवाज में बोल रहे हैं। यहाँ सबसे अहम बात है कि नागालैंड की टेरीटरी को वे अपना मानते हैं, लेकिन जो नागा विद्यार्थी कह रहे हैं उसको सुनने के लिए वे तैयार नहीं हैं। उनसे पूछिए, आप दिल्ली को 'इण्डिया' क्यों कह रहे हैं, सुनिए उनकी बात, तो इतिहास समझेंगे आप नागालैंड का।

नागालैंड हमारा है, कश्मीर हमारा है, लेकिन कश्मीरी, नागा, हमारे नहीं हैं? यह माना जा रहा है कि नागालैंड और कश्मीर की धरती पूर्व रूप से 'भारत' नामक प्रदेश में शामिल है, भारत के लोग बाद में आये। ऐसे में ये माना जा रहा है कि राष्ट्र लोगों से पहले है या राष्ट्र का जन्म लोगों से पहले हुआ है। ऐसे राष्ट्रवादियों के दिमाग में 'मुर्गी या अण्डा' वाला सवाल है ही नहीं! उनके दिमाग में बहुत स्पष्ट है कि इण्डिया, जिस तरह हम उसका नक्शा बनाते हैं, वो इण्डिया किसी ईश्वर ने दिया है, या जैसे बारिश धरती पर पड़ती है, उसी किस्म के प्राकृतिक नियम या तरीके से बना है।

यदि आपने *हिमाल पत्रिका* पढ़ी है तो देखा होगा कि उन्होंने एक नक्शा बनाया है जिसमें भारत को उल्टा दिखाया गया है। श्रीलंका ऊपर है, कश्मीर नीचे। उस नक्शे

को देखते ही लोग कहते हैं कि ये उल्टा नक्शा आप क्यों रख रहे हैं। लेकिन हम सब जानते हैं कि धरती गोल है। उल्टा कुछ भी नहीं है। उल्टा इसलिए लगता है, क्योंकि नक्शा बनाने के लिए कुछ कनवेंशन्स हैं। उत्तर ऊपर, दक्षिण नीचे, दिखाया जाता है। लेकिन उत्तर को नीचे करने से दुनिया की तस्वीर ग़लत नहीं हो जाती है, सिर्फ अजनबी–सी हो जाती है। हमें तथ्यों के बारे में दुबारा सोचने पर मजबूर करती है।

अब आप ये सोचें कि उस आम नक्शे पर, जिसे हम सब पहचानते हैं, उस पर कैसे "भारत माता" की छवि को बनाया गया है जो कि बिल्कुल प्राकृतिक लगता है, कश्मीर सर है, गुजरात और बंगाल बाहें हैं, इत्यादि। प्राकृतिक ही नहीं, राष्ट्र को एक शरीर (माता के शरीर) जैसा दिखाने से, देश का हर भाग उसका अटूट हिस्सा बन जाता है। शरीर के किसी अंग को काटके क्या इंसान ज़िन्दा रहेगा? क्या देश ज़िन्दा रहेगा, अगर कोई भाग उससे छूट जाये? लेकिन इस नक्शे को "उल्टा" दिखाएँ तो वह भारत माता नहीं लगेगी, शरीर नहीं लगेगा।

राष्ट्र कोई प्राकृतिक शरीर नहीं है, इंसानों द्वारा बनाया गया ढाँचा है। राष्ट्र को हमें जनतंत्र के नज़रिए से देखना चाहिए, जिससे समझ में आयेगा कि हर समस्या का हल बातचीत और समझौते से हो सकता है।

तीसरी कहानी ये है कि मेरी एक दोस्त लेह (लद्दाख) में पाठ्यपुस्तकों के संशोधन पर काम कर रही थी, तो उसने पाया कि उन किताबों में लेह की जगहों या पेड़–पौधों और जानवरों की जानकारी नहीं थी। वहां के बच्चे वही पढ़ रहे थे जो इण्डिया की और जगहों पर पढ़ाया जाता था। स्थानीय कोई जानकारी नहीं थी उन किताबों में। पर सब से मज़ेदार बात यह थी कि पीढ़ियों से लेह के बच्चे पढ़ रहे थे कि 'हिमालय हमारे उत्तर में है'।

ऐसे में ज़ाहिर है राष्ट्र समावेशी नहीं है। राष्ट्र ज़्यादा लोगों को शामिल करने की कोशिश भी नहीं करता, बल्कि राष्ट्र के नाम पे बोलने वालों का प्रयास ये रहता है कि ज़्यादातर लोगों को ज़बरदस्ती बदल कर अपने जैसा बना डालो, यानी उन मुट्ठी भर मर्दों, हिन्दी–भाषी क्षेत्र के, सवर्ण मर्दों जैसे। उन जैसे अगर बनो तो यहाँ रह सकते हो, वरना धरती हमारी, तुम लोग पाकिस्तान जाओ।

तो क्या हमें कहना चाहिए कि हमें ज़्यादा समावेशी राष्ट्रवाद चाहिए? हमारे राष्ट्र के मायने में ज़्यादा से ज़्यादा लोगों को शामिल करना चाहिए?

लेकिन सवाल यह उठता है कि क्या ऐसा हो भी सकता है? ये 'हम' बड़ा ही अजीब शब्द है, क्योंकि हर कोई 'हम' शब्द इस्तेमाल नहीं कर सकता। नागा विद्यार्थी नहीं कह सकते, भारत के नाम पर, 'हम', वे चाहें भी अगर। वो नागा हम नहीं है। लद्दाखी हम नहीं है। हम, 'हम' ही कह सकते हैं। हम जो निपट भारत के इलीट हैं। हम बड़े उदार दिल के हैं। हम सबको शामिल करना चाहते हैं, बशर्ते आप हमारी तय

की हुई नीतियों के आधार पर रहें। हम जो कहते हैं, पहनें; हम जिसे दिव्य मानते हैं, उसे आप भी मानें; हम जो कहते हैं, खायें; हम जो ठीक समझते हैं, करें।

आप देखें कि कब 'हम' का इस्तेमाल होता है।

'हमारे पास परमाणु बम है'।

'हम मैच जीत गये'।

लेकिन क्या कोई कह सकता है कि 'नर्मदा पर बने बाँध से हम, भारत, डूबने वाले हैं'?

अब संख्या को देखें।

आख़िर सिर्फ ग्यारह मर्दों ने मैच जीता। (मर्द ही कहें क्यों कि हम ये भी जानते हैं कि महिला क्रिकेट में किसी को कोई दिलचस्पी नहीं है!)। एक मुट्ठी–भर लोग जो न्युक्लियर एस्टैब्लिशमेंट चलाते हैं, उन्होंने परमाणु–बम बनाया और उनके हाथों में है उस बम के बारे में सारे निर्णय। फिर भी इन मामलों में देश के नागरिक कहेंगे "हम"।

अब नर्मदा के बाँधों को लें। हजारों की तादाद में लोग नर्मदा घाटी में बेघर हुए हैं। लेकिन वे नहीं कह सकते हैं कि 'हम' (यानि हिन्दुस्तान) नर्मदा के पानी में डूब रहा है।

हम बार–बार इण्डिया–इण्डिया कहते हैं। क्या भारत का सही इतिहास सबको बताया जाता है? क्या हमें सिखाया जाता है कि भारत में कश्मीर का विलय कैसे हुआ? स्कूल में पाठ्य पुस्तकों में भी सही इतिहास नहीं बताया जाता है। स्वयंघोषित राष्ट्रवादी लोग इतिहास पर इतना बड़ा हमला क्यों करना चाहते हैं? क्योंकि इतिहास अगर हम जान गये तो राष्ट्र के सारे रहस्य खुल जायेंगे। राष्ट्रवाद की पोल खुल जायेगी! यही है असली समस्या।

बात ये है कि 15 अगस्त 1947 में, उस वक्त कई जगहें ऐसी थीं, कई क्षेत्र ऐसे थे इस महाद्वीप में, जिनके अपने स्वायत्त इतिहास थे। वे सीधे ब्रिटिश सरकार से डील कर रहे थे, बातचीत कर रहे थे। लेकिन इन प्रक्रियाओं को एक तरफ़ करके स्वतंत्र इण्डियन राष्ट्र–राज्य ने इन क्षेत्रों को 'इण्डियन टेरिटरी' घोषित कर दिया।

कुछ उदाहरण लीजिये। मणिपुर 1947 में एक स्वतन्त्र संवैधानिक राजतन्त्र बना था, जनतांत्रिक तरीके से चुनी विधान सभा सहित। ब्रिटिश के साथ बातचीत से, बिल्कुल जनतांत्रिक तरीके से, एक संवैधानिक राजतन्त्र मणिपुर में तय हुआ था। लेकिन स्वतंत्र भारत बनते ही, मणिपुर के राजा को गिरफ़्तार कर लिया गया और मणिपुर का इण्डिया के साथ ज़बरदस्ती विलय कर लिया गया।[1]

नागालैण्ड को देखिए। हैदरी समझौते के तहत नागा नैशनल कौंसिल और ब्रिटिश सरकार के बीच बातचीत से नागालैण्ड को दस साल का प्रोटेक्टिड स्टेटस दिया गया। उसके बाद उनको जनमत या रायशुमारी का हक़ दिया गया था। लेकिन ब्रिटिश सरकार के जाते ही इण्डियन राष्ट्र–राज्य ने नागा टेरीटरी को अपनी घोषित किया।[2]

उत्तर–पूर्व के सारे क्षेत्रों के ऐसे ही इतिहास हैं, और वहाँ भारत का राज कायम रखने के लिए तब से आज तक ज़बरदस्त सैन्य मौजूदगी की आवश्यकता रही है। यहाँ तक कि मिज़ोरम की राजधानी आइजॉल पर 1966 में भारतीय वायु–सेना द्वारा बम गिराए गये। यानी, भारतीय राष्ट्र–राज्य ने अपने ही निहत्थे, सिविलियन नागरिकों पर हवाई बमबारी की।

कश्मीर की कहानी मुझे बताने की ज़रूरत नहीं है। आप सब जानते हैं कि जो सिद्धान्त बाकी रियासतों के लिए अपनाया गया, वो यह था कि जो समुदाय बहुसंख्या में था, उसकी राय ली गयी, कि भारत में रहे या पाकिस्तान के साथ जाये। मसलन जूनागढ़ को लीजिए। जूनागढ़ के शासक मुसलमान थे, लोग हिन्दू थे। शासक चाहते थे कि पाकिस्तान के साथ जायें। लेकिन सिद्धान्त यह दोहराया गया कि 'लोग क्या चाहते हैं'? लोगों ने चाहा कि वहाँ हिन्दू बहुसंख्यक हैं, इसलिए वे हिन्दुस्तान के साथ रहेंगे। जूनागढ़ हिन्दुस्तान में आ गया। ऐसे ही हैदराबाद रियासत के साथ भी हुआ। कश्मीर में मुसलमान बहुसंख्यक थे, और राजा हिन्दू थे। विलय के बारे में चर्चा चल ही रही थी, कि पाकिस्तानी हमले हुए। राजा ने भारत से मदद माँगी, और इस मदद के लिए भारत के साथ विलय की शर्त रखी गयी। लेकिन कश्मीर की तरफ़ से भी एक शर्त थी, कि जब स्थिति शान्त हो जायेगी तब जनमत संग्रह होगा। आख़िर यही सिद्धान्त बाकी रियासतों के साथ भी अपनाया गया था, कि बहुसंख्यक समुदाय की राय को वज़न दिया जायेगा। लेकिन तब से आज तक जनमत संग्रह नहीं हुआ है।[3]

हमें अच्छा लगे या बुरा, लेकिन हम सब जानते हैं कि दुनिया–भर में ये माना जाता है कि भारत ने कश्मीर को अवैध तरीके से अधिकृत किया है। इस का एक संकेत है, भारत के नक्शों को लेकर विवाद। आपने ग़ौर किया होगा, अक्सर सुनने में आता है कि कोई विदेशी पत्रिका, जैसे *टाइम* या *न्यूज़वीक*, या *दी इकोनोमिस्ट*, के किसी अंक को भारत में आने से रोका गया क्योंकि उनमें भारत का 'ग़लत' नक्शा छपा गया है।[4] गलत नक्शों का क्या मतलब है? मतलब यह है कि कश्मीर की कुछ जगहों को पाकिस्तान और चीन के अन्तर्गत दिखाया गया है। इसका मतलब है कि सारी दुनिया में जो नक्शे चलते हैं, भारत की सरहदों के, इन नक्शों में, और हम जो नक्शे इण्डिया में देखते हैं, उनमें बहुत बड़ा फर्क है। और भारतीय राष्ट्र–राज्य हर सम्भव कदम उठाता है कि उसके नागरिक ये नक्शे न देखें।

मज़े कि बात ये है कि हाल ही में, मार्च 2015 में, राष्ट्रीय स्वयंसेवक संघ की पत्रिका *ऑर्गनाइज़र* को सार्वजानिक माफी माँगनी पड़ी, जब मार्च 15 के अंक के पृष्ट 32 पर, भारत का नक्शा ग़लत दिखाया गया। वही ग़लती, कि कश्मीर के कुछ भाग पाकिस्तान के अन्दर दिखाये गये। अगले अंक में माफ़ी दर्ज की गयी, यह कहते हुए कि दक्षिण एशिया का नक्शा किसी वेबसाईट से उतारा गया था, और उस नक्शे की

ग़लती पर *ऑर्गनाइजर* को बहुत खेद है क्योंकि वे हमेशा जम्मू–कश्मीर को भारत का अटूट अंग मानते चले आये हैं।[5]

जब *ऑर्गनाइज़र* की विचारधारा के लोग भी भारत का नक्शा इन्टरनेट पर खोजते हैं, उनको वही नक्शा मिलता है जो 'ग़लत' है। यानि अगर हर आम स्रोत में पाये गये नक्शों में और भारत के अन्दर उपलब्ध नक्शों में ये फ़र्क है, तो क्या हमें नहीं सोचना चाहिए कि भारतीय नागरिकों को जो समझाया जा रहा है, वो दुनिया नहीं मानती? भले ही हम बार–बार कहें कि कश्मीर भारत का अटूट अंग है, उसकी स्थिति दुनिया की निगाहों में दरअसल अति विवादास्पद है।

अगर कश्मीर में आज़ादी का नारा उठता है, तो हम कम–से–कम ये समझें कि दुनिया में 'इण्डिया' को किस तरह समझा जा रहा है। इण्डिया बिल्कुल एक साम्राज्यवादी देश की तरह माना जाता है। तो क्या हमें इस पर गर्व होना चाहिए? और ज़ाहिर है कि जब मैं आज़ादी के नारे को तवज्जो दे रही हूँ, मेरी राय यह नहीं है कि कश्मीर पाकिस्तान का है, बल्कि ये कि कश्मीर के लोगों को अपना भविष्य खुद चुनने का हक है।

कश्मीर में आज़ादी के कई मायने हैं, और आज़ादी क्या है, इस पर कश्मीरियों में बहस जारी है। कई लोगों के लिए आज़ादी का मतलब है, साफ साफ भारत से आज़ादी। लेकिन कई ऐसे हैं जिनके लिए इसका मतलब है कश्मीर का असैनिकीकरण, अफस्पा को रद्द करना और कश्मीर की प्राकृतिक सम्पदाओं पर, ख़ास कर पानी पर, कश्मीर के लोगों का नियंत्रण।

हम जानते हैं कि अफस्पा के ख़िलाफ लोगों की जनतांत्रिक भावनाएँ बुलन्द हैं, वे चाहे नार्थ–ईस्ट में हों या कश्मीर में हों या छत्तीसगढ़ में हों। अफस्पा एक बहुत ही महत्वपूर्ण ब्रह्मास्त्र है जिससे भारतीय राष्ट्र–राज्य किसी न किसी तरह सामाजिक व्यवस्था (सोशल ऑर्डर) को कायम रखता है। अफस्पा के तहत इलाक़ों में एक निरन्तर रोज़ाना की इमरजेन्सी है। जहाँ अफस्पा है वहाँ हमारे नाम पर यानि कि, भारत के नागरिकों के नाम पर, हमारे चुने हुए जनप्रतिनिधि अफस्पा चला रहे हैं। हम सब इस अन्याय में शामिल हैं। यह हमारे नाम पर किया जा रहा है।

सात राज्यों में अफस्पा है, और मई 2015 तक आठ राज्यों में था, त्रिपुरा सहित। यानी भारत के राज्यों में से करीब एक चौथाई राज्यों में अफस्पा चलता है। अफस्पा के अन्तर्गत संविधान के सारे जनतांत्रिक अधिकार रद्द होते हैं, और भारी सैनिक मौजूदगी हर जगह देखने को मिलेगी।

इसके अलावा करीब 680 में से 101 जिलों में 'डिस्टर्बड एरियाज़ एक्ट' के तहत सैन्य ताकतों को ख़ास पावर दिये गये हैं। लिहाज़ा हम ये कह सकते हैं कि भारत

की आबादी के करीब 30 प्रतिशत लोग किसी न किसी तरह सैन्य ताकतों के नियंत्रण में हैं।[6] और हम अपने आप को दुनिया का सबसे बड़ा जनतंत्र मानते हैं!

भारत का जो चेहरा कश्मीर देखता है, नार्थ–ईस्ट देखता है या छत्तीसगढ़ का आदिवासी देखता है वह है इण्डियन आर्मी।

यह हमें याद रखना चाहिए।

एन्टीनेशनल किस–किस को माना जाता है, इस सवाल से हम बात को खत्म करें। एक वो हैं जो काउण्टर नेशनलिज़्म प्रकट करते हैं और दूसरे वो जो विकास के ख़लाफ़ हैं, क्योंकि ज़ाहिर है कि बड़े बाँध, फ्लाईओवर और मॉल्स, ये सब ही 'विकास' हैं और साधारण लोगों की रोज़मर्रा की ज़िन्दगी में और उनके मसलों में 'विकासवादियों' को ज़रा भी दिलचस्पी नहीं है। तो जो इस तरह के विकास के ख़िलाफ हैं, वे भी एन्टीनेशनल ठहराये जाते हैं। मतलब काउण्टर नेशन्लिज़्म और तथाकथित विकास के ख़िलाफ जो बोलते हैं, वे सब एन्टीनेशनल हैं।

अगर हम कभी एन्टीनेशनल लोगों की लिस्ट बनाने की कोशिश करें तो वह बढ़ती जायेगी, लगातार बढ़ती जायेगी।

नर्मदा–बचाओ आन्दोलन और सारे आदिवासी एन्टीनेशनल हैं। पूरा का पूरा नार्थ–ईस्ट एन्टीनेशनल है। कश्मीर तो है ही, मुसलमान तो सारे ही एन्टीनेशनल हैं। अब ईसाई भी एन्टीनेशनल बन गये हैं। अम्बेडकरवादी एन्टीनेशनल हैं क्योंकि कबीर कला मंच के बहुत सारे लोग जेल में हैं। वे गाना गाते हैं जातिवाद के ख़िलाफ। तमिलनाडु तो है ही क्योंकि हिन्दी नहीं बोलेंगे। ये तमिलनाडु बहुत दिनों से एन्टीनेशनल है। भूमि–अधिग्रहण के ख़िलाफ जो किसान और आदिवासी बोलते हैं वे भी एन्टीनेशनल हैं। जो औरतें जीन्स पहनती हैं, शराब पीती हैं, पितृसत्ता को नहीं मानती हैं, वे भी एन्टीनेशनल हैं। जो समलैंगिक प्यार करते हैं वे भी एन्टीनेशनल हैं ।

अगर हम इन लोगों की राष्ट्रवाद की परिभाषा के हिसाब से सोचेंगे तो शायद 24–25 लोग रह जाते हैं जो सच्चे देशभक्त हैं।

हमें राष्ट्रवाद की इस परिभाषा के बारे में बहुत चिन्ता करनी चाहिए!

*

Notes/References/Bibliography

1. Namrata Goswami, 2014, *Indian National Security and Counter-Insurgency: The Use of Force vs Non-violent Response*, Routledge.
2. Sanjib Baruah, 'Nations within Nation States', *Hindustan Times*, 13 October 2005.

3. Balraj Puri, 1993, *Kashmir. Towards Insurgency,* Orient Longman, Hyderabad.
4. 'Kashmir Map in the *Economist* Sparks India Censorship Row'; AFP (2011) http://www.theaustralian.com.au/news/world/kashmir-map-in-the-economist-sparks-india-censorship-row/story-e6frg6so-1226062121063; *The Australian*, 24 May 2011; Prabhu Chawla, 'Magazines: Holding Action', *India Today*, 22 July 2013.
5. 'RSS Mouthpiece *Organiser* Apologizes for PoK Map Error', *The Times of India*, 14 March 2015.
6. Gautam Navlakha, 'Armed Forces as Livelihood and State Power', Kafila https://kafila.org/2015/12/02/armed-forces-as-livelihood-and-state-power-gautam-navlakha/, 2015.

Picture credit: Sorit Gupto, *Down to Earth*

Civil Liberties and Indian Nationalism

Mridula Mukherjee

(24 FEBRUARY 2016)

WELL, FRIENDS AND, OF COURSE, ALL my dear students and former students, I would like to begin by saying that, as all of you know, this is one of the toughest times that JNU and perhaps the country is going through. I was rather worried when I read a report in today's newspaper about a function held yesterday for a book written by our former home minister and finance minister, P. Chidambaram. The report said that in his speech Chidambaram noted that in the history of independent India, there were three moments where there has been such polarization: the first was during the Partition in 1947, the second was the Babri Masjid demolition and what happened around it in 1992 and the third moment is what is happening around us now.

I am beginning with this to try and bring to you the significance of what is happening today. What is happening is not *just* about JNU, as I'm sure all of you are aware. It is about JNU, it is about Kanhaiya, it is about all our other students, it's about Anirban, it's about Umar, and yet it's much, much bigger than that, and I think increasingly we all need to get a sense of what we are fighting for, what is it that we are standing up for and how important it is that we continue to stand up for it. Because I do think that JNU has been chosen for this attack precisely because of its significance and the symbolism that it embodies. I think the powers that be feel that if they can cow us down, if they can silence us, if they can frighten the JNU students, they have won the battle. They don't have to go to every university in every town to tell them, 'Don't speak against us and our ideology, don't speak against our idea of India.' The message will go loud and clear. People will say, if JNU couldn't stand up to the pressure, if JNU with its renowned faculty could not stand up to it, if JNU with its wonderful students could not stand up to it, with all the support that it can get internationally, from Nobel laureates, from the best universities, and nationally, from the media, from the parliament, if JNU can't stand up to it, the battle is lost.

So, I think the significance of this battle for all of us is that we are fighting for the nation, on behalf of the people of this nation, and we are lucky in a way that we are the ones who have been chosen for this because we do have the capacity to fight. In difficult times like this, it is privileged places like JNU, and I don't mean privileged in the ordinary sense of the term, that we have more money or we have more facilities, I mean privileged because of the education that we get over here, privileged because of the quality of the faculty and the students, privileged because of our traditions which have been established by the founders of this university, which have given us a very solid grounding. It is very important that each one of us understands this significance and therefore brings to our struggle that seriousness and gravitas, sobriety and sense of purpose.

I also want to use this opportunity to say that a great responsibility devolves on us to be true to the slogans we are putting out and the principles which we are talking about, that we embody: debate, discussion, difference. We are telling the world every day that we are not anti-national, in fact we are nation builders. We are telling the world every day that we believe in debate and in respecting difference, we believe in discussion, we believe in actually sorting out all our problems through our own institutional mechanisms, we are fighting for our autonomy, we are criticizing those in our administration who have been compromising our autonomy. But that puts a very great responsibility on us: that we do actually live these principles. We also need to look inwards, introspect. Where we have been intolerant, we have to ask ourselves, do we need to change? Do we need to become more accommodative of difference? Do we need to engage in more debate and dialogue instead of just tolerating difference? These are some of the things I would like to talk to you about today, linking it with the tradition of the Indian freedom struggle or national movement.

As you know I am not a theoretician, I am not an ideologue, I am an ordinary historian and our craft is a very mundane craft. We wade through very boring archives and we try to make sense of them. We try to bring you some of the excitement of that past. So what I'm going to do is tell you some stories, especially about those parts of our past and of the past of our long battle for freedom which are not so well known. There may be times when you wonder why we need to go back to these old stories. Admiral Ramdas just said we are in the twenty-first century, nationalism is a concept that came up in the seventeenth century, forget it.[1] It's a very nice talking point, but it's actually too serious – nationalism and its power – to be forgotten. How it's being misused, how it's being flung in our face, how in less than two weeks, the image of this university has been changed in this country. You know it when you go out and want to return to JNU and auto drivers ask you if you want to go to Pakistan. (By the way, my answer to that is, 'Why should I want to go to Pakistan when you're making a Pakistan here. Very soon, I wouldn't need to go across the border.') But I think we need to take the idea of nationalism seriously, understand its resonance amongst the people, and try and appropriate to ourselves what I have called, revolutionary nationalism. I also wrote about it recently, arguing that there is a progressive nationalism, a revolutionary nationalism, and there is a regressive and jingoistic nationalism.[2] It's the jingoistic, aggressive nationalism which is calling us anti-nationalist, and we are going to reply to that by telling people, by telling our people, that we stand for the humane, compassionate, pro-people, revolutionary nationalism which our freedom struggle has given us. It's that tradition which we are going to assert and throw in the face of those who are challenging our nationalism.

For my talk today, I have chosen to concentrate on the issue of civil liberties. Because I think it is at the heart of the debate and the attack on us today, and especially on our students, raises the issue very clearly. Every TV channel, every discussion, everywhere you go, they're saying: 'But aren't there limits that must be placed on civil liberties?' 'Is there no restriction on freedom of speech?' What are those limits? What are those restrictions? These are not absolutes, these are not things which you can answer with a yes or no. I think we need to look back at our tradition and see how those who fought and led the struggle that brought this nation into being, how they addressed these issues. What was the nation they envisioned? And how did they see to it, through their own practice and their struggles, that these ideas were embedded and went deep into Indian society.

But just a little caveat before I get on to civil liberties. The legacy of the freedom struggle is manifold but the crucial elements in that are a commitment to secularism, a commitment to democracy and civil liberties, with civil liberties being seen as an essential part of democracy, you cannot have one without the other. But I'm not going to talk about democracy today, I'll focus on civil liberties. There is also the tradition of an egalitarian social and economic order or a pro-poor orientation and there is the tradition or legacy of sovereignty and independence. These are some of the crucial legacies that we have from our freedom struggle, which are embodied in our Constitution. This Constitution was not a gift of the British, democracy was not a gift of the British, we fought for it every inch of the way. As early as 1895, Lokmanya Tilak had published a Constitution of India Bill, in which he had asked for universal adult suffrage, for both men and women, no property qualification, no educational qualification. In Britain, women got the vote after the First World War; in India, of course, as we know we got it in the Constitution. Even before 1895, the struggle for the Constitution of India had been going on, so the Constitution wasn't a one-shot affair, actually much of what the Constitution was finally had been worked out through at least the fifty years before that, through debate, discussion, struggle and long deliberations between the different streams of the Indian national movement.

Coming to civil liberties, I'd like to begin by saying, and this should strengthen all of us, that this tradition goes back at least to Raja Ram Mohan Roy, who is also called the Father of Modern India, and I'm talking about 192 years ago, so when you're fighting this battle for civil liberties, don't feel weak. You have that whole tradition and that whole legacy behind you. (I don't know what's going to happen to the lights, but to the extent I can, I want to share some very interesting quotes with you.) This is in the year 1824, Raja Ram Mohan Roy protested against a regulation restricting the freedom of the press. The regulation did not come earlier because there was no press, so as soon as the modern press started to emerge, the regulation started to emerge. He wrote in a memorandum to the Supreme Court, every good ruler 'will be anxious to afford every individual the readiest means of bringing to his notice whatever may require his interference. To secure this important object, the unrestricted liberty of publication,' please note the words, '*the unrestricted liberty of publication*', 'is the only effectual means that can be employed.'[3]

So this goes back to the early nineteenth century. Even before the establishment of the Indian National Congress in 1885, which we usually take as the beginning of the modern national movement, right from the 1860s, 1870s, 1880s, the demand for civil liberties, and particularly for freedom of the press was an invariant part of the programme of Indian nationalists. In fact I would say Indian nationalism actually began in the Indian-language press. The earliest manifestations of Indian nationalism, and the earliest example of the intelligentsia identifying with the peasant, which becomes a very interesting and important feature of Indian nationalism, began in the 1860s. It is Dinabandhu Mitra who wrote *Neel Darpan*, a play about the Indigo revolt as early as the 1860s, just a few years after the revolt of 1857. Over time, the anti-British nationalist tone of the Indian-language press went on strengthening, to the point that in 1878 the British had to pass the Vernacular Press Act. Why did they have to pass a Vernacular Press Act? To restrict the freedom of the Indian-language press, and not the English-language press. The Indian-language press was far more radical and revolutionary than the English-language press, so they brought in a bill, they passed an act that severely restricted the liberty of the Indian-language press. There was a huge agitation by nationalists and the nationalist press against this act.

In fact, all the early nationalist leaders made maintenance of civil liberties and their extension an integral part of the national movement. They fought against every infringement of the freedom of the press and speech and opposed every attempt to curtail them. I will try and give you a few examples. In fact it was said at that time that the press played the role of the institutional opposition to the government. In the absence of democracy, it was the Indian press, which fought for its freedom every day, which performed this task. The motto of the press had three words, 'Oppose. Oppose. Oppose.' And please remember, I'm talking about the period before the establishment of the Indian National Congress. Every act of the government was subjected to sharp criticism. Lord Dufferin, who was the viceroy in March 1886, barely three months after the formation of the Indian National Congress, said, and I quote, 'Day after day, hundreds of sharp-witted babus pour forth their indignation against their English oppressors in very pungent and effective diatribe.' Would anyone say that of our press today? He continued in the same vein two months later, I quote again, 'In this way there can be no doubt that there is generated in the minds of those who read these papers, a sincere conviction that we are, all of us, the enemies of mankind in general, and India in particular.'[4] That was the tone of the press even before the Indian National Congress was officially founded. However, as we all know now very well in JNU – perhaps the most well-informed place about Section 124A; I'm sure all of you dream about it in your sleep, have it for breakfast, rehearse it at lunch – Section 124A had been brought on to the Indian Penal Code in 1870. So for the press, people who were writing in this press, to preach disloyalty was no easy task, because this section could be used against them. The punishment could go up to transportation for life, and not only imprisonment for life, as it is now.

I would like to make a little caveat here, to point out that the Indian press at this time and the journalists who were there were mostly nationalists, though there was a small pro-British press as well. The nationalist press was all established by very middle-class people, who usually put all their life savings and their family jewellery which they sold happily, and set up this press. Most of them were ruined, their families suffered a lot. It was not big business houses that set up these newspapers.

These nationalist journalists perfected a variety of subterfuges, how to work around Section 124A. They prefaced their vitriolic writings with effusive professions of loyalty to the government and to the queen. So before the abuses it was all presaged by loud professions of loyalty. Some historians have taken that seriously and said that the moderates or early nationalists were loyalist. Another device resorted to was to publish extracts from British newspapers, often without giving the quotation marks and the source, to fool the bureaucracy into contemplating action which of course the bureaucracy had to give up once they discovered the source. The Indian journalists would say we are just repeating what came out in the *London Times* or some such newspaper, and since the British hadn't prosecuted those in Britain, they couldn't very well start prosecuting them here. This was a very, very popular game that they played, and, apart from everything else, it made the bureaucracy look very foolish. Another favourite strategy was that an article in a British newspaper which was, say, sympathetic to terrorist activities against Czarist Russia, would be republished as a means of drawing attention to Indian revolutionary activity, without ever naming the Indian revolutionaries. And you could not be accused of sympathy for them because again you were repeating a British newspaper which was talking about Czarist Russia and not about India. I could go on telling you stories of this kind. Tilak particularly had perfected this art and had a lot of fun at the expense of the police and the bureaucracy.

In fact, the first big mass demonstration in the form of a huge public meeting was organized in Calcutta in the Town Hall on the issue of civil liberties. So modern mass politics in India begins with defence of civil liberties, to oppose the Vernacular Press Act, which I have already mentioned to you, passed in 1878 to gag the Indian-language press. In fact the protests were so powerful that Viceroy Lord Ripon, who had succeeded Lord Lytton, the author of this Act, actually repealed this Act in 1881. This was by no means a small victory for the nationalists.

Surendranath Banerjee, one of the founders of Indian nationalism, was the first to go to jail for his journalistic writings. In an editorial in his newspaper, *Bengalee*, on 2 April 1883, he criticized in sharp tones, a judgment of the Calcutta High Court. He was sent to jail for two months for contempt of court. Vigorous protests followed, there was a total hartal in many parts of Calcutta. Students demonstrated outside the court, they threw stones at the police and smashed the windows of the court. One of the rowdy young men was Ashutosh Mukherjee who later became the famous vice chancellor of Calcutta University. (Who knows some of you may become vice chancellors a few years down the line! Life has a way of turning everything around.) Protests spread to many cities in Bengal and elsewhere, to Lahore, Amritsar, Agra, Faizabad, Poona, all across north India. The first open-air mass meetings were held in Calcutta. This tradition of open-air mass meetings, which is what you are doing here in JNU today, goes back to this period and it became the staple of the Indian national movement. If any particular form of protest is identified with India's freedom struggle, it is the mammoth open-air mass meetings, and this tradition started with the protests against Surendranath Banerjee's arrest in 1883. Surendranath Banerjee is also very significant because he wrote an autobiography which he tellingly titled *A Nation in the Making*, which articulated the early nationalists' conception of India, not as a pre-made, preordained nation which originated in the deep past and was infallible, but a nation that was in the process of being made.

I'm sure you've all heard of Lokmanya Tilak, who went to jail, charged with sedition under Section 124A. Why was he sent to jail on the charge of sedition? Because in his newspaper *Kesari*, which was a Marathi-language newspaper (in English he published *The Mahratta*) on 15 June 1897, he published a poem titled 'Shivaji's Utterances' and also a copy of the speech which he had given at the Shivaji festival. He was tried by Justice Strachey and a jury of six Europeans and three Indians. The verdict: all six Europeans for the sentence and all three Indians against. A barbarous sentence of eighteen months of rigorous imprisonment was passed, and this when Tilak was a member of the Bombay Presidency Legislative Council. The reaction was instantaneous. Again, do remember, this was still before the onset of the Swadeshi movement of 1905–08, when the real mass movement began, so I'm deliberately telling you the story of the pre-mass-movement phase to let you know how deep this tradition is. Widespread countrywide protests followed against this attack on civil liberties, led by the group of nationalists who were called moderates. Who was Tilak? He was a leader of the group which was called extremist. So his political rivals in the freedom struggle were the ones who organized and led the protests against his arrest. Because they believed that civil liberties were sacrosanct and you had to defend your opponent if that opponent was attacked on the ground of suppression of civil liberties. Newspapers came out with black borders. I could go on and on with the story of the protests, but suffice it to say that at the annual session of the Indian National Congress which was held as usual in December that year, Surendranath Banerjee eloquently summed up the mood of the people in a simple phrase, 'a whole nation is in tears'.[5] That was the reaction to Tilak's imprisonment which was seen as an assault on the freedom of the press.

Once again, eleven years later, on 24 June 1908, Tilak was tried on the grounds of sedition, again under the same Section 124A. This time for having published a series of articles called 'On the Arrival of the Bomb'. The timing is important, as this was the last phase of the Swadeshi movement, and within it a political strand had emerged, which was called revolutionary terrorism, and which had now started using bombs and violence against individual government officers, etc. In these articles, while criticizing and condemning the use of violence and the use of the bomb, his whole emphasis was on why this was happening. And he lay the blame squarely at the door of the British, saying, because you do not permit dissent, because you are not giving us freedom, you are pushing our youth into these channels. For writing these articles, even though he condemned the violence, he was charged again under this section. A few days before he was arrested when he was warned by a friendly police officer of the impending action, he laughed and said, I quote (and you will all, I'm sure, relate to this), 'The government has converted the entire nation into a prison, and we are all prisoners. Going to prison only means that from a big cell, one is confined to a smaller one.' He was sentenced to transportation for six years and sent to Mandalay in Burma. Repression of the kind that was happening earlier was not possible. So that one incarceration had a very profound impact on the national movement as a whole. Public reaction to Tilak's arrest and sentence was stupendous, that's the only word I can use. Workers of textile mills and railway workshops in Bombay went on a strike for six days, and this was a completely political strike, as there were hardly any trade unions at that time. It was spontaneous action by the working class. Markets remained closed for a week. So by all sections of society, all over India there were protests. To force the workers of Bombay back to work, first the police were called, they failed, the army was then called out, and sixteen workers died in that clash. Lenin, hearing about this, hailed this as the entry of the Indian working class on the political stage. And he called Tilak a revolutionary.

Echoes of Tilak's trial were heard in 1922 when Gandhiji was tried for the same offence of sedition under the same Section 124A. So there is a very long and glorious tradition of those who have been tried under this section. In 1922, after the Non-Cooperation movement had ended, Gandhiji was charged with sedition. The government did not have the courage to arrest Gandhiji while the movement was on. Here was a leader who had led the biggest mass movement against the British, in which millions had participated, lakhs had gone to jail, but they charged him for sedition for writing articles in his paper, *Young India*. Such is the beauty of governments. Anyway, the judge told him his offence was the same as that of Lokmanya Tilak and therefore he was going to give him the same sentence of six years. Gandhiji replied, 'Since you have done me the honour of recalling the trial of the late Lokmanya, I just want to say that I consider it to be the proudest privilege and honour to be associated with his name.'[6]

I would like to draw your attention at this stage to the very remarkable and interesting difference between 1908, when Tilak was charged under Section 124A, and 1922, when Gandhiji was charged. It shows you the long path that the national movement had travelled in this period and how Gandhian politics brought a completely new idiom, not just idiom, it brought a completely new framework into Indian nationalism. Even the great Tilak, courageous, brave, not afraid of the British, willing to go to jail, *defended* himself against the charge of sedition. Gandhiji said, I plead *guilty* to the charge of sedition. This was the territory that the movement had traversed by then, because Gandhiji said, yes indeed, this is a Satanic government and I am proud to oppose it. These became acts of Civil Disobedience whereby you proudly and openly defied laws that you thought were unjust and took the punishment for them.

Coming to Gandhiji, I would like to share with you a couple of very fine quotations. As we all know, in his work and in his actual practice in the freedom struggle, Gandhiji showed a tremendous commitment to the values of democracy, civil liberties and dialogue, including dialogue with his opponents. His whole ethic of politics was that you do not leave even your opponent out of a dialogue. But still I think it's important that we also get a flavour of the beautiful language in which he could express his ideas. I am quoting from an article he wrote in *Young India*, in 1922, in

January, at the height of the Non-Cooperation movement. Even at the height of the Non-Cooperation movement he was telling people that the most important thing is civil liberties. I quote, 'We must first make good the right of free speech and free association before we make any further progress towards our goal. We must defend these elementary rights with our lives.' That's how important the struggle for civil liberties is, he said, that you must be willing to even sacrifice your lives for it. I quote from another article he wrote soon after: 'Liberty of speech means that it is unassailed even when the speech hurts. Liberty of the press can be said to be truly respected only when the press can comment on the severest terms upon and even misrepresent matters. Freedom of association is truly respected when assemblies of people can discuss even revolutionary projects.'[7] The only line that he drew was that of non-violence, as will become clear in the next quotation that I read to you. I quote again: 'Civil liberty, consistent with the observance of non-violence is the first step towards Swaraj. It is the breath of political and social life, it is the foundation of freedom. There is no room here for dilution or compromise, it is the water of life.'[8] So in civil liberties, there are no limits. It is the water of life, he said. The imagery of water I think is very significant, because there is no life without water, and civil liberty is like water. But it also cannot be diluted. You can't say I give you this freedom, but I put restraints on it, but I put limits on it. In fact, the Supreme Court of India also, in the way it has defined Section 124A and what constitutes it, has very clearly put in non-violence as a Lakshman rekha, that is, as long as you remain within those limits you cannot be accused of sedition even if you are discussing a revolutionary project.

Jawaharlal Nehru, Gandhiji's lieutenant in the battle for freedom and India's first prime minister, after whom this university is named, was perhaps the most vociferous believer in civil liberties. I quote from him. This is in 1936.[9] He said, 'If civil liberties are suppressed, a nation loses all vitality and becomes impotent for anything substantial.' In 1940: 'The freedom of the press does not consist in our permitting such things as we like to appear. Even a tyrant is agreeable to this kind of freedom. Civil liberty and freedom of the Press consist in our permitting what we do not like, in our putting up with criticisms of ourselves, in our allowing public expression of views which seem to us even to be injurious to our cause itself.'[10] That's why I said, look within, introspect, do we match up to these standards of what is really civil liberties? Nehru attached as much importance to civil liberties as he did to economic equality and socialism. In 1931, he drafted the Karachi resolution of the Indian National Congress, which I'm sure all of you know about. It was like the charter of the Congress, it was the precursor of the Constitution of India, which guaranteed freedom of expression and freedom of association. I'm sure you have all heard of the People's Union for Civil Liberties. Well, the man whose statue is there in front of us[11] and has become such a potent symbol, he was the one who was the strongest force behind founding the Indian Civil Liberties Union in 1936 as a non-party, non-sectarian organization. As prime minister, we know that he upheld these freedoms consistently and if I start telling that story we'll be sitting here the whole night.[12]

I now want to give you a few different examples of defence of civil liberties. Not just statements of faith in civil liberties but actually living out these conceptions which I have just talked about. That is defending people with whom you do not agree, defending your opponents, defending people with whom you may have sharp differences. The first example I want to share with you is from 1929. You have all heard, perhaps, of the Meerut Conspiracy Case? In March 1929, the British government was very worried that the left and communist activities were increasing in India. They were worried that the left forces were becoming powerful in the working class, setting up the Girni Kamgar Union in Bombay, the workers' and peasants' parties in different parts of India, for example the Kirti Kisan Party in Punjab, the Kisan Mazdoor Party in Bengal. There was a flourishing of left-wing activity and organizations in India, especially between 1927 and 1929. Subhash Bose and Jawaharlal Nehru had both committed themselves to socialism. They had formed Youth Leagues all over the country. So this was a time when the government was for the first time becoming worried about growing left-wing activity. So what they did was very interesting, and has very contemporary resonances. They picked up those who they thought were the extreme wing of the left, hoping thereby to divide the left and the national movement. They arrested thirty-two people, among whom were trade union leaders, political leaders, including three British communists who had come to India to help in the organization of the trade union movement. They were put up for trial in Meerut, a small town in UP, and very soon the Meerut Conspiracy Case became a national cause. The British had thought that they would isolate the left-wing activists, suppress them, convict them and send them for long terms to jail and thereby finish off the movement. Instead, what happened was that Jawaharlal Nehru, M.A. Ansari and M.C. Chagla took up their defence, became their lawyers. They said we will defend the communists. Gandhiji himself, I wonder how many of you know this, visited the Meerut prisoners in jail to show solidarity with them. (And lest I forget, Jawaharlal Nehru had visited Bhagat Singh and his comrades in jail to show solidarity with them.) Speeches of defence made by them in the court were carried in major nationalist newspapers, and this was how, for the first time in fact, ordinary Indians became familiar with communist ideas. Because they came to the court and in their defence they talked about what their ideals were. Just as our police today is learning about subaltern studies and Indian history from our students and getting very educated in the process. (I hope they don't apply for admission. Though we welcome genuine students no matter from where they come. In the Centre for Historical Studies, we had a marine, an actual US marine, as our student three or four years ago and he was a brilliant student.)

I want to give you another example of the practice of this idea of not just tolerating difference, not just accommodating difference, but actually encouraging it, and when necessary protecting those who differ from you. It is a wonderful example of this tradition of the national movement and exemplified by Gandhiji himself at the highest level. You have all heard of the Quit India movement, or the August Revolution of 1942, as it is often called. Many of you will also know that this was during the Second World War, when the draconian Defence of India Rules were in place, and political activity, including all public assemblies, were banned. Yet the Congress, in its session held in Bombay, to take a decision on the Quit India movement, held its meeting in an open maidan. It's called the Gowalia tank, those of you who know Bombay probably recognize it, it's right in the heart of the city. So this is supposed to be a meeting of the All India Congress Committee, which consisted of maybe about 250 or 300 people, but actually there were thousands of people who turned up despite the ban on assemblies. This was the mood, a fiery mood. People were very angry against the British for what was happening during the war years. And this was a day before the entire leadership of the movement was picked up and thrown into jail and then the movement broke out, what is called the revolution of 1942 broke out, this is one day before that. I'm sure many of you and probably all of you also know that Indian communists were opposed to the Quit India movement, their line was that of Peoples' War, their understanding was that this was a war against fascism. Soviet Union was on the side of the allies and we must support that war, they believed. There were thirteen communist members in the All India Congress Committee. I hope you all know that communist and socialists were never barred from the Indian National Congress. So there were three communist members of the AICC who came to the meeting. The main resolution was in favour of launching a movement for the British to quit India. It was on this occasion that Gandhiji made his famous 'Do or Die' speech. The communists pressed amendments to the resolution and, in fact, asked for a division and voted against the Quit India resolution. Try and imagine that atmosphere. You are not even a thousand people here today, and this was at least ten to fifteen thousand people, all in favour of the movement. Thirteen communists get up and oppose.

And what does Gandhiji do after they oppose the resolution? He says, 'I congratulate the thirteen friends who voted against the resolution, in doing so, they had nothing to be ashamed of. For the last twenty years we have tried to learn not to lose courage even when we are in a hopeless minority and are laughed at. We have learnt to hold on to our beliefs in the confidence that we are in the right. It behoves us to cultivate this courage of conviction for it ennobles man and raises his moral stature. I was, therefore, glad to see that these friends had imbibed the principle which I have tried to follow for the last fifty years or more.'[13] What was Gandhiji doing by this statement? He was not only establishing the right to dissent, he was also providing a protective cover in this situation of mass enthusiasm for Quit India. Imagine these thirteen communists in this large crowd of enthusiastic revolutionaries. Imagine a few people showing up just now and saying that they oppose everything that's going on here. Not going to be a very easy situation for them, right? But this is how the best of our national leadership and Gandhiji himself inculcated in the Indian people the notion of democracy. It is not just about the parliamentary system of government, it is not just about elections. As Nehru said, democracy in the final analysis is about dialogue, it's about whether you are willing to listen to your opponent or not, whether you are willing to give your opponent the same space that you demand for yourself.

I've carried on for a long time, and I'd like to end by saying that particularly from Gandhiji, we get many examples of actually practising democracy and respect for democracy in its most extreme form. He taught Indian people not to attack the enemy, but to attack the system. We are fighting not against the British people, he taught, not even against the British officials, we are fighting British imperialism. I will give you an example from the interview of a lady who was a young woman in 1942 and who later spent her whole life as a Gandhian activist. At the height of the Quit India movement, she was there in Bombay where a procession was being taken out. And there was a British soldier who was hurt because somebody threw something at him. The processionists stopped, took the soldier home, treated his wounds, looked after him. He was astounded and said, what is this? And they said, this is our nationalism. We are not against the British people, but against British rule. And I can tell you hundreds of stories of this kind, not one.

That is why I think our tradition in this country is so powerful and I am not afraid that it can be easily snuffed out. See the response to you, see the response to JNU, have you gone and mobilized? How much mobilization have you done? There is a spontaneous response because this is inside people. People do not like civil liberties to be suppressed, they don't like democratic principles to be suppressed, they don't like an aggressive nationalism to be flung at them as the genuine Indian nationalism. So this tradition is very deep, but we have to continue to fight for it. There's a lot of it there which will come to our aid if we have the courage to stand up. Gandhiji could open a dialogue with the revolutionaries when he emerged as the leader of the national movement during the Non-Cooperation movement. The revolutionaries' methods were totally opposed to Gandhiji's, as they believed in violence, they believed in targeting individuals. And yet he called them for a dialogue. What are we saying in JNU? Dialogue with those who don't agree with us. Dialogue with those who are even going outside the pale of what we may think is correct or not correct. Gandhiji called them for a dialogue, they had long discussions. Believe it or not, he said to them, I don't know whether in the long run my methods will prove to be the right ones or yours, but in order for me to experiment and try out my method of non-violence, it is necessary that you suspend your violent actions, because if at the same time violent incidents happen, my method will not really get a chance to be tried out. So I ask you to suspend your politics for the period of this movement, the Non-Cooperation movement. Give me a chance to try out my methods; if I fail, you take forward your methods. And would you believe it? They did.

This was the level of dialogue that existed between opposing political strands within our national political struggle, which is why we won the battle for freedom. Because people differed but worked together. Communists went in and out of the Indian national movement. Sometimes they had one theory, sometimes they had another, but they worked together! They were in the peasants' movements, they were in the workers' movements, they were in the civil disobedience movements, the Satyagraha movement. And the politics which they evolved was a politics in which their aim also was to bring the masses, the peasants and the workers into the freedom struggle. Of course there were some differences. Nobody had greater differences than Gandhi and Nehru amongst themselves. Do please read Nehru's autobiography, half the book is a criticism of Gandhiji. Gandhiji's reaction was, the more you criticize me, my love for you grows. What was poor Nehru to do with an opponent like that, who could always disarm him? Who refused to get annoyed by anything he said and tried in fact to absorb and learn and continued to change? The crucial point was that he was constantly evolving and changing in a radical direction, absorbing from other strands even at that late age.

I'll end by saying, how many people could have the courage that Mahatma Gandhi showed as exemplified in the last year before his assassination.[14] He went to Noakhali, on 4 November 1946, when he heard that communal violence had erupted there. This was an area with a Muslim majority. The people were not sympathetic, the government was not sympathetic to him. And yet he decided that if these are my people and I'm saying this is my nation, I have to try and talk to them, I cannot not talk to them, I can't condemn them as communalists or whoever. So he went there and stayed there for four months, in one of the remotest districts of India, he didn't even come back to any town, he walked through village paths, through dense jungle area. When people threw excreta in his path, he took off his sandals. He said: Do what you can, torture me, crucify my flesh, something must be wrong with me that my people are behaving like this, that I cannot communicate with them. And after some time people did start listening. Every evening he would have his usual open-air prayer meeting, where anybody could come. We have examples of his prayer meetings in other parts of Bengal, in 1946, in remote areas, where two lakh people would turn up. This was at the height of communal antagonism, and yet he insisted that dialogue must happen. On 15 August 1947, where was he? He was not in Delhi, celebrating independence, but that was not because he was not proud of Indian independence, though some people interpret it like that, but because he saw his task as being where the situation was tough. Suhrawardy, the chief minister of Bengal, asked him to be in Calcutta, because he feared that on 15 August, when Partition took effect, and Calcutta went to India, and his government would no longer have any power, Hindus would take revenge for the Great Calcutta killings of 1946. And Gandhiji said to Suhrawardy, I will stay provided you and I sleep under the same roof. On 15 August, he walked through the streets hand-in-hand with his opponent Suhrawardy. They had nothing in common, but he would dialogue even with his opponent. That is the tradition which we have and which we have to fight for, to save, to keep up and to take forward. Thank you.

*

Notes/References/Bibliography

1. Admiral Ramdas, a prominent social activist, had addressed the JNU students just before the lecture by Mridula Mukherjee.
2. See my interview in the *Times of India*, 21 February 2016.

3. Cited in J. Natarajan, 1955, *History of Indian Journalism*, New Delhi: Publications Division, p. 15.
4. Dufferin to Secretary of State, 21 March and 17 May 1886, Dufferin Papers.
5. G.P. Pradhan and A.K. Bhagwat, 1958, *Lokmanya Tilak: A Biography*, Bombay: Jaico, pp. 117–18.
6. M.K. Gandhi, *Collected Works*, Vol. 23, p. 120.
7. Ibid, Vol. 22, pp. 142 and 176-7.
8. Ibid, Vol. 69, p. 356.
9. Jawaharlal Nehru, *Selected Works*, Vol. 7, p. 414.
10. Ibid, Vol 11, p. 367.
11. The reference is to a statue of Jawaharlal Nehru that is situated facing the Freedom Square (as the site of the JNU protests was named), and which became a rallying point for protests.
12. For a detailed treatment, see Mridula Mukherjee, 'Indian Democracy: Debt to Jawaharlal Nehru', *Mainstream Weekly*, 1 June 2014.
13. M.K. Gandhi, *Collected Works*, Vol. 76, p. 384.
14. For a fuller treatment of the theme, see Mridula Mukherjee, 'Legacy of Anti-Communal Struggle: Gandhiji and Nehru', *Mainstream Weekly*, 31 January 2016.

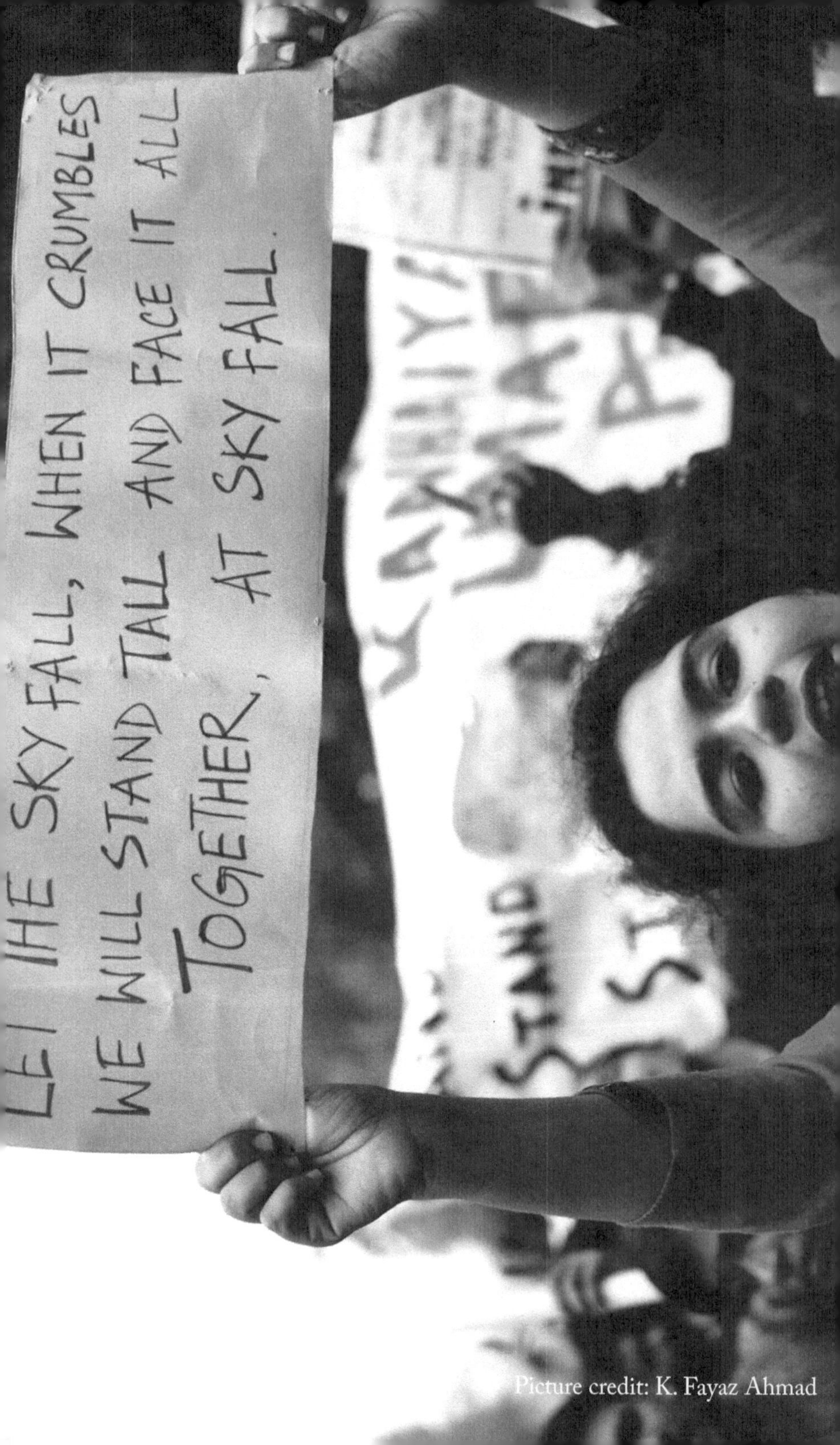

Picture credit: K. Fayaz Ahmad

Gandhi's Nation

Tanika Sarkar

(25 FEBRUARY 2016)

WITH ALL THE LECTURES THAT HAVE gone on so far, all of you are, by now, thoroughly familiar with multiple definitions of nation. We have, for instance, a British variant – Rule Britannia, rule the waves – where nationalism is driving colonization. We have the Nazi kind – my nation above all others, my nation above humanity, reason, morality. There is, moreover, religious nationalism that identifies the nation with the religion of the majority community, and which excludes religious minorities from full entitlement to it. On the other hand, we also have had vast popular upsurges in Asia and Africa fired by anti-colonial, anti-racist nationalism. There is not always a hard and fast line, though, that separates all these different kinds of nationalisms, and often we find a lot of overlap. I will take up just one instance today. I will briefly contrast Gandhi's national vision with a few alternative or competing concepts that were available among Indians of his times. The contrast is meant to show how Gandhi himself sometimes changed his ideas through open and honest debates with his adversaries. It also helps us to see more clearly the distinctiveness as well as some of the problems in his own understanding.

It has so far been one of the great traditions of this university – or all universities that matter – that we exercise our critical and analytical faculties openly, even when they problematize figures that we deeply respect ourselves; and I say whatever I say in that spirit. Since we are pressed for time I will dwell on just two interrelated aspects of Gandhi's perspective on the nation: the place of poverty and caste. I will not discuss the place of Adivasis as there are better people here to do that, or of women in Gandhi's nation, which I would have loved to discuss had I time for that, nor will I discuss his secular nationalism. Gandhi was so uncompromisingly secular that there is very little to discuss here, though there is of course a lot to learn and remember from that. Gandhi, let me remind ourselves, always acknowledged his moral and spiritual debt to Christianity. He said with unwavering consistency that people of all faiths are equal in the eyes of God and nation. He also said that though he himself worshiped the cow, he would never force the worship on those who do not, nor would he tolerate the violence in the name of cow protection. He said that Hindus must bear the primary responsibility for ensuring communal peace for they are the dominant community, and people of other religions are vulnerable in comparison.

For most nationalists, the nation indicates a single monolithic supra-entity that must rank above all other commitments and identities. The problem, however – and this is the critical problem – is that this paramount identity is always undercut by diverse and very deep internal contradictions within national life. What distinguishes one kind of nationalism from another, what sets them apart, is how each manages such internal divisions. V.D. Savarkar, the powerful ideologue of Hindutva, defined the nation in admirably clear terms. Perpetual antagonism against an 'Other', in his view, is the basis of the nation: the Other, presumably, is always to be defined by the self-appointed guardians of the nation. Antagonism, he said, creates and consolidates national identity and nothing unites a nation more than the presence of a common enemy. The nation, therefore, actually needs an enemy. The presence of the anti-national, in fact, is the first and also the supreme condition for the existence of the nation. His Indian nation was – and once again he was admirably clear about this – unambiguously Hindu in its cultural essence as he postulated that the faith of all true Indians must be born on the Indian soil. So, immediately, without his having to mention it, this definition excludes Muslims and Christians from full entitlement to the nation.

But was a single Hindu nation possible, imaginable, given its internal contradictions? Here Savarkar had some interesting things to say. He did refer to caste divisions among Hindus. He admitted that upper-caste power is founded on a historical act of conquest of indigenous people. But, having accepted the foundational role of power and violence in the making of caste, he immediately dismissed caste inequality as a problem not worth going any further into. He argued that over centuries the blood of 'high' and 'low' castes had mingled, creating thereby a shared identity, a single family, whose differences do not matter. His family metaphor was a subtle and powerful one as it both admitted and evaded hierarchy in the same breath. It also made inequality appear as a relationship of intimacy.

Where does Gandhi stand? He organized vast anti-colonial movements, with all possible social classes and categories in India, despite their many mutual conflicts and divisions. Each Gandhian upsurge represented and concretized a single people in miniature. Gandhi used two images to describe his ideal nation, both very far from Savarkar's insistence on perpetual antagonism. These were trusteeship and Ram Rajya. Both admitted that there are inequalities among Indians, yet both suggested that love and mutual care are still possible between those who have power and those who have none. But this was a hope that was mightily difficult to sustain, except at peak points of anti-colonial upsurges which drowned out all these differences temporarily. It is very important to see how Gandhi tried to come to terms with the intractable problems of social conflict and injustice and we must give it to him that he always struggled with difficulties, he never evaded them. We do not, necessarily, see either total consistency or a clear pattern of evolution. There were different tonalities, jostling with one another in his thinking, but a few strands, I think, did become more and more pronounced over time.

Let us begin with poverty and the class question. He wrote in 1921 and I quote, 'To a people famishing and idle, the only acceptable form in which God can dare appear is work and promise of food as wages.'[1] Having acknowledged the pervasiveness and the centrality of Indian poverty, Gandhi then takes a somewhat surprising route. He attributes it, in *Hind Swaraj*, to a moral failing among the poor. Machine-based production of an infinite number of objects breeds infinite greed, which in turn creates poverty. While everyone shares this craze for modern and useless objects, the poor pay most dearly for it and their poverty is consolidated by their own unworthy aspirations. The poor, therefore, are held responsible for their own plight. The question of class power and class struggle becomes irrelevant, and Gandhi tries to resolve poverty in two ways: one, by asking the poor to be content with what they have and what they do; second, by reorienting the moral vision of their masters. His trusteeship principle asked property owners to regard their property as a trust that they hold for the benefit of the poor. He admitted – and this is a very important admission – that the rich acquire property by 'exploiting the masses'. At the same time, what allows them to do so, he said, is their greater competence. So they deserve, in a sense, what they have. I quote from him again, 'Those who are capable wish to acquire more, it is natural.'[2] The poor, by implication, are less able. So, no structural change in production or property relations, but a change in some of the lifestyle and moral practices of both rich and poor is all that is required. This is where his differences from the Left of those days began.

Trusteeship can be better understood in terms of Tulsidas's *Ramcharitmanas* whose concept of Ram's realm or Ram Rajya provided the pattern for Gandhi's ideals for Swaraj. I quote from him, 'We call a state Ram Rajya when the relationship between the two [that is between the ruler and his subjects] is as good as that between father and a son. The people are not as wise as he (the ruler) is.'[3] So, once again, ruler and subject are divided on the basis of superior and inferior capabilities. Gandhi, thereby, translates power into hegemony – hegemony which is built on the active consent and will of the governed – even while the hierarchy between the king and subject remains clear and fixed.

Gandhi sometimes tried to short-circuit a social process by his personal example. His self-sufficient communes and ashrams did not exploit, nor even employed labourers. Inmates were their own cultivators, bakers, cooks, scavengers, sweepers, tailors, shoemakers, etc. – everything that can possibly be needed from labourers – overthrowing distinctions and taboos about 'clean' and 'unclean' work totally. The example, however, was confined to ashrams, it was not the pattern for society at large. This was very important as an exemplar, but, what Gandhi and his associates did was a matter of personal choice. The poor, in contrast, are forced to live a life of non-possession.

The self-chosen poverty of the great leader did not address or resolve the brutal privations in their life. On the contrary, it morally privileged and aestheticized them. He assumed the leadership of Champaran and Khera satyagrahas in Bihar and Gujarat almost as soon as he returned to India. They powerfully challenged European planters and state appropriation of surplus from peasants. So, the uncomfortable question of Indian oppressors didn't arise. With these movements Gandhi learnt how to bring social opposites together on the basis of a shared concrete grievance against a state that unifies different classes and castes. This creates unity across classes and avoids social conflict. On the other hand, he almost never allowed the Congress to address or struggle against issues of rent and cess that Indian landlords imposed on tenant cultivators, nor against the exorbitant agrarian interest rates that cultivators were forced to pay to moneylenders, not even in the terrible years of agrarian depression in the mid-1930s when indebted cultivators were evicted from their land for defaulting on interest and rent payments.

Gandhian resolutions for poverty – the homespun, village schools, sanitation – did help the poor peasants to augment their meagre incomes in small but very meaningful ways. But neither did it help those who faced dispossession from land, nor did the rich behave as trustees or protectors as he had hoped. As the moral economy of trusteeship failed to appear, Gandhi reprimanded the peasant or the Adivasi who rebelled, rather than the landlord who failed to discharge his paternal responsibilities. Gandhi, of course, valued the peasant as the perfect satyagrahi, just as he said the woman was one. Both served others without any thought of the self. But in order to be so perfect, both peasant and woman had to provide selfless service endlessly.

So Gandhi knew, and none better, how to speak to the peasant: but he did not always speak for the peasant. At the same time, and this is just as important, Gandhi was the first Indian leader who solicited the peasants' entry into the political nation, and the role of the peasant satyagrahi in nation-making did create the basis for future democracy in India. It eased in universal adult franchise into our polity without any obvious strife and that is a huge achievement.

Gandhi was always critical of urban life, condemning the urban rich and the urban poor in equal measure. But at the same time, he deplored the strike weapon, denounced class conflict, distrusted collective bargaining through trade unions – once again inhibiting class protests while leaving mill owners to pursue their methods of control and exploitation. But – and this is what I want to emphasize – things changed somewhat, and his vision unravelled tragically towards the end of his life.

His faith in trusteeship was corroded in the dark days of 1946, when he travelled through Bengal villages, trying with his frail body to stop the communal violence. He came to realize, first-hand, how class inequalities were mapped onto communal divisions, and what a terribly potent brew it was. In June 1947, almost at the end of his life, he suddenly recalled his early attraction towards socialist ideas – class revolution without violence – to which he had never much referred before. He also said that peasants have to struggle for justice for themselves and landlords can help by fleeing. He said that trusteeship had failed and he said that Ram Rajya was really beyond realization. He was big enough to give up on, or admit failure of some of his most cherished, most dear visions.

I come to caste now, via racism. Gandhi, surprisingly, did not characterize racism as an innate property of white-skinned people. He saw it, instead, as unequal distribution of power which exists in different forms in different contexts. I will give you two examples. In his autobiography, he drew a startling analogy between Hindu untouchability and racism. A barber in South Africa had refused to serve him and Gandhi couldn't be angry, and I quote from him, 'We do not allow our own barbers to serve our untouchable brothers, the conviction that it was the punishment for our own sins saved me from becoming angry.' He coupled untouchability and racism together again in the case of the Jallianwala Bagh massacre. Referring to General Dyer who gave the order to shoot upon an unarmed crowd in Amritsar in April 1919, and to Michael O'Dwyer, the infamous governor of Punjab, Gandhi wrote immediately after the events in 1921, 'Has not nemesis taken us for the crime of untouchability, have we not practised Dyerism and O'Dwyerism on our kith and kin? In fact, there is no charge that the pariah cannot fling in our faces, which we do not fling in the faces of Englishmen.'[4] He described, therefore, the massacre as penance, equating the open violence of colonialism, with the structural violence of untouchability.

In his early life, we all know, Gandhi showed a remarkable irreverence for caste orthodoxy, courting outcasting without penance, the ritual penance, when he went abroad. In South Africa he worked closely with 'low caste coolies' and invited untouchables into his home on equal terms. He made his family and associates engage in labour that was considered profoundly polluted – shoemaking, leatherwork, cleaning of toilets. The preoccupation with the cleaning of toilets, one might even say obsession – work most awfully reprehensible to savarna or caste Hindus – persisted all his life. At Durban, a Dalit Christian clerk stayed in his house as a guest. We all know of this famous event, when Gandhi commanded his wife to clean his chamber pot and when she refused, in a fit of rage, Gandhi almost turned her out of the house, although he later repented his rage. Once back in India, a Dalit family joined his ashram in Ahmedabad and his patrons immediately withdrew funds to punish him, and there were rumours of a citywide boycott of Gandhi and the ashram. Gandhi resolved to relocate the ashram in untouchable quarters of the city rather than expel the family from the ashram.

But he had to moderate his activities as he was simultaneously pressured by two contrary forces – orthodox Sanatanis on one hand and emergent non-Brahman and Dalit politics on the other. For quite a long while, he was more eager to persuade the Sanatanis, whom he saw as friendly adversaries, sharing the same religious world view. He, moreover, believed that untouchability could be abolished by moral reasoning – that he could teach good Hindus in time that hereditary caste divisions were part of their faith; true, but untouchability was not.

We must take, I think, one thing, very seriously. Gandhi was a very sincere, very devout Hindu, and Hindu scripture was genuinely sacrosanct to him, to the point of being non-negotiable. He could not play around with them. He, therefore, could not, in all honesty, deny that caste constituted an essential part of dharma. So he worked endlessly around two incompatible poles: his own passionate repugnance to untouchability and his equally strong commitment to varnashram dharma as a religious principle sanctified by scripture. Compromises were inevitable. Pollution taboos were totally abolished in his South African farms and communes. In Indian ashrams, however, their known observance was voluntary, though not mandatory. From 1918, he began to systematically distinguish between varna and jati. Varnadharma or the fourfold, hereditary, hierarchical division of society and labour forms, he said, was the core of dharma. It was immutable. I quote from him, 'It would be violation from the laws of nature and of God.'[5] Brahmans were higher in status than Shudras, who must do menial work but at the same time, Shudra labour should be valued as selfless service. Jati or multiple subdivisions within a varna, on the other hand, was extraneous and irrelevant to true dharma. Untouchability, however, was beyond both, a horrible perversion of Hindu faith. He said that respect for all forms of labour, however degraded, was a must, but so was the hereditary division of labour. It was a rational social principle and in its absence anarchy will reign.

He also strongly upheld the taboo against inter-varna marriages and dining till the late 1930s or even later. In 1924, he plunged into the Vaikom Satyagraha, which had been started by Ezhavas for temple entry in the Hindu princely state of Travancore. In a very conciliatory mood he told Brahman authorities, and I get this from my late colleague M.S.S. Pandian, that low castes were already penalized by the gods for their misdeeds in past births and man should not add to their sufferings. He, therefore, echoed the theological justification of hierarchy that low castes were made 'low' by their own actions in past births. He also described Brahmans as, and I quote again, 'the finest flowers of Hinduism and Humanity. I will do nothing to wither it.'[6]

But the more he defended the varna order as benign and just, the more urgent it became to salvage it from the harshness of untouchability and here lay the problem. He tried out many ways to achieve respect for untouchables. He renamed them Harijan, children of God, which did not please all of them or politicize them. He tried to render them physically cleaner by suggesting that they avoid eating leftover food and carrion or the meat and flesh of dead animals, which are filthy as well as sinful habits; that they should not touch carcasses of dead animals, and that they should bathe and change frequently. He believed that it was their handling of physical filth which made them dirty in the eyes of the world and this lay at the root of pollution and avoidance taboos. Once their bodies were cleansed, the stigma would vanish, even though, they would continue to do the same work. But untouchable children told him if they did not consume leftover food or carrion, they would starve, that they did not have access to water to bathe in or clothes to change into. Reform, clearly, was not easy.

In despair, then, he turned to A.S. Altekar, the great scholar of Hinduism, and tried to inquire whether scripture could be reread to provide any usable loopholes. He wrote that he knew that the *Smritis* did endorse the avoidance rituals taboos and, possibly, also the Vedas. But he hoped that Altekar would be able to translate scripture in such a way that pollution taboos would appear as the consequence of 'external practice' and not of birth. Once again, he tried to attach impurity taboos to impure work. He sought to render them a temporary and not a permanent inherited condition. So work and purity/impurity had to be separated. Work had to be done by the same caste in the same way but impurity should go.

The new Dalit politics, however, severely disturbed his definitions and methods. As Dalit leaders began to negotiate with the state about separate electorates, spurning their Hindu identity, and as they became relentlessly critical of the Congress temporizing on caste, Gandhi's debates with B.R. Ambedkar now began to assume the proportions of an epic confrontation. Ambedkar's threat to defect from the Hindu fold dangerously narrowed down the space for manoeuvre. Ambedkar overthrew Gandhi's distinction between acceptable varna dharma and impermissible untouchability, insisting that the two are integrally connected. He demanded the annihilation of caste itself as social and economic system, as ideology, as ritual practice. He demanded a politics of distribution as well as of recognition but he also said that it was Gandhi who first brought the issue of untouchability to the forefront of national politics and no one could have done it the way he did.

Gandhi's responses to Ambedkar were more complex. Initially, he took Ambedkar to be an upper-caste person because of his educational achievements and social confidence. He was not the typical abject Dalit. His first comments on Ambedkar were somewhat patronizing and I quote, 'He has received a liberal education, he has more than the qualifications of an average educated Indian. His exterior is clean, though his interior is a mystery.'[7] I do not know why he had to refer to Ambedkar's cleanliness as that is not how he described his first acquaintance with others. Obviously, that was the first thought that occurred to him on meeting a Dalit intellectual. He insisted that untouchables did not need Ambedkar as they had the Congress to lead them. At the second Round Table Conference he went further, and I quote, 'I, myself, in my own person claim to speak for the whole of untouchables.'[8] He asked them to forget their own grievances and to serve the nation and the national movement first. In reply, Ambedkar asked him an unforgettable question: do I have a country?

The issue of representation brought about a deadlock as Ambedkar made it clear that the Congress could not represent nor lead untouchables. They have to throw up their own leaders. Gandhi, on the other hand, objected till the mid-1930s to an independent sphere of politics. They should seek neither legal redress nor political autonomy, nor activism on their own. The burden of social transformation should lie with the upper caste alone, they will repent first and then reform society and nation. The burden, however, is actually a privilege. Just as it underlined upper-caste guilt – and underlined it very powerfully and passionately indeed – it also vested political agency solely in them, rendering the Dalit a passive victim. Rejuvenated and redeemed by penitence, upper castes would then rightfully reclaim their trustee status and reform low castes. It was, therefore, a return to hierarchy on a higher plane.

But neither the Sanatanis nor the upper castes showed any signs of relenting or repenting, and this now put his faith, more precious to him than his life, in a state of total crisis. He wrote poignantly in 1933 and I quote, it's a very moving quote, 'There is nothing so bad in all the world as untouchability'. Also, 'My life would be a burden to me if Hinduism failed me, but then I cannot tolerate it with untouchability.'[9] He now began to say that it was better for untouchables to fight against low-caste savarnas than to live as, and I quote him again, 'wretched slaves'. And most significant of all for a person like Gandhi, '...if this kind of untouchability were an integral part of dharma, that religion has no use for me'.[10]

Gandhi was beginning to change. At the end of his life he became ready to accept a legal, constitutional prohibition of untouchability. Earlier he had never endorsed inter-varna marriages, at the most intra-jati marriages – marriages within the same jati. Now he advised upper-caste girls to marry untouchable men. Previously firmly committed to prohibitions on intermarriage, he now spoke in favour of pratiloma or hypogamous marriages, so very loathsome to Hindu orthodoxy. Ashis Nandy has argued that it was this blow to caste that made him such a dangerous man to his enemies – along, of course, with his defence of equal rights for Indian Muslims and Christians. His assassin, Nathuram Godse was an orthodox Maharashtrian from the purest of Brahman categories.

Gandhian anti-colonial movements prefigured one kind of nation, populated with class- and caste-divided subjects, who, nonetheless, possessed political agency, and hence had democratic entitlements, even if he continued to endorse inequalities till almost the end of his life, prescribing, at most, caste and class with a human face. More strikingly, however, I find, his nation was capable of recognizing its own contradictions and oppressions and feel guilty about them. This capacity for introspection, for recognizing evil within the self, was the most important thing about Gandhi's nation. A nation that refuses to feel guilty about itself is a nation to fear deeply.

*

Notes/References/Bibliography

1. Gandhi's letter to Tagore, *Young India*, 13 October 1921.
2. Interview to Charles Petrasch, London, 29 October 1931, *Collected Works of Mahatma Gandhi*, Vol. XLVIII, p. 241-42.
3. Speech at Morvi, 24 January 1928, *CWMG*, XXXV, 1969, pp. 489-491.
4. M.K. Gandhi, 1927, *An Autobiography or the Story of My Experiments with Truth*, Ahmedabad: Navjivan Trust, 2006 Reprint, p 177.
5. *Harijanbandhu*, 19 April 1933, *CWMG*, Vol 54, pp. 348-49.
6. Cited in M.S.S. Pandian, 2007, *Brahmin and Non-Brahmin: Genealogies of the Tamil Political Present*, Delhi: Permanent Black, p 191.
7. *Harijan*, 11 March 1933, in M.K. Gandhi, 1950, *Hindu Dharma*, Ahmedabad: Navjivan Publishing House, p. 319.
8. Cited in David Hardiman, 2003, *Gandhi in His Times and Ours*, Delhi: Permanent Black, p. 131.
9. Letter to Jawaharlal Nehru, 2 May 1933, *CWMG*, Vol. 55, p. 96.
10. *Harijanbandhu*, 19 March 1933, *CWMG*, Vol. 54, p. 127.

Picture credit: Samim Asgor Ali

Nationalism: Its Power and Limits

Achin Vanaik

(26 FEBRUARY 2016)

I WANT TO START BY SALUTING you students for two reasons. First, students have from time to time been a spark for very positive and progressive transformations worldwide. This was very much the case in the 1960s and '70s. In the US, for example, the two great mass movements – the Civil Rights movement against racism and the anti-Vietnam War mobilizations – which transformed that country in a progressive direction, did not come from the political parties. They came from outside and then the parties had to accept them. In India, Europe, everywhere, you had huge anti-Vietnam war movements. These were a real tribute to what students can achieve. In 1968, the spark that the students of France ignited shook France like never before; so much so that President de Gaulle actually ran away because he thought he might have to get out of the country.

If you look at the 1980s, you see students doing the same thing in South Korea, where they helped to overthrow a dictatorial regime. In the 1990s, you have students from Indonesia doing the same. After 2000, you had students involved in the uprisings in the Middle East and in North Africa. You saw them in the Occupy Movement of the US. Students cannot do everything on their own but they can be a very important spark and that is why we have to keep on struggling in this country. It's very easy and very normal, when there is repression against the student community and against this university, to fight against it via demonstrations, morchas, legal aid, dharnas, and that's very important. But the second reason why I wish to salute you is that besides the usual forms of opposition, legal aid, etc., you have – and this is very remarkable – insisted on having a series of teach-ins to debate about what kind of nationalism we want.

You've in fact made something of a declaration that we have to try and fight for the 'soul of Indian nationalism', because today – let's have no doubts – there is a fierce battle for its appropriation. On one side there is a systematic attempt to elaborate and instil a very anti-democratic, intolerant, belligerent and aggressive nationalism to which we have to respond with a much more humane, democratic and inclusive nationalism. This discussion in JNU is something that the political parties outside, the parliament, the media, and others can and should learn from.

Now, in this fight we have to understand the complexity of this notion of nationalism. Let me start by saying that this is one of the most complex terms ever, and we have to understand why there are competing nationalisms and decide what direction we have to take. Is nationalism old or new? Is nationalism based on objective characteristics or is it subjective? Is nationalism civic or ethnic, or can it be either? Is nationalism universal or particularist, or both? Is nationalism inclusive or exclusive, or both? Is it doctrine or sentiment, or both? Is it cultural or political, or both? Is it good or bad, or both? And sometimes if it's good, isn't there some element of bad in it? And even if it is very bad, maybe sometimes there is something good in it?

Let me start by saying nationalism is a modern phenomenon. Even if you have an ethnic nationalism, the ethnic community or ethnie may be old. If it's based on language, the language can be old. If it's based on religion, the religion can be old. But nationalism always emerges in modern times. Once you understand this, how do we go about trying to understand nationalism? There have been basically four ways which have been the starting points for trying to understand this modern form of nationalism.

First, 'changes in social structure' – that's the starting point for you to try and understand what nationalism is about. What does this mean? A great exponent of this view was the renowned sociologist Ernest Gellner who argued that nationalism emerges in relation to the processes of industrialization.[1] Nationalism and what it brings with it are functional and necessary for the process of industrialization to take place. But of course, you also know that many countries which do not have serious processes of industrialization do have nationalism!

The second approach starts from 'changes in political structure'. Those who are international relations students would have read and would have been taught that 1648 and the peace of Westphalia is the beginning of the modern nation state. Wrong! Why did they say that? They say it because in 1648 you have the emergence of the tax-office state which bases itself to a great extent on tax collection. You had some agreement on centralized administration over a rough territory even if the borders were not completely demarcated. You had a centralized bureaucracy. You have a standing army, a standing diplomacy, and all of these are features of the modern state. So surely, this must be the modern state? No! The states involved in the 1648 peace settlement were absolutist states. What does that mean? Before 1648 you had feudal states, and all feudal states are characterized by three things. They are decentralized – they are all over the place. They are personalized – there is the king or royalty of some sort; and they are sacralized. There is the 'divine right of kings'. In India, we had, as written in the ancient texts, the concept of rajdharma. Kingship must be accepted, but he should be a good, religiously sanctioned king.

Now we reject the notion of 'divine rights of kings'. We have changed. The feudal state was decentralized, personalized, sacralized. In 1648 the absolutist state was centralized but personalized and sacralized. After 1648, the modern system of nation states comes about but that too only through two hundred years of imperialism, colonialism and exploitation. Note that the modern nation state is centralized, but it is also de-personalized and de-sacralized. The power of the nation state comes from the fact that it is supposed to belong to the peoples constituted as different nations unlike in the past when the state was supposed to belong to this or that royal family. So it is important not to take changes in political structure as the starting point.

The third point of analytical departure is 'changes in political consciousness'. It's when people become politically conscious and mobilize and act – that's when nationalism emerges. Not quite! You will find that before political nationalism there is always a certain kind of process of culturally trying to come together. In India, for example, it's not the political nationalism or the political movement that comes first but a consciousness developing among elites to begin with, of us belonging to a separate culture and that we are different from the British and must assert ourselves culturally-politically in some way. It is some sense of cultural unity that first emerges and then becomes an important, even if subsequently contested, part of the emerging political nationalism.[2]

It's the fourth approach that I would suggest is the most important, and that is 'changes in social consciousness'. The most outstanding figure is Ben Anderson, whose book *Imagined Communities* many of you must have read.[3] His book was very important and wonderful. But the best definition of nationalism did not come from him. It came from the liberal tradition before him, but Anderson powerfully developed its implications. And that definition which I want to leave with you was given by Hans Kohn who wrote *The Idea of Nationalism* in 1944. What did he say? He said nationalism or the nation is a 'cultural entity, lodged above all in consciousness, striving to become a political fact'.[4] You take nationalism seriously because it has a political thrust. It's a cultural entity lodged above all in consciousness. Now this is very important because what it means is that there is only one thing that is common to all nationalisms and all nations throughout the world and that is the question of consciousness.

Let me elaborate a bit on this. Do not make the mistake of thinking that there is some sort of a checklist, where this plus this constitutes nationalism – because you will not find this anywhere. It is not common territory. You will find nations and you will find peoples who do not have the same common territory but who believe they are part of one nation. Hawaiians believe that they are part of the United States. Among the Puerto Ricans however, there are many who do not agree to this. The Falkland Islanders say that they are part of Britain even though they are closer to Argentina. You had, after 1947 in India – if it were not for the huge mistakes made by Yahya Khan – East and West Pakistanis, though territorially separated, who felt for some time that they were one nation. It's not common history. It's not language; it's none of these things. The

Canadians and the Americans have the same language. Germans in Germany and Austrians in Austria – they both speak German but the Germans and Austrians don't want to come together. Lichtenstein, a tiny principality where the majority language is German and whose economy is totally dependent on those of its neighbours, has been for decades and still wants to remain a separate sovereign state.

So what's my point here? Once you realize that nationalisms in different parts of the world arise from different combinations of various objective factors, it becomes easier to recognize that the only factor common to *all* nationalisms is that in one way or the other people come to think of themselves – the imagined community – as being a collective belonging to the same nation! It is this cultural dimension lodged in consciousness that is decisive. So to understand nationalism – and there are two ways of going about understanding nationalism – we have to understand culture which is another very complicated term. Here you could think of culture as a thing, an attribute or you can think of it as a process. Even when you think of it as an attribute – which up to a point is okay – there is often also a process of change within that. In other words, when we talk about a 'common culture' we can think of it as something commonly shared – language, religion, etc., which is what the preoccupation with endorsing multiculturalism does and whose conceptions of 'cultural equality' presses for a project of generating equal respect across different 'cultures'. But more importantly, we can also think of it as something that is commonly *fashioned*, indicating that there is also of a collective project of improvement to be undertaken. There is something called cultural exploitation. There is cultural oppression. There is cultural empowerment and disempowerment. But unlike the 'politics of multiculturalism' the emphasis here is on a project whereby there is the promotion of capacities to overcome these cultural inequalities in a more collective effort to *produce* a more common culture and future!

If you understand culture in this way, it means culture is five things – it is plural, open, ordinary, changing, expanding. It is plural – we have multiple identities of being Malayalee or Punjabi or whatever and have cultures associated with those respective identities. We are a plurality not just at the level of language or region. There is the culture of the schools that we go to, the culture of JNU, all kinds of cultures that we have.

A plurality is not about looking at the world through one particularly important prism, for example, religion. Modern life is about recognizing how we have to shift from identity to identity and use those different prisms to look at different things at different times in different places.

Culture is open. It is open to global influences. If culture has something to do with the way we dress, speak, talk and all the rest, isn't this obvious? It's ordinary. What does this mean? There's so much talk about the wonderful culture of the ancient past whether it's India or any other country. But let's understand that literacy is a very powerful tool for better or worse, for cultural empowerment or cultural oppression. In the past, when you only had Brahmins and a small number of people who had the power of literacy, you did not have cultural equality or serious possibilities for such greater equality. You live in a world today where the ordinary products of people – a book by Wendy Doniger or by Salman Rushdie – can cause uproar. It's changing. In the past you had two kinds of cultures: elite culture, the beautiful monuments, the classical music and all of that; and you had folk culture. Then comes what is called 'popular culture' which has a wider spread than folk culture. But it is only in the twentieth century with the emergence of mass communication that you now have 'mass culture' and the three most important products of this are spectator sports, dance and music, films.

Culture expands because the notion of 'rights to culture' and of a 'culture of rights' has emerged in modernity where both the 'goods' and the 'bads' of modernity are qualitatively of a much higher order from those of the past. We, therefore, have to pursue a critical and modest modernity. Please note that with the emergence of health care the average lifespan of people has increased. So, for the first time we divide it in a way we could not do before. We talk about childhood, of adolescence, of adulthood, and old age and of their respective rights. If it was not for the extension of the lifespan you could not have talked about child rights and that they should be able to have play and leisure and go to school, and all that. In other words, our understanding of the various dimensions of culture changes in and through modernity.

I say all this is because you must not have an essentialist conception of culture which is profoundly dangerous. You – and this is connected to the question of nationalism – will have people who will be saying 'you

Mr Hindu in Bangladesh', 'you Mr Muslim in India', 'you Mr Ahmadiya in Pakistan', 'you Mr Jew in Germany', 'you Mr Asian in Britain', 'you Mr Black Person in the US', 'you had better understand that this is the essence of our culture and if you do not accept this, if you do not respect it, if you do not help to strengthen it further, you are dangerous. We don't like it. You are weakening us and we will not tolerate it'. This is a profoundly dangerous conception of culture which then gets connected to a sense of nationalism of a dangerously exclusivist and intimidating kind.

I had said earlier that you can think of nationalism in two ways. That is to say you can think of nationalism as an inheritance from the past; or you can think of nationalism as something that belongs to the present and the future. All nationalisms, as you know, invent traditions. But my point here is that if you really believe that it belongs to the past and that it is an inheritance, there will always be disputes about what the proper inheritance is, and who the proper inheritors are. 'You in India understand that our essence is Hinduism and not just Hinduism but a particular kind of Brahmanical Hinduism. And you Mr Lower Caste, or you Mr Muslim or Christian, or you Communist, better recognize and accept this.' But nationalism actually belongs to the present and the future and what that means is that nationalism is what we will make of it.

This means that in the Indian context there must be *different* ways of being and feeling Indian. Now, how can a person in Manipur, Nagaland, Tamil Nadu, Kashmir or Punjab feel Indian if you do not have any respect for their culture, their language or their interests? Therefore, you cannot separate the question of building a decent, humane and democratic nationalism from the larger context of building a democratic society. And in a society which is multi-religious you have to have a secular conception of nationalism which is not biased in favour of any group. But even secularism is not enough. Much more important is the question of the democratic character of nationalism. The relationship between secular and democratic is that you can have a secular state which is undemocratic but you cannot have a democratic state which is not secular.

Let me say something about the power of nationalism. Nationalism has an extraordinary power as a form of belonging. Nothing matches it. Those of us on the Left have long advocated the international solidarity of the working class but this has repeatedly broken on the shoals of nationalism. There are those who talk about international sisterhood; it's broken on the shoals of nationalism. Those who talk about the Islamic umma cannot overcome the divides of nationalism. In Afghanistan, you have any number of Muslims but in different tribes that fight with each other. The second longest war of the twentieth century was between Iran and Iraq, in which on both sides the majority were Shias. In the case of Buddhism, you have Sri Lanka and Myanmar but they don't want to come together. In the case of Hinduism, for all the talk of an Akhand Bharat, can you imagine the response if someone were to say to Hindus in Nepal: forget Nepal and join Hindu India? The response will be: 'We are Hindus and proud of it, but you Mr Big Brother India do not tell us to abandon our Nepaliness!'

Why is religion less powerful than nationalism? So much so that religious organizations usually do not try to confront nationalism but to co-opt it? This is where you have to remember what Ben Anderson said when he talked about imagined communities. He did not simply say the nation is an imagined community but said it is an 'imagined *political* community' which is different from merely imagined communities like religion or some other grouping. Nationalism, like religion, is a community of believers. These are the two entities for which most people are willing to fight and die. They seem like 'communities of fate', of 'destiny'. Yes, people will fight for feminism and for socialism and so on, but not at the same scale or depth of intensity. But nationalism has one great edge over religion. It's not just a community of believers, it's a political community of citizens! This is an extraordinary, powerful thing because it means that the nation belongs to you. Even dictatorships, whether in Pakistan or elsewhere, are no longer like those of the past. They don't say that this state belongs to my family. Even a dictator will say, I am doing this for the people of Argentina or for the people of Pakistan. Even if it's not a democracy, it's still answerable to you in some particular way.

Nonetheless, the structures of religion and nationalism are in many ways quite similar. They both have myths about themselves. They both have their heroes and heroines, their symbols, their rituals, their doctrines and so on. So when they merge, they powerfully reinforce each other. This can be quite dangerous because a powerful love also sometimes means a powerful hate. Religious nationalism, because it is not a secular nationalism by its very nature, is dangerously undemocratic. But it is different from a communal nationalism. A religious nationalism as in Iran where almost everybody is Muslim will oppose the non-religious or secular. But when in a multi-religious society you have a communalized nationalism, there will be not just opposition to the secular or the non-religious nationalist, there will also be hostility to some religious 'other'. That makes it even more dangerous, and this is what's happening here. We have to fight it, but that fight cannot be separated from the fight at various levels to make this country in so many ways a much more humane and decent society. You cannot separate the struggle against communalism from other struggles. To succeed in the struggle against communalism we will have to fight against more than communalism! To succeed in fighting a militarized nationalism we have to fight against more than militarism.

There are limits to nationalism. This is very important. Even an inclusive nationalism can be very dangerous. It can manipulate you. The idea of 'my country right or wrong' is mistaken. Incidentally, what is realist thinking in international relations? It is a sophisticated justification of this sentiment of 'my country right or wrong'. But government, state, country are all different. 'My country right or wrong' usually means 'my government right or wrong'. Soldiers don't like to hear this. Most of the time soldiers do not die for their country, they die for their government which is not the same thing. Sometimes the 'national popular will' is so great – fighting an invasion or overthrowing a dictatorship – that they do come close together, even though there will still be small sections that are not part of this more general will.

But even when there is mass support, you have to be careful. There was and is mass support for America's dropping bombs on Hiroshima and Nagasaki – the two greatest acts of terrorism in human history. In other words, the question of morality and of righteousness has to come in. You can't just excuse anything in the name of nationalism. The democratic government of the US supported the apartheid regime in South Africa. But there were whites who aligned themselves with the fight against apartheid against the declared national interests of the US government. We are not prisoners of any particular identity. We also have an international identity and thus the ability to empathize with the just struggles of others against our own governments. We can empathize with the struggle of the Vietnamese. We can be men and empathize with the struggle of women. We can be upper caste and empathize with the struggles of lower castes.

But I will also say that there are limits to nationalism. There's a lot of talk about the unity and the integrity of India. What we are referring to here is simply a territorial space, and a religious nationalism tries to *sacralize* this space. To even question existing borders or territorial acquisitions then becomes blasphemous, let alone 'anti-national', and therefore, you must be punished. And to curtail free speech and carry out such punishment, laws must be made much stricter, harsher and undemocratic. This is what the current government is trying to do. Former police commissioner Bassi of Delhi called the opposition to expanding the scope of Indian sedition laws blasphemous![5]

I want to clarify this point here. When I talk about Palestine – and I support Palestine because Israel has been terrible – I ask students, 'Does Israel have the right to exist?' And even those who are pro-Palestinian will say, yes Israel has the right to exist. Then I'll ask them, in that case, if Israel ceases to exist, will that be a great wrong? And they will say yes. Then I ask, does the Soviet Union or East Germany or Czechoslovakia or Yugoslavia or East Pakistan exist? No. Is that then a great wrong?

My point is simple – that sovereignty lies with the people, not a territory. The fundamental moral principle here is not whether Israel and any of these countries have the right to exist but that the people who live there have the right to exist! You can certainly argue, if you wish, that for Israeli Jews to exist, Israel must exist as a territorial space. But that's a secondary level of argument on which there can be disputes. The point is that it's the people and their collective consciousness that creates the basic foundation for what we call the nation. What then are you going to do when for whatever reason some people say that they don't want to be a part of that existing territorialized nation? You can resort to mass repression. You can also move in the direction of Czechoslovakia which peacefully separated the Czech Republic and Slovakia; or of Canada which held a referendum on Quebec; or of Britain where the Scots and the Welsh have a choice to remain in or leave the UK.

In many democracies there is powerful constitutional protection of the principle of free speech as long as there's no question of violence. In the United States you have groups that say 9/11 was a CIA conspiracy. You can even burn the flag in the United States. You have Welsh and Scottish nationalists in Britain. You have Basque and Catalonian separatists openly active in Spain. In many ways, this is a testimony to their more open and democratic characters. Let me give you one more example. There are also leftists and liberals in Pakistan universities. What if a Pakistani stood up in a university there and said, 'Pakistan murdabad, India zindabad' or 'Pakistan *ko tootna chahiye*'? Why? Because Pakistan does not have as strong a democracy as India's. Pakistan oppresses Ahmadiyas; it has the Hudood ordinance which is oppressive. That there is a Punjabi–Pathan nexus that dominates and oppresses Baluchis and Sindhis who have their legitimate nationalist aspirations. If that student is accused by the Pakistani establishment of being anti-national, terrible, etc., and even punished, what would many Hindutva supporters, who label JNU students anti-national, say? They would say, well what do you expect? That's an undemocratic country compared to us.

Finally, there are just three more things I want to say. We are living in a world where for the first time in human history we are faced with three new developments that have never existed before and which represent a huge threat to human existence on a transnational scale and have to be addressed internationally. For the first time in human history, we have the continuity of mass inequality, mass deprivation, mass suffering, basic needs being unmet – and basic needs today are not just the issue of malnourishment but include adequate leisure, health, education, freedom from fear, dignity and respect, but not because there is a scarcity of resources on the global level.

Second, for the first time in human history we have the capacity to destroy the metabolic relationship between nature and humans thereby destroying substantially or fully, the human species itself. These two things are in my view, connected to the nature of capitalism. The strength of capitalism which gives rise to its technological dynamism is the never-ending pursuit of profits. But this is also its key weakness. You cannot have the continuous pursuit of profits unless there is the continuous pursuit of growth, and this is a huge problem. It was one early ecological economist called Kenneth Boulding who said, 'Anyone who believes exponential growth can go on forever in a finite world is either a madman or an economist.'[6] And he's absolutely right. Conventional economics has no theory of limits given its belief in the substitutability of all factors of production. This is a huge danger. How are we going to address it? India is the fourth largest carbon emitter, soon to become the second largest. But our security experts go on about, above all, promoting our 'national interests' so we can't think too much about what will happen to the small island nations through rising sea and ocean levels but must, like China, pursue Western-style average living standards which will guarantee such rises.

The third thing, of course, is that we have the capacity through nuclear weapons and nuclear winter to blow up the world. It's extraordinary that this is something that is accepted in the name of national security. There is a profound moral issue that is involved here. If you are not a complete pacifist, you can use a gun or a tank or whatever for what you legitimately believe are good purposes. But you cannot use nuclear weapons for any good purpose. Even to possess them is immoral since their morality is not determined by the goodness or the badness of the people who have them. When you have them, thereby threatening to use them, what you're saying is that for our national security we have the right to threaten the existence of future generations and of the human species itself. What an extraordinary state of affairs. You have two scientists in India with very different perspectives because scientists were and are divided. People like Niels Bohr, Richard Feynman or Einstein were horrified by nuclear weapons. But why go far? In India you had your middle-class hero Abdul Kalam saying how wonderful it is that India has them. But there was another Indian scientist who won a Nobel Prize not by working in the laboratories of the West, like so many other Indians who have won Nobel Prizes in the sciences, he won it here in India itself, and his name is C.V. Raman. In 1957, he said that scientists should be willing to starve rather than work on nuclear weapons.[7]

My point is simply this. The struggle to build a democratic and humane nationalism, to build a democratic and humane world, means we must recognize the kind of nationalism we have to fight for even as we must go beyond that nationalism to fight on an international scale against these great evils. If this debate on nationalism can continue and develop, maybe there is some hope. Throughout history there have been two kinds of people. There are those who fight for power and there are those who fight for justice, dignity and decency. These are not parallel paths. They meander; and sometimes they come close together and merge. When this happens, for example, in a movement for national liberation or against a dictatorship, it's wonderful because power is being harnessed towards a fundamentally just and humane purpose. And then, when the paths diverge, people will have to choose which to follow. That's the choice your generation will have to make to shape the kind of India and the world that you want. Thank you very much.

*

Notes/References/Bibliography

1. Ernest Gellner, 2009, *Nations and Nationalism*, Second edition, New York: Cornell University Press.
2. For the second and third approaches, see Benno Teschke, 2003, *The Myth of 1648: Class, Geopolitics, and the Making of Modern International Relations*, London: Verso; and Elie Kedourie, 1960, *Nationalism*, Oxford: Blackwell.
3. Benedict Anderson, 1991, *Imagined Communities: Reflections on the Origin and Spread of Nationalism*, London: Verso.
4. Hans Kohn, 1944, *The Idea of Nationalism*, New York: Macmillan, p. 19.
5. Times News Network, 'Bassi at it again, wants stricter sedition law', http://timesofindia.indiatimes.com/city/delhi/Bassi-at-it-again-wants-stricter-sedition-law/articleshow/51113742.cms, accessed on 24 February 2016.
6. www.fdnearth.org/youth/quotes/, accessed on 24 February 2016.
7. Lawrence S. Wittner, 1997, *Resisting the Bomb: 1954–1970*, Stanford, CA: Stanford University Press, p. 80.

Picture credit: Samim Asgor Ali

A Gadfly Jurisprudence of Dissent

Lawrence Liang

(28 FEBRUARY 2016)

THANKS FOR HAVING ME HERE. IT'S always fantastic to be in JNU, but particularly so in the last two weeks when, in a way, the nation is watching you, but not necessarily in the way that many people on TV make that declaration. My initial plan was to talk in Hindi, but there are some technical elements to what I'm going to talk about and my Hindi is so notional that I'm very worried that I'll be declared an anti-notional because of my Hindi, so I'm going to stick to the safe ground and speak in English. I'm going to talk today about the relationship between the right to dissent, freedom of speech and expression, and sedition – the key issues that have been at the heart of the debate for the last two weeks.

But I want to begin with an image, an image that a number of you will be familiar with, and one that many of us have seen: of sculptures of kings and leaders perched on top of a horse. Usually they have a sword in their hand, marching ahead. But often, if you've noticed, a lot of the kings seem very nervous and appear as though they are going to fall off. They appear precariously perched on the edge of the saddle and there is a good reason for that. While the horse has always been the companion of power and of imperial ambition, the horse is also extremely susceptible to one small irritating insect, a little fly called the gadfly. The gadfly has this habit of getting into the ears of the horse and disorienting the horse, making it move wildly, resulting in the dislodging of the arrogant sovereign.

I like to think of the gadfly as the form of speech that is unacceptable to the sovereign. The sovereign's ears are closed to what the gadfly has to say, and yet the smallest of whispers threatens the arrogant sovereign because sedition doesn't always scream out loud – sedition sometimes speaks in whispers. The gadfly also lends its name to a certain ethos of dissent. If you take, for example, Plato's apology which is about Socrates's death, he describes Socrates as a gadfly – a gadfly that speaks to the slow, dim-witted horse called the state. Socrates himself says, 'I am the gadfly who you can easily swat but if you kill me you do it at a very high cost to yourself.'[1]

I would like to offer the gadfly as the first instance of an idea of political dissent inaugurating, if you'd like, a gadfly jurisprudence. A gadfly jurisprudence is what we have to return to today because the last thing that Socrates said before he died was, to paraphrase, 'I am the gadfly that attaches itself to the state, arousing, persuading, annoying and constantly reproaching you. I advise you to spare me.' We know that didn't happen and his life was taken, but that was not the first instance where political dissent was trampled upon. If you look at the history of gadflies, centuries later you have another gadfly in the anti-colonial movement, a gentleman called Mahatma Gandhi who was also charged under Section 124A of the Indian Penal Code (IPC) for sedition and in a remarkable trial, Gandhi said, 'Affection cannot be manufactured or regulated by the law. One should be free to give full expression to their disaffection unless it incites violence.'[2]

What is really remarkable is that Gandhi's interpretation of Section 124A has really become in some ways what the Supreme Court has, over the last sixty-three years, laid down the interpretation to be, and I'll come to this in more detail. The trial itself was quite incredible in the way that it was conducted. The judge in the trial, Broomfield, was so embarrassed about having to sentence Gandhi, because he didn't believe Gandhi deserved to be charged with sedition, that he apologized for his job. Gandhi said, unfortunately you have only two options – you can either resign from your job or give me the harshest punishment, and at the end of the trial Gandhi thanked him for the courtesy that was afforded to him.

If ever there was an example of grace, civility and style in a criminal court, this was the best example of it, something that the Patiala House lawyers spectacularly failed in, even as they see the image of Gandhi every day as they enter the portals of law. But returning to the fact of Gandhi and Socrates being charged as traitors, what is remarkable is that neither Gandhi nor Socrates ever saw themselves as traitors. Socrates, for instance, spoke the language of love, and he said that he was dissenting out of love. Now, it's not a coincidence that we are talking about love because Section 124A is a provision that talks about, amongst other things, the excitement of disaffection towards the state. Disaffection is an emotive category, it is a category about love, and therefore, when we talk about the idea of what it means to be seditious, let's take it away from the language that's been given to us – of national, anti-national, of traitor, of betrayer, etc., and argue instead another kind of politics that reclaims what we may mean to think about a different form of love.

Because if you want to look at the idea of what it may mean to think about a commitment to principle rather than a commitment to power or a commitment to the state, we have a situation where one can articulate a politics of radical citizenship which does not cede the ground in any easy manner to those who claim a monopoly over determining who is an anti-national. The problem with the entire polarized debate about nationalism is that it creates an idealization of the nation where there is a kind of wounded narcissism whenever there is any criticism – internal or external – of the state, and this extreme polarization borrows itself from the language of the friend and the enemy; and this is something we have to absolutely reject.

This is a polarization which is fake. It does not allow us to talk about the real issues, and one way of doing that, if you've read Professor Upendra Baxi's article in yesterday's *Indian Express*, is a distinction he makes between constitutional patriotism and a statist patriotism. So, a dissenter, to my mind, is someone who articulates this politics of citizenship where you're looking to articulate what it might mean to be committed to a set of principles – equality, justice, dignity, etc., rather than to the trappings of a formal state; and that's the reason why any criticism that's grounded on substantive politics is negated by the symbolic politics of nationalism.

But the dissenter, at least in the Indian context, has always found a safe home and the safe home to my mind is one way of thinking about Article 19(1)(a) of our Constitution, or the provision for freedom of speech and expression. If you look at the history of case law in India, there are many kinds of normative justifications for free speech: some of them are about the intrinsic value of free speech (what some would describe as the autonomy argument), while others are about the instrumental value of free speech and there are different kinds of instrumental values. You could argue, for example, about the marketplace of ideas; you could argue about the watchdog function of free speech in maintaining truth, but the most important ideal that has been consistently upheld to justify why one needs to have a very broad standard for free speech in India has always been the democracy argument. The courts have been unequivocal in their belief that it is only free speech that guarantees democratic rights and democratic institutions.

If you look, for example, at a case, *LIC vs Manubhai Shah*,[3] the court says freedom of speech and expression is the lifeline of any democracy, and stifling, suffocating or gagging this would sound a death knell to democracy and usher in autocracy and dictatorship. So, one way of thinking about the relationship between free speech and politics is to think of it as what allows or gives you a certain breathing room. It provides a safe space for you to exercise any political opinion that you want – and there have been no safer spaces till now than universities in this country as the safeguards for this right to dissent – and on that count JNU, if universities are a mirror of the health of a democracy, presents an extremely healthy picture in which a diversity of opinion, a healthy regard for disagreement, and a tradition for dissent has been the marking features of JNU. It is for this reason that I think we need to ensure that JNU fights for the freedom of speech and expression not only for this university but for everyone else in this country.

Now, what is substantively this idea of freedom of speech and expression, and what does it entail? Because we always invoke the term, but I think it's important to nuance it to understand that freedom of speech and expression only makes sense if you think about freedom before, freedom during, and freedom after speech. The problem that we have in the contemporary era is that this idea of freedom has been hijacked. It has been hijacked by two primary trends: it has been hijacked, on the one hand, by the heckler or the stone thrower, so there is no freedom if there is always fear of someone attacking you, of someone violently usurping your ability to speak; and it has been hijacked by the paparazzi. If the press played a crucial role in developing the history of freedom of speech and expression, it is unfortunate that these freedoms have been severely compromised by the news channels of today. So how are we to bridge this gap, this huge gap that now exists between our commitment to free speech principles on the one hand and our actual free speech practices in which you see that the greatest violators of freedom of speech and expression today are actually the press?

How are we to make sense of the gap that exists, for example, between the good Supreme Court judgments that we have, the jurisprudence of free speech that we have, versus the daily reality where Kanhaiya Kumar can be picked up overnight over charges of sedition even though there is nothing seditious that he has said? What do we make, then, of this gap? Are these principles, therefore, useless and exist only in a domain of some utopian politics, or are there ways in which we can really actualize them with what is happening right now in JNU and other parts of the country? To my mind there are some practical ways in which one can think about how one can bridge this gap, and those practical ways include, for example, decriminalizing any form of dissent by making any speech offence automatically bailable. The process is actually the biggest problem and the biggest fear. Ninety-five per cent of all sedition cases will not lead to a conviction, they will lead to acquittals. But if the process is the punishment, you need to ensure that there are some changes in the process that ensure that speech is not expropriated even before it finds its legal arguments in a court. So one way to think about this will be in procedural reform. The other will be to think about this in substantive terms because if there is something that has happened in the last week, it is a very sad reminder of something that had happened during the Emergency where the courts had not responded to the political crises of the times, where the courts had abdicated their responsibility in actually responding as guardians of fundamental rights, and maybe it is important to go back into the judicial history of free speech as a reminder and with a hope that the courts will not abdicate their responsibility this time around.

If we look at the history of freedom of speech and expression in this country, specially concerning sedition, during the Constituent Assembly debates, sedition was initially included in the restrictions clause of free speech but it was dropped, and the reason it was dropped is that it found vociferous opposition from all sides – from the left and from the right – because a large number of people who were part of the anti-colonial struggle had all been charged under Section 124A – so from people like T.T. Krishnamachari, to Nehru and K.M. Munshi, all of whom opposed the inclusion of sedition in the restrictions clause on speech.

So what happened, why is it that Section 124A remained then, and what is the problem? If the Constituent Assembly was so clear that sedition should not be included in the Constitution, what was the problem of it continuing? One problem that some scholars like Jaya Nandita Kasibhatla identify is that the Constituent Assembly debates happened in the aftermath of Partition. Partition is the haunting presence in the Constituent Assembly debates, and Kasibhatla argues that while there are no memorials to the partition in India, unlike let's say the Holocaust memorial, the partition is memorialized, unfortunately, as the Emergency laws in the Constitution, and memorialized in the form of laws like Section 124A, and the idea of the nervous state that emerged is something that sixty years later we now need very seriously to revisit. For Kasibhatla, the incorporation of historical crisis (Partition and/or 'communalism') into the constitutional framework results in an infinite deferral of the citizen effect and the idea of the Emergency swallows the conception of the present moment in history by isolating it under the sign of 'crisis' – that time 'out of time', with no end in sight.

What is the problem with sedition? Sedition belongs in Chapter 6 of the Indian Penal Code, which are offences against the state. Look at what the companions of sedition are in the Indian Penal Code: they are the most serious offences in the IPC. So you have Section 121 which is on waging war against the state, Section 122 which is on collecting arms for the waging of war against the state. Sedition is the only speech offence in the chapter of offences against the state, but if you compare this to other speech crimes under the IPC – equally draconian but benign compared to Section 124A – you get a sense of just how serious Section 124A is.

The punishment under Sections 153A and 153B of the IPC – which deal with hate speech provisions – is three years' imprisonment for each; the punishment for sedition is life imprisonment. So we are talking about a scenario in which an extremely draconian law exists on paper, but which has thankfully been diluted over the years. If we do a quick milestone visiting of what the Supreme Court has said over the years about the law of sedition, you get a sense of what the standards should be for some speech to be considered seditious. In the very first case in 1957, which was not about Section 124A but about public order, the Ramji Lal Modi[4] case, it was clear that this was a very narrow test that the court applied. The question they asked was: Is there a tendency to cause public disorder? Now, this is a very, very vague phrase. What does not have a tendency to cause public disorder? Arnab Goswami is a walking example of a tendency to cause public disorder.

So this was a very narrow test that the public has applied. Why is this idea of public order crucial? It is crucial because Article 19(1)(A) of our Constitution, which is about freedom of speech and expression, is a fundamental right. It cannot be narrowed or taken down except under the condition laid down in Article 19(2), and as we have established, Article 19(2) does not have the word 'sedition', the only phrase that is closely proximate to sedition in Article 19(2) is 'public order'. So, 'what do you mean by public order?' became the crucial question for the courts over the years. And then in a very important judgment in 1960 in the Ram Manohar Lohia case,[5] they interpreted the term 'reasonable restrictions' in relation to public order to mean that there should be a proximate connection, not a far-fetched connection, between speech and consequences. You had to show a real, actual effect that was going to take place. And the second thing they established was that there had to be a proportionality between the measures that attempted to restrict speech and what it sought to achieve. How do you then justify, for example, the difference between three years' imprisonment under Section 153A and life imprisonment for sedition? This question of the constitutional validity of sedition, a lot of friends earlier said, we need to challenge. The question of constitutional validity was in fact raised in 1962, in the Kedarnath judgment, in which the court managed to save Section 124A very narrowly.[6] And the reason they were able to save Section 124A was that they interpreted the section to be a very, very narrow domain in which, unless there was an incitement to public disorder and violence, there was no way that it could be held to be constitutional. The court had to do this because there were already three High Court judgments that ruled Section 124A to be unconstitutional. So, the court comes in to save Section 124A but it saves it only on the very strict ground that satisfying the criteria of incitement to violence can be the only ground that you can actually have sedition. There have been a number of subsequent judgments, very important ones like Rangarajan,[7] and Arup Bhuyan in 2011,[8] all of which have further clarified what the standards are for actually measuring sedition. In the most recent judgment in 2015, in the Shreya Singhal case[9] that invalidated Section 66A of the Information Technology Act, the court made a distinction between a discussion, an advocacy, and an incitement and it's very clear that a large number of politicians and a large number of those who were not even habituated within an ethos of debate and discussion cannot make out the distinction between the three. For them there is no distinction between a discussion, an advocacy, and an incitement.

It will do well for them to spend a little more time in places like JNU and other universities to know that a heated debate, a strong disagreement between people, is not necessarily an incitement and this distinction is what we really need to press. This is a judgment that is crucial because it also introduced a new element in overruling a law on the grounds that it violates Article 19(1)(A) of the Constitution and it says if there is a law that has the consequences of having a chilling effect or creating in a way a condition in which speech cannot be exercised because of an ecology of fear that you will be punished, that you will be beaten up – this chilling effect is a very critical ground in which we should think about what it means to revisit a challenge to Section 124A of the IPC. After the Shreya Singhal judgment came out, the noted feminist lawyer Indira Jaising tweeted congratulating Shreya Singhal, saying that it was only someone from the under-thirty generation who could obtain this judgment. Apart from this being a very generous compliment from a very seasoned legal campaigner, it's also interesting to note because we were reminded in the Rajya Sabha of us being children and this is an instance that we should take to heart.

We need to take this to heart because if you look at the history of children and of young people leading the fight for freedom of speech and expression and on dissent, you'll find a glorious history there, because if Shreya Singhal was a twenty-two-year-old student who could get Section 66A of the Information Technology Act invalidated, there are a whole range of other children in the global history of dissent that we need to learn from. And one such child was a thirteen-year-old girl who during the Vietnam War, in 1969, had gone to school wearing a black band on her arm. She was asked by her school in Iowa to remove the band, but she refused, as a result of which she was suspended from the school, much like some of the students here have been suspended from JNU. Having been suspended from school, she went home and after learning that there were thirteen other children who had done the same thing that day in school and all of them had been suspended from their schools, she raised a constitutional challenge to their suspension, arguing that this was a violation of their right to dissent. This led to a judgment called *Tinker vs Des Moines*[10] in 1969. There are other children who have done similar things. In 1987, in India, in a case called *Bijoe Emmanuel vs State of Kerala*,[11] a case in which a group of children belonging to the Jehovah's Witnesses sect in Kerala had refused to stand up for the national anthem. They were suspended from their school for violating the Prevention of Insults to National Honour Act. The Supreme Court in this case held that the right to freedom of speech and expression includes the right to remain silent, and there is no greater act of dissent than remaining silent when the cacophony of ultra-nationalism surrounds you. So let's take this advice to heart and let's think about how these 'children' actually teach us a lot about the right to dissent in contrast to this conservative idea that somehow these young students don't know what they are doing, practising some sort of immature politics, because the real politicians are the ones who are sitting in parliament.

Let's not forget that the history of freedom of speech and expression is a history in which these rights have not been granted to you by the courts; courts have merely affirmed the existence of these rights. These rights, instead, were born out of individual struggles, they were born out of social struggles, they were born out of extremely charged political moments, in which questions of nation, nationalism, anti-nationalism were all up for grabs. So let's take back in a way the authorship of freedom of speech and expression because ideals of free speech are not some abstract, normative ideals that have been created out of thin air. They are the products of extremely rooted, local struggles like the one that is happening today. At the same time, I would warn you about relying too much on the judiciary to be your saviour because there is also an equally long history of the judiciary creating or recycling extremely conservative categories. For example, after the 1992 Mumbai riots, Joseph Bain D'Souza, the chief secretary of Mumbai filed a case against Bal Thackeray under Section 295A of the IPC for incitement of hatred. The matter went up to the Bombay High Court, and the articles that had been written by Thackeray were presented as proofs. The court in this case, in an extremely regressive judgment, made a distinction between ordinary Muslims and Muslims who are traitors, and said that the provision is about incitement of hatred for the entire community but not for those members of the community who are traitors. There is, therefore, a real danger that in the given current political climate, when the debate around nationalism and anti-nationalism is so polarized, relying solely on courts as some kind of saviours of the right to dissent could also run the risk of creating, in a way, a judicial discourse of nationalism and anti-nationalism. So that's something we should keep in mind, i.e., just to say that one shouldn't rely on a juridical politics entirely.

What I want to conclude with are some important questions that we all need to ask ourselves, because while we are all absolutely clear with where we stand in relation to this false question of the national and anti-national, we are not engaging this in relation to the absolute loony right. Over the last week, from what I have heard in a number of conversations with ordinary people whom you would consider to be reasonable people, I have a feeling that such people are upset by what is happening in JNU. Of course, at one level this is about countering the media falsities that have been perpetuated, but at another level, what if indeed there are a large number of people who feel some kind of hurt, some kind of an injury? How are we to reach out to them, to engage and have a conversation with them? And to what extent are the slogans, the campaigns, the strategies that we currently have able to do what they intend to? How are we to think of more creative campaigns, more creative slogans that are actually able to converse with a large number of people?

Because the greatest danger, I think, is to actually accept the polarization, because the politics of sentiment will always trump the politics of reason, and right now we are relying entirely on the politics of reason. How may we bring a more intelligent politics of sentiment in the way that we lead our campaigns themselves?

The second thing I want to think about is that, as we began with the idea of the gadfly as a symbol of dissent and as one of the most powerful metaphors of the right to dissent, what we have in JNU is a swarm of gadflies. How do we think about the way the swarm moves in its contagion beyond the walls of JNU? JNU is already a safe space for the exercise of certain types of speech but what does that mean vis-à-vis actually supporting initiatives in other universities? M.S. University, Baroda, is facing a very severe crisis posed by the right. In what ways can JNU move out to ensure that this swarm of gadflies that we have actually becomes a contagion across the country, which is one of the great things that the last two weeks has demonstrated, despite how politically bleak it seems outside. The way in which – some people may say that this is delusional or that this is romantic idealism – a certain politics of hope is practised within JNU reminds me of what one of the great dissenters of the twentieth century, Vaclav Havel, had once said. Havel, while in jail, wrote an important tract which said: 'One has to lead one's life and one's politics, "as if".' As if the conditions that do not allow us were not there, as if it were not impossible, as if we can get whatever we demand and that's the only way in which one can have or practise a politics of impossible hope, because to be hopeful in these difficult times is not just foolishly romantic, it is also subversively and compassionately so. Because it reminds us that human history is not just a history of cruelty but also a history of compassion, of courage and of kindness. Dissenters often have very, very tiny feet but the little steps that they take are already a marvellous victory over the political despair all around. So, as you march on the streets of Delhi and onto parliament in two or three days, remember that these tiny feet are the ones that are paving in some way a much more radical idea of dissent in this country which will finally do away with the law of sedition.

*

Notes/References/Bibliography

1. Plato, 2011, *Apology*, CreateSpace, independent publishing platform.
2. http://bombayhighcourt.nic.in/libweb/historicalcases/cases/TRIAL_OF__MAHATMA_GANDHI-1922.html. See also A.G. Noorani, 2008, *Indian Political Trials 1775-1947*, New Delhi: Oxford University Press.
3. (1992) 3 SCC 637.
4. AIR 1957 SC 620.
5. AIR 1960 SC 633.
6. AIR 1962 SCC 955.
7. (1989) SCC (2) 574.
8. (2011) 3 SCC 377.
9. (2015) 5 SCC 1.
10. 393 US 503.
11. AIR 1987 SC 748.

Picture credit: Samim Asgor Ali

Tagore's Take on 'the Self-Love of the Nation'

Ranabir Chakravarti

(29 FEBRUARY 2016)

ONE CANNOT BUT BE DEEPLY SADDENED and anguished by the nearly unstoppable and interminable hectoring by the current political bosses of India and their stooges on who is a true nationalist. This is propounded not to highlight the virtues of nationalism or the qualities of a nationalist, but to identify, profile, abuse, bully and punish (unconstitutional and extra-legal measures not excluded) those who are arbitrarily dubbed as 'anti-national'. The label of 'anti-national' is flaunted to gag and browbeat any voice of dissent and critique. Even the mildest alternatives to certain pet ideas of the current ruling group invariably receive the intemperate and violent outpour from the self-appointed guardian angels of nationalism in India. It results in systematic silencing of political opponents, endless torture of women and ostracization and oppression of the Dalits. No less menacing is the emergence of the self-proclaimed upholders and protectors of cultural nationalism, one of the foundational premises of Hindutva. These culture vultures have been using nationalism and cultural nationalism as instruments of propagating hate culture and hate speech. Any one critiquing the government and the dominant ruling party is branded as an anti-national and a friend and spy of Pakistan. Any blatant wrongdoing is laundered white, if the miscreant chanted the name of Bharat Mata and/or gau-rakshan. This is, to say the least, an alarming scenario for the sustenance and longevity of democracy in India. To critique and dissent are the basic ingredients of a democratic polity, especially in the very long pluralist cultural traditions in India. It is in this painful and frightening scenario of crying hoarse on nationalism, patriotism and the anti-national that one needs to take a close look at Rabindranath Tagore, one of the most hallowed cultural icons of India.

Tagore (1861–1941) is mostly remembered for being a Nobel Laureate, for composing the *Gitanjali* (The Song Offering) and for his '*Janaganamana adhinayaka*', which became the national anthem of India. It is also customary to recite his iconic poem 'Where the mind is without fear'. Also, repeatedly cited as a marker of his patriotism is his momentous decision to relinquish the knighthood, conferred upon him in 1914 by the British emperor, in protest against the mowing down of peaceful protestors at Jallianwala Bagh in 1919. Tagore's Indian roots and his championing of the quintessential Indianness to the wider world immediately make him a national icon.

Was he a nationalist? The answer is an unequivocal *no*. He was never a nationalist and never projected himself to be so in his entire creative oeuvre. He repeatedly denounced nationalism as a menace. He also said that he would not fit the bill of a patriot in the usual and ordinary sense of the term. In the Hindutva agenda, Tagore will surely stand accused as an anti-national; had he been alive today, he would have been jailed for utterances unfit for a deshbhakt, a word now gaining increasing currency and sanctity. Professor Harbans Mukhia, former professor in JNU and Professor Sugata Bose, an MP (of Trinamool Congress) and a distinguished professor in Harvard, unequivocally stated that Tagore would have languished in a jail in India for his steadfast opposition to nationalism, by inviting the wrath of the current Indian government.[1] Going a step forward, Bodhisattwa Kar wrote with lacerating sarcasm that the government could well put him behind the bar posthumously, since the government confers posthumous honour on one it deems fit.[2] Is this a mere coincidence that three eminent historians found that Tagore would not have passed the litmus test of deshbhakti? Is there also not in vogue a grand design to brand a large number of historians, respected universally for their professional competence and commitment, as anti-nationals, pseudo-secularist, Marxist and suchlike stereotypes by the champions of Hindutva?

Let me come back to Tagore and his stand on nationalism. Nationalism, no doubt, has a stellar history in inspiring colonized people all over the globe to bring down colonial rule of European powers. The irony is that these European powers justified their colonial rule from the point of the aspirations of their respective nations. One of the relatively modern political concepts, nationalism is rooted to an assumption of identity of a group of people primarily on the basis of territory, language, religion and culture. Nationalism often consolidates what Anderson (2006) called 'the imagined communities'. This bonding on the basis of assumed identity is a primary factor in nationalism which, therefore, has an in-built exclusionary element and programme. It is this exclusionary feature and self-aggrandizing nature of nationalism that Tagore abhorred. Repeatedly denouncing nationalism, he pointed out that it is nurtured by pride, chauvinism, aggressive posturing and a hate culture against an imagined or actual Other who is to be seen and targeted as an enemy. Tagore, therefore, bares before us that the greater the bombastic noises for nationalism, more is the revelation of its inherent hollowness and its fear of the different. It is to stamp out the dissident, the deviant and the different that nationalism becomes the potent tool for its dubious handlers. Put succinctly, he viewed nationalism as synonymous with parochialism and hate culture; at its core it is an 'engine of cowardice', to borrow an expression of Ruchir Joshi.[3]

Tagore's misgivings about nationalism are not merely India-specific, but spread out to situations worldwide. This is particularly evident from his collection of essays, anthologized as *Nationalism* (1918). These originally formed part of his lectures in Japan and the USA in 1917 when he sharply critiqued the nationalist posturing and policies devouring and destroying the world. It is no wonder he was completely misunderstood. This rubbishing of nationalism is the dominant theme of his Bangla essay 'Loraier Mul', or 'The Root Cause of War', written at the onset of the First World War in 1914. He categorically diagnosed therein that the malady lay in the insatiable greed of the European nation states, mostly

Britain and France and subsequently Germany, to espouse colonialism for furthering their competing interests that inevitably resulted in unprecedented hostilities and destructions affecting the entire world. He found that this war was actually a contestation among European nation states which turned it into a global war by dint of their possessing far-flung colonial empires. One may go back even further and take a close look at a poem 'The Sunset of the Century', composed on 31 December 1899 (the quote below is available in his 1918 book, *Nationalism*). Its backdrop was the Boer War.

> The last sun of the century sets amidst the blood-red clouds
> Of the West and whirlwind of hatred.
> The naked passion – the self-love of the nation in its drunken
> Delirium of greed, is dancing to the clash of steel and the
> Howling verses of vengeance.
>
> The hungry self of the Nation shall burst in a violence of fury
> From its own shameless feeding.
> For it has made the world its food.
>
> ...
>
> The crimson glow of light on the horizon is the light of
> Thy dawn of peace, My Motherland
> It is the glimmer of the funeral pyre burning to ashes the vast
> Flesh – the self-love of the Nation – dead under its own
> Excess.[4]

The above quote also speaks of his concerns about his Motherland. The deep attachment of the poet to India is writ large particularly in the torrent of patriotic songs which cascaded from his pen during the period of the Swadeshi movement in the wake of the partition of Bengal in 1905 (which was annulled in 1910 under the pressure of a celebrated mass movement, known as the *Banga-bhanga Andolan*). Tagore was at the forefront of this movement and composed one of his immortal songs, '*Ekla chalo re*' (Walk Alone). As the movement broke out in 1905, Rabindranath was at Giridih (now in Jharkhand). Among many songs he created then, several were put to the tune of Baul songs, an inseparable aspect of the folk life and culture in Bengal. Perhaps the earliest of such patriotic songs, in Baul tune, was '*Amar nai ba holo pare jawa*'. Tagore, at the mature age of forty-four, deliberately brought in for the first time in his music the Baul tune and format, which was steeped in the folk culture, to coincide with the upsurge of the mass movement. The choice of Baul form and tune in his Swadeshi songs was indeed a political act. His love for his native land, his upright stance against the imperial colonialist and his deep faith in humanism stand out in these songs, inspiring countless people to plunge into the anti-British movement.

Yet, soon after this, Tagore withdrew from active politics and devoted himself to the onerous task of spreading education and espousing internationalism. Did he remain a patriot and/or a nationalist? His unquestioned love for and ties with his motherland never vacillated. Interestingly enough, Tagore mostly preferred to use the term *Swadesh*, one's homeland, nuanced with the idea, if one has/had a home in land. He virtually desists from using *Jatiyatavad* and *Rashtravad*, usually considered equivalent to nationalism. There is an ambivalence in his attitude towards nationalism. If and as long as this creed raised its voice against the inhuman exploitation of India by the colonial power, the utter impoverishment of the country and the indignity of the colonized, Tagore was certainly in league with the nationalists. But if the nationalists primarily aimed at and sought for mere political freedom and mimicking of the Western ideas of the nation state, he would underline the limitations of mere political freedom. That's why he raised the issue of freedom within the family structure, exposing the severe gender inequality in the patriarchal Indian family; he asked the uncomfortable question on the degree of freedom accorded to children in the family. This was perhaps drawn from the experiences of his own childhood when he felt the vacuity of the school education and dropped out of school. From this time onwards, Rabindranath would devote his life and energy to two complementary issues: rural reconstruction through poverty alleviation and mass education. He withdrew from the Swadeshi movement, yet remained ever active as what has been labelled as 'constructivist swadeshi' by Sumit Sarkar.

Before delving a bit more into Rabindranath's ideas of rural reconstruction and education as his programme on Swadesh, it may be in order to look into his '*Janaganamana adhinayaka*', which became the national anthem of the independent nation state of India. There has been consistent allegation from certain quarters that this was composed by Tagore in honour of King Emperor George V at the time of his Delhi Durbar (one of the latest to join this chorus is Kalyan Singh, the governor of Rajasthan in July 2015; he was the chief minister of UP at the time of the demolition of Babri Masjid on 6 December 1992). The Delhi Durbar was held on 12 January 1911. Sabyasachi Bhattacharya has demonstrated that the song was composed on 11 January 1911. How a song composed less than twenty-four hours before the ceremonial Durbar could even be conceived for presentation/singing during a state ceremony of strict protocol defies both imagination and logic. The song was presented for the first time on 27 December 1911 on the second day of the twenty-sixth session of the Indian National Congress, held in Calcutta (Kolkata). Two English dailies belonging to the Anglo-Indian press, namely *The Statesman* and *The Englishman* respectively reported:

> The Bengali poet Rabindranath Tagore sang a song composed by him specially to welcome the Emperor (*The Statesman*, 28 December 1911).
>
> The proceedings began with the singing by Rabindranath Tagore of a song specially composed by him in Honour of the Emperor (*The Englishman*, 28 December 1911).

This is being lapped up for more than a century by the people of Tagore's own country. In sharp contrast to the stories published in *The Statesman* and *The Englishman*, the *Amritabazar Patrika* and *The Bengalee* reported:

> The proceedings of the Congress party session started with a prayer in Bengali to praise God (Song of Benediction). This was followed by another song sung welcoming King George V (*Amritabazar Patrika*, 28 December 1911).

> The annual session of Congress began by singing a song composed by the great Bengali poet Rabindranath Tagore. Then a resolution expressing loyalty to King George V was passed. A song paying a heartfelt homage to King George V was then sung by a group of boys and girls. (*The Bengalee*, 28 December 1911).

The second song sung after '*Janaganamana adhinayaka*' has been identified as '*Hamare badshah*', composed by Rambhuj Chaudhary. First, there is not an iota of truth that '*Janaganamana adhinayaka*' was composed by Tagore to welcome George V. Second, the Anglo-Indian press deliberately concocted the two separate presentations and dished out a blatant lie maligning Tagore. The hard-core nationalists of today still prefer to swear by the report of the Anglo-Indian press of the colonial times, completely ignoring the factually correct report published by the *Amritabazar Patrika* and *The Bengalee*. This is one of numerous instances where the nationalist images and ideas of Indianness are an aping of the perceptions of the former colonial masters! Tagore had to confront this non-issue time and again in later decades. In 1937, one of his most trusted lieutenants, Pulin Bihari Sen, wrote a letter to Rabindranath on this matter. Tagore's reply may be partly quoted here:

> A certain high official in His Majesty's service, who was also my friend, had requested that I write a song of felicitation towards the Emperor. The request simply amazed me. It caused a great stir in my heart. In response to that great mental turmoil, I pronounced the victory in Jana Gana Mana of that Bhagya Vidhata [ed. God of Destiny] of India who has from age after age held steadfast the reins of India's chariot through rise and fall, through the straight path and the curved. That Lord of Destiny, that Reader of the Collective Mind of India, that Perennial Guide, could never be George V, George VI, or any other George. Even my official friend understood this about the song. After all, even if his admiration for the crown was excessive, he was not lacking in simple common sense.[5]

Tagore's sharp tone and anguish remain unaltered in a letter of 1939:

> I should only insult myself if I cared to answer those who consider me capable of such unbounded stupidity as to sing in praise of George the Fourth or George the Fifth as the Eternal Charioteer leading the pilgrims on their journey through countless ages of the timeless history of mankind.[6]

Let us now pick up our thread on Tagore's ideas on education and rural reconstruction. The very foundation of Visva-Bharati in 1921 as a co-educational, residential university was an immensely courageous and extraordinary effort towards Tagore's greatest experiment. This emerged out of what he had earlier planned as the Brahmacharya Vidyalaya at Santiniketan. This was his alternative to the colonial education system, which was geared to produce loyalists for the colonialists. The sharpest critique to the colonial education system took the form of the parable-like short story, entitled 'Tota Kahini' (1917). It was translated first as the 'Parrot's Training', but a recent English translation is easily accessible on the internet under the title 'Parrot's Tale' (superbly translated by Palas Baran Pal).[7] It will perhaps take tomes to write on Tagore's educational ideas and programmes in his Visva-Bharati. Three points need to be stressed here. The first and foremost feature in Tagore's Visva-Bharati was the unbound celebration of creativity, steeped in nature. Its second sterling quality is that it embraced the world as its home (hence its motto: where the world becomes its single home – *yatra visvam bhavatyekanidam*), upholding internationalism from its very inception. Tagore was critiqued in India for his championing of internationalism when the country was engaged in nation's freedom from foreign yoke. Tagore remained undeterred as he viewed internationalism as the bulwark against the petty and narrow-minded nationalism, that too having been mostly practised by members of the upper echelons of the society. The third feature, Tagore envisaged for Visva-Bharati, was rural reconstruction. We may here take a close look at his rural reconstruction programme in which the core idea was the rejuvenation of the Swadeshi Samaj. This Swadeshi Samaj in Tagore's idea was far more important than the state, especially the nation state; his discomfiture and distrust of the nation state are well known. The centre-staging of the Swadeshi Samaj was in true spirit of eternal India which gave greater priority to society than to the state. Intent upon rural reconstruction he created an agricultural wing of Visva-Bharati, located at the village called Surul and christened as Sriniketan (the Abode of Grace), in proximity to Santiniketan. Tagore felt that this reconstruction must be taken up by rural populace themselves, not to be led by the urbane, middle-class bhadralok group. He always encouraged the application of the appropriate technologies and scientific apparatuses, if necessary to be borrowed from the Western world. This prompted him to send his son and son-in-law to learn agricultural science and technologies from Illinois in USA. Coupled with this programme were his steps to form a cooperative society at the rural level and introduce rural banking system. To give a distinct shape to his ideas of rural reconstruction at Surul he invited the agro-economist Leonard Elmhirst to Visva-Bharati. Among various measures undertaken by Elmhirst, one was to improve upon the sanitation in this remote village and to insist upon the use of the nightsoil as natural manure in the fields. Reminisces Elmhirst in his diary, on 23 February 1922, in the context of digging a trench of a specific measurement in which were to be buried 'all the waste from kitchen, garden and latrine':

> ... the boys all come up to my room for a discussion, this time on trenching. I told them that until they'd each had the experience of emptying their own latrine buckets in trenches on their own garden plots ... they could not consider themselves farmers. ... Since the Poet himself emptied his own bucket why shouldn't they?[8]

Mahatma Gandhi would have surely joined this chore had he been in Sriniketan at this time. These two celebrated makers of modern India shared certain things in common but also maintained sharp differences of opinion on many matters. This is a fairly well-known and documented aspect of the Gandhi–Tagore interactions and does not require revisiting here. Differences notwithstanding, the two harboured the highest esteem and respect for each other. On the question of untouchability in Indian society, both were committed to its eradication, albeit in their own ways.

For Gandhiji, untouchability was an evil emanating as a result of the corruption and degeneration of the pristine varnasramadharma which was viewed by Gandhiji as an ideal social norm of an ordered society. Tagore had little attachment to merits, if any, of the varnasrama system. In 1932, when Gandhiji was on his epic fast unto death in the Yeravda jail, Tagore was hugely anxious about the Mahatma's failing health. He urged all inmates of Visva-Bharati to practise the acceptance of drinking water from the 'Harijans' of the nearby villages as a mark of solidarity with the Mahatma. Sujit Kumar Mukhopadhyay, then a student of Visva-Bharati and later a noted scholar/academician in Sanskrit, Chinese and Tibetan, further urged Tagore that food needed to be cooked by scavengers in the Visva-Bharati kitchen and the same food ought to be served by the same scavengers to all inmates. Tagore gave his immediate nod to this proposal which, Mukhopadhyay tells us, was a challenging test even to many of the closest compatriots of Tagore.

It was with these acts of breaking taboos and boundaries that Tagore tried to give new life to India and not by chanting the mantras of narrow nationalism. The growing urge of nationalism in India seems to have begun from the second half of the nineteenth century. This seems to have coincided with the increasing championing of the Bhagavadgita as the ideological plank of selfless act and sacrifice (*nishkama karma* based on the tenet *karmanyevadhikaraste ma phaleshu kadachana*) to ensure the emancipation of the country. The Gita was the bedrock for the Mahatma in propagating, pursuing and practising non-violence (ahimsa) and/or what he called passive resistance. In the narrative of nationalism in India, both in the colonial and the postcolonial period, the Gita is invariably taken as the foundational ideology of the Indian nation. Tagore, however, viewed the sacred text in quite a different way. An instance of this is available in his 1932 travelogue during his trip to Iran. This text, *Journey to Persia and Iraq: 1932* (the original Bengali piece is called *Parasye*), begins with Tagore's journey from Calcutta (Kolkata) to Busheir in Persia by plane. This was the second time that Tagore boarded an aircraft. He detested the flight, not because of his fear of an aircraft, but due to his utter disgust about this machine. A long quote from this account is unavoidable here:

> As the aeroplane rose higher, our relationship with the earth became narrowed down from that of the five senses to one – of sight, and even that no longer intimate. In such a state of mind, I realized, man can grow cruelly destructive if he is out to rain bombs from the aeroplane. Then, delicate calculations as to the offence of the victims no longer paralyse his raised arms, for the very basis of that calculation has vanished.
>
> The doctrines of the Gita are an aeroplane of this sort. They took the compassionate mind of Arjuna to that distant region from where the slayer and the slain, stranger and friend, could no longer be distinguished. Those hapless survivors – for them only remains the consolation: na hanyate hanyamane sarire. (The full verse reads: 'For the Soul there is neither birth, nor death at any time. He has come into being, and will not come into being. He is unborn, ever existing and primeval. He is not slain when the body is slain [*Na jayate mriyate va kadachinnayam bhuta bhavita va na bhuyah/Ajo nityah sasvato'yam purano/Na hanyate hanyamane sarire*]).[9]

This is a stunning critique, almost a parody, of the Gita, the like of which could have been essayed by only another icon of twentieth-century India, B.R. Ambedkar. What is even more striking is that the Gita verse he so scathingly mocked at belongs originally to the *Kathopanishad*. Tagore, in one stroke, not only de-sanctified the Gita, but also an Upanishad text. The common belief is Tagore had been steeped in the Upanishads from his childhood and Upanishadic ideas and ideals formed the very core of his creativities. The above quote amply bears out that Tagore defies categorization. One may be permitted an aside at this juncture. If Upanishadic ideas and spiritualism were the essence of Tagore's creations, including his music, how does he provide immense inspiration to the making of Bangladesh, both in its struggle for liberation and the making of a sovereign nation state, which is a Muslim-majority country? As we all know, Tagore's song, '*Amar sonar Bangla*' (created during the movement against partition of Bengal 1905–10), is the national anthem of Bangladesh. No less significant is the fact that the Sri Lankan national anthem, '*Sri Lanka Matha*', is also associated with Tagore. It was either penned by Tagore or by Ananda Samarakoon (1940) who, as a pupil of Visva-Bharati (till 1938), was inspired by Tagore to compose it. He is the only person in the world whose songs have become national anthems of two sovereign nations (if not also a third one, if we include Sri Lanka), and yet the man ever remained a sceptic of nationalism. This celebration of contradictions is an essential aspect of the life and activities of Tagore. Thus he once said, albeit in a jocular mode, that his greatest virtue lay in inconsistency and his greatest weakness too was the same, i.e. inconsistency.

An extremely significant anecdote about Tagore's non-conformist stand is captured by Amartya Sen. The context is Gandhiji's visit to Santiniketan in 1940, at the invitation of Tagore – in fact, Tagore's last meeting with the Mahatma. During the elegant receptions accorded to Gandhiji by Tagore, a lady from Calcutta, attired in a silk sari, paid her homage to the two great men on the first day. She went again on the next day, but clad in a khadi sari and carrying an autograph book. As she placed the autograph book before Gandhiji, the Mahatma did notice the change in the dress material. And he then scribbled, 'Never make a promise in haste. Having once made it, fulfil it at the cost of your life'. Seated next to him was Rabindranath who immediately reacted to it; in an agitated mood the poet immediately wrote a short Bangla poem with the essence that none can be made a 'prisoner forever with a chain of clay'. Tagore then realized that this Bangla poem won't be intelligible to Gandhiji. So he scribbled further, this time in English: 'Fling away your promise if you found it to be wrong.'[10]

The anecdote sums the impossibility of appreciating/judging Tagore on the yardstick of crass nationalistic commitments and agenda. I would like to end this endeavour with a situation in 1940. The stage is set in Paris, on 13 June, just on the eve of the fall of Paris before the Nazi army. The radio broadcast Tagore's play, the *Post Office* (originally composed in Bangla as *Dakghar* in 1912; translated into French by Andre Gide). Where lies its significance and message? The drama revolves round a terminally ill boy, named Amal, confined to bed which is beside a window, his only aperture to the wider world. The stricken boy makes friends with all unknown passers-by, including the head constable and the mendicant (Fakir). He learns about the establishment of a post office nearby and yearns for a letter from the King. In this allegorical play, the boy is destined to die, but his spirit is indomitable and unfettered even in the face of death; his spirit overcomes death and the fear of death as he sores into eternity. The plot of the drama became charged with the undying wish for emancipation when humanity encountered one of its darkest days during the high noon of Nazism and fascism. The drama was translated into Polish by Janus Korczak and enacted in Polish ghetto during the holocaust. The crux of the matter is the invincible human spirit which nationalistic frenzy cannot curb. To this humanism, far beyond the confines of the nation state, Tagore paid his homage in his 'Religion of Man' (1933) and 'Crisis in Civilization' (1941).

In a remarkable BBC television series, the *Ascent of Man*, Jacob Bronowski (mathematician and biologist who also authored the book of the same name) raised a crucial issue: what is the essential message in science – to espouse knowledge or to reach certainties? Bronowski pays his tributes to the seekers of knowledge, which is generated by repeated questioning of the established ideas.[11] In other words, knowledge courts uncertainty. Certainties, on other hand, are the very end of inquiry, of freshness, of innovations – in short, ensuring a complete closure of the mind. Tagore invariably would embrace uncertainty and open-ended situations. He provides us with alternatives to the established binaries of national and anti-national, devotee and dissident, enemy and ally. Time is ripe now to discard the supremacist and majoritarian stances inherent in the idea of the nation. That's why we need to examine Tagore, not to seek his validity for the current scenario, but his relevance to the critical time around us. Never to be fettered by the demands of the nation state, Tagore wrote a brief poem in Bangla in 1932 to observe the twelfth anniversary of the foundation of *Anandabazar Patrika*. The last two lines of this poem assume enormous significance at this hour: If you wish to endear your homeland, go above and beyond it/ Don't belittle human beings for the sake of the nation (*Swadesere chao jodi taro urddhve otho/ Koro na deser kachhe manushere chhoto*).

*

Notes/References/Bibliography

1. http://timesofindia.indiatimes.com/india/Nobody-is-the-univocal-spokesperson-for-the-nation-Full-text-of-speech-in-Lok-Sabha-by-Sugata-Bose-on-Rohith-Vemula-suicide-and-JNU-row/articleshow/51128201.cms, accessed on 24 February 2016.
2. https://kafila.org/2016/02/25/come-on-man-be-clear-what-comes-first-nation-or-democracy-bodhisattva-kar-translated-by-ahona-panda/, accessed on 29 August 2016.
3. http://www.telegraphindia.com/1160731/jsp/opinion/story_99712.jsp#.V6IBlpN97-Y, accessed on 29 August 2016.
4. Rabindranath Tagore, 1918, *Nationalism*, New York: Macmillan Company.
5. Ibid, 1961, Rabindra Rachanavali, vol. XIV, Kolkata: Govt. of West Bengal (Centenary Edition), pp. 1049–52.
6. Ibid, p. 1052. Further discussion is available in Prasanta Pal, 1982–94, *Rabi-Jibani*, Kolkata: Ananda Publishers, Vol. IV (in Bangla).
7. http://www.parabaas.com/translation/database/translations/stories/Rabindranath_parrot.html, accessed on 29 August 2016.
8. Leonard K. Elmhirst, *Poet and Plowman*, Kolkata: Visva-Bharati, 2008.
9. Rabindranath Tagore, *Journey to Persia and Iraq: 1932*, Delhi: Orient Blackswan, 2003.
10. Amartya Sen, 'Tagore and His India', www.nobelprize.org, accessed 2 August 2016.
11. J. Bronowski, *The Ascent of Man*, London: BBC, 1975.

Picture credit: Gayatri Balusha

One Hundred Years of Tamil Nationalism

A. Mangai

(1 MARCH 2016)

GOOD EVENING TO ALL OF YOU and thank you so much for this opportunity. These three weeks at JNU have been really intense – anxious on the one hand and highly inspiring on the other. I think the hope of tomorrow lies in all of you. It is wonderful to see that we can resist and offer a creative counter-resistance. I am sure these few days have been exhausting, to say the least. There are a lot of things to do, life takes over, and we have our lives to live and that is what we want to do. And in order to lead our lives the way we want, we have no other go but to struggle. I am amazed at the sense of responsibility exhibited by all of you young people, who are not usually considered responsible enough! One refers to youthful fervour and passion, but here I am actually witnessing utmost responsibility along with fervour and passion and I feel extremely happy. I am visiting JNU briefly and am happy to be part of you at this moment of crisis.

My solidarities from Tamil Nadu, where we are historically by default 'anti-national'! Some of the things that I read in the papers here and the interpretations that are given provoke laughter in me. Because we grew up hearing anti-Sanskrit, anti-Hindi, or anti-north India, or anti-Central government slogans. It is such a given that you almost feel like a foreigner in the rest of the country. The year 2016 is the centenary of the Dravidian movement. In 1916, Thenninthiya Nala Urimai Sangam (South Indian Liberal Federation) was founded by the non-Brahmin middle- and upper-class leaders in Tamil Nadu. It was reorganized as the Justice Party later. Periyar who was in the Congress at that time broke away from it in 1925. Since he fought with the Congress on issues of caste and communal representation, he founded the Self-Respect movement in 1925. In due course, this movement consolidated itself as Dravida Kazhagam. It got split into Dravida Munnetra Kazhagam (DMK in 1949) and *Anna Dravida Munnetra Kazhagam* (ADMK) much later. Everybody has to add a 'D', a 'Dravidian' tag in Tamil Nadu, otherwise it's very difficult to exist on the public platform. We are going to face our elections in May and whether it is the Congress or the BJP, they have to find their alliances. In Tamil Nadu, without the tag line, Dravidian, nobody can enter, and this has been made possible through one whole century of various struggles at different points of time over various issues.

I shall focus on Tamil nationalism, on the basis of two major nodal categories that organize and give shape to Tamil nationalism, namely, language, which is Tamil, and the other – caste. Both these categories were central to Tamil nationalism. It is a misnomer to imagine that the Tamils do not accept 'outsiders'. History tells us another story. There have been Telugus, Marathas and Nizams who have ruled Tamil Nadu at different points of time and stayed on in the state. There are, however, a lot of interstate issues with Kerala, Andhra, and Karnataka over water and migration.

I would like to historicize this Tamil context or identity. Why did it become important in the early twentieth century? The colonial Indological studies, undertaken through the Royal Asiatic Society, framed India through Sanskrit language and literature. Therefore, most Indologists began with the idea of Sanskrit. It is pervasive even today and also among many Indian scholars (even a scholar like Amartya Sen, while tracing the culture of argument in India would refer to Sanskrit and probably add Pali, but never really refer to Tamil). That's because of the legacy of the colonial scholars with their Orientalist philosophy that built up Sanskrit as pan-Indian and the only classical language. This framework collapsed in 1856 with Caldwell's study. He was a missionary in Tamil Nadu, in a remote corner, and a philologist. He published his *Comparative Grammar of Dravidian Languages* in 1856. He classified Dravidian languages as a separate family of languages as against Indo-Aryan, and that in turn extended to the question of who were these Dravidians, who spoke these languages and what was their habitat. History is yet to ascertain the spread of Dravidian culture in the geo-space called India.

In the late nineteenth century and the early twentieth century, we also had the rediscovery of the classical Tamil canon. I am referring to it as rediscovery because for a long while these texts were in palm-leaf manuscripts which were not available to everyone. Collecting these palm-leaf manuscripts, editing and publishing them was almost a missionary activity undertaken by scholars. It took about three decades from the late nineteenth century and early twentieth century to accomplish this. I am not going into the details of that exercise. But we retrieved, classified and published the Sangam corpus of poetry, spanning from the second century BC to about second century AD – about four to five centuries. It has to be internally periodized, which is still a contested terrain. The textual sources reveal a completely new perspective about life built around the concept of *Tinai*, which can be translated as 'ecoscape', even though it was translated as 'landscape' by A.K. Ramanujan. We have multiple translations of various Sangam texts available today. This was a culture that roughly divided itself according to the landscape and the occupations of the landscape and the rituals and deities connected with each landscape, and it also divided the whole thematic terrain of life into *akam* and *puram*, translated as love and war. I would prefer to translate it as interior and exterior. These texts talked about an alternate way of looking at life in conjunction with nature, and a society which has nothing to do with the Ramayana and the Mahabharata. You have a few rare references to the Mahabharata and the Ramayana in *Cilapatikaram*, which is dated to the second century AD. We can consider Sangam texts as having echoes of mainly non-Vedic religions like Jain and Buddhist teachings. But one can't be very sure. But we know that in Tamil we have five epics, two of which are available as full texts. One is *Cilapatikaram*, and the other is *Manimekalai*. *Cilapatikaram* is a Jain epic and *Manimekalai* is a Buddhist epic. So we have nothing to do with this Hinduism that's being talked about as *the* Indian culture.

This is not to say that the Tamils were a peace-loving people. Far from that. There were a lot of references to war in Tamil Sangam and post-Sangam texts. There is a whole genre of literature called *Barani* that talks about warfare, much later. There were chieftains and communities that were fighting with each other. The most ancient grammar available in Tamil, titled *Tolkappiyam*, could be equated to Panini's grammar in Sanskrit, and within *Tolkappiyam*, there is a chapter titled '*Meypattiyal*' that refers to basic bhavas and rasas. *Cilapatikaram* has detailed references to everything you find in *Natyashastra*.

In the early twentieth century, one became aware that Tamil is a language which was as classical as Sanskrit, but it was also modern because it was a living language, unlike Sanskrit. This created two kinds of turns – one was Iyothithasar, about whom V. Geetha and S.V. Rajadurai talk in their *Non-Brahmin Millennium*, prescribed at JNU. The other was the romanticization of Tamil language and culture which was made into political mileage. What Iyothithasar did was to talk about *adi tamizhar*, the original inhabitants of the region speaking *adi tamil*. He also argued that the religion practised in this region was Buddhism. So the people were also adi Buddhists. So it is adi tamil and adi Buddhist, both forming the axis of Tamil identity. But Iyothithasar himself was discovered only about two decades ago. His works were collected by Aloysius. It brought a new perspective to the question of Tamil nationalism. As early as the early twentieth century, Iyothithasar ran a journal called *Thamizhan* and sold it for 1 paisa, so it was called *Oru Paisa Thamizhan* (1904–14). Iyothithasar was a Dalit and an intellectual. The other trend that followed all these discoveries was to romanticize the glorious, ancient past of Tamil. We have this adage in Tamil that 'a Tamil belongs to that ancient clan that lived even before sand and stone came into being on this earth!' Therefore, the Tamils were probably the first apes!

The differing significance ascribed to Tamil and Sanskrit and the resulting power relations was read as parallel to north and south India. This in turn can be read as parallel to Brahmin and non-Brahmin discourse. Sanskrit was primarily learnt and hailed by Brahmins. These Brahmins, as M.S.S. Pandian observes, quoting the historian N. Subramanian, speak a kind of slangish Tamil. One can mark them by their slang and I hear a lot of that Tamil in Delhi (probably 'Tam-Brahms' left Tamil Nadu much earlier and settled in Delhi, and their migration to California, Toronto or wherever continues, and they speak that specific Tamil language). In the public world, as lawyers and judges and officers holding major positions in governance, they spoke impeccable English. They spoke that British English and only rattled off about the supremacy of Sanskrit. Very few of course knew Sanskrit, to be honest. Thus, Sanskrit remained a classical language. Tamil language, on the other hand, had to wait till 2004 to achieve classical status officially by the Indian government. The Congress regime, because of their electoral alliance with DMK and the certification given by Prof. George Hart from University of California, Berkeley that Tamil is an ancient language, deigned to confer that status onto the Tamil language. How much more colonial could we become!

It is in this context that Periyar should be understood. He began as everyone did at that time – as a Congress person – and broke out of the National Congress over differences vis-à-vis caste and religion. He openly criticized the Congress for practising caste discrimination. We have many aspects/phases of Periyar: the Periyar of the Congress party leading temple entry in Vaikkom; one who is influenced by his visit to the Soviet Union; one who announces that he will fight superstition leaving the other fights to fellow-travellers. He was the founder member of the Self-Respect movement and Dravida Kazhagam as well. The old man with his stunning beard also had his own complex graph of how he negotiated his terms with powers that be. Iconicity does not help in historical understanding.

He insisted on three things in everything that he said and did – atheism, anti-Brahminism and gendered understanding are the cornerstones of his philosophy. He clearly announced himself to be an atheist, thereby getting away from any of the religious clutches. He proclaimed himself to be anti-Hindu, because Hinduism is based on *Manudharma* which practises caste hierarchy. So he was anti-Hindu, therefore anti-Brahmin and, therefore, anti-caste discrimination, and anti-Hindi. His notion of anti-Hindi did not stem from the primacy of Tamil. He didn't have any love lost for Tamil. He did not agree with anyone living on the business of building up a glorious past. He saw that Tamil was very closely connected to the Saivite and the Vaishnavite cults and the bhakti literature that comes with it. He wanted to get away from that. *Thirukkural* is the only ethical literature he propagated in the Tamil canon for its secularism. At the same time, because Tamil was the language of the people, he also advocated reformation of the Tamil script, but not in a way that the later Dravidian movement would make it out to be. Periyar's anti-Hindi position was because of the Aryan–Dravidian question, and the question of the north flourishing and the south diminishing. Because both Hinduism and the Aryan culture were practising patriarchy, and imposing the notion of chastity on women – he was anti-patriarchy, in a non-reformative sense. He wanted things to change, he told women to organize themselves. He asked women not to bother about reproduction. This is not the space to dwell on gender in detail, but Periyar incorporated gender as an integral part of his perspective.

Periyar considered the Ramayana as the manual that practises Manudharma, and therefore he shamed the statues of Rama with slippers, and burnt copies of the Ramayana. In terms of language, of course, he opposed Sanskrit outright, because it was considered to be the *devabhasha*, and also because it was a dead language for all practical purposes. He denounced the hegemony of Hindi. There is, however, a difference in the way Periyar opposes Hindi and Sanskrit. He also critiqued Tamil's connections to religion and the glorious, ancient past. But at the same time, he kept in touch with whatever had to be done vis-à-vis the Tamil language.

There are three major anti-Hindi agitations that we can talk about in the twentieth-century history of Tamil Nadu. In Tamil we refer to it as *mozhi por* – 'struggle for our language'. The earliest is 1937–39, when we had the provincial governments and Hindustani was proposed as an official language by Rajaji. There was a huge opposition to that move. Two people lost their lives in this struggle and are hailed as 'martyrs of this first war for Tamil' to be recognized as the official language. One of them was Thalamuthu, a Dalit, and the other was Natarajan. That was in the 1930s, before Independence.

In 1947, when India became independent, Periyar observed it as a black day. It caused a rift in the DK – Dravida Kazhagam. The overtly spelt reason for Annadurai breaking away from Periyar's party and forming Dravida Munnetra Kazhagam was essentially this. Annadurai wanted to work within the Indian state, within the federalism of the Indian state and believed that it was possible, while Periyar did not subscribe to it. DMK was formed in 1949.

Between 1949 and 1952, there was a continuous struggle against the Central government's imposition of the three-language formula in schools. We grew up without learning a word of Hindi. If we study in Tamil medium, we learn English as a second language, or if you study in English medium, which was rare at that point, you study Tamil as the second language. English hadn't become a status symbol as it is now. That was the pattern. The three-language formula was imposed by the Congress and when there was resistance, Rajaji came up with an alternative plan. The alternative was *Kula Kalvi* – the varnashrama education. Rajaji advocated that people practise the occupations that one was born into and the hours of education could actually match the kind of occupation one did. Therefore, the struggle was to fight both Rajaji's *Kula Kalvi* as well as the three-language formula. And finally, at that time the Central government and Prime Minister Jawaharlal Nehru agreed that in states where Hindi was not the language spoken by the people, till they accepted it, they could continue with the two-language formula. I think today's governments should learn from these past instances. Nehru actually negotiated with the differences that were there. He listened to the demands of the people. We only had the two- language system in Tamil Nadu, but the threat was always there – that there would be the three-language formula and Hindi would be imposed on the Tamil people.

In 1956, there was a big movement to rename the erstwhile Madras Presidency as Tamil Nadu. In Tamil language it has always been called Tamilagam. So there was no problem in Tamil. It is not like the struggle to change Bombay to Mumbai. Because in Tamil, Tamil Nadu or Tamilagam was always in use and Madras was a colloquial usage. There are creative writers who have used it, there are many people who have used it in everyday language, there was a newspaper called the *Madras Mail*, but still when you speak in Tamil formally, you refer to it as Tamilagam or Tamil Nadu. The struggle was to rename it – Madras Presidency to be renamed as Tamil Nadu, and Periyar was in the lead.

The third struggle came in 1965, when Bhaktavatsalam, the then chief minister of the Congress government, tried to bring back the imposition of Hindi. The struggle at that point was taken over by the students. The students of Annamalai University rallied around the cause of Tamil. Annamalai University was the hub of activity in 1965 and most of the first ministers of the DMK came from Annamalai University, because that was where Tamil language and literature, Tamil music, Tamil culture, and related fields were studied under the tutelage of renowned scholars. This was also the time when we saw Karunanidhi distinctly because he fought for the renaming of Dalmiapuram as Kallakudi and laid his head on the railway tracks, and that shot him to fame. That's when he became the trusted leader in 1965.

So this is the background against which DMK was swept into power in 1967. Once in power, the dynamics began to change. As soon as Annadurai became the chief minister, he passed two major laws. One was to legalize Self-Respect marriages, I'll come to that towards the end, and the other one was to implement what they called communal representation, which is actually reservation as we understand it today. He also legitimized the name of the state as Tamil Nadu. Annadurai passed these major legislations, and after his untimely death, Karunanidhi became the chief minister.

The DMK adopted the *Tamil Thai Vazhththu* – invocation of the Tamil mother as the official anthem of Tamil Nadu. The song they chose is the song of benediction from the play titled *Manonmaniyam*, written in the late nineteenth century. It is considered the first modern Tamil play that was written by Sundaram Pillai who was a Saivaite Tamil scholar and was part of the early Dravidian movement. The song places Tamil Nadu as part of India, within which the Dravida region has a great space and the Tamil language reigns supreme in her evergreen youth. DMK, however, chooses to omit two lines of the original song. They are:

> Kannada, Telugu and Malayalam / have born out of you and multiplied /
>
> But you have not, like the Aryan language / lost your everyday usage /...

The reference to Sanskrit, which has lost its everyday usage among the people, unlike Tamil which is youthful and still in use, was conveniently omitted by the DMK regime. We still continue to have it as our state anthem. The same song is sung in other countries that have a sizable Tamil population like Malaysia or Singapore, and Tamil is one of their official languages. They have not edited the lines about other Dravidian languages and Sanskrit! In Sri Lanka, where the ethnic war between the Sinhalas and the Tamils for over three decades has ruined the lives of people, Tamil is one of the official languages. So you get off at the airport and you will see boards written in Tamil and other official languages, but not in Tamil Nadu. This clearly reveals what DMK wanted to do. They wanted '*Manila suyatchi; mathiyil koottatchi*' – autonomy in the state and federalism in the Centre. The question of Tamil nationalism is kept alive for popular sentiment even today.

One has to look at the question of caste as parallel to that of language. As early as in 1927, when the provincial legislative council was led by Subbarayan, the Communal Government Order was implemented in Tamil Nadu. It was the precursor to the reservation policy. Tamil Nadu is one of the states that implemented this communal representational reservation in education and employment till the country got its independence in 1947. It meant that representation was given to different communities. Out of twelve parts, non-Brahmins get five, Brahmins two, Muslims two, Anglo-Indians and others of European origin two, and Scheduled Castes (SCs) one. This was the way by which the education and employment sectors were addressing representational politics based on caste and religion. It was in keeping with Periyar's ideology and recognized that caste discrimination is at the core of the Hindu hegemonic way of life and therefore it has to be addressed. The question of social justice began as early as that.

After Independence, there was a lawsuit by one Mrs Shenbagam Duraisami, who had applied for a medical seat and did not get it. She was a Brahmin, and she thought that she did not get it because of the reservation system followed in the state. Both the High Court and the Supreme Court judged in her favour. Then the whole agitation for reservation started. They wanted representations for all the sections of people in the society. The Indian government had to relent and the first legal amendment made to the Constitution in 1951 was provoked by the demands made by Tamil Nadu. Ambedkar was the law minister and the amendment pointed out that for socially and educationally backward communities, the respective state can implement ways and means by which it can actually include them into the social strata. Now this amendment was not used by any other state, except Tamil Nadu till DMK came to power. And when DMK came to power, they implemented it as a law. Even before that, even during the provincial government, till Independence, the employees were given jobs based on this kind of representation, including in the Central government offices, like post office.

So when the Mandal Commission report was released and the whole country had a huge uproar, it was a non-issue in Tamil Nadu. In Tamil Nadu, none of these arguments regarding merit would work because we have proven right from the mid-1920s onwards that reservation is a must. Clearly, one cannot hope to achieve social justice without that in a society stratified by caste hierarchy. We had a whole stream of young, first-generation voices that came up and changed the whole topography, and the ethos and the ecology of public discourses. From the 1960s, once DMK started implementing it, it became a given. Even now, we have a separate category in Tamil Nadu called MBC – Most Backward Class, given to the denotified tribes and within the SC community, there is a separate quota for Arunthathiyars. They are at the last strata amongst the Dalit communities and are organized. They have 1 per cent within the SC quota. There is also 1 per cent reservation for Muslims and also for women. Therefore, the reservation debate does not really echo anything of what is happening in the rest of the country. I mean, the whole Hyderabad Central University struggle could be rethought if we can actually think of this history that has been part of a neighbouring state in south India.

There were also other cultural measures undertaken because of this caste question being addressed seriously. Taking a caste surname is almost out of vogue in Tamil Nadu. One can be an Iyer, Iyengar, or whatever, but only the first letter of the father would prefix or suffix one's given name. (Father provides the initial!) Of late, the PMK (Pattali Makkal Katchi) wants to highlight the Vanniyar caste identity. I am constrained by time to go into the details of the changes that are happening now. Reservations are interpreted as caste quota, like in any other part of India, forgetting the progressive history of social justice built over time. Social justice seems to be taking the back seat. None of the road names have any of the caste appendages. Even the person who is outright casteist will at least feel ashamed to use it publicly. You will probably find people using the caste name in their wedding cards! (How can marriages happen without caste purity?) These cultural struggles go along with the administrative issues in Tamil Nadu. One cannot happen without the other.

I would like to end with a caveat on gender in this discourse. Periyar had a radical feminist vision. Self-Respect marriage is perhaps one of its kind, where two individuals get married out of love, affection, attachment and shared interests. There were no garlands, no thaali – the mangalsutra, no priests chanting in Sanskrit or Tamil. Periyar said, marriages are platforms of propagation. Everyone wore black and if the bride too belonged to the Dravida Kazhagam or the Periyar lineage, she would also wear black. There was no other paraphernalia or expenditure. He actually said that people can donate to the organization. Self-Respect marriages were liberating marriage from Brahminical rituals and economic pressures. And it was so different from Gandhi's idea of relationship, especially regarding widow remarriage. We had many inter-caste, inter-religious, widow remarriages, all of them documented in the newspapers of the movement. Thanks to the research done by Geetha, Valarmathi and Anandhi, we actually have a record of these measures. Women were in the public space and actually questioned the social norms.

In one of the plays written by Geetha and directed by me titled *Kaala Kanavu* (A Dream of Time), we raised the question: What happened to these women of the 1940s? That's how we ended the play, what happened to all those women out there in the public, speaking and discussing? These are not anonymous people. We can actually locate them and some of them are still active in public life. We tried to address that question in another play titled *Aanmaiyoo Aanmai* (Macho o Macho), also written by Geetha and directed by me. It tries to address the discourse of gender that came into vogue in the Dravidian movement, in DMK especially, after they came to power.

True, they were negotiating with the Centre in terms of caste and language and there was a subaltern masculinity that was made visible and there were a sizeable number of women who were also part of the movement. And yet the question of patriarchy never really got addressed. I want to give you a sample of the way patriarchy operated in the very rubric of the psychology of the DMK. One of the wall writings during the anti-Hindi struggles, was:

Athai magal Tamizh irukka
Aasainayaki Aangilam irukka
Ur thevadiya Hindi ethukku?

Tamil, your cousin sister whom you are entitled to marry is right here;
English, your kept-woman is round the corner;
Why do you then need the whore – Hindi?

Such was the hyper-masculinity of the Dravidian movement, once they came to power. That is why when actress Khushboo made a comment about premarital sex, there was a huge outcry against her. She was seen as a Gujarati settled in Tamil Nadu and therefore was not Tamil enough, and she has no clue about Tamil *karpu* (chastity)! Dalit Panthers, the Dalit political party, organized its women to rally towards Khushboo's house with broomsticks. More recently, we had the issue regarding Perumal Murugan's novel *Madhoruhagan* (One Part Woman). It was published four years ago in Tamil. No one had any problem with the novel. It was translated into English and within two months, the Gounder community organizes itself. The book gets torn to pieces and Perumal Murugan intimidated. The fear is very palpable in the public domain. And we are also witnessing honour killing in Tamil Nadu which is unimaginable to our generation. Inter-caste weddings are facing violent attacks. It is clearly against the Dalit youth who are becoming slightly upwardly mobile. The PMK leader Dr S. Ramadoss talks about Dalit young men with their 'modern' T-shirts and jeans going around and taking their young girls away. Perhaps all Tamil young men should wear 'traditional' dhoti and shirt with a towel on their shoulder! The situation seems dangerous.

What I have traced here is not a rosy picture of a counter-regionalism to the question of Indian nationalism. There are inherent complexities within Tamil nationalism. But I think what we have managed is to speak out for ourselves, and speak out as a public and not as a small group of intellectuals. Whether it is about language identity, or caste question, we have not let the relations of power and the violence go unnoticed. Those are lessons that states like Tamil Nadu have declared to the Central government. We all know it's not going to be easy. Most of us have short-term memory. But I think it is important for us to remember – to remember moments of resistances of all kinds. We need to garner every single fragment of resistance that we can hail into our service, today.

Thank you for listening patiently.

*

Notes/References/Bibliography

Bate, Bernard, 2009, *Tamil Oratory and the Dravidian Aesthetic: Democratic Practice in South India*, New York: Columbia University Press.

Daniel, E. Valentine, 1984, *Fluid Signs: Being a Person the Tamil way*, Berkeley: University of California Press.

Dirks, Nicholas B., 2001, *Castes of Mind: Colonialism and the Making of Modern India*, Princeton, N.J.: Princeton University Press.

Fakhri, Abdul Khader, S.M., 2008, *Dravidian Sahibs and Brahmin Maulanas: The Politics of the Muslims of Tamil Nadu, 1930-67*, Delhi: Manohar.

Geetha. V and S.V. Rajadurai, 2008, *Towards a Non-Brahmin Millennium: From Iyothee Thass to Periyar*, Kolkata: Samya.

——. 'End of Dravidian Era in Tamil Nadu', 1999, *Economic and Political Weekly*, Vol. 34, No. 24, pp. 1483–88.

Gorringe, Hugo, 2005, *Untouchable Citizens: Dalit Movements and Democratisation in Tamil Nadu*, New Delhi: Sage Publications.

Hardgrave, Robert, 1969, *The Nadars of Tamilnad: The Political Culture of a Community in Change*, Berkeley: University of California.

——, 1965, *The Dravidian Movement*, Bombay: Popular Prakashan.

Hikosaka, Shu, 1989, *Buddhism in Tamilnadu: A New Perspective*, Madras: Institute of Asian Studies.

Hirudayam, Ignatius, 1977, *Christianity and Tamil Culture*, Madras: Dr S. Radhakrishnan Institute for Advanced Study in Philosophy, University of Madras.

Irschick, Eugene F., 1977, *Politics and Social Conflict in South India: The Non-Brahman Movement and Tamil Separatism, 1916-1929*, Berkeley: University of California Press.

Kailasapathy, K., 1968, *Tamil Heroic Poetry*, London: Oxford University Press.

Kanakasabhai Pillai, V., 1966, *The Tamils Eighteen Hundred years Ago*, Madras: Saiva Siddhanta Publications.

Ludden, David, 1985, *Peasant History in South India*, Princeton: Princeton University Press. (Paperback edition, Delhi: Oxford University Press, 1990.)

Nambi Arooran, K., 1980, *Tamil Renaissance and Dravidian Nationalism – 1905-1944*, Koodal.

Pandian, M.S.S., 1992, *The Image Trap: M.G. Ramachandran in Film and Politics*, New Delhi: Sage.

——, 2007, *Brahmin and non-Brahmin: Genealogies of the Tamil Political Present*, Delhi: Permanent Black.

Sivathamby, Karthigesu, 1981, *Drama in Ancient Tamil Society*, Chennai: New Century Book House.

——, 1986, *Literary History in Tamil: A Historiographical Analysis*, Thanjavur, India: Tamil University.

Seneviratne, H. L., 1997, *Identity, Consciousness and the Past: Forging of Caste and Community in India and Sri Lanka*, Delhi: Oxford University Press.

Subramanian, Narendra, 1999, *Ethnicity and Populist Mobilization: Political Parties, Citizens, and Democracy in South India*, New Delhi: Oxford University Press.

Trautmann, R. Thomas, 2006, *Languages and Nations: The Dravidian Proof in Colonial Madras,* Berkeley: University of California.

Viswanath, Rupa, 2014, *The Pariah Problem: Caste, Religion, and the Social in Modern India*, New York: Columbia University Press.

Zvelebil, Kamil, 1973, *The Smile of Murugan: On Tamil Literature of South India*, Leiden: E.J. Brill

(There is also a substantial reading list available in Tamil language on this subject.)

Picture credit: Gayatri Balusha

गाँधी का आख़िरी ठिकाना

अपूर्वानंद

(4 मार्च 2016)

अक्सर दिल्ली यूनिवर्सिटी और जेएनयू के बीच एक प्रतिद्वंदिता का रिश्ता रहता है। और दिल्ली यूनिवर्सिटी के छात्र इस बीच कई बार, और मेरे सहकर्मी भी, मुझसे पूछते रहे कि भई इतने नकचढ़े जेएनयू वालों के साथ खड़े होने की जरूरत ही क्या है। और मेरी क्लास में एक छात्र ने कहा, कि जेएनयू वालों की समस्या यह है कि उनके भीतर बौद्धिकता का अहंकार बहुत है। और मैंने कहा बौद्धिकता का अहंकार विश्वविद्यालय परिसर में ही होना चाहिए, उसके बाहर नहीं। मैं उसको अहंकार नहीं कहता लेकिन बौद्धिकता का अभिमान जरूर होना चाहिए। ख़ासकर ऐसे समाज में जहां बौद्धिकता पर हमले हो रहे हों, और विवेक पर हमले हो रहे हों।

तो जवाहरलाल नेहरू विश्वविद्यालय जो इस परिसर में है, दरअसल उसे एक ख़याल में बदल जाना चाहिए। और भला हो इस सरकार का... अगर हम कार्ल मार्क्स को उलट कर कहें, उसने भौतिक यथार्थ को एक ख़याल में तब्दील कर दिया है। और इस ख़याल की एक ताकत है, और यह ख़याल ही दुनिया को बदलकर रख सकता है। परसों शाम, जब हम संसद मार्ग पर खड़े थे जहां जुलूस जाकर रुका, वहीं ये खबर मिली, कि कन्हैया को ज़मानत मिल गई है। इससे बहुत राहत मिली, जितनी खुशी नहीं उससे ज़्यादा राहत मिली। क्योंकि हम अपने छात्रों को जेलों में नहीं परिसरों में देखना चाहते हैं। लेकिन उसके बाद जब ये पता चला कि ये ज़मानत नहीं अंतरिम ज़मानत है, तो कल शाम को हम, कुछ जज और कुछ लीगल कोरेसपॉन्डेंट्स मिलकर मगजपच्ची कर रहे थे कि ये अंतरिम ज़मानत नाम की चीज़ क्या होती है।

तो जैसा आपने कहा कि ये एक इनोवेशन है जिसके लिए कन्हैया को मुबारकबाद देनी चाहिए। हिंदुस्तान के जूरिसप्रूडेंस के इतिहास में ये आपका भी एक योगदान है। इसे भी दर्ज कीजिए कि ये भी जवाहरलाल नेहरू विश्वविद्यालय का ही योगदान है। उन्हें छह महीने के लिए अंतरिम ज़मानत दी गई। लेकिन कल जज साहिबा का जो आदेश है, ज़मानत का, उसको पढ़ते हुए, और उस बीच में इस पूरे प्रकरण पर जो बहस हो रही थी, उसमें बार–बार सुना कि यहाँ भी हमारे कुछ सहकर्मियों का ख़याल है कि विश्वविद्यालय परिसर में छात्रों को केवल पढ़ने आना चाहिए। हम एक बहस में थे और राष्ट्रीय स्वयंसेवक संघ के एक बहुत ही वरिष्ठ नेता ने कहा: 'स्टूडेंट्स शुड कम टू कैंपसेस टू लर्न'। और मेरा ध्यान बहुत पहले, 1931 के दिसंबर में, प्रेमचंद के लिखे एक लेख पर चला गया।

प्रेमचंद दो कॉनवोकेशन एड्रेसेज़ का ज़िक्र कर रहे हैं। और ये कॉनवोकेशन एड्रेसेज़ इलाहाबाद और लखनऊ विश्वविद्यालय के दीक्षांत समारोहों में दिए गए थे। एक दीक्षांत भाषण सर सी. वी. रमन ने दिया, और दूसरा दीक्षांत भाषण दार्शनिक राधाकृष्णन ने दिया। प्रेमचंद इन दोनों दीक्षांत भाषणों का ज़िक्र करते हैं, और मैं वहाँ से अपनी बात शुरू करना चाहूँगा और फिर अपने विषय पर आऊँगा। प्रेमचंद सी. वी. रमन को उद्धृत करते हैं और मैं वह उद्धरण आपको सुना रहा हूँ। 'हिंदुस्तान के विद्यार्थियों का ये धर्म नहीं है कि वह इस क्रांति और परिवर्तन की गति को और तेज़ बना दें, बल्कि उनका वास्तविक धर्म है, कि वह जातीय विकास की द्रुत गति के लिए एक ब्रेक का काम करें।' आप देख रहे हैं सर सी वी रमन बहुत नज़दीक हैं हमारे जज साहिबान के, और बाकी तमाम लोगों के। बहुत बड़े वैज्ञानिक हैं...प्रेमचंद इस पर टिप्पणी करते हैं, 'हमारी क्रांति हमारी खोई हुई आत्मा को, अपने त्याग, सरलता और आदर्श को वापस लाना चाहती है। सहयोग और सहृदयता की इच्छुक है'। और उसके बाद वे दूसरे दीक्षांत भाषण को उद्धृत करते हैं। राधाकृष्णन के । और मैं ये नहीं कहूँगा कि प्रेमचंद किनके साथ खड़े हैं। ये फैसला आप खुद कर सकते हैं। पहला उद्धरण मैं दे चुका हूँ। राधाकृष्णन का उद्धरण थोड़ा लंबा है, लेकिन आप सुन सकते हैं, धैर्यवान हैं, इतने दिनों से धीरज धर के यहाँ बैठे हुए हैं। राधाकृष्णन यह कहते हैं, 'बुद्धिमान व्यक्ति का यह दावा नहीं होता कि हर एक विषय पर वह कोई न कोई राय दे सकता है। न वह किसी लेखक का सार एक वाक्य में और न किसी संस्कृति का तत्व एक व्यंग में प्रकट कर सकता है। बुद्धिमान व्यक्ति में दृष्टि का विस्तार, विचारों की स्वाधीनता और अन्य मनोभावों को समझने की शक्ति होती है। वो हमेशा उन विचारों से सहानुभूति रखने को तैयार रहता है, जिनसे उसे मतभेद है'। आगे वे कहते हैं, 'प्राचीन काल में विद्यालयों के संस्कार की उपमा एक मशाल से दी जाती थी। जो एक हाथ से दूसरे हाथ और एक युग से दूसरे युग तक चलती रहती थी। यह मशाल एक भयंकर वस्तु है, इसने कितने ही आंदोलनों को जगाया है,

कितनी हलचल जगाई है। यह क्रांति भावना की द्योतक है, वह आग है जो घास–फूस और गंदगी को जलाकर साफ कर देती है। अगर हम उन सामाजिक, आर्थिक और राजनैतिक आंदोलनों से भयभीत हो जाएं जो इस आग के फैलने से पैदा होते हैं तो हमें विद्यालयों से दूर ही रहना चाहिए', ये राधाकृष्णन कह रहे हैं।

और उसके बाद प्रेमचंद ये कह रहे हैं, 'विश्वविद्यालय में युवावस्था का जोश और सजीवता होनी चाहिए। अगर विश्वविद्यालय ऐसे मनुष्य पैदा करता है जो अपनी जान की ख़ैरियत मनाते हैं, जो ऐशो–आराम के बंदी हैं, जो जोख़िम से बचते हैं, तो वो विद्यालय अपने धर्म का पालन नहीं कर सकता। अगर वह उत्साह और पौरुष से भरे हुए युवकों को लेकर – जेंडर इनसेंसिटिविटी को माफ कीजिएगा – उन्हें बोदे, स्वार्थी और आकाओं का गुलाम बना देता है, अगर वो उनके विचारों को कठोर कर देता है, और अगर वो उनके आगे बढ़ने की शक्ति को निर्जीव कर देता है तो वह अपने धर्म से दूर चला गया है'। ये प्रेमचंद हैं। मैं कह सकता हूँ कि आप प्रेमचंद के सच्चे वारिस हैं। और जवाहरलाल नेहरू विश्वविद्यालय प्रेमचंद का सच्चा वारिस है। और वह राधाकृष्णन का भी सच्चा वारिस है। और वह सी.वी. रमन जैसे वैज्ञानिकों को कह सकता है, कि दरअसल हमारा काम आज्ञाकारी लोगों को पैदा करना नहीं है। और हम कोई राष्ट्र का, या राज्य का उत्पादन बढ़ाने के कलपुर्जे नहीं हैं।

लेकिन आज की हमारी बातचीत का विषय है, गांधी का खोया हुआ पता। जब मुझे पता चला कि यहाँ कक्षाएं या बातचीत राष्ट्रवाद के विभिन्न पहलुओं पर चल रही है, तो मुझे लगा कि राष्ट्र की कल्पना हम किस रूप में करते हैं। अंततः राष्ट्र एक समुदाय है। या ये कह सकते हैं कि राष्ट्र एक प्रकार की सहमति है, एक रज़ामंदी है। जिस रज़ामंदी पर हम एक–दूसरे के साथ अलगाव रखते हुए, मतभेद रखते हुए, जिस रज़ामंदी पर हम पहुंचते हैं। ये रज़ामंदी की जगह ऐसी हैं जिसमें हम सब एक दूसरे के साथ इज़्ज़त और बराबरी को बरकरार रखते हुए रह सकते हैं। राष्ट्र का मतलब एक लगाव भी है या हम कह सकते हैं एक ठिकाना भी है। वह हमारी जगह है, या वह हमारा पता है। और मुझे ध्यान आया कि हम बचपन से पढ़ते चले आए हैं कि गांधी के बारे में ये कहा जाता था कि उनके नाम जो चिट्ठी लिखी जाती थी, वह गांधी या बापू इंडिया या भारत, जहां भी हों। और मैं ये सोचने लगा कि फर्ज़ कीजिए आज एक चुट्ठी लिखी जाए बापू, इंडिया या गांधी, भारत तो वो कहाँ पहुंचेगी? इस प्रश्न पर हम थोड़ी देर ठहर कर विचार कर सकते हैं, कि वह चिट्ठी कहाँ पहुंचेगी। गांधी से हमारे मतभेद बहुत सारे हो सकते हैं, लेकिन गांधी को राष्ट्रपिता कहा जाता है। गांधी के इस योगदान को कोई अस्वीकार नहीं करता कि जिस राष्ट्र की कल्पना को हमने स्वीकार किया है, उसमें गांधी का काफ़ी कुछ हिस्सा है। लेकिन वो कहाँ पहुँचेगी, और अगर मैं आपको दिल्ली के बीच में ले जाना चाहूँ – इत्तेफ़ाक़ से वह इनकमटेक्स चौराहे के आसपास की जगह है, और ये बहुत अजीब बात है। और आप

जब उधर से गुज़र रहे होंगे तो देखेंगे कि पुलिस मुख्यालय पर गांधी की मुस्कुराती तस्वीर भी है, जिसको दिल्ली पुलिस शायद देखती ही नहीं! लेकिन वहाँ ढेर सारे पते हैं जो दावेदारी करते हैं कि गांधी की चिट्ठी वहाँ पहुँचनी चाहिए। मैं गांधी के वारिसों की बात कर रहा हूँ। गांधी ने अपने जीवन काल में स्वयं कई आश्रम बनाए, दक्षिण अफ्रीका से लेकर भारत तक। तो एक पता वह है गांधी का। यानी गांधी के आश्रम। दूसरे गांधी को संस्थाएँ बनाने का बहुत शौक था। उन्होंने बहुत सारी संस्थाएँ बनाईं, दूसरी दावेदारी इन संस्थाओं की है, कि गांधी का पता इन संस्थाओं में है। लेकिन गांधी के विचार के साथ या गांधी के साथ जो सबसे बड़ी दुर्घटना हुई, वह यह कि भारतीय राज्य ने सबसे ज़ोरदार दावा पेश किया कि गांधी का असली पता दरअसल भारतीय राज्य है। अब गांधी के साथ और कोई इससे बड़ी नाइंसाफ़ी नहीं हो सकती थी। क्योंकि गांधी बड़े अराजक व्यक्ति थे और राज्य नाम के किसी विचार को अपना ठिकाना बना लेना गांधी के लिए बड़ा मुश्किल था या दुविधाग्रस्त था। लेकिन गांधी की विडंबना यह थी कि वो जो काम कर रहे थे, उस काम की परिणति या उसका एक पड़ाव भारतीय राष्ट्र राज्य के निर्माण में ही होना था। और यह गांधी के पूरे संघर्ष का एक द्वंद्व या आप उसका उसकी एक विडंबना के रूप में देख सकते हैं कि गांधी जो स्वयं किसी जोर–ज़बरदस्ती के यंत्र के अधीन रहने को तैयार नहीं थे, जो संघर्ष कर रहे थे, उसका नतीजा दरअसल एक राष्ट्रराज्य के निर्माण में होना था जो आगे चलकर ज़ोर–ज़बरदस्ती के एक औज़ार के रूप में विकसित होने ही वाला था। तो गांधी पर सबसे ज़्यादा दावा पेश किया इस राज्य ने यानी गांधी का सबसे बड़ा वारिस भारतीय राज्य ने खुद को घोषित कर दिया। तो ये जो आधिकारिक पते हैं गांधी के क्या गांधी के ये पते हैं? या नहीं हैं?, इसकी जाँच की जानी चाहिए। अगर आप गांधी के आश्रमों को देखेंगे तो गांधी के वह आश्रम जिनको छोड़कर गांधी निकल गए थे और वापस नहीं गए। साबरमती आश्रम में, 2002 में जब अहमदाबाद में मुसलमान मार खाते हुए, और अपने कातिलों से भागते हुए साबरमती आश्रम के दरवाज़े पहुंचे, तो आश्रमवासियों ने दरवाज़ा उनके मुँहपर बंद कर दिया।[1] वह दिन था जब ये कहा जा सकता है कि साबरमती आश्रम अब गांधी का पता नहीं है। वर्धा में आप अगर आप सेवाग्राम के आश्रम में जाएंगे, मुझे ऐसा मौका मिला सन् 2000 से लेकर सन् 2002 तक सेवाग्राम में काम के सिलसिले में लगातार आने जाने का और उस आश्रम के यात्री निवास में ठहरने का और मैंने देखा ये वो मौका था जब नेशनल डेमोक्रेटिक अलाएंस, एनडीए की सरकार सत्ता में थी। और मैंने देखा कि बापू कुटी के आश्रमवासी या सेवाग्राम के आश्रमवासियों को कोई परहेज़ नहीं था हेडगेवार भवन जाकर उनके साथ मंच की साझेदारी करने में। और मैंने उनके कर्ता–धर्ताओं से कहा कि अगर आप ये कर सकते हैं, यानि यदि आप अपने बापू की हत्या का जश्न मनाने वालों के साथ मंच की साझेदारी कर सकते हैं, तो सेवाग्राम का आश्रम भी बापू का

पता नहीं हो सकता। अगर आप यहाँ के आश्रमों को देखेंगे तो यहाँ के आश्रम ज़्यादा से ज़्यादा सरकारी आश्रमों में तब्दील हो चुके हैं यानि गांधी की चिट्ठी वहाँ भी ठीक से नहीं पहुँच सकती। इस तरह गांधी के नाम पर बने हुए जो आश्रम हैं, वे आश्रम गांधी का ठिकाना नहीं हैं। और अगर वे गांधी का ठिकाना नहीं हैं, गांधी का ठीक ठीक ठि. काना क्या है, अगर हम इसको समझने का प्रयास करें तो हमें गांधी के आख़िरी दिनों पर नज़र दौड़ानी पड़ेगी। आख़िरी दिन यानि अगर हम 1946 से 1947 और 1948 के गांधी को याद करने की कोशिश करें।

या अगर हम उससे पीछे चले जाएँ और हम देखें कि 1915 में जब गांधी हिंदुस्तान वापस पहुंचते हैं, उसके बाद उनका कोई भी एक स्थाई ठिकाना नहीं होता है। गांधी उसके बाद यायावर या भारत में श्रमण परंपरा में आने वाले महात्मा के रूप में दिखलाई पड़ते हैं, जो निरंतर भ्रमण करते रहते हैं। उनका कोई एक ठिकाना नहीं होता है। लेकिन गांधी की ये बेचैनी, उनकी यात्रा की ये बेचैनी बढ़ जाती है 1946, 1947 और 1948 में। अगर 1946, 1947 और 1948 के गांधी को हम देखें तो वो भटकने वाला गांधी है जिसका कोई एक ठिकाना नहीं है और जिसे पता नहीं है कि वो किसी एक जगह रुकेगा या नहीं रुकेगा। हम जिस दिल्ली में बात कर रहे हैं, उस दिल्ली में आख़िरी बार गांधी पहुंचे 9 सितंबर 1947 को। गांधी आ रहे थे बंगाल से और उनको जाना था पंजाब। बंगाल में गांधी आग बुझा कर आ रहे थे। और गांधी को आग के बीच रहने का एक तरीके से शौक पैदा हो गया था। हम ये कह सकते हैं कि गांधी में एक तरह की आत्मघाती प्रवृत्ति बन गई थी। वे ये कह भी रहे थे कि मैं, मुझे ऐसा लगता है कि मेरे चारों तरफ़ आग लगी हुई है और मैं उसके बीच में बैठा हुआ हूँ। मुझे पता नहीं कि मैं इस आग से निकल पाऊंगा या इसमें भस्म हो जाऊंगा । लेकिन मेरे पास इसके अलावा कोई उपाय नहीं। 1946 और 1947 में गांधी की यात्रा बिहार, नोआखाली, कलकत्ता की यात्रा थी। नोआखाली की यात्रा ख़ासकर मानीखेज़ है, इसलिए कि नोआखाली मुस्लिम बहुल इलाका था और वहाँ हिंदुओं पर हमले हो रहे थे। ऐसा कहा जाता है कि हज़ारों–हज़ार हिंदुओं का कत्ल हुआ और गांधी ने ये फैसला किया कि वे नोआखाली जाएंगे। ये बहुत मुश्किल फैसला था। और जब वे नोआखाली पहुंचे तो उनका स्वागत नहीं हुआ। उनके मुसलमान दोस्तों ने उनपर आरोप लगाया कि आप नोआखाली क्यों आए हैं। नोआखाली से ज़्यादा बदतर घटनाएं दूसरी जगहों पर हुई हैं और मुसलमानों पर हमले हुए हैं, आप वहाँ क्यों नहीं गए, आप नोआखाली क्यों आए हैं? गांधी का उत्तर अक्सर जटिल नहीं होता था, निरस्त्र करने वाला उत्तर होता था, जिसमें कोई सैद्धांतिक जटिलता नहीं जान पड़ती थी। लेकिन गांधी ने कहा मेरे लिए इससे कोई फ़र्क नहीं पड़ता कि हिंदू मारे जा रहे हैं और मुसलमान नहीं मारे जा रहे हैं। मुझे मेरे मन ने ये कहा कि मुझे नोआखाली जाना चाहिए और वहाँ रहना चाहिए। मैं आपके बुलाने से नोआखाली नहीं आया हूँ।

और आपके कहने से भी नोआखाली से नहीं जाऊँगा। मैं नोआखाली में तब तक रहूँगा जबतक मुझे इसका यक़ीन न हो जाए कि यहाँ अल्पसंख्यक हिंदू बहुसंख्यक मुसलमानों के साथ रह सकते हैं। नोआखाली की यात्रा का विवरण पढ़ने लायक है क्योंकि उसमें गांधी ने लगभग अपने आपको असुरक्षित कर लिया था। और गांधी को लेकर एक भ्रम ये है, चूंकि उन्हें महात्मा कहा जाता है, तो हमारे दिमाग में तस्वीर यह है कि गांधी की स्वीकृति चारों तरफ थी, जबकि गांधी के जीवन को अगर ध्यान से देखा जाए तो ऐसे शख़्स बहुत कम हैं जिनका विरोध इतना ज़्यादा हुआ हो। और नोआखाली में भी गाँधी का सफर विरोध से आज़ाद नहीं था।

ख़िलाफ़त आंदोलन में गांधी की शिरक़त और उनके सहयोग की बहुत आलोचना की गई है। जबकि उसके पीछे के सिद्धांत को समझने की कोशिश बहुत कम की गई है। गांधी कहना क्या चाहते हैं? गांधी ये कहना चाहते हैं कि भौगोलिक सीमाबद्ध राष्ट्रवाद के साथ, भौगोलिक सीमा से परे किसी प्रतिबद्धता को स्वीकार किया जा सकता है। यह प्रतिबद्धता उम्मा के प्रति हो सकती है, यह प्रतिबद्धता अंतर्राष्ट्रीय मजदूर आंदोलन के प्रति भी हो सकती है, यानि भौगोलिक सीमाबद्ध राष्ट्रवाद किसी व्यक्ति की सीमा नहीं हो सकता। ये गांधी ख़िलाफ़त आंदोलन के जरिए बताने की कोशिश कर रहे थे, जिसको यह समझा गया कि गांधी दरअसल धर्म का घालमेल कर रहे हैं। उसको लेकर बहस हो सकती है लेकिन उस वक्त उन्होंने नारों की बात की थी। गांधी ने कहा कि जो नारा सबसे पहले लगाना चाहिए हिंदुओं और मुसलमानों के साथ मिलकर, वह नारा है 'अल्लाह–ओ–अकबर' का नारा। और इसलिए उन्होंने कहा कि इसमें एक उदात्तता की भावना की अभिव्यक्ति होती है, 'अल्लाह–ओ–अकबर' कहने से। और फिर उन्होंने बाकी दो नारों के बारे में कहा कि मुझे सोचना पड़ेगा कि क्या हम 'वंदे मातरम्' कहें दूसरे नारे के रूप में या 'भारत माता की जय' कहें। और फिर उन्होंने कहा कि मैं थोड़ा सा पक्षपाती हूँ। गांधी की मुस्कुराहट को याद कीजिए वो ख़ासी दुष्टता से भरी हुई मुस्कुराहट है और गांधी में हास्य–बोध बहुत ज़्यादा था जिसे अंग्रजी में आजकल लोग सेंस–ऑफ–ह्यूमर कहते हैं। तो गांधी ने कहा कि मैं इन दो नारों के बीच चुनाव करना चाहता हूँ, 'वंदे मातरम्' और 'भारत माता की जय', लेकिन मेरा बंगाल के प्रति पक्षपात कुछ ज़्यादा है, इसलिए मैं 'वंदे मातरम्' को रखना चाहता हूँ दूसरे नारे के रूप में। और तीसरा नारा क्या हो? तीसरे नारे के लिए वो कहते हैं, 'हिंदू–मुसलमान की जय'। ये तीन नारे वो प्रस्तावित कर रहे हैं। 'अल्लाह–ओ–अकबर,' 'वंदे–मातरम्' और 'हिंदू–मुसलमान की जय'। 'वंदे मातरम्' को लेकर लंबी बहस है, मैं उसमें नहीं जाना चाहूँगा। गांधी भी उसपर बहस करते हैं और वो बहस आगे चलती है और वो इन तीन नारों की बात कर रहे हैं। और मैंने कहा कि वो पहला नारा कहते हैं 'अल्लाह–ओ–अकबर'। इस नारे में उन्हें कोई संकीर्णता नहीं दिखाई पड़ती है, इस नारे में उन्हें एक फैलाव दिखाई पड़ता है। इस

नारे में उन्हें उदात्तता दिखलाई पड़ती है। और यह नारा भी ध्यान रखिए, राष्ट्रवादी नारा नहीं है, यह राष्ट्र की सीमा से परे जाने वाला नारा है। तो गांधी जब यहाँ पहुँचते हैं, बंगाल से दिल्ली और वो शहादरा के स्टेशन पर उतरते हैं, उनको वहाँ लेने आए हैं सरदार वल्लभ भाई पटेल। बाद में गांधी अपने एक मित्र को ख़त लिखते हैं, कि मैं जब ट्रेन से उतरा तो मेरी सरदार से मुलाकात हुई। और सरदार के चेहरे पर मुर्दनी छाई हुई थी। यह वो सरदार नहीं थे जिन्हें मैं जानता था, पूरे मज़ाक़, खुशदिल और हमेशा चुटकुले सुनाने वाला सरदार। ये ग़म से भरा हुआ सरदार था और ये वो दिल्ली नहीं थी जिसे मैं जानता था। यह दिल्ली जैसे श्मशान हो गई थी। सरदार ने कहा कि दिल्ली के हालात बहुत खराब हैं। और ऐसा लगता है कि ये हमारे संभाले नहीं संभलेगी और आपको यहाँ रुकना होगा। गांधी ने पंजाब जाने का इरादा मुल्तवी किया। गांधी का इरादा यह था, और यह बहुत दुस्साहस से भरा हुआ इरादा था, कि वे जो हिंदू और सिख अपने–अपने घरों, अपनी–अपनी ज़मीन को छोड़कर नए बने हुए मुल्क पाकिस्तान से हिंदुस्तान चले आए हैं, उन्हें लेकर वापस जाएँ, और वहाँ जो मुसलमान चले गए हैं उन्हें वापस लेकर वो हिंदुस्तान आएँ, खासा दुस्साहस था। लेकिन गांधी जब ऐसा कर थे तो मुझे जो शब्द याद आया जो राष्ट्र के बरक्स रखा जा सकता है। वास्तव में वो दो शब्द हैं, एक है वतन और दूसरा है देस। और ये शब्द चार दिन पहले मुझे फिर याद आये, जब आपकी इस पूरी जद्दोजहद के बीच, आपके परिसर के एक बहुत अज़ीज़, जिन्होंने आपके परिसर में एक नाट्यदल की स्थापना की, बहुरूप नाट्यदल, शाहिद अनवर, लगभग उतने ही दिनों तक वो लड़े, ज़िंदगी और मौत के बीच झूलते जितने दिनों तक आपकी लड़ाई चल रही थी और आख़िरकार उनके सांस की डोर टूट गई। और सवाल ये हुआ कि शाहिद अनवर को दफ़न कहां किया जाएगा। दिल्ली उनकी जगह थी एक तरह से, कर्मभूमि थी। लेकिन शाहिद अनवर की माँ सासाराम में हैं, गया के करीब, और उनके भाई और उनके रिश्तेदारों का ख़याल था कि शाहिद अनवर का वतन, उनका देस सासाराम है। और उस वक्त, और गांधी के उस अभियान को देखकर मैं सोच रहा था, गांधी दरअसल कह क्या रहे थे। गांधी दरअसल राष्ट्र के बरक्स देस, तालव्य श से नहीं, दंत्य स से, देस और वतन इन दोनों की कल्पना रख रहे थे, उनका कहना ये था कि आबादियों का तबादला एक नकली चीज़ है और मैं इसको कबूल नहीं कर सकता। इंसान अपनी मिट्टी से जुड़ा हुआ होता है। और उसको उखाड़ कर किसी दूसरी जगह नकली ढंग से स्थापित नहीं किया जा सकता। यह काम अक्सर तानाशाहों ने किया है, यह काम स्टालिन ने भी किया। यह काम दूसरी जगहों में भी, दूसरे मुल्कों में भी हुआ, जहां आबादियों को बदल कर, एक जगह से दूसरी जगह डाल कर एक नए राष्ट्र की भावना का निर्माण किया गया। लेकिन गांधी राष्ट्र की इस भावना से लड़ रहे थे। और उसके सामने वो एक स्थानीयता की

धारणा प्रस्तुत कर रहे थे, वतन और देस की। इंसान को वो एक ऑर्गेनिक वस्तु के रूप में प्रस्तुत कर रहे थे, एक जीवित ऑर्गेनिक चीज़, जो सिर्फ किसी सैद्धांतिक विचार से बंधी हुई नहीं होती है। यह सच है कि इंसान सफ़र करता है। यह सच है कि इंसान अपनी हद से पार जाता है, लेकिन यह भी सच है कि इंसान लगभग वैसा ही जीव है, जिसके जड़ें होती हैं, जिसके पंख होते हैं। जो उड़ना भी चाहता है लेकिन जो जुड़ना भी चाहता है। और इसलिए गांधी का अभियान पंजाब जाने का था जहाँ से, जहाँ वे उन लोगों के बीच रह सकें जिन्होंने सबसे ज़्यादा ज़ुल्म और अपमान झेला है। लेकिन गांधी दिल्ली में थे। और गांधी ने अपने मित्र को ख़त लिखा और उसका सार मैं आपके सामने प्रस्तुत कर रहा हूँ। उन्होंने लिखा कि मैं ये देख रहा हूँ कि मैं एक ऐसी दिल्ली में हूँ जहाँ मैं तो इत्मीनान से चल सकता हूँ लेकिन ज़ाकिर हुसैन सिर उठाकर नहीं चल सकते। और मुझे ऐसी दिल्ली में रहने में शर्म आती है। और इसलिए मुझे इस दिल्ली में रहना ही होगा क्योंकि अगर ये दिल्ली हाथ से निकल गई, और ये उनके शब्द हैं, अगर दिल्ली हाथ से निकल गई तो हिंदुस्तान हाथ से निकल गया समझो। और अगर हिंदुस्तान हाथ से निकल गया तो दुनिया के लिए कोई आशा नहीं बचती है। ये शब्द गांधी ने क्यों कहे, ये कोई हिंदुस्तान के प्रति मिथ्या गौरव की भावना से वो नहीं कह रहे थे, ये वो इसलिए कह रहे थे कि गांधी और उनके सहयोगियों ने हिंदुस्तान की जिस कल्पना को सामने रखा था वह एक नई कल्पना थी। उस कल्पना में एक दुस्साहस था, हालांकि उसकी प्रतिद्वंदिता ठीक बगल की एक कल्पना से थी जो मोहम्मद अली जिन्नाह पेश कर रहे थे। गांधी का द्वंद्व मुहम्मद अली जिन्नाह से है और ध्यान रखिए, नेहरू का द्वंद्व मुहम्मद अली जिन्नाह से इसलिए नहीं था – जैसा बहुत दिनों तक वामपंथी भी सोचते रहे, और दूसरे लोग भी सोचते रहे, और आजतक प्रचारित किया जाता है – कि गांधी को सत्ता की, नेहरू को सत्ता की हवस थी। वे जल्दी से प्रधानमंत्री होना चाहते थे। जी नहीं। इसलिए जो लोग नेहरू और गांधी पर मुस्लिमपरस्त होने का आरोप लगाते हैं, वे उस इतिहास और उस बहस को भी देखें। उनकी पहली बहस मुहम्मद अली जिन्नाह से हो रही है। और ये बहस चलती है जिसमें वे मुहम्मद अली जिन्नाह के जिस सिद्धांत को चुनौती दे रहे हैं वो ये है कि मुसलमान का प्रतिनिधित्व सिर्फ मुसलमान ही कर सकता है। ये कोई राजनीतिक ज़मीन पकड़ने की कोशिश नहीं थी, ये दरअसल एक बुनियादी, इंसानी उसूल को स्थापित करने की कोशिश थी। मैं अपनी हद से बाहर जा सकता हूँ। मैं नए रिश्ते बना सकता हूँ। और मैं अपनी नई पहचान बना सकता हूँ। मैं अपनी दी हुई पुरानी पहचान का कैदी नहीं हूँ और न मैं उससे बंधा हुआ हूँ। इसलिए जिस नए भारतीय राष्ट्र की कल्पना पेश की गई जिसे समझ में आने वाले शब्द का इस्तेमाल अगर हम करें तो सेक्युलर भारत कहते हैं। गांधी और नेहरू, इन दोनों की प्रतिबद्धता इस विचार से थीः वह सेक्युलर भारत कैसा भारत होगा। और

इसे 9 सितंबर 1947 दिल्ली में रहते हुए, दिल्ली की शरणार्थी बस्तियों में जाते हुए, दिल्ली की अपने प्रार्थना–सभाओं के वक्तव्यों में गांधी ने बहुत अच्छे से स्पष्ट किया।

गांधी ने कहा कि सेक्युलर भारत का मतलब यह है कि यहाँ आबादी में हिंदू भले ही ज़्यादा हों, लेकिन हिंदू मुसलमानों के सरपरस्त नहीं होंगे। अक्सर हिंदुओं की सदिच्छा की अपील करते हुए कहा जाता है कि हिंदुओं को मुसलमानों का ख़्याल रखना चाहिए, उन्हें बड़े भाइयों की तरह पेश आना चाहिए। गांधी कहते हैं कि नहीं, बड़े भाई और छोटे भाई का कोई रिश्ता नहीं होगा। संख्या में आप भले ही ज़्यादा हों, लेकिन आप सरपरस्त नहीं हैं। ना ही आप बड़े भाई हैं। आप दोनों एक सतह पर खड़े हैं। आप दोनों के शहरी हक़, आप दोनों के नागरिक अधिकार, और आप दोनों के इंसानी हक़ बराबर हैं।

गांधी को इसको लेकर भी कोई अस्पष्टता नहीं थी और उन्होंने कहा कि दरअसल ये बात मैंने दक्षिण अफ्रीका में सीखी अपने दोस्त से कि जब भी शक हो तो हमेशा अल्पसंख्यक का पक्ष चुनना। बहुसंख्यक का कभी नहीं। उन्होंने कहा कि इस बात को मैंने गांठ बांध लिया, कि अल्पसंख्यकवादी होना अच्छा है। और उन्होंने ये कहा उन्होंने कि दिल्ली में मुझपर आरोप लगाया गया कि आप दरअसल मुस्लिम–परस्त हैं। गांधी ने कहा कि हां मैं मुस्लिम–परस्त हूँ, मैं कबूल करता हूँ कि मैं मुस्लिम–परस्त हूँ। मैं भारतवर्ष में या हिंदुस्तान में मुस्लिम–परस्त हूँ और पाकिस्तान में हिंदू–परस्त हूँ।

ध्यान दीजिए, गांधी उस वक्त एक ऐसे व्यक्ति के रूप में बात कर रहे हैं और उनका ये विश्वास है कि पाकिस्तान में भी उनकी स्वीकृति उतनी ज़्यादा है कि जिसे लेकर दूसरे लोगों को शक हो सकता है। गांधी को ऐसा विश्वास है। वे कह रहे हैं कि मुहम्मद अली जिन्नाह भी ये कह रहे हैं कि हिंदुओं के साथ नाइंसाफी नहीं होनी चाहिए। हालांकि मुहम्मद अली जिन्नाह के साथ दिक्कत ये हुई – पुनः गांधी के उस सिद्धांत को हम याद कर लें, जिसका हम बहुत ज़्यादा मज़ाक़ उड़ाया करते थे, कि साध्य पवित्र हो, उसको हासिल करने के लिए साधन भी पवित्र होने चाहिए – कि पाकिस्तान के निर्माण के बाद जिस सेक्युलर पाकिस्तान की अवधारणा प्रस्तुत की वह प्राप्त नहीं की जा सकती थी क्योंकि जो साधन उन्होंने अपनाया था, वह साधन उस सेकुलर पाकिस्तान को बनने नहीं देता। इसलिए साध्य और साधन के बीच एकता या अभेदता या दोनों की पवित्रता की वकालत जो गांधी करते थे, उसे न मानने की विडंबना आप जिन्नाह के साथ देख सकते हैं। जिन्नाह अंततः एक आधुनिक व्यक्ति थे। उन्होंने राजनीतिक गोलबंदी के लिए एक सिद्धांत अपनाया, जिसमें शायद उनकी आधुनिकता विश्वास नहीं करती थी। लेकिन जब उन्होंने उससे अलग रास्ता अपनाने की कोशिश की तो उनके साधन ने ही उनको खींचकर नीचे डुबा दिया। गांधी उसके ठीक उल्टा प्रस्ताव कर रहे थे। और इसलिए जब वो दिल्ली में थे, 1947–48 की दिल्ली में और उस दिल्ली की आप सिर्फ कल्पना कर सकते हैं, जामा मस्जिद, पुराना

किला और ऐसी तमाम जगहें, मुसलमानों से भरी हुई थीं। मुस्लिम बस्तियों पर हमले हो रहे थे। दिल्ली और उसके आस–पास के इलाके हिंदू और सिख शरणार्थियों से भरे हुए थे। ये शरणार्थी नए बने पाकिस्तान से लुट–पिट कर आए थे। औरतों का अपहरण हुआ था, बलात्कार हुआ था, धर्म परिवर्तन हुआ था। जबरन निकाह हुआ था। अपमान, क्षोभ और गुस्से से भरे हुए हिंदू और सिख दिल्ली की सड़कों पर घूम रहे थे। और वे इस बात से अंदर से जल रहे थे कि एक तरफ़ हमें अपने वतन से निकाल दिया गया, हम दर–बदर भटक रहे हैं और यहाँ मुसलमान क़ाबिज़ बैठे हैं। और मुसलमानों पर हमले शुरू हुए और वे इन जगहों पर शरण लेने के लिए बाध्य हुए। और गांधी ने कहा, कनॉट प्लेस की मस्जिद में मूर्ति रख दी गई और कनॉट प्लेस की मस्जिद पर झंडा फहरा दिया गया, महरौली की ख्वाजा चिश्ती की दरगाह पर कब्जा कर लिया गया है,। और वहाँ से खादिमों को भगा दिया गया है, मैं ये कहना चाहता हूँ, अगर ये मस्जिद खाली नहीं की गई और ये दरगाह खाली नहीं की गई तो यह हिंदुओं के लिए ही अपमान की बात है। लेकिन इसका जो जवाब गांधी को मिला, वो था गांधी मुर्दाबाद, बूढ़े को मर जाने दो। मरता है तो मरने दो। ये नारे गांधी को रोज़–रोज़ सुनने पड़ते थे। इसलिए गांधी के बारे में यह ख़याल दिमाग से निकाल दें कि गांधी की पूजा होती थी इस देश में। गांधी का विरोध कहीं ज़्यादा होता था। गांधी इन नारों को सुन रहे थे, और उसके बाद उन्होंने फ़ैसला किया 12 जनवरी 1948 को, कि वे उपवास करेंगे, ये गांधी के जीवन का आखिरी उपवास होने वाला था। क्योंकि उसके अठारह दिन बाद उनकी हत्या होने वाली थी। लेकिन 12 जनवरी 1948 को जब उन्होंने उपवास का फैसला किया तो इस उपवास से उनके सारे सहकर्मी बुरी तरह से हिल गए। उनको गांधी की ज़िद का पता था कि एक बार ये बूढ़ा ठान ले तो उससे हटने वाला नहीं है। लेकिन इस बार सबसे पहले चिट्ठी लिखी उनके बेटे ने। देवदास गांधी ने उनको चिट्ठी लिखी और कहा कि आपका ये फैसला ग़लत है। आप अभी उपवास की कह रहे हैं जबकि काम मुसलमानों की जिंदगी को बचाना है। और अगर आप ज़िंदा रहेंगे तो हो सकता है लाखों मुसलमान बचें, लेकिन अगर आप इस उपवास में गुज़र जाते हैं तो उनके लिए उम्मीद ख़त्म हो जाती है। और गांधी ने देवदास गांधी के इस पत्र का बड़ा ही औपचारिक उत्तर दिया। उन्होंने कहा कि आप मेरे शुभेच्छु हैं, और मैं आपकी शुभकामनाएँ समझता हूँ, लेकिन ये फ़ैसला मैंने बहुत सोच–समझकर लिया है। और गांधी के साथ एक दूसरी दिक्कत ये भी थी – हालांकि वे काम इंसानों के बीच करते थे, लेकिन उनका वार्तालाप ईश्वर से चलता था। और वे जब ऐसे फैसले पर पहुँच जाते थे तो इसके लिए वो ईश्वर का सहारा लेते थे कि मेरी उनसे बातचीत हो चुकी है, फिर उसमें आप दख़लंदाज़ी कैसे कर सकते हैं। इसका मतलब यह कि मैं जिस अहिंसा के उपकरण के प्रयोग की बात कर रहा था, उसका अब तक सही प्रयोग नहीं हुआ है। और अहिंसा दरअसल इस्तेमाल ही नहीं की गई।

और अगर यह हो तो परीक्षा किसे देनी चाहिए? गांधी ने कहा कि मेरे पास, मेरे शरीर के अलावा कुछ नहीं है कि मैं दे सकूं। और यह वक्त है 1947 का जब गांधी दोबारा उस नारे का इस्तेमाल करते हैं जिस नारे का इस्तेमाल 1942 में हुआ था। वे कहते हैं, 'करो या मरो'। ये 1947 में दोबारा वे कहते हैं, 'दिस इज़ अ मवूमेंट फॉर मी, टू डू ऑर डाइ'। करो या मरो। बीच का कोई रास्ता नहीं है। लेकिन जो होने वाला था वो ये कि करते हुए मरना था, गांधी को। और गांधी ने अक्सर कांग्रेस के लोगों से पूछा जो उनके पास आते थे। और उसके पहले, दिल्ली के पहले उनसे नोआखाली में चिटगाँव सशस्त्र विद्रोह के भागीदार, जो बाद में कांग्रेसी हुए, गाँधी से बातचीत करते हुए उन्होंने कहा कि दरअसल चिटगाँव सशस्त्र विद्रोह में जो लोग शामिल थे, लोगों ने उनका सम्मान नहीं किया। गांधी ने कहा कि मैंने, मैं चिटगाँव सशस्त्र विद्रोह में शामिल किसी को हथियार नहीं दे सकता था, लेकिन मैं कायरता की किसी को सलाह नहीं दे सकता हूँ। गाँधी ने ये भी कहा कि चिटगाँव के विद्रोहियों की विफलता यह थी कि वे पूरे लोगों को 'इन्फ़ेक्ट' नहीं कर पाए, पर्याप्त इन्फेक्शन नहीं फैला सके, इसलिए वे कम रह गए। ज़्यादा नहीं हुए, ये उनकी कमज़ोरी थी। और गांधी का जो अहिंसा का चुनाव था, हिंसा का विरोध था, उसके पीछे एक बहुत बड़ा कारण यह था। और इस पर मैं कोई बहुत लंबी बात नहीं करना चाहता हूँ लेकिन ठहर कर इसपर ध्यान देने के लिए कह रहा हूँ। क्योंकि हम अक्सर हिंसा और अहिंसा पर बहुत सरल ढंग से विचार करते हैं। गांधी एक बहुत ही चतुर राजनेता थे, बहुत ही चतुर। और ईमानदार। गांधी ने *हिंद स्वराज* किताब लिखी। वह किताब कोई ग्राम स्वराज का प्रचार करने के लिए नहीं लिखी गई थी। वह किताब दरअसल इंग्लेंड में बैठे हुए क्रांतिकारियों के साथ बहस का नतीजा थी। जिसमें गांधी हिंसात्मक सशस्त्र संघर्ष का विरोध कर रहे थे। उस बहस में, ध्यान रखिए, सावरकर भी शामिल थे। गांधी हिंसा का विरोध क्यों कर रहे थे?, और क्यों इसको समझना हमारे लिए ज़रूरी है? क्योंकि हिंसा का सहारा लेकर जब हम राजकीय या सामाजिक परिवर्तन की बात करते हैं तो अंततः हिंसात्मक संघर्ष को छोटा होने की बाध्यता होती है। ज़्यादातर सशस्त्र संघर्ष में लगे दल गोपनीय होते हैं। गोपनीय कार्रवाइयों में ज़्यादा लोग हिस्सा नहीं ले सकते, ये मजबूरी है। गोपनीय कार्रवाइयों में आपको स्वेच्छा से हिस्सा लेना होता है। आप क्रांतिकारी दलों के इतिहास पढ़ें और उनकी बहसों को पढ़ें। इसके अलावा आप अल्बेयर कामू के नाटक *न्यायी हत्यारे* को भी पढ़ लें। आपको खुद को पेश करना होता है कि मैं इस कार्रवाई में हिस्सा लूँगा क्योंकि उस कार्रवाई में हिस्सा लेने का मतलब है आपकी जान का जाना। आपकी गिरफ्तारी का होना, आपको फांसी या सूली होना। फ़र्ज़ कीजिए कि एक क्रांतिकारी दल में पचास लोग हैं और एक कार्रवाई का फैसला किया गया, और उन पचास लोगों में सात लोग ही अपने आपको स्वेच्छा से पेश कर रहे हैं। बाकियों ने पेश नहीं किया। जिन्होंने पेश

नहीं किया है वे एक तरह से शक़ के दायरे में आ जाते हैं। और वे सात लोग उस कार्रवाई में हिस्सा ले रहे हैं तो ये तय है कि उनमें से कुछ लोग पकड़े ही जाएंगे। और मानवीय कष्ट सहने की सीमा है, इसलिए हो सकता है उनमें से एक या दो टूट ही जाएंगे, और मुखबिर बन जाएंगे। अगर वो मुखबिर बन जाएंगे तो उस क्रांतिकारी दल की बाध्यता है कि वो उस मुखबिर को ख़त्म करें। ये एक ऐसा दुष्चक्र है क्योंकि जनता ये देख रही है कि आप उसके नाम पर काम कर रहे हैं लेकिन उस काम में शामिल होने की इजाज़त जनता को नहीं है। इसलिए कोई भी हिंसात्मक संघर्ष अनिवार्यतः अपने स्वभाव में जनतांत्रिक नहीं होगा। और उसके जनतांत्रिक नहीं होने के कारण गांधी को वह संघर्ष का रास्ता स्वीकार नहीं है। हिंसात्मक संघर्ष में एक प्रकार का अभिजातवाद भी है, इलीटिज़्म है। वह इलीटिज़्म भी गांधी को स्वीकार नहीं है।

*

नोट्स/संदर्भ–ग्रंथ

1. http://www.telegraphindia.com/1021214/asp/nation/story_1479888.asp; http://eprints.lse.ac.uk/28476/1/WP64.2.pdf.

Picture credit: Gayatri Balush

On Anti-National Economics

Jayati Ghosh

(5 MARCH 2016)

TO BEGIN WITH, I REALLY HAVE to thank all of you students. This month, February 2016, I will have spent three decades teaching at this university, and before that I was a student here for some years. So I have a very long association with this campus; but even so, I feel that I have never been prouder of this university than I am today. We have always said that this university is made by its students, and we also know it in our hearts. But to know it once again in this way, in this time of stress, to realize how much we teachers and others are learning from all of you – in terms of your political understanding, your discipline, your maturity, your creativity – is just amazing. In particular, your courage and resilience – please keep that courage and resilience – we're going to need it, because we all know that it's not over, that there may be a long struggle ahead. Despite that I have huge faith and optimism when I see how smart you all are. You surprise me, and please continue to keep surprising all of us with this incredible smartness and political savviness. So thank you all, really, from the bottom of my heart.

I am going to talk about anti-national economic policies, even though I know that 'anti-national' is not necessarily a term that many of us find very useful. Especially in the last few years, it has really been a term used by those in power to fix any dissident voices, any opponents of government policies. For example, protestors against Kudankulam nuclear plant are called 'anti-national'; those who are fighting for the human rights and citizens' rights of displaced people are 'anti-national'; those who are struggling against mining companies that degrade and pollute the environment for local tribal residents without compensation are 'anti-national'.

This is typically how the term has been used in the public discourse by those in power and by the media trying to serve those interests. And now, of course, it has been further extended, and we are told that this entire university is 'anti-national'. But as the air grows thick with accusations of this type, it is worth taking a step back to consider what this term actually means. After all, to characterize someone as 'anti-national' you must first define what a nation is. Doing so in any meaningful way makes it clear that a nation is much more than territorially defined: a nation is ultimately its people. The nation remains the terrain on which rights of citizens can be demanded of the state, even though obviously the notion of universal human rights extends much beyond national boundaries. And the construction of the nation is dependent upon social contracts that are forged by the will of its people and their interactions over time.

Once you recognize that, it becomes evident that nationalism – and indeed anti-nationalism – must have deeper and more nuanced meanings than the more trivial attributes typically ascribed to it. To begin with, a person cannot be anti-national. Rather, whatever goes against the interests of the people (especially in terms of the defined social contract) is anti-national, which in turn means processes and policies can be anti-national, not individuals.

The nation of India may be nearly seven decades old, but it is still a nation in the making in terms of meeting the social goals defined in our Constitution. That remarkable document, for which Dr Ambedkar is justly venerated, was also very much the product of the freedom struggle that defined nationhood in a positive, inclusive sense in contrast to the divisive categories utilized by the colonial power. It defined a positive concept of the nation, not a negative one defined in terms of some 'other' – some enemy who must be defeated, but rather in terms of what this newly independent nation would offer to its people. So in looking for the essence of the Indian nation, it is worth examining the Preamble to the

Constitution, since the framing of the goals defined there can be seen as providing the essential building blocks of the idea of India.

Consider, then, what the Preamble to the Constitution of India promises. It declares that this nation will ensure for its citizens four essential features. First, justice – in social, economic and political terms. Second, liberty – of thought, expression, faith, belief and worship. Third, equality – of both status and opportunity. And finally, fraternity – expressed first in terms of ensuring the dignity of the individual and then in terms of the unity and integrity of the nation. These, then, are the essential building blocks of our nation, which explains why it is still a work in progress.

But these goals also define what we value in our country: to the extent that we love our flag, to the extent that we actually are proud to be Indian, we are thinking also of this vision of India. To the extent that we see ourselves as nationalists, we believe in that vision. So, I would argue that working towards achieving these goals is nationalist. And by the same token, policies and processes that undermine these goals are really anti-national, because they are against this idea of the nation, they are against the promise of this nation, they are against these essentials that define us as India.

Indeed, it could be argued that very little else defines all of us as Indians, because of the very diversity of our society, economy, polity. We are mostly very proud of how diverse we are and how many different types of everything we have; and indeed it is true that in India we manage to contain everything, however contradictory. There's this famous professor I had in England (the economist Joan Robinson) who would say, 'Whatever you can say of India, the opposite is also true.' And this remains true in many ways. So, even today, if you can say there is fascism in India, you can also say, thank heavens, that there is anti-fascism in India.

Seen in this light, if these goals are the defining building blocks of our nation, it becomes evident that many policies of the recent past can be described as anti-national. Let us examine only the economic content of some of these very broad overarching goals. While citizenship can be a problematic concept, it is still significant because it is the terrain on which we can demand rights for our people. The social, economic and political rights that we demand, that must be recognized and realized by our state, are defined in terms of the notions of citizenship.

Economic justice can be defined in many ways, but whichever way you slice it, it is relatively easy to identify its opposite. And there can be no denying that our society is rife with the myriad forms of economic injustice. We know that there are deep structural inequalities, some of which are very old indeed, as the histories of caste and gender oppression and their economic ramifications will testify. But recent economic policies and processes have greatly added to such injustice.

Let's look at the condition of workers. India is the only country in the world where we have such a loose definition of whom we call a 'formal worker'. To be classified in this way, a worker needs to have only *one* of these three: a written contract, paid leave, or any type of social security provision (pension, medical coverage, anything). In most countries you would need all of these to be called a formal worker, but we use this very loose definition. Even so, more than 96 per cent of all workers in India are informal. And that doesn't even count those workers who are not recognized as workers, but who do a lot of work (I'll come to those). Imagine – only 4 per cent of those recognized as workers are formal workers.

And what is even more incredible is that over the last three decades that proportion has gone down – believe it or not. The proportion of formal workers fell from about 5 per cent to slightly under 4 per cent, actually 3.8 per cent, if you look at the latest National Sample Survey (NSS) data. So here is a way in which we are happily recognizing that not only do most of our workers – the dominant, overwhelming proportion of our workers – not have any of these things, but their proportion is actually increasing. Those who have even one of these things, their proportion is falling. Then you find that the share of the national income that is going to wages has been falling continuously in the past decades. This is evident from our national income data and it is even coming out from data on organized manufacturing industry. So, even in organized establishments, wage shares have been falling, and the share of profits, interests and so on has been rising. This shift has been really sharp in the last ten to fifteen years. In fact, over the last two decades, the share of workers in the value-added organized manufacturing has gone from about 14 per cent to about 8 per cent, which, by the way, is one of the lowest in the world.

The largest category of workers in India are still those who get their livelihood from the land, whether as owner or tenant farmers or farm workers. We certainly don't provide justice to the huge category of farmers who are not classified as working for anybody else, they are part of the self-employed group. The share of national income from cultivation has been falling continuously. This government has promised – both the prime minister and the finance minister have done so – to double farmers' income in five years. This may seem like a big promise, but, if it's the money income, that's not really an achievement because in this economy, with some inflation, most money incomes double in five years. If it is in terms of real income, that too is still a modest ambition, because currently, the average farmer in the country receives less than three thousand rupees a month as net income from cultivation. This really means that most farmers are unable to survive solely on farm income. My colleague, Vikas Rawal, who has done a lot of surveys across the country, will tell you that for farmers across India who have negative income from farming the only way to survive is by somehow doing other work or other forms of activity that will enable them to get an income.

What has happened in the past twenty years is that farming has become less and less viable. After some recovery during United Progressive Alliance (UPA)-1, things are getting worse and worse for cultivators, to the point that this government has really made an all-out attack on agriculture, in fact. There was a deep crisis in farming from the mid-1990s, with big increases in farmers' suicides and other signs of severe agrarian distress. In the middle of the first decade of the new millennium, when UPA-1 came to power, there were some attempts to revive farming through more credit, more public expenditure on agriculture and so on. So there was a slight improvement in conditions at the margin, in terms of what farmers were receiving and their ability to get remunerative prices for their crops and some provisions of inputs and access to new knowledge.

But this government has actually systematically eroded many of those gains. Under the guise of fiscal responsibility, it has massively cut the

Central government funding for agriculture. Because of public outcry, as they realized this was not so popular or politically savvy, in the latest budget, they have pretended to reverse this.

Why do I say, pretended? Because it's a false increase, achieved through a simple shifting of budget heads: a subsidy that used to go to banks that provided credit for agriculture (not all of which actually goes to farming) was moved from the finance ministry to the agricultural industry. So there was a ₹15,000 crore increase in the agriculture budget, but actually this implied no increase at all. Even the total increase in budgetary allocation to agriculture was tiny – only 0.01 per cent of the GDP, so really negligible. This is most certainly not enough to make any kind of difference to the crisis that we know farmers are facing because of rising input costs and terrible climatic conditions, with two drought years in a row, and the much greater difficulties in terms of marketing. Farmers reeling under the adverse effects of agrarian crisis have yet to receive the minimal economic justice due to those who work towards ensuring the food security of the country under risky and increasingly adverse conditions. Meanwhile, the lip service paid to their needs actually rubs salt in their wounds because the policies of the government make cultivation less viable.

Other self-employed workers in non-agricultural activities are forced to function in extraordinarily difficult conditions, without access to formal institutional credit (of which they get less than 2 per cent) or basic infrastructure and facilities, access to technology, and inputs or assistance in marketing. And they too face not just neglect by official policy but downright attacks on their livelihoods because of state policies based on the belief that only large corporate players deserve incentives. The term that is popular now is MSMEs: micro, small and medium enterprises. A micro-enterprise is one person – so you know that lovely old man who sells fruit on the road just beside us over there is a self-employed micro-enterprise. This is the kind of employment that now accounts for more than half of the non-agricultural workers. They are self-employed, which means they're running their own businesses, if you can call that a business, surviving in whichever way they can. Even for the entire informal sector taken together, the share of that in the national income has been falling systematically, and very sharply in the last five years. Economic policies designed for this catch-all informal sector that employs the huge bulk of workers remain non-existent; in fact, if anything, they are against them. For example, informal enterprises get only 2 per cent of the bank credit in the country. Just 2 per cent!

So now, is the Jan Dhan scheme going to give them access to bank credit? Unfortunately, no. What it does is to create no-frills bank accounts, into which money can be put and withdrawn, but nothing else – no cheque facility, no other uses that are typically associated with bank accounts. For a proper account, all the old requirements remain – and even those do not guarantee access to credit. Because of the rush to create such accounts, many multiple and fictitious accounts were created, and indeed, most of the accounts have been dormant since they were opened. The idea of the government is to provide subsidies and 'direct benefits transfers' through such accounts – which would be fine if they did not replace public provision of essential goods and services. In any case these Jan Dhan accounts do not actually ensure access to institutional credit; so all of the holders of such accounts are still typically forced to survive on informal credit sources with very high interest rates. Given that, and all the other difficulties that small and micro-enterprises face in terms of lack of infrastructure and essentials like electricity and running water, not to mention access to markets, it is almost a miracle that so many of them still survive. It is certainly hard to imagine our big companies surviving if they had to pay the 25–30 per cent rates of interest that all informal enterprises have to pay as a norm. Certainly, we are not providing them anything like minimal economic justice.

Similarly, migrant workers are routinely robbed of their basic rights as citizens because so much public provision remains residence-based, and so they and their families miss out on many basic services and amenities. In addition, because of poor bargaining power, they typically face terrible living and working conditions in their destination. Women migrant workers face even more severe problems that also affect their physical security. Yet, the National Democratic Alliance (NDA) government seeks to bring in legislation that will further reduce the bargaining power of all workers, and relies on cynical subcontracting and other subterfuges (such as, not considering women anganwadi workers and accredited social health activists [ASHAs] to be workers) to deny workers their basic rights even in public employment.

In fact, we ignore these other workers, which is to say the entire group of people who are not recognized as workers at all, predominantly women, but often men as well. We often think that unpaid work is only what happens in households, and it's true, a lot of it does happen in households, but a lot of it also happens in communities. Millions of unpaid workers (predominantly, but not only, women) continue to be essential contributors to the economy and society, but without recognition, respect or remuneration. Our own survey data tell us that, while recognized work participation of women is really low at around a quarter of women above the age of fifteen years, actually nearly 90 per cent of women in the country are engaged in work, but most of them are in unpaid work relating to various household tasks. This unpaid work is in fact work that is critical for the survival of a society and is also critical for production. It's not just what we call social reproduction. Of course the care economy is an important part of this: looking after the old, the young, the sick, and so on. But there is also a whole range of production services inside households, which actually enable households to process foods themselves, to cook and clean and get the benefit of other services, collection of water, collection of fuelwood, collection of various other essential items. There is this massive reliance of the formal economy on this unpaid, unrecognized, informal economy. But the conditions of those workers have actually got worse over time, because we are making it more and more difficult and more time consuming – for example, to collect water, or to collect fuelwood. We are not thinking of policies that will actually provide piped water, piped fuel, ease the burden of unpaid work, and so on and so forth. The conditions of such workers have also been made much worse by cuts in public spending that deny people access to basic amenities and essential public services, forcing households to rely on more unpaid labour by family members, especially women and girls.

And then there is the whole category of what I will call underpaid workers. You would have heard that Kanhaiya's mother was an anganwadi worker. Anganwadi workers are part of this huge increasing category of underpaid workers, underpaid by the state. They use the fact that so much of women's work is not recognized, not paid, to actually provide women with so-called paid work at well below the minimum wage. Anganwadi workers get three thousand rupees a month, anganwadi helpers get fifteen hundred rupees a month which really is something like one-fourth of the minimum wage in most of the states that they are operating in. And yet they are expected to do an entire range of activities, they are expected to do a huge amount of work in a day, fulfilling seventeen different roles and functions that they have officially been assigned. The National Rural Health Mission operates on the back of an even more exploitative relationship, based on ASHAs. They get paid even less per month: five hundred rupees in some states, a thousand rupees in some others. Therefore, even the government does not call this a wage, they call it an honorarium – based on the assumption that ASHAs are activists, they are volunteers, they are doing this because they love helping the people, which perhaps they do. Not because they need or deserve a minimum wage. And yet our public health systems and our public maternal and child nutrition systems run entirely on this.

Then there is the injustice meted out to those who are displaced from their land, habitat, resources and livelihood, not only by 'development' projects like roads and irrigation schemes but also by urban spread and the expansion of luxury real estate. And those who are displaced do not have access to the minimum kinds of compensation or rehabilitation. The NDA government has sought (unsuccessfully) to worsen such injustice by weakening the provisions of the Land Acquisition Act – and it has not bothered to implement the just provisions of the Scheduled Tribes and Other Traditional Forest Dwellers (Recognition of Forest Rights) Act 2006. This is all part of this tendency of not recognizing the need for justice to those who are affected by particular growth strategies and development.

The second promise – of liberty and freedom of expression, thought, faith, belief and worship – is being much discussed currently, and so there is no need to belabour the obvious point that such freedoms are hugely under threat in India today, and that this government has become much more of a threat to such liberties than the previous government, and in many different ways.

The third promise, of equality of status and opportunity, is in many ways linked to the first. It is also as hard, maybe even harder, to achieve. This is partly because in India we have probably the most complex and highly developed systems of hierarchy, discrimination and exclusion in the world, developed over millennia, using caste, gender, ethnicity, religion and language among other criteria. Yet in some ways, things may have got worse.

We know that India is a very unequal society, we know that India is a very unequal economy. Nonetheless, economists often trumpet the fact that at least in terms of the Gini coefficient (a measure of inequality), we have relatively low inequality in India. But this is very misleading. First, our estimates are based on surveys of consumption, and we know that incomes tend to be more unequal than consumptions expenditure. Also, our surveys tend to leave out both ends of the distribution, the very rich and the very poor. They do not survey, for example, the consumption of the Ambani family; nor do they capture the pitifully small consumption of the homeless. So they tend to underestimate inequalities even in consumption. This, in turn, means that we actually have a much higher inequality than our official data suggest; everyone who has actually gone out to local areas and actually done income surveys has found much, much higher inequality. Maybe double that which the official surveys give us.

Of course, most of us don't really need to be told this, we know that it's there because we can see it. Just to give you an idea of how things have changed, consider the dollar billionaires that our media are so proud of. One-third of the world's dollar billionaires now come from India. Last year we had 111 dollar billionaires, and according to the latest report that measured this, the dollar billionaires' income went up by 25 per cent in India. Now just imagine, our GDP growth was only 7 per cent, but our dollar billionaires got 25 per cent hike in their wealth.

Clearly, our system is doing all right for the dollar billionaires in our midst; somehow, we're delivering for them. One of the ways in which we do this is through fiscal policy. Because we have relatively very low tax rates that we don't even attempt to implement and administer properly, there is no real attempt to raise tax revenues from the rich. We are proud of being in the BRICS and the G-20, but we have the lowest ratio of tax incomes to GDP among all the countries of these two groups. No wonder we don't have money for public services, no wonder we don't have money for schools and hospitals, or your scholarships, or proper public universities and so on, because we do not raise those taxes. And along with not raising those tax revenues, what we do is also to provide massive tax breaks. It used to be called 'revenue foregone' in the budget, but then it was probably realized that this is showing us up a bit, that we are foregoing revenues, so it was changed to 'statement of revenue impact'. So what are these implications of tax incentives? Well, in the past year, according to the budget, it amounted to ₹611,128 crore. That's 20 per cent more than the fiscal deficit.

Let me put this number into perspective. This is around twenty times what was spent on the rural employment guarantee programme, which was underfunded and had chief ministers begging for the money that should have come automatically, while millions of workers were not paid their wages in time. It was nearly twenty-seven times what was spent by the Ministry of Agriculture, and more than ten times what was spent by the Central government on women and child welfare and school education taken together. This is the amount that was just the officially declared giveaway to corporates through various kinds of tax concessions. I'm not even talking about the unrecognized giveaways, such as cheap land or low-cost infrastructure or other facilities. I am not even entering into the question of all the bad corporate debts that the public sector banks were encouraged or pushed into loaning. So there is a huge way in which we massively subsidise the rich: the rich corporates, the rich personal elites, the rich in general.

However, these massive giveaways are never mentioned when we talk about subsidies. Subsidies are always described only as the things that affect the poor. So food is a subsidy, whereas what we are actually doing is trying to ensure sufficient production of food in India so that every household gets a minimum amount of grain required for human consumption, so as to feed some of the largest number of nutritionally deprived people in the world. As it happens, food subsidies are not a big deal globally: the United States and countries in Europe have been doing this for a very long time. The east and south-east Asian tiger economies have also been doing this for a long time, over the course of their industrialization and development process. Every country that has developed to rich country status has had strategies to ensure local food production and the distribution of minimum required food to its people. Yet we are planning to dismantle this system and cut this 'wasteful' subsidy.

Meanwhile, the Central government cuts public spending on all the things that provide the basic needs of people. This has happened for over two years now: big cuts in the budgets for health, education, nutrition, even sanitation (a bit of an irony given the declared emphasis on 'Swachh Bharat'). Now, what happens when you actually reduce these, when you cut, say, health spending? Do people say: well, too bad, now I just won't take my mother to the doctor but will just let her die? It doesn't work that way – people turn to private services. In India, we have the highest proportion of private, out-of-pocket spending on health in the world. On this one indicator, we've beaten sub-Saharan Africa, we've beaten Pakistan. Unbelievably, even this terrible situation has now got worse. We now have many states in the country that are not able to run the primary health clinics because money from the Centre has dried up and their own resources are simply insufficient. Education at all levels has been massively affected and is being in effect privatized, because of the failure of the public sector to deliver. This is a huge way of creating inequality. Universal access to good-quality education is not just good for the economy and society – it is critical for improving inter-generational social mobility and thereby reducing inequality. Yet this government is pushing young people to more privatized education, especially higher education, even as employment opportunities for graduates remain dismal.

Education goes to those who can afford it, health goes to those who can afford it, sanitation goes to those who can afford it, clean drinking water goes to those who can afford it. Now we know, even clean air goes to those who can afford it, because otherwise you have to live and work in the polluted environment and so you are more vulnerable to lung disease, compared to the people who travel in the cars with filtered air.

The economic strategy of the past decade was in fact based on inequality, premised on the idea that incentives to large corporations would generate investment that would pull the Indian economy up by its own bootstraps. This meant that large capital was allowed and even encouraged to get natural resources and labour cheap, thereby generating both 'scams' and greater inequality. Contrary to their own propaganda, the proliferations of scams has not diminished at all during the NDA regime thus far – and given the tendency to run roughshod over matters like environmental clearances and labour rights, matters are likely to deteriorate further.

So there have been dramatic increases in inequality in India as a result of policy, not just because of some inescapable pressure of the world out there and the forces of globalization but as a result of domestic policy. So, in that sense if you are looking at equality as the third, major peg in what we want to define as our nation, these are deeply anti-national policies.

Finally, consider a major plank of this fourth promise: dignity. There are many aspects of ensuring dignity to the individual, and only some of them can be affected by state policies. But in so far as a government can indeed work towards ensuring greater dignity for all of the people, the performance of this government may actually be going counter to this.

The rights-based movement was a critical movement for ensuring dignity. It also relates to the awakening of oppressed groups and communities – of Dalit awareness, of women's movements, and so on. The rights-based demand is not from the 'mai-baap' state, i.e., the demand is not a plea for help and charity, it is instead a demand of a citizen for her basic rights. This is being sought to be eroded very, very systematically, particularly by this government. What is notable about the NDA government is its distaste for any rights-based legislation or economic policies. The prime minister was open in his contempt for the employment guarantee scheme until quite recently; the government has ignored the need for speedy implementation of the Right to Food law; it is actively trying to scuttle or enfeeble the Right to Information Act; after making promises on the right to health it has actually made massive cuts in the Central health budget and offered in its stead a trivial sop in the form of health insurance through private providers. So one basic plank of reducing inequalities – the universal provision of good-quality public services and basic goods – has already been dealt a big blow by the policies of this government.

As a result, rights are also being removed from the public discourse. There is almost nothing in the government's statements that talks about rights anymore. In fact, bureaucrats who are usually very quick to sense these changes in the wind are quick to respond when rights are mentioned, 'No, no don't talk about all that. That's all kind of ... very last year, let's move on to the new things, the JAM, and things like that.' So, what is the new strategy? It is providing benefits – direct cash benefits. Please note, it's not a right, it's a benefit – the government will give the people some goodies. It's going straight to their bank accounts, the government will not check whether it actually ensures that people have food to eat, or whether it actually substitutes for the price they would pay for an essential good or service, or whether it is actually something that will enable the child to go to school or someone to access a health service, because the chances are that the money will not be enough for that. It will just not be enough.

Across the world, wherever cash transfers have been successful in reducing poverty and improving dignity of recipients, they have simultaneously been part of a strategy of increasing public expenditure on food, health and education – rather than reducing it. Yet this government seeks to cut such spending (passing off the responsibility to state governments that do not have anywhere near the required resources) and substituting public provision with direct transfers into bank accounts. Quite apart from the many difficulties of such targeted transfers, such as unfair exclusion or unjustified inclusion of beneficiaries, not keeping pace with price increases, and so on, this also attacks the rights-based notion that saw such provision as the right of every citizen.

So, in the Indian case, the move towards direct benefit transfers (or cash transfers) has come as a substitute for public provision in essential areas. 'Decent-quality, good-quality health care, good-quality education as a right to every citizen? No. We'll give you a little bit of money and you go out there and find it. See how good we are, we're giving you some money, you should be grateful to us. It's a benefit, a gift from the government.' Instead of a government that must deliver on its responsibility to realize the rights of its citizens, we are back to the mai-baap sarkar, where anything that is provided must be accepted by grateful 'beneficiaries' as a benevolent gift from the government. This also involves a fundamental denial of dignity to citizens. The erosion of that dignity comes in addition to the millennia of indignity in various social forms that we impose on so many of our people. It's a worsening and, therefore, in that sense it's a strengthening of that peculiar form of inequality that we have in India – and it is a complete reversal of the promise of dignity that was so essential to the hope inspired by the Constitution and indeed by the nationalist movement.

By these criteria, then, the NDA's economic policies have been profoundly anti-national. Sadly, this form of anti-nationalism is not seen to be a crime; nor does it appear to generate the violent antipathy that is directed to dissenting opinions even in the popular media. But for most of the Indian people, it is likely to be the most harmful form of anti-nationalism that can exist.

Picture credit: Gayatri Balusha

The Past as Seen in Ideologies Claiming to Be Nationalist

Romila Thapar

(6 MARCH 2016)

I AM DELIGHTED TO BE HERE on this occasion, having been invited to participate in the teach-in on nationalism. When I come to JNU these days, I feel a bit like a dinosaur – having been one among the founding generation of teachers. We belong to another age as we were here at the start of JNU. I joined in November 1970. We left the various universities where we were teaching to build the new JNU. Our main concerns were two: one, that it must have an impressive academic quality so that it would be recognized as a centre of academic excellence, as a place for serious study and thoughtful interactions; two, that it must be a place where there is free discussion and debate. Over the years, as I worked in JNU, observing the university and its methods and content of teaching and research, I felt proud of being at JNU. For the last month or so, when the attack on JNU began, I must confess that I have been deeply depressed by what happened on the ninth of February, because I saw this as an attempt to break JNU by those that regard themselves as 'the authorities'. But I feel much more positive now that I have seen how JNU reacted to defend itself. I just want to say, thank you for being JNU, and I continue to be proud of belonging to this university.

Now, having spoken like a dinosaur, let me come to something that is much more topical and that is the connection between history and nationalism. This is a connection which is very close, and it is particularly so because nationalism has much to do with the question of understanding one's society and identifying as a member of that society. The question of identity is central and history has much to do with arriving at an identity. Eric Hobsbawm has a rather interesting description of the relationship between history and nationalism. He writes that history is to nationalism what the poppy is to the opium addict.[1] What does he mean by that? What he means is that history is a source and history is also that which gives the nation its identity. And it's these two questions that I'm concerning myself with this evening.

Nationalism emerges as a concept or an idea in modern times as a response to historical changes. It is difficult to locate it in pre-modern societies. So, we don't look for nationalism in the centuries-long past, we look for it when society changes to the point where it is required. When it emerged in Europe in the seventeenth and eighteenth centuries, it was a time of emerging capitalism and the start of colonialism, both of which were to expand. Together with this came the growth of the middle class and its aspiring to participate in governance through democratic representative systems. Small territories were integrated within larger territories. It brought together many groups and encouraged a secular identity to ensure inclusive unity. This is characteristic of most nationalisms. Defined by a new sense of social awareness and identity, there is in nationalism inevitably an inclusive and overarching identity. History is essential to a national ideology but it has to be a shared history that binds people together. History has to be the bond. It cannot be a history dominated by only one identity because nationalism doesn't exist only on one identity. It has to be all-inclusive. National history of course locates a golden age in the past, a utopian age which is the exemplar. It is often the kind of society that is held forth as being the ideal society, not realizing of course that whatever society you take as the Utopia from the past, remains in the past, it belongs to the history of the past.

But what we are dealing with today is in a sense the history of the present which is in some ways a rather different history. National identity supersedes existing identities. If it is inclusive, draws everyone in, it is generally much healthier. But if it is exclusive, and leaves out some sections of society, it can be disastrous. We have had an example of the latter – a very severe example – of exclusive nationalism in the case of Germany in the 1930s. It propagated the theory of the purity of the Aryan race that resulted in the genocide of the Jewish population and the justification for the genocide.

But where it has been inclusive, even if scattered, it has had quite a positive effect. For example, the kind of nationalism that we never refer to, but is pertinent in terms of comparative history to the Indian situation, is African nationalism, sometimes referred to as Negritude. It was propounded in the Caribbean by Aimé Césaire and Léopold Senghor, and it brought together an African consciousness that stretched from Africa to the Caribbean to North America.[2] It was an inclusive nationalism of a very extraordinary kind, and I think we would do well to study it, with both its positive and negative features. If nothing else, it would make us aware of the different varieties of colonialism and how these differences impacted the idea of nationalism.

But let me turn to the Indian situation. The evolution of nationalist ideas in India was tied to colonialism. Therefore, the influence of the colonial interpretation of Indian history is present in all kinds of nationalism to a lesser or a greater degree. In pre-colonial times there were multiple identities of caste, language, religious sects and regions. Political ambitions that caused constant wars kept changing the borders of kingdoms. Patterns of caste that differed from the north to the south, from the east to the west throughout the subcontinent, gave each region a certain kind of identity. Religious identities, I would like to argue, were not based on large monolithic religions but on a range of religious sects. And the religious sect is what we should give much more attention to when we talk about the history of religion in India. In sum, we now recognize that diversity characterized Indian cultures. Up to a point it can be said that modern anti-colonial nationalism drew the diversities together.

But we can't stop there, because if diversity is characteristic, the next question is: How did diverse groups negotiate their space and their relationships? This is a fundamental question where some explore these relationships whereas others project a single identity, argue that it is the identity of the majority and should therefore have priority. Let's look at how this came about.

The colonial reading of Indian history denied the diversity of India. The first modern history of India was the well-known one by James Mill, published in the early nineteenth century, *The History of British India* (1818–23). Two theses from this history have been influential in Indian politics and continue to be so. One was periodization. Mill divided Indian history into three periods – the Hindu civilization, the Muslim civilization and the British period. This periodization was based on just one feature – the religion of the ruling dynasties. This feature as a source of periodization is now rejected in current historical research. Mill projected Indian history as that of two nations, and right through the nineteenth century colonial scholarship wrote and spoke about the Hindu nation and the Muslim nation. This was entirely the invention of colonial historiography. It was also said that these two nations were permanently hostile towards each other, therefore it required the intervention of the British to prevent these hostilities.

There were no histories, of course, of India as a unified territory prior to colonial rule. Colonial history tried to tidy up the diversity, not by asking how these diversities related to each other, but by envisioning all religions in India as large monolithic religions and fitting the sects into one or the other, instead of seeing them as autonomous or only partially allied to another religion. Colonial scholars dramatized the confrontation of what they called the Hindu religion and the Muslim religion in order to support the two-nation theory, required by colonial policy. Relationships between religious groups are never so simple. There can be both accommodation as well as conflict between them. The historian has to investigate both and explain the reason, and the reasons can be multiple. But with colonial scholarship the interpretation of Indian history appropriated the two-nation theory, a theory that has been politically so influential and continues to be influential in some ideologies today. From this perspective, Hindu–Muslim antagonism became axiomatic to Indian history.

The two-nation theory persisted and was strengthened by the introduction of the concept of the majority community and minority communities after the British Indian census. It divided Indians and encouraged Indians into thinking about their identity as distinct, consolidated, monolithic religious identities. This suited colonial policy and therefore was encouraged. Nationalist historians writing substantially a century later, the great stalwarts such as H.C. Raychaudhuri, R.C. Majumdar, Nilakanta Sastri, challenged some colonial theories such as Oriental Despotism, but curiously accepted the periodization without questioning it. It was merely updated by calling it ancient, medieval and modern, but the parameters remained the same. I remember many arguments that we had at the start of our courses and syllabi here in JNU as to whether we should keep to these labels because ancient was the old Hindu period, medieval was the old Muslim period and modern was the old British period. The labels had been changed, but the divisions and the reasons for the divisions – the religions of the ruling dynasties – had been questioned. We were questioning them in our structuring of the courses. We kept the boundaries fluid, resulting in the discovery of interesting overlaps.

The two-nation theory was one that came out of colonial scholarship. The other is a more complicated one but nevertheless, has its roots in colonial history and came to be called the theory of Aryan race. We have to keep in mind that what was called 'race science' was very influential in Europe at this time.[3] In the mid-nineteenth century, European philology became interested in Vedic Sanskrit and its links with Indo-European languages. Many philologists and Sanskritists, such as Friedrich Max Müller and others, projected the idea that the Vedic corpus, authored by the Aryans was the foundation of Indian civilization. The history of the origin of the Aryans and their innate superiority became an important aspect of colonial scholarship and of nationalist historians. It was popularized, initially by the theosophist, Colonel Olcott.[4] He maintained that not only were the Aryans indigenous to India, but that they also migrated westwards and eventually civilized the West. This was useful in projecting the idea that India has always had a singular history, of which the most important has been that of the ancient Hindus.

Various theories were put about on the origins of the Aryans. Max Müller said they came from Central Asia; Dayanand Saraswati preferred Tibet. Tilak, as we all know, was much more adventurous in suggesting the Arctic regions. When it became fashionable in the 1920s and

'30s to talk about the Aryans being indigenous to India, it was a little embarrassing to have Tilak placing them in the Arctic. So someone had the bright idea of saying that in those days the North Pole was actually located in Bihar.[5] Various Indo-European languages from Sanskrit to Celtic were said to be of the same language family. It was assumed that those who spoke the same language were biologically related.

One may well ask why there was the need to project an indigenous descent for the Aryans. It was important to the theory that there was a direct link between the Aryans and the upper-caste Hindus that followed generation after generation up until present times. Max Mueller in England and Keshab Chandra Sen in India argued that since both the British and the upper-caste Indians were Aryans, they were all eventually kin-related and, therefore, were like 'parted cousins' now coming together.

This theory met with an obstacle in the 1920s with the discovery of the Indus Valley civilization or the Harappa culture as it is also called. This was prior to the Aryans and it was not Vedic. Therefore, this had now to be the foundation of Indian civilization. This naturally created a problem for those who believe that Vedic Aryanism is the foundation. That is one reason why today, some archaeologists and Sanskritists are trying to take the dates of the Vedas back to pre-Harappan times. Newspaper reports have stated that attempts are being made to take it back at least to 7500 BC. But the other problem is the unknown origin of the Harappans and that their language remains undeciphered. It's much simpler now to maintain that the Harappans were also Aryans. There were many archaeological cultures in the subcontinent, so were they all Aryans?

How do these ideas and problems connect to the question of nationalism? By the late nineteenth century, there was an established middle class in India. The colonial economy was tied into British capitalism, and much of the middle class, largely upper caste, had emerged as professionals, managing the administration of the colony and its colonial economy. The idea of nationalism began to emerge from this group. So once again it is the particular historical situation in modern times that leads to the emergence of nationalist ideas. At first, the nationalists requested greater representation in governance and then gradually, as we all know, it grew into a mass movement and the mass movement then finally ended up by demanding an independent nation, which was a logical outcome. Anti-colonial nationalism endorsed the idea of a nation and defined it as a democracy with a secular, egalitarian society. This anti-colonial nationalism maintained that the primary identity of all citizens was being Indian, irrespective of whatever identities they may have claimed prior to this. Being Indian was an overarching and inclusive identity incorporating people of all religions, castes and languages on an equal basis with equal rights, and this is the central component for what was originally projected as secular, anti-colonial Indian nationalism. This was a new identity obviously, and was seen and projected as such.

But given the history that was written by colonial scholarship and taught to the colonials by the colonizer – the fundamentals of which had not been fully challenged – there inevitably arose two kinds of what some people call religious nationalisms and some people prefer to call communalisms – the Hindu and the Muslim – and some may even refer to them as pseudo-nationalisms. Both endorsed the old, British two-nation theory. One aimed at establishing a separate Islamic state and managed to establish Pakistan, the other aimed at uniting the subcontinent under Hindu rule – what was to become the idea of the Hindu Rashtra. Unlike anti-colonial secular nationalism that was inclusive of all as equals, for these communal ideologies those of their own religion had priority, and to that extent these nationalisms were exclusive. They were not anti-colonial – some of them regarding the colonial power as their patron. But their hostility was towards each other.

These views were basic to the two organizations that propagated these ideas: the Muslim League and the Hindu Mahasabha. The latter was gradually superseded by the RSS and later there emerged a conglomeration of organizations referred to as the Sangh Parivar. The ideology that has come to be associated with it is Hindutva. The RSS took shape from the 1930s, as a disciplined organization, its discipline reflecting influences of Italian fascism which it regarded as the exemplar.[6]

As with all nationalisms of all kinds, Hindu religious nationalism also turned to history. But interestingly, it appropriated the two dominant colonial theories – the Aryan foundation of Indian civilization and the two-nation theory. These they now describe as the indigenous history of India. Ironically, it is claimed that these histories are cleansed of the cultural pollution of Indian historians influenced by Western ideas! That their own ideas are rooted in colonial theories is conveniently ignored.

The core of this ideology is the identity of the Hindu. The Hindu is the only one who can claim the territory of British India as the land of his ancestry – *pitribhumi*, and the land of his religion – *punyabhumi*. Muslims and Christians are described as foreigners since they came from outside the territory of British India and their religions originated in other lands. The ancestors of the Hindu and his religion having been indigenous to India – he therefore, is the primary citizen. The true claimants to the ancient civilization can only be Hindus, descendants of the Aryans, and this is one reason why it has to be proved that the Aryans were indigenous to India, irrespective of whether they were or not. Being indigenous, they are the inheritors of the land. There are, however, glitches in this argument. Those of us who have pointed out the problems get our daily dose of abuse on the internet, and we are described as ignorant JNU professors and worse, even if in fact most are not from JNU.

The history of the Aryans as it stands today, on which much of the basic ideology of Hindutva hinges, has now become extremely complex because it has come to involve many disciplines. Information on the subject comes from specialized studies of texts in Vedic Sanskrit, distinct from classical Sanskrit, the study of which requires a substantial input from linguistics in addition to just the study of language; the archaeology of multiple sites in the north-west of the subcontinent of varying cultures and their contact with adjoining areas; hydrology for information on the rivers that changed the contours of the landscape; and most recently, genetics, to map the population structure of those millennia. DNA samples are being taken by some in the hope of locating the Aryan. It is difficult to convince those supporting a variety of theories that Aryan is not a biological entity but a language category, a shorthand for 'Aryan-speaking people'. The confusion over biology and language creates its own problems.

The questions that historians of a different ilk are asking have moved away from the obsession of whether the Aryans were indigenous or foreign. Cultures do not grow in isolation, so we need to know which other cultures coexisted, and which contributed to the cultural beginnings of Indian history, and how did this cultural mixture, amalgam, juxtaposition, evolve.

Then we come to the two-nation theory, taking history back to medieval times. This theory is being questioned in various ways by modern historians. The history of religion, as many argue, covers a range of religious sects and social groups with a variety of different relationships between them. Those relationships resulted in some degree of conflict or of accommodation or a mix of both at different levels of society and in different spheres of activity. The history of religion has to be seen as the history of these sects, and not the history of monolithic religions in confrontation, as I have argued earlier.

It is commonly said by people who should know better, but obviously don't, that for the last one thousand years, Hindus have been enslaved and victimized by the Muslims, and now finally they are free. That is not what history tells us. In the last one thousand years when the status of Hindus in the subcontinent is investigated, there emerge some very interesting ideas, events and personalities. Sanskrit learning continued to thrive at many centres in the subcontinent because Sanskrit learning had spread at the end of the first millennium and this was not discontinued. It had the impressive patronage of maharajas, sultans, and Mughals among royalty, as well as among wealthy landowners. The patronage of Sanskrit and Persian was a sign of being cultured among such groups.

Centres of learning referred themselves to a variety of Hindu and other sects. There were commentaries on and digests of earlier Sanskrit texts such as the Vedas, the Ramayana, the Mahabharata, and the Dharmashastras, all discussing crucial issues pertinent to contemporary times and their mixed society and the situations that emerged. For example, was there a difference in status between the shrotriya brahmana and the priest performing the daily rituals in the temple? Temples in some cases were endowed with money and land, and those associated with their functioning were financing other activities. This resulted in various new categories of functions having to be performed by brahmanas other than those traditionally associated with them. Some new rituals of worship had entered religious practice, not unconnected with the new sects. Important questions arose related to forms of worship and who legitimized the forms, given the multiplicity of sects that were working out their practices.

The scholar Sayana wrote a fascinating commentary on the Rig Veda, which is actually an interesting insight into the medieval mind, and how the medieval mind of the fourteenth century looks back three thousand years on the Rig Veda, and provides a commentary on it.[7] Among texts discussing philosophical schools, one that was highly regarded was the *Sarvadarshanasamgraha* of Madhavacharya, where the Charvaka philosophy of materialism constitutes the first lengthy chapter. The author explains that although he disagreed with it, but given that it was being discussed by scholars, he thought it necessary to discuss it in this compendium of philosophical schools. This attitude to knowledge and the form of discussion needs to be observed in our time too.

Many books on mathematics and astronomy were written and Indian astronomers and mathematicians, many of whom were Hindu, were praised, discussed and quoted in Arabic texts. Did these mathematicians on both sides know Sanskrit and Arabic? Otherwise, how could they have had these discussions? What happened to that tradition, why isn't it reported, why don't we learn about it in school?

There were also compositions of high quality in the regional languages, such as the Tulsi Ramayana and the Bengali Ramayana, not to mention the huge range of highly popular bhajans and dohas, sung by people of all religions who understood the languages in which they were composed. The dohas of Ras Khan in praise of Krishna are sung by classical musicians to this day. The beginnings of Hindustani classical music in the form of Dhrupad was nurtured in this period at the courts of Muslim rulers.

The shape and form taken by Hinduism as we recognize it today draws a great deal from developments during these thousand years. Bhakti sects were becoming more common in parts of north India and bhakti tradition and worship became an extremely important part of what we today call Hinduism. The Shakta-Shakti worship expanded and popular sects such as the Nathapanthis were to be found from Bengal to Hinglaj in Sindh. This is what I sometimes call the Guru-pir religion because it is the religion of the majority of the people who followed it, and still do

– the teachings of the gurus and the pirs, the sants and the babas – and that is really the religion we should be looking at.

These are not the cultural forms taken by people who have been enslaved and victimized. These are the articulations of a rich and many-faceted civilizational tradition. We need to put these facts into a historical context and see them as part of that historical context and not spend our time only searching for confrontations between Hindus and Muslims. That's an approach which, apart from being invalid in most instances, does not help in understanding medieval history. We have far more important things to investigate and discuss. There were religious and cultural forms arising out of the characteristic features of the time even in the last one thousand years. As in the previous millennium, it was a time that hosted differences, it had an attitude to all kinds of differences, and they could either coexist, get amalgamated or create new forms, or confront the other. So, there was a range of choice on how sects and differences were played out in the society of the time. This range is what we should be investigating and trying to understand.

And once again we need to see the interactions of the various cultures and explain their mutations, and be sensitive towards the spaces they have created, and observe the emergent identities that came out of them. This can be seen if we don't restrict the study of religion to texts alone but also explore religions expressed in the oral traditions, because we have to keep in mind that the vast majority of Indians could not read, and oral traditions were their source of belief and their source of social goals. For the historian, religion in pre-modern India is an extremely challenging study precisely because it is not a case of two monolithic religions confronting each other all the time, as we have been made to believe. It makes far more sense to see religion as an array of religious sects that cover the range from the orthodox to the heterodox. The sects have their own relations with each other – some friendly and some not so. The religious sect was also linked to caste, and that remains common to all religions in India. Let me give you a couple of examples of what I mean by this.

Arab traders came in large numbers and over the last twelve hundred years settled along the west coast and established new religious sects, which were an amalgam of Hindu and Muslim ideas and practices. But each one kept its distinct identity, despite the fact that some of them had common Islamic elements, or had inducted the same Hindu deity. They maintained their separateness largely because they had intermarried into different local castes and adopted local customs. Thus a Gujarati Bohra would not have married a Malayali Mappila, and yet they had some similar origins, but they evolved with different beliefs and custom, living in different geographical areas.

The other striking feature is that all formal religions in India – based on religious books and texts – discriminate against Dalits, even those Dalits that belong to their own religion. Muslims and Christians outside India do not observe this segregation, but in India they do. One cannot study any religion in pre-modern India without studying its links with caste. Those who were always marginalized like the Adivasis and the Dalits and the lower castes, when they were not converted to formal religions, had their own forms of worship and these are rarely commented upon in modern histories of religion.

Sources from early times seldom mention monolithic forms of religion. From Ashoka to Al-Biruni, a period of fifteen hundred years, references to dharma are said to consist of two streams – Brahmanism and Shramanism. Ashoka refers to '*bahmanam-samanam*', Megasthenes the Greek visitor to India writes of the *Brachmane*s and the *Sarmane*s, Al-Biruni mentions *brahmana*s and *samaniya*s. The brahmanas believed in the gods, in the divine sanction of the Vedas and in the immortality of the soul. The shramanas – such as the Buddhists, Jainas, Ajivikas and such like – rejected all of this and were therefore called by the brahmanas as the *nastikas* / non-believers.

Each of these two dharmas hosted a range of sects covering variants of belief and worship. Some of them were accommodating towards each other, some were confrontational. There are references, for example, to Shaiva sects, more than the others, sometimes being hostile to the Jainas and the Buddhists. But interestingly, Patanjali, the great Sanskrit grammarian of the early centuries AD, also refers to the two dharmas – that of the brahmanas and that of the shramanas – and adds that the relationship between the two can be compared to that of the snake and the mongoose. I think that's a very telling statement.

The point that I am trying to make is that the reading and interpretation of the past requires a trained understanding of the sources and a sensitivity to understanding what has been written. The political requirements of today cannot be imposed on the history of the past. To maintain a generalized statement that the period of the last thousand years was one of the victimization and enslavement of the Hindus by the Muslims is historically unacceptable. This kind of generalization feeds communal nationalism. That is why I am cautioning against it. Unfounded generalizations have to be replaced by analytical history.

At the time of Independence and soon after (when none of you were born!), we had no problems defining nationalism and the definition was widely accepted. Nationalism meant declaring every Indian as an equal citizen of India and upholding the rights of every citizen to that equality. Today, efforts are being made to obfuscate it. Nationalism draws on reliable history and not on the contorted history that feeds communal ideologies. Reliable history demands critical enquiry which, as we all know, is essential to the advancement of knowledge. It is expected of a university to critically enquire into what may publicly be claimed. Nationalism gives an identity to the citizen. The citizen is pre-eminent but no citizen or group of citizens can claim superiority over others as citizens, irrespective of what may be the basis of the claim. Citizenship is founded on the equality of all and the equal rights of all. Incisive debates on this are part of the nationalist enterprise, and this is an ongoing enterprise in the relationship between history and nationalism. Universities are the obvious places for such debates. We in India have had a head start due to our Constitution and with our commitment to making the nation a secular democracy. This is what we are committed to as Indians and what we were committed to when we became independent, and this commitment has to continue as the hallmark of our nationalism.

*

Notes/References/Bibliography

1. Eric Hobsbawm, 1998, *On History*, London: Abacus, p. 6.
2. Peter Benson, 1986, *Black Orpheus: Transition and Modern Cultural Awakening in Africa*, Berkeley: University of California Press.
3. A. Montagu, 1997, *Man's Most Dangerous Myth: The Fallacy of Race*, Walnut Creek: AltaMira Press; Stephen J. Gould, 1996, *The Mismeasure of Man*, New York: W.W. Norton.
4. H.S. Olcott, 'A Glance at India Past, Present and Future: the Past', *The Theosophist*, March 1881, Vol. II, p. 124 ff.
5. On the North Pole being in Bihar, see, M.S. Golwalkar, 1935, *We or our Nationhood Defined*, Nagpur: Bharat Publications, p. 45; E.F. Bryant, 2001, *The Quest for the Origins of Vedic Culture: The Indo-Aryan Migration Debate*, New York: Oxford University Press, p. 273
6. On RSS and Italian fascists, see, Marzia Casolari, 'Hindutva's Foreign Tie-up in the 1930s', in *Economic and Political Weekly*, 22 January 2000, p. 218 ff.
7. E.B. Cowell (ed.), 1996, *Sarva-darsana-sangraha of Madhava Acharya: Review of Different Systems of Indian Philosophy*, New Delhi: Satguru Publications (reprint), first published 1882. See also, S. Radhakrishnan, 1929, *Indian Philosophy*, Vol. I, London: George Allen and Unwin.

Picture credit: Gayatri Balusha

Reinstituting the Colonial History of Medieval India

Harbans Mukhia

(6 MARCH 2016)

WELL FRIENDS, MY YOUNG FRIENDS, AS a dinosaur, I'm just a few months younger than Romila is. We came here in the beginning of JNU, and therefore it was very, very exciting to be here. JNU was in its formative phase, and the formative phase is always extremely exciting. JNU was not merely an institution where we worked and got our salaries from and so on and so forth. JNU is something that resides in our hearts; anything that happens here, any call from JNU, and one responds immediately. When I was invited here I began to wonder – lots of doctors, medical doctors around the world, institutions around the world, they are doing very expensive research on what is called age fighting, no, anti-ageing process, on finding an anti-aging treatment; I think the best anti-ageing treatment is to come to JNU, interact with the students of JNU. Nothing sheds off more decades from your age than interaction with JNU students. It's so wonderful because JNU was meant to be a different university, even as any university should be, but JNU, above all, was meant to question received wisdom, was meant to question established truths. Questioning does not mean demolishing, questioning does not mean opposing; questioning nationalism does not mean becoming anti-national, questioning patriotism does not mean you become anti-patriotic. Questioning means trying to understand phenomena. When you question nationalism, you are trying to understand the phenomenon of nationalism, and nationalism is not just one phenomenon; it is a very, very diverse and complex set of phenomena, it is a whole host of phenomena. Whether it is nationalism or patriotism or any other ism that you talk of, it's a whole host of phenomena and therefore understanding that, questioning that is trying to understand that ensemble of phenomena, and that's why JNU promotes so much of questioning. Please forgive me for a little autobiographical note, I think it was 30 or 31 January 2004, my last working day in JNU, and I was to give my last lecture to my class, after teaching history for forty-four years – eleven years in Delhi University and thirty-three years in JNU. Believe me, I still prepared my last lecture for three hours before I delivered it, because in JNU you can't go to class without preparing your lecture. So that's JNU, that's why we love JNU so much.

Now I'll take off from a point that Romila touched upon, that's very, very crucial. By the way, before I go on to that let me bring in Fernand Braudel, who was one of the landmark historians in the world in the twentieth century, and his last book is called *The Identity of France*.[1] He opens that book by virtually asking, in the twentieth century: Is France one country? Is France one society? Is France one nation? He traces the immense diversities of every kind through France's history in Vol. 1, and concludes in Vol. 2 that France began to develop as a society and as a nation only after the coming of the radio and, later on, television when French became the language of all of France, when French nationalism came to be accepted by all of France. Yet, even in the twentieth century, there is still a region called Bretagne (Brittany in English) whose inhabitants resent being called French, though they are French obviously; they speak French, they still resent being called French just as the Scots resent being called British or English. The Soviet Union never became a nation even under a very strong state and the most powerful bureaucracy. One can go on with examples. So, nationalism is a concept which is still evolving even in the most advanced nations; it's not a settled question in any country, in any region of the world, and therefore, it has to be understood, it has to be questioned, it has to be queried all the time.

But I'll come back to James Mill, whom Romila referred to. James Mill, as she said, and as we all know, divided Indian history into three periods – Hindu period, Muslim period, British period, with his notion of 'civilization' as the analytical category.[2] Prior to that there was no notion of periodization in Indian history. The difference between past and present was known, naturally, as it is in every society, the difference between what transpired ages ago and what is happening now. That change has occurred in the past through to the present was obviously known, but there was no notion of ancient and medieval past, there was no such notion, not only in India but anywhere else except in Europe. In Europe, this tripartite division which is so familiar now had come only towards the end of the seventeenth century, in 1688 to be precise,[3] and then it spread to the rest of the world in the nineteenth and early twentieth century. Its spread around the world was not due to its innate intellectual vigour but had a great deal to do with the emergent global power relations. It reached Japan and China towards the end of the nineteenth century and got incorporated in the study of history there in direct or modified form.[4] In India it was used for the first time – the ancient/medieval/modern model – in 1903. But it was used in a different form – it coincided with James Mill's division of historical time into the Hindu, the Muslim and the British periods.[5] The change in nomenclature established no change in the substance; for that Indian historians were to wait until after Independence.

What is the implication of this tripartite division – Hindu, Muslim and British? The implication is that James Mill, as a utilitarian, was against all religions; he had very, very great contempt for Islam, but he had even greater contempt for Hinduism. The 'Hindoos' he characterized as 'dissembling, treacherous, mendacious, to an excess which surpasses even the usual measure of uncultivated society'. He believed that modern states should function with modern institutions, modern rational thought, etc., emulating Europe's post-Enlightenment rationality. So he had contempt for any earlier forms of state functioning and, therefore, he declared that earlier forms were Hindu and Muslim; that is to say, nothing else mattered prior to the coming of the British rule. All that mattered was whether the religion of the ruler was Hindu or Muslim, that's all. Therefore, James Mill essentialized one notion, that of religious identity. Kanhaiya Kumar very rightly reminded us JNU people that we use too much of jargon, which is often not intelligible. Essentialization is not much of a jargon, but let me, nonetheless, taking advice from him, explain what essentialization means. It means that if Kanhaiya Kumar stands up and says my name is Kanhaiya Kumar, immediately we understand that he is a Hindu, he is a boy. That he is also a Marxist by persuasion, that he is a political and social activist, that he has a certain social, economic and family background, that he has certain aspirations for himself and for his society – all that becomes irrelevant. What remains relevant is that he is a Hindu boy, that's about all, nothing else matters. Our friend Umar Khalid has been shouting from housetops that he is an atheist; in fact, when he was charged with being sympathetic to Jaish-e-Mohammed, his young sister said on TV that he didn't bother even about Mohammed himself, much less about Jaish-e-Mohammed. And yet he will be projected as a Muslim, because his name is Muslim; that's what essentialization means.

All of us have many, many different aspects to our existence: we are male, we are female, we are urban, we are rural, we are educated, we are uneducated, we are devoutly religious, we are devoutly atheistic, this, that, and the other, all kinds of facets – each one of us is an ensemble of all kinds of facets. Our existence is not just one identity, it has many, many identities. But all of those identities are reduced to just one, namely, the religion, and that in history to the religion of the ruler. Therefore, Hindu and Muslim periods means that nothing else mattered but the religion of the ruler. He was a Hindu or a Muslim ruler. Whether he was a good ruler, a bad ruler, efficient ruler, inefficient ruler, whether he conquered territories, didn't conquer territories, whether he cared for the development of agriculture, industry, towns, trade, none of that matters. So Mill essentialized the study of pre-British history in these terms of Hindu and Muslim, and therefore justification of colonialism, that colonialism brought modernity, modern institutions, enlightenment, etc., to India. He also asserted that Indians were alien to the notion of change, any change, until the British brought it home to them.[6] This notion indeed was predominant among all major European thinkers in the eighteenth, nineteenth and good part of the twentieth century and was the unquestioned premise for understanding India – indeed of the whole of the Orient – among such intellectual giants as Montesquieu, Hegel and not least Karl Marx.[7]

Now, it's not as if the identities of Hindu and Muslim were not known earlier, obviously they were known. Professor Romila Thapar has written that excellent book, *The Past Before Us*, and she has also talked about the theme for a while now, where she shows an enormous range of perceptions of the history of India, a huge range. There's not one perception of the past. History has been seen in many, many different ways in early India, sometimes intertwined with religion, sometimes independently of it. Let me talk of medieval India. In medieval India, history takes a different form from that in early India; it has a very strong Islamic colour to it, in the sense that one historian, Arab historian Tarif Khalidi, writes that Islam brought not only a new religion to the world, but also a new concept of history.[8] The pre-Islamic Arab world was not illiterate: there was poetry in it, there was arithmetic, accounting, there was genealogy, etc. But there was no concept of history as we or as anybody understood it in the seventh century. So Islam brought a new discipline there, that of history, and from there it spread to wherever Islam spread. In medieval India also historians were imbued with this idea of Islam as an aspect of history writing, and therefore, the era that they used, mostly, though not all of them, was the Hijri era. So, Islam is present in history writing in medieval India, but is history writing a branch of theology in India? No, it is not a branch of Islamic theology. Why not?

When is history a branch of theology? Let me illustrate this first and then I'll explain why medieval history writing is not a branch of theology. In medieval Europe, the historians were all ecclesiasts, for that was the only literate class in Europe then. The rulers were generally illiterate, it was from the second or the third generation of a dynasty that the rulers began to read and write. But the literate class was only the church fathers; they were thus the only historians. Being church fathers, not only did they live in the precincts of the church, but their mindsets also were entirely shaped by their religion. In their religion, God is omnipresent, God is omniscient, God knows everything. Whatever has happened in the past, whatever is happening today, whatever will happen in the future, God knows all that. In God's mind, everything is clear – past, present and future are clear. We humans do know a little bit of the events of the past, a little less of what is happening before us in the world and nothing whatsoever of what the future has in store for us. But God knows everything because what's happened in the world in the past, is happening now or will happen in the future is a manifestation of God's will, of divine will. God has willed this war to take place, this flood to take place, this earthquake to take place, this fellow to succeed to the throne, etc. It is God's will which is manifesting itself in historical events. So there are two aspects here: one is that all of history is universal history, for all events in the world happen as parts of God's design. History thus is a single universal whole, a single unit. And the second is that all historical events merely unfold a divine pattern, God's will, which is actually a causative force extraneous to human beings and to history.

In medieval India, neither of these facets occurs in history writing. Interestingly, even as history is visualized as world history within the fold of Islam, the 'world' that this history comprises is histories of several regions, chiefly where Islam had already spread and established its supremacy. It is thus not a universal history, but is the history of either different, often adjacent, regions or, in most cases, of single regions. Within regions it is reduced to dynastic history, within dynasty, there's regnal history – wherein each reign is a single unit, and when you come to the current sultan, each year becomes a single unit. It's a stupendous craft of reduction from 'world' history to regional history, further down to dynastic history, to regnal history, to annual history; it's a reduction of superb craftsmanship.

The second distinctive aspect is chronology. The Arab–Muslim historians are very strict about sticking to the exact chronological sequence of events. This feature has been passed on to the craft of history writing wherever Islam spread. In its Indian version, each event is treated as a single, individual event; no event is related to any other event. Even their narration is like this. 'In this year, this event took place'; they would narrate that event and then move on to the next event by announcing 'and another event that took place was this' and they would describe that event. There is no connection between one and the other event; each event is a single, individual entity, which is contrary to European history where everything is part of a pattern; here, there is no pattern in history. The second thing is that in Europe, medieval Europe, history, as has been emphasized again and again, is a manifestation of divine will, God's will; in medieval India, history is a manifestation of the will of the ruler, or at best, the nature of the ruler, i.e., individual will, human will, not divine will. Therefore, you have people like Alauddin Khilji, who was a very strong ruler and therefore he conquered lots of territories; Firoz Shah Tughlaq was a very weak ruler and hence didn't conquer any territory; Akbar was very liberal and therefore he followed a very liberal religious policy, etc. You must have, in your undergraduate days, read about this – weak ruler and strong ruler. All of this comes from medieval Indian historiography, the notion of ruler's will or ruler's nature being the determinant of historical events or indeed history in general. In this sense, medieval Indian historiography is very fundamentally different from medieval European historiography and, therefore, it is not a branch of theology, notwithstanding the use of Hijri era, and the fact that it owes its origin to Islam, in Arabia.[9]

Now, once you have human nature as the determining element of the events you are narrating, you have a whole range of natures among rulers; no two persons have the same nature. I just mentioned to you, Alauddin Khilji was a very strong ruler, Firoz Shah Tughlaq was a very weak ruler. You have even theorization on this. The most important historian of the fourteenth century, Ziauddin Barani, posits that man's nature comprises contradictory qualities.[10] It's only a balanced mixture of these contradictory qualities that leads to success, and an imbalanced mixture leads to failure. And in fact he says even God's nature comprises contradictory qualities. And those of you who remember your chapter on Muhammad Bin Tughlaq would recollect that Muhammad Bin Tughlaq's nature, according to Barani, was an unbalanced mixture of contradictory qualities, and that is why he failed as a ruler. But you have other rulers who are very strong, tough and ruthless, like Balban, who would cut down dense forests to chase and punish rebels, or others like Firoz Shah Tughlaq who undertook construction of lots of canals to improve irrigation for cultivation, and so on and so forth. Everyone's nature is different and therefore you have a range of explanations that are given to you by medieval Indian historians. What James Mill does is that he reduces this great range of explanations to one single explanation – the fact that the ruler is a Muslim is all that matters. Period. That's all that needs to be understood, nothing else needs to be taken into account. No variation, no change, no range, nothing. The ruler is a Hindu or a Muslim, that's all. And therefore, we began to adopt that periodization and that mode of history writing in the nineteenth century, and for a part of the twentieth century, we kept going along that path.

To illustrate what it does to history, I'll give you two examples, what this reduction to essentialization does. Annette S. Beveridge translated *Babur-Nama* into English and it is an excellent translation, absolutely fabulous translation. Now it has been superseded by another translation, but for about a hundred years this was a standard translation and a good translation. In the *Babur-Nama*, Babur mentions twice on the same page that he went to Ayodhya, he notes the administrative arrangements he made there and does not forget the shikar he undertook. However, he doesn't mention any Ram temple, he doesn't mention Ram, he doesn't mention any temple, he doesn't mention the demolition of any temple, doesn't mention the construction of the Babri Masjid, or any masjid by him.[11] However, in the translation, there is an appendix inserted by Mrs Beveridge, the translator. It says, in this year Babur went to Ayodhya. There he must have come across a very old, sacred temple of the Hindus, and as a faithful follower of his faith – I'm just paraphrasing, I don't remember the exact words – he must have destroyed that temple and given the order to erect a mosque.[12] Now this is what follows from essentialization – because Babur was a Muslim, he must have done all of this. That he actually demolished an existing temple, there is no evidence of that, and even Mrs Beveridge is not sure, but she presumes that Babur must have done all that because he was a Muslim![13]

But let me take up a bigger example than this. You see, as an essentially Muslim ruler, or rulers, what would be their primary duty when they are ruling over India, such a vast territory as India, with a massive non-Muslim population? Their primary duty would be to convert these non-Muslims to Islam; that would be expected of a very faithful follower of Islam, essential Muslim, etc. That is required, naturally, and follows from the essentialization of a Muslim ruler. Now, let us look at the process of conversions to Islam, I don't want to go into many details, but touch upon it very briefly.[14] The Muslim population in the Indian subcontinent before Partition – India, Pakistan, Bangladesh together – is the largest population in the whole world; now the region is divided, so Indonesia has the largest Muslim population but, if you put the three countries together, it is the largest Muslim population in the world. And yet there is not a single book on how these conversions took place, the largest population, and we don't know how these conversions have taken place in India.[15] Why is there no book? It's not that historians haven't thought of writing a book, but because there is no data available to let the historians do research on this massive theme. Why is there no data available? It is interesting that of the numerous court histories written in the Persian language from the Delhi Sultanate to the end of the Mughal Empire, covering a period of some six centuries, there is very scant reference to conversions undertaken by the rulers. Most histories were written by Muslim authors, some by Hindu historians. Among them was a range of historians – some very highly charged Muslims like Mulla Abdul Qadir Badauni, Akbar's courtier, and others like Abu'l Fazl, who discounted Islam as the only true religion, and several others in-between, but it is extremely rare that any one of them, zealot or 'liberal', Muslim or Hindu, refers to proselytization by the ruler. Nor is there much data on it in popular, vernacular literature, which abounds in medieval India. But knowing that massive conversions did take place, why are references to it so scarce? The only reasonable explanation is that had conversions taken place at the hands of one single agency by force or otherwise, or in one short period of time, there is no way it could have escaped getting into record of one sort or another at the hands of one writer or the other. Conversions took place over very long stretches of time and through a number of agencies and for a number of motivations; hence the absence of a dramatic element lets these off the record.

There is a second aspect of the problem. In the last census before Independence, 1941, the Muslim population in India was estimated to be just short of 25 per cent, i.e., one in every four Indians was a Muslim. In 1826, one Bishop Hebbar mentions that one in every six Indians was a Muslim. Going by this data there was a 50 per cent rise in Muslim population in over a century when the British were ruling here.

Then again let us look at the demographic distribution of the Muslim population in the undivided subcontinent. The massive majority of the Muslim population is concentrated in four peripheral regions: Kashmir, what is now Pakistan, what is now Bangladesh, and in Malabar in Kerala, isn't it?

Now, these are the four geographical peripheries of the subcontinent which were also the political peripheries of the medieval Indian state, where the hold of the state was either non-existent (as in Kerala) or very sporadic and far from firm over long periods. Thus in the heartland of the Muslim rule – Bihar, Delhi, UP, East Punjab – the Muslim population never exceed 10 per cent; if it was around 15–16 per cent in 1941, it was obviously much lower than that earlier – at best 7–8 per cent, 10 per cent, whatever. Therefore, the argument that the Muslim state was converting people to Islam falls flat on its face if you look at the demographic map of India. I'm not suggesting that the state had no hand in it – the state also had its hand in it. In fact, my Muslim friends here might not be very pleased to hear this but nonetheless, as a historian let me just say that the state converted people to Islam as a kind of punishment; that is to say, if you commit a crime against the state, the only punishment for crime is your beheading, but if the ruler is kind or the ruler considers past services or usefulness of the man himself, he'll say, okay I will not kill you if you convert to Islam. So it's a second-level punishment being given to them. Second, sending people to Hajj is the second-biggest punishment you can give them. Whenever the state is angry with some Muslim noble, they send him to Hajj. So, it's not as if the state did not have a hand in conversions, but that the simple explanation flowing from essentialization of 'Muslim' rule is extremely tenuous. So, you get a distorted picture of history. You lose a whole range of explanations of history, you get one explanation which is a false explanation in terms of historical data. Therefore, you get a bad kind of history from this, just one monolithic kind of history.

Now, this sort of history lasted until about the 1950s. Fortunately or unfortunately, this is also the kind of division that our historians,

Indian historians, have adopted, as Romila has already pointed out. But things began to change in the late 1950s, early '60s. I happen to be one of those who belong to that fortunate generation. I was a student of the undergraduate and postgraduate programmes at Delhi University in the second half of the 1950s. I studied that kind of history which I am now describing, Hindu and Muslim and so on and so forth. It was called medieval India but it was actually Hindu and Muslim periods, that kind of history. Suddenly, from the late 1950s, early '60s there was a wave of change; suddenly you started talking of class at the mass level, rather than religious identity of the ruler, as the driving force of history.[16] Religious identity as a category of analysis was central to that kind of history; that was suddenly replaced by a new category called class, which had nothing do with religion and was no longer centred on the individual ruler. History found its explanation in terms of class exploitation and class upheavals and so on. You take peasantry as a whole, and not divide it into Hindu and Muslim peasantry and so on. Thus started a new kind of historical explanation; history's landscape changed in the late 1950s and early '60s and the colonial legacy began to give way quickly within under a decade. In the late 1980s and the 1990s, a new threshold was crossed again and a fascinating range of themes emerged. Themes like the history of the notion of time, for example, history of the notions of space, history of interpersonal relationships, intercultural interactions, history of the household, history of gender, ecology, the natures of states and so forth.[17] Therefore, a fascinating new world emerged from the late 1980s onwards and then in the twenty-first century, alternatives to old chronicles and court histories and texts, etc., began to be explored in the vernacular literatures, folklore, folk songs, etc., not as sources of history but as alternative perspectives of history in some outstanding recent works. A new world is opening up, so we have left colonial history far, far behind. And I must say that the British are themselves revisiting their earlier generations' assumptions and conclusions under the influence of Indian historians; they are themselves giving up this kind of colonial, historical writing. But that's the problem with the RSS and the BJP: they want us to ignore all the recent marvellous developments in history and go back to James Mill, go back to colonial history understood exclusively in terms of Hindu and Muslim, that's all. Nothing else matters, except

Hindu and Muslim, to them. The religion of the ruler is all that matters and of course all Muslim rulers are essentialized as cruel, perverse and oppressive. Do you want to go back to that kind of history?

[To a resounding 'No' from the audience, the speaker concludes,] 'That is why you are under attack!'

*

Notes/References/Bibliography

1. Fernand Braudel, 1988, 1990, *The Identity of France: Vol. 1: History and Environment*; *The Identity of France: Vol. 2: People and Production*, London: William Collins.
2. James Mill, 1817, *History of British India*, London: Baldwin, Cradock and Joy.
3. Harry Elmer Barnes, 1963, *A History of Historical Writing*, Oklahoma: University of Oklahoma Press, pp. 16, 172, 348.
4. See the special issue of *The Medieval History Journal*, 1,1, 1998, devoted to the history of the notion of the 'medieval' across Europe, China, India, Japan, the Arab Muslim world and Central Asia.
5. Stanley Lane-Poole, 1903, *Medieval India Under Mohammedan Rule (A.D. 712-1764)*, London: G.P. Putnam's Sons, 1903. On the opening page itself, Lane-Poole observes 'Distinct and clearly marked as the Medieval or Mohammedan period is...', p. iii.
6. For Mill, the Asiatic social system was 'one in which all progress had ceased thousands of years ago'. *History of British India*, p. 107.
7. Montesquieu cited in Perry Anderson, 1974, *Lineages of the Absolutist State*, London: Verso, p. 464; W.F. Hegel, 1944, *The Philosophy of History*, New York: Willey Book Company, p. 163; Karl Marx, 1960, 'The Future Results of the British Rule in India', K. Marx and F. Engels, *The First Indian War of Independence*, Moscow: Foreign Languages Publishing, pp. 33-34.
8. Tarif Khalidi, 1995, *Arabic Historical Thought in the Classical Period*, Cambridge: Cambridge University Press, p. 115.
9. For a detailed discussion of this theme, Harbans Mukhia, 1976, *Historians and Historiography During the Reign of Akbar*, New Delhi: Vikas Publishing House.

10. Ziauddin Barani, *Fatāwā-i Jahāndārī*, English Translation by M. Habib and Afsar Khan as *The Political Theory of the Delhi Sultanate*, Allahabad: n.d., pp. 85–89.
11. A.S. Beveridge (tr.), 1970, *Babur Nama* (from the original *Tuzuk-i Baburi* by Babur), Delhi: Oriental Books, p. 602.
12. Ibid. Appendix U.
13. See Harbans Mukhia, 2010, 'The Ram Janmabhoomi–Babari Masjid Dispute: Evidence of Medieval Sources', in his *Exploring India's Medieval Centuries: Essays in History, Society, Culture and Technology*, New Delhi: Aakar Books.
14. For a more detailed discussion, see Harbans Mukhia, 2004–05, *The Mughals of India*, New Delhi: Oxford University Press, pp. 27–39.
15. There are two excellent books on Kashmir's transition to Islam and one on Bengal by M. Ishaq Khan, Ashraf Wani and R.M. Eaton. There are also some brief essays on some regions like Rajasthan, but no single book on India as a whole.
16. The catalyst for this transition was undoubtedly D.D. Kosambi's *An Introduction to the Study of Indian History*.
17. Some of the recent explorations of several of these themes are Aditya Behl, 2012, *Love's Subtle Magic: An Indian Islamic Literary Tradition 1379-1545*, (Wendy Doniger ed.), New York: Oxford University Press; Allison Busch, 2012, *Poetry of Kings. The Classical Hindi Literature of Mughal India*, New York: Oxford University Press; Rajeev Kinra, 2016, *Writing Empire, Writing Self*, New Delhi: Primus Books; Tanuja Kothiyal, 2016, *Nomadic Narratives: A History of Mobility in the Great Indian Desert*, New Delhi: Cambridge University Press.

Picture credit: Gayatri Balusha

India's Uncivil Wars: Tagore, Gandhi ... JNU ... and What's 'Left' of the Nation[1]

Makarand R. Paranjape

(7 MARCH 2016)

Ideas Rather than Ideologies: JNU's 'Alternative' Performative

FELLOW JNU-ITES AND FRIENDS, I HAVE followed most of the talks in this series with great interest. While I don't wish unthinkingly to join in the chorus of self-praise in proclaiming how great we are, what does make us special, even important, to the nation is precisely this alternative performative, this staging of ideas. This is as vital to who we are as the theatre, *theatrics*, of JNU politics. We are known for our vibrant political culture – some would say it's too vibrant – but what also makes us distinctive is JNU as a place of creative and intellectual possibilities. I

(Editors' Note: After several long and detailed discussions with the author, the editors have retained this considerably altered version of the lecture/article, including references as provided by the author, for which he takes responsibility.)

have learned a lot from the previous speakers; you too, I hope, have found them informative, provocative, inspiring. I thank JNUTA for organizing this series and our students for attending these 'classes'; attendance, as we all know, is not compulsory in JNU, but it's heartening that so many have shown up for this 'teach-in'.

Now let me come straight to my topic: 'India's uncivil wars: Tagore, Gandhi,' then there is an ellipsis, followed by the second half of the topic, 'JNU ... and What's "Left" of the Nation'. To put it simply, on one side of the debate we have Tagore and Gandhi, and on the other, what's left of the nation. Right in between is JNU. Is there anything 'left' of the nation following the stance that some take here? That is the question I pose to you.

In this regard I am reminded of a witticism attributed to John ('Jack') Gallagher, late professor of imperial history: 'Revolutions devour their children, nationalism eats its parents.' The source of the first part of the quip is Jacques Mallet du Pan's remark on the French Revolution. In today's altered state it almost seems as if nationalists are eating their children and revolutionaries their parents!

If, however, we are not cannibalistically oriented in either direction, where do we stand? Neither ultra-nationalists nor self-styled revolutionaries, naturally, we might feel distressed to find our entire lives, including our academic pursuits, not to speak of this campus itself, being held hostage to positions we do not share even if we respect their right to be heard. What is lost is precisely the nation that our forebears, from Ram Mohan Roy to Mahatma Gandhi, strove so hard to build. It is the imagining of this India that I tried to convey in my book *Making India.*[2] It is this India that needs so sorely to be recuperated.

Intermediality: An Answerable Hermeneutics for Our Times?

Friends, I suggest that what we need today, especially those of us who wish neither to be ultra-left nor ultra-right, is a hermeneutics of mediality. *Medium*, *medial*, *median* go back to ancient Indo-European roots from whence also spring common Indian words like *madhyam.* Those interested in classical Indian thought will immediately see the connection with the Mahayana Buddhist school, *madhyamaka*. It is a rather powerful tradition, with hundreds of years of continuity and development, from the famous master Nagarjuna (c. 150-250 CE) to our own contemporary, the Dalai Lama, who is perhaps its most famous living exponent.

The question is how to mediate between these polarities of radical left and extreme right? What kind of hermeneutics do we have for mediation – call it a medial hermeneutics, if you will. We must recognize the imperative to stand between the two opposite poles of the political spectrum. Can the two sides speak to one another without one trying to defeat or obliterate the other? What ensues from such a negotiation is a dialogic rather than dialectic exchange.

To begin with, our project may be intermedial, but if it is truly to succeed, it must also be remedial. The idea of remedy (*svasthya*) is connected with what we consider our self-state (*sva+avastha*), our natural state of well-being (*svasthi*).[3] Return to a healthy state, likewise, is predicated upon restoring equilibrium, which of course can be very difficult during conflicts. That is why I propose such an intermedial hermeneutics as the need of the times.

In contemporary thinking, there is a similar methodology, diatopical hermeneutics, recommended by the Portuguese social scientist, Boaventura de Sousa Santos. Diatopical hermeneutics calls for 'placing oneself simultaneously inside and outside what one critiques, and thus making possible ... the doubly transgressive sociology of absences and emergences'.[4] In today's charged and contentious environment, it is much easier to relate to reductive formulations. But when conducting academic discourse, rigorous, intellectual, rather than polemical, we must open our minds to both sides. As Santos puts it:

> Diatopical hermeneutics is based on the idea that the *topoi* of an individual culture, no matter how strong they may be, are as incomplete as the culture itself. Such incompleteness is not visible from inside the culture itself ... The objective of diatopical hermeneutics is, therefore, not to achieve completeness – that being an unachievable goal – but, on the contrary, to raise the consciousness of reciprocal incompleteness to its possible

> maximum by engaging in the dialogue, as it were, with one foot in one culture and the other in another. Herein lies its *diatopical* character.[5]

According to this view, no topoi, no ideology is complete in itself. It is only when we accept that there are difficulties, problems, absences, misunderstandings, and factual errors in our own position that we can engage in diatopical understanding or dialogue. You may call this an epistemology of dispassionate compassion rather than the 'epistemicide' that often substitutes for academics these days.

The 'Nation' of Tagore and Gandhi

In keeping with such a line of thinking, the challenge of intermediality or diatopicality is to arrive at non-reductive understandings not just of Tagore and Gandhi, but of the nation and nationalism. What I shall try to do is trace the genealogy of that middle ground we are trying to retrieve today that made the very idea of India possible.

Let us look at Tagore's idea of nationalism by focusing on two moments in his very complex life and creative career. These two moments, though part of a space–time continuum, are also intermedial in that one presents the poet as polemicist, while the other the novelist and creative artist.

The first instance would be Tagore's trip abroad in 1917 when, just over fifty-five and towards the end of the Great War, he gave a series of lectures on nationalism in Japan and then in the United States, published in book form soon after. In these lectures, Tagore takes an unequivocal stand against nationalism: 'Nationalism is a great menace. It is the particular thing which for years has been at the bottom of India's troubles.' The poet contends that the Nation (with a capital N) is an inhuman, predatory machine:

> Have you not seen, since the commencement of the existence of the Nation, that the dread of it has been the one goblin-dread with which the whole world has been trembling? Wherever there is a dark corner, there is the suspicion of its secret malevolence; and people live in a perpetual distrust of its back where it has no

> eyes. Every sound of a footstep, every rustle of movement in the neighbourhood, sends a thrill of terror all around. And this terror is the parent of all that is base in man's nature. It makes one almost openly unashamed of inhumanity.[6]

Clearly, this idea of the nation signals a harsh critique of totalitarian, authoritarian and imperialistic regimes, conflicts between whom were threatening the peace and stability of the world. Tagore was also aware of the dangers of nationalist ideology becoming almost a religion, full of lies, propaganda and jingoism: 'Clever lies become matters of self-congratulation. Solemn pledges become a farce.' It is possible to think that Tagore was a staunch anti-nationalist, and on the strength of a few other texts quoted out of context, many have appropriated Tagore's legacy to the cause of post- and anti-nationalism. But this would be a simplistic reading where, nationalism, as E.P. Thompson points out in his Introduction to *Nationalism*, mostly stands for imperialism.[7] Rather than an anti-nationalist, we may understand Tagore better as an *alter*-nationalist, unless we are to coin new phraseology such as 'no-nation-ism', 'anti-politics' (to recall Thompson again), or 'vernacular' nationalism to better characterize his position.[8]

Professor Sabyasachi Bhattacharya shows at least five distinct phases, not necessarily progressive, of the deepening and enlarging of Tagore's views on nationalism: 1890–1904 (conventional nationalism), 1904–1907 (Swadeshi agitation), 1907–1916 (disillusionment and criticism of militant nationalism), 1917–1930 (critique of imperialism), and 1931–1941 (reconciliation of antinomies).[9] In addition, there are at least two different, though interrelated, personae that operate through his vast and complex oeuvre: the English, outward-facing, international Tagore, and the distinctly Bengali Tagore, more inward and Indian, as aesthetically–spiritually reflective as socio-politically conscious. We must resist the temptation of slotting him according to our requirements as Tagore demands a methodological anti-essentialism, reflective of the hermeneutics of mediality. Remember Tagore's more constructive essays on swadeshi samaj, where he believes that self-sufficient and self-supporting village societies would be the backbone of the new India?

Tagore was deeply distrustful of all ideologies that destroy the human spirit, our finer qualities and inner creativity as individuals. This brings us to the second part of my discussion on Tagore. The intermedial challenge in reading Tagore is not only to reconcile the diachronic and paradigmatic, but also to cross several genres, languages, and creative media. Not just non-fiction, but stories, novels, plays, songs, and an astonishing range of art works, from doodles and cartoons to the mysterious oil paintings, need to be taken into account along with their mutually influencing interactions. This is a huge challenge but must be undertaken to get a more complex picture of Tagore, including his idea of nationalism.

To illustrate, let us briefly consider his three major political novels, *Gora* (1909), *Ghare Baire* (1916), and finally, *Char Adhyay* (1934), the last of his thirteen novels.[10] First, *Gora*, which was serialized in *Prabasi*, soon after the partition of Bengal. Through his eponymous protagonist, Tagore rejects both the extremes of religious ultra-nationalism and comprador elitism. While the first part of the book shows the inadequacy of the former, British imperialism comes under attack somewhat later.

In *Ghare Baire*, Sandip, as Indranath in *Char Adhyay* – the figures who represent the passion of politics and the fanaticism of nationalism – are depicted as self-serving, unscrupulous and manipulative. In the former, Bimala is misled, her marriage destroyed; later Amulya, her ardent admirer, almost a foster-son, loses his life. Not only does ideological enthusiasm come under attack, but it is also shown to be insincere and opportunistic.

Georg Lukacs, the Marxist critic who reviewed *Ghare Baire* in *Die rote Fahne* in 1922, dismissed it with an epithet: 'a petty bourgeois yarn of the shoddiest kind'. He accused Tagore of not voicing the aspirations of an enslaved people rebelling against imperialism; alleged that Tagore's task was to save the Indians spiritually and to protect their souls from the dangers posed by the violence, deceit, etc., with which they were waging their struggle for freedom. He scorned such spirituality, saying, in sum, that this stance represented nothing less than the ideology of the eternal subjection of India. Lukacs calls Sandip a caricature of Gandhi which is obviously a mistake because the novel was written before Tagore met Gandhi in 1915. But from such a perspective, we see that Tagore's is not so much an anti-national as anti-revolutionary position, something that his bhadralok admirers would not relish.

Was Tagore really anti-national when almost every Indian sees him not only as a great patriot, but as one of the founders of modern India? As Brojendranath Seal remarked to Edward J. Thompson on Tagore's critique of nationalism, 'Yes, but he has a right to criticize us. He has been a nation-builder'.[11] The same paradox might explain how, in *The Creative Ideal*, Tagore is as sarcastic about patriotic, as he is of religious, poetry:

> ...when some storm of feeling sweeps across the country, art is under a disadvantage. In such an atmosphere, the boisterous passion breaks through the cordon of harmony and thrusts itself forward as the subject ... For a similar reason most of the hymns used in churches suffer from lack of poetry. For in them the deliberate subject, assuming the first importance, benumbs or kills the poem. Most patriotic poems have the same deficiency.[12]

This, coming from the author of two, perhaps three, national anthems and innumerable devotional poems, shows the complexity of his creative genius.

Now, let us move to Gandhi. Again, I want to focus on two moments in Gandhi's long and challenging life.[13] Let us first consider November 1909, when Gandhi was aboard the *S.S. Kildonan Castle*, sailing from England back to South Africa. Clearly, he had an epiphany: he wrote *Hind Swaraj*. As he confided in a letter to his friend Kallenbach, Gandhi had had a 'profound experience of illumination' and produced 'an original work'. *Hind Swaraj*, written in Gujarati, was first published in *Indian Opinion*, a broadsheet that he edited, then translated into English by Gandhi himself and published in early 1910. It soon ran into many editions and was banned by the British authorities in India.

What was Gandhi's great illumination? We know that when Gandhi was in England he had met Indian freedom fighters of every stripe and hue. One or two of these meetings took place at the India House, founded by Shyamji Krishna Verma, and between 1905 and 1910 (until it was shut down by the British authorities) offered a platform to Indian revolutionaries, both from the left and the right.[14]

What is more germane to our discussion is that Gandhi probably met Vinayak Damodar Savarkar at India House. Savarkar, an avowed revolutionary, was also the author of *India's First War of Independence*, offering a counter-narrative on the Great Revolt of 1857 to established imperial historiography. Incidentally, like *Hind Swaraj*, it was also published in 1909 (in clandestine edition in Netherlands, reportedly with *Pickwick Papers* as the false dust jacket) and banned by the British authorities. While Savarkar believed in armed revolution, Gandhi abhorred the use of violence for political ends. Perhaps, this was the beginning of their lifelong antagonism that persisted right till Gandhi's assassination by Nathuram Godse, an admirer of Savarkar. Another of Savarkar's protégés, Madanlal Dhingra, who had shot Sir Curzon Wyllie at point-blank range, was tried at Old Bailey in London and hanged on 17 August 1909, when Gandhi was in London.

Gandhi's great discovery was that India could not, *should not*, win its freedom through armed struggle. He presented in *Hind Swaraj* an alternative method, based on age-old Indian traditions, of fighting *bahubal* (armed might) with *atmabal* (soul force), offering the blueprint of new India and, indeed, a new world order based on self-restraint, non-aggression, cooperation, restricted consumption, and enhanced moral as opposed to material development. Gandhi advocated satyagraha, truth-force, as the right and proper means to swaraj – not just political freedom, but complete self-mastery and emancipation.

Gandhi tried and tested satyagraha in his struggle for the rights of Indians in South Africa. The fight culminated in the long march of November 1913. Gandhi led over 2,000 striking miners and sugar plantation workers, along with 127 women and fifty-seven children, from Natal to Transvaal, resisting colonial authorities, defying prohibitory orders, filling jails. This great satyagraha led to the Indian Relief Act in 1914, with the repeal of harsh taxes and recognition of native marriages. Gandhi left South Africa later that year, but his struggle for the oppressed Indians in that distant theatre of resistance turned him into a Mahatma.

In India too, Gandhi's ideas met with widespread support. Arguably, Indians were divided, disarmed and demoralized; they might never have beaten the British at their own game.[15] Perhaps, that was the reason they supported Gandhian methods so ardently. What Gandhi did was not so much to kick out the British, as make India too difficult to govern. After World War II, the British were sapped, exhausted, and the Indian empire seemed no longer profitable or viable.

The freedom struggle led by the Mahatma in the loincloth, ethically empowered Indians enormously, partly through their own suffering and partly through their rulers' discomfiture. Gandhi, through ahimsa and satyagraha, wrested the moral and media advantage; Indians lost not only their respect for their colonizers, but what is more important, ceased to fear them.

Gandhi proclaimed that women better suited satyagraha temperamentally, having honed their skills in patience, suffering, and surviving over generations in a patriarchy. Hard-headed votaries of realpolitik, even feminists, may well scoff at these Gandhian ideas, but the victories he achieved in the realms of the spirit bore concrete results in the material, political plane. Mass awakening, non-cooperation, widespread civil unrest and unprecedented participation of women and depressed classes in the freedom struggle, complemented by a string of rebellions, mutinies, and finally, the assault of Subhas Chandra Bose's Azad Hind Fauj in the north-east, albeit repulsed – all these not only shook the very foundations of the British Empire in India but made freedom and political independence imminent, inevitable.

Gandhi's great discovery, then, was quite contrary to Marx's observation that British rule in India was a regrettable but necessary phenomenon, fulfilling 'a double mission … one destructive, the other regenerating – the annihilation of old Asiatic society and the laying of the material foundations of Western society in Asia.' Marx had little understanding and less respect for India's traditional Hindu civilization, which he regarded as 'a brutalizing worship of nature, exhibiting its degradation in the fact that man, the sovereign of nature, fell down on his knees in adoration of Kanuman [sic], the monkey, and Sabbala, the cow'.[16]

Let's proceed to the second Gandhi moment, not of victory but failure, when he bore witness right unto his martyrdom (*balidan* or *shahadat*), to the Partition and the incredible bloodbath that accompanied our Independence. In the second half of my book, *The Death and Afterlife of Mahatma Gandhi,* I have focused on Gandhi's last 133 days in Delhi.[17] After dousing the communal conflagration in Kolkata, brokering an amazing peace accord between feuding Hindus and Muslims, the frail and sick-in-the-soul Mahatma arrives in Delhi on 9 September 1947. It is raining and his normal place of residence, the sweepers' colony, is no longer available because of security concerns. He is sent to the palatial Birla House, where less than five months later, on 30 January 1948, he is shot dead. Gandhi thus performs his last yagna or sacrifice, saving India from perpetual, never-ending civil war. He stops the recurring re-enactment of the Partition in endless and mimetic cycles of internecine bloodletting. Prepared to die, he actually offered his own life as *ahuti*, oblation, to this sacred task.

How does Gandhi accomplish this? On the one hand, he appeals to Hindus not to drive Muslims out of Delhi in retaliation for the Hindus and Sikhs forced out of Pakistan. 'You cannot secure justice,' he says, 'by doing injustice to the Muslims.'[18] On the other hand, he exhorts Muslims in Delhi to 'unequivocally condemn the Pakistan Government where it had departed from the civilized conduct and demand that all those Hindus and Sikhs who had to leave their homes in Pakistan should be invited to return with full guarantee of their safety and self-respect'. He insists on replacing the cycle of reciprocal violence with one of reciprocal peace. In making such a demand, Gandhi admits: 'I am told that the whole thing was started by the Muslims. It is true. ... But,' he adds in the very next breath, 'what is the point in harping on it all the time?'

Though exhausted and deeply distressed, Gandhi devotes all his energies to saving the newly independent, fragile nation, which he likens to a wrecked boat. Partition, he acknowledges, is a big mistake: 'I realize what a blunder we have committed in partitioning the country...' but '... we continue to make more and more blunders.' In a letter to an unnamed correspondent, he cries in anguish, 'If heart unity is not restored in Delhi, I can see flames raging all over India. ...Hence, night and day, I turn to Him. I say: "O God, come. Gajaraja[19] is sinking – India is sinking – save her."' He is sure that if Delhi is won, Pakistan will also turn; he did not see his peace mission ending in Delhi: 'When I go to Pakistan I will not spare them. I shall die for the Hindus and the Sikhs there.'

Before he was assassinated, Gandhi went on a five-day fast, his last. The doctors predicted that it will kill him, but that did not deter him. Only a written pledge from all of Delhi's warring factions to end violence persuaded him to break it. Delhi's Muslim citizenry, which had fled from Chandni Chowk and Daryaganj, now returned to their homes. Eyewitness accounts attest to the miraculous change in atmosphere. Delhi, nay, India was saved. A few days later, cleansed in body and spirit, when peace was restored, Gandhi fell to his assassin's bullets, having co-scripted his own end-game.

JNU... and What's 'Left' of the Nation

Let us, using Gandhi as our link, now turn to JNU and our present situation. From his lifelong advocacy of the immediacy and ultimacy of ahimsa, Gandhi in his final phase came to admit that very few had understood non-violence. For most Indians it was merely passive resistance, the only weapon of an unarmed and fearful subject people against a vastly superior adversary. When the authority of the colonial state was suspended, Indians fell upon each other with shocking barbarism and cruelty, forgetting non-violence. Gandhi was therefore willing to settle for the limited violence of the state in maintaining law and order. That, to him, was preferable to mob violence. He even approved the sending of troops to Kashmir to protect innocent civilians and fend off the invading mercenaries led by Pakistani army generals, who had already laid waste to several towns and killed thousands. Perhaps, those advocating azadi for Kashmir today have forgotten those days of terror, when some of their own ancestors in the Valley were saved from great harm by Indian troops.

Muslim Kashmiri separatists from the Valley, on behalf of whom some of our students have been shouting slogans, would do well to ask where they were when their Kashmiri Pandit brethren were driven out of the Valley just for being Hindus. When the Kashmiris treated their own minorities so badly, didn't they damage their moral right to be treated better as minorities themselves? There is a proxy war going on in Kashmir since Independence; how come azadi-chanters conveniently fail to mention that or speak of Pakistan-occupied, the so-called 'Azad' Kashmir? How 'Azad' is it really? Are even proper elections held there?

When the Kashmiri Pandits were evicted out of Kashmir at gunpoint, their lives and properties threatened, why were there no protests in JNU?

Why are there no agitations when a Sujith – and hundreds of other RSS/BJP workers – are lynched or attacked in north Kerala? Why no morcha for Hindus who are raped, killed, or converted in Pakistan? Or, for the slaying of Hindu priests and leaders in Bangladesh? Similarly, why no protests against Chinese repression in Tibet while Israeli occupation of Palestine is condemned again and again? Clearly, our agitations are neither fair nor even-handed, but divisive and deeply biased. They lack integrity, whether ideological or ethical.

Closer to the trigger for the recent regrettable incidents, whether we agree with the Supreme Court verdict or not, Afzal Guru received due process in the Indian legal system. His trial went on for eight years; there was even the final appeal for a presidential pardon. What due process do Maoists, militants, religious fanatics, and terrorists give to their opponents? These same radical groups, who attack Indian democracy, claim the right to dissent and free speech, guaranteed by the very state and its Constitution that they do not respect and intend to overthrow. Actually, which communist state has given any separatist group the right to secede? They have, contrarily, been imperialists themselves, taking over other people's territories and nations. Look at China's record in Tibet and elsewhere. Surely, this is a major contradiction in our Leftist, anti-statist intellectuals that should be evident to all thinking people.

Some of you have been shouting slogans for azadi. I invite you to consider the difference between Gandhi's idea of swaraj and the separatists' call for azadi. Swaraj is based not just on the demand to be freed from some external power but on self-restraint and self-mastery. Azadi, a word of Persian origin, has the original sense of manumission, of being freed from bondage. It may not be fashionable to admit it, but Islam sanctions slavery; Arabs were among the earlier slavers in Africa, long before the Europeans joined the game. You may burn the *Manusmriti* a hundred times, but how many of you have condemned other holy books for sanctioning practices more heinous and unacceptable, including extermination of infidels, enslaving and raping of captives, and consummation of marriages with minors? Why such double standards? Why selective and motivated condemnation? Is this your idea of azadi? Swaraj, on the other hand, implies a highly responsible, highly evolved personal behaviour and social arrangement. It was not just anti- this or that, it is not just licence to criticize and demand, but a commitment to oneself and to others. Swaraj, clearly, does not end with political independence; it is an ongoing struggle, a daily plebiscite, as a previous speaker rightly said.

What was Gandhi's method to attain swaraj? It was satyagraha, insistence on truth. We must deeply ponder over this because today it seems as if truth is our first casualty. An unprejudiced pursuit of truth is what is meant by the famous phrase, 'scientific temper', that Jawaharlal Nehru, Gandhi's chosen heir and India's first prime minister, advocated. I needn't remind you that our university is named after him. According to the First Schedule of the JNU Act, the university 'shall endeavour to promote' a 'scientific approach to the problems of society'. Scientific temper' is also in the Directive Principles of our Constitution. But do we maintain and pursue it here? More often than we care to admit, don't we resort to half-truths, cover-ups, even outright lies to achieve our ends? Can any ideology justify deceit, duplicity, hypocrisy and insincerity? In the name of perfectly good causes such as equality and social justice, aren't we oftentimes promoting dangerous, divisive and unethical practices? Pitting one community or caste, one class or section of society against the other, aren't we exploiting and misdirecting the gullible, even romantic, idealism of youth? At least we must ask such hard questions.

Of course, when we study human beings and society, we must also have compassion. That is, to me, the essence of the kind of remedial hermeneutics that I have been recommending. Satyagraha implies compassionate dispassion just as ahimsa implies love, not just non-injury. We who seek justice, Bapu famously said, must learn to do justice. Today, we are eager to condemn our opponents; far from doing them justice, we use every occasion to target and attack them. This is a zero-sum game of assured mutual destruction. I have dubbed this polarized state of constant strife in India as our *un*civil war. It is this culture that needs to change, whether inside JNU or outside, in the body politic of India. Let us therefore ask not just 'What the Nation Really Needs to Know', but also what JNU really needs to understand. When the JNUSU president thundered, '*Hum unko bataaenge ki rashtravaad kya hai*!' I wanted to ask, '*Kya hum subko sunate hi rahenge? Hamein kuch bhi sunna nahin hai? Humko sunna bhi chahiye*' – shouldn't we listen too?

Some comrades even go further to say that they don't believe in this bourgeois democracy. If so what is left? Kanhaiya Kumar said yesterday, '*Humara sabse purana sangathan hai, aur humne is desh ke liye bahut ladaai kari hai.*' But I want to ask him, what about the flip-flop of the communists in 1942 when, at their Soviet masters' behest, they declared practically overnight that the imperialist war was suddenly the peoples' war? Soon after Gandhi's assassination in 1948, didn't B.T. Ranadive, the Communist Party of India supremo, coin the slogan, '*Yeh azadi jhooti hai*' (this freedom is fake), and advocate an armed overthrow of the elected government? Again, in 1962, when the Chinese invaded India, didn't E.M.S. Namboodiripad, the communist leader, support the cause of China, branding India as the aggressor? If you don't believe me, go check the record for yourselves.

Similarly, I ask Kanhaiya, who is right here? Didn't you say that Golwalkar[20] met Mussolini? But did you check your facts? It was Dr B.S. Moonje who met Mussolini, not 'Guruji' Golwalkar. Moonje was a Congressman, who later became president of the Hindu Mahasabha, as was Dr Hedgewar, founder of the RSS, also once a member of the Congress party. Moonje met Mussolini in March 1931. According to his diary entries, he was impressed by the discipline and organization of the fascists. No doubt, fascism is anti-democratic, but so is Stalinism, isn't it? Why do you condemn one and not the other? For your information, Gandhi also visited Mussolini later in the same year, 1931, after the Round Table Conference in London. For that matter, Tagore, the other protagonist of our narrative, also met Il Duce, twice, even earlier, in 1926. Does that make them fascists? Guilt by association is quite a lame way of discrediting your ideological opponent.

My point, Kanhaiya-ji, is that you have to check your facts, know what you are talking about. Similarly, when you advocate communism or even socialism, what do you make of the conundrum that the Chinese state, run by the Communist Party of China, recreated private property after abolishing it under Mao? Deng recognized that communism simply didn't work as an economic system and turned China into a capitalist powerhouse, without the labour unions and other safeguards that Western democracies have. Then why are you promoting a failed ideology here? Your call for economic equality is laudable, but how do you propose to enforce it? Through the ballot or the bullet? If the former, aren't you part of the same electoral process that you condemn and discredit? If the latter, then you don't respect the Indian Constitution; then why should the Indian state grant you the rights you demand from it? Aren't such paradoxes of history and ideology worth exploring rather than mouthing the same tired slogans and shibboleths over and over again, as if we are stuck in a time warp?

For my part, I am proud to belong to a country where one so-called 'judicial murder' created such a huge ruckus. Do you know how many judicial murders were committed from 1920 to 1950 in Stalinist USSR? There were over four million political sentencings, out of which 799,455 were executions! As opposed to this, the non-political judicial killings only amounted to 34,228. And how many people do you suppose were sent to gulags and concentration camps in Stalinist USSR? According to official Soviet records, over fourteen million! How many perished there? About 1.7 million.[21] My submission is that communists were clearly anti-democratic. Stalin certainly was; he killed almost all his political opponents; he had Trotsky murdered as well.[22]

What about China's record? What happened during the 'Great Leap Forward' and the 'Cultural Revolution'? Have we forgotten Cambodia's killing fields, instituted by the communist red scourge better known as Khmer Rouge? How many millions perished in such misadventures? I'm not even sure if these unprecedented tragedies of history are properly studied in our Left-dominated JNU.[23] Consider North Korea, probably the only 'orthodox' communist state that still remains in the world. Find out how many people perish there not just from malnutrition, but simply trying to cross over to South Korea.

Look around you: we've hung placards and statements from all over the world endorsing our struggle. But can you show me a statement from north Korea, or for that matter, from China? China, even today, is thirsting for freedom and democracy. I've been there five or six times. I've met many Chinese intellectuals; in a café or over a drink, or in private, they can tell you what they really think. But ask them to take out a morcha, put up a placard or poster in Tiananmen Square, and see what happens! Even an ordinary departmental faculty meeting in any

Chinese university must have a representative of the Communist Party present to enforce the party line. Is that democracy? A recent survey in Hong Kong shows a surprising percentage of the population wishing to emigrate. Though the former British colony is one of the most prosperous parts of the world, so many of its citizens don't want to live under an authoritarian regime.

Indeed, closer home, take the trouble to read the joint resignation letter of Umar Khalid, Anirban and their associates; they quit DSU because there was no room for dissent, no democracy in the so-called *Democratic* Students Union. They felt stifled by the lack of freedom! Are the adherents of such ideologies, with their totalitarian and authoritarian DNA now suddenly going to be champions of freedom and azadi in India? Shouldn't they be unmasked in JNU?

It was not always that we were so one-sided or unquestioning. If you study the history of JNU itself, in the 1970s, Anand Kumar, standing for the 'Free Thinkers', challenged Comrade Prakash Karat, even wresting the post of JNUSU president. The erudite and passionate Trotskyist Jairus Banaji became the leader of JNU's own left opposition, tearing to shreds the reactionary and ill-informed views of veterans like Sitaram Yechury and D.P. Tripathi, who still supported and justified Stalinism.

When Kanhaiya questions the legitimacy of Prime Minister Narendra Modi, saying that the BJP polled only slightly over 30 per cent of the votes, might we also not ask where Kanhaiya derives his own legitimacy from? Kanhaiya secured 1029 votes out of a possible 8000+, which, according to our former vice chancellor, is the student strength of JNU. That's less than 13 per cent. The runner-up, AISA's Vijay Kumar, got 962. So Kanhaiya won by a margin of just sixty-seven votes. Does that make him more legitimate than the prime minister of India? Similarly, when some of you say that you wish to overthrow the elected government of India, from where do you derive you legitimacy? Is it that all the peasants and workers have been polled to give you the right to speak on their behalf?

That is why I invite you to join me in questioning whether JNU is as truly democratic as it is vaunted to be. Isn't it rather a Left-hegemonic space? My own experience in my sixteen-year stint here is that you are subjected to the five 'B's if you dissent from the dominant ideology:

brainwashing, branding, boycott, bullying, browbeating. It's a form of incremental exclusion.[24]

It is well known how the system of patronage works in many Centres and Schools; you can't go against the ruling ideology or clique. The system of academic inbreeding, not tolerated in any good university abroad, is the norm here, ensuring that deeply entrenched interests reproduce and perpetuate themselves. Just check the faculty lists in most Schools; the majority of the faculty, perhaps close to 70 per cent, have degrees – PhDs, not to speak of MPhils, MAs – from JNU. Some came even earlier, to get their BA, and never left. A few of our residents live here year after year without earning a single degree, so welcoming is the system, what with ridiculously low fees and next to no hostel charges, plus subsidized boarding.

A few days back, I was touched to find a fellow JNU-ite carrying a placard on a bicycle that said 'I am not an anti-national'. I hope that no one who questions or critiques the dominant view in JNU is forced to carry a placard saying 'I am not anti-JNU'. Though I have questioned left-hegemonic, bordering on left-dictatorial practices, I love JNU too, no less than any here. Every single book of mine acknowledges JNU, my colleagues, my students. If you allow me to invoke Freud, not just the Thanatos of politics and propaganda thrives here, but also the Eros of all that is creative and life-enhancing; in fact, the former flourishes precisely because it is so deeply tinged with the latter. *Yahan siyasat-bazi ki ek alag masti hain.*

But just so that you have no doubts about where I stand, let me unequivocally express my solidarity with all those who want to protect the autonomy not just of JNU but all educational institutions in our country; I also stand in solidarity with those who demand due process, who believe in democratic institutions not just within a university, but in the whole country. I too hold that genuine freedom, such as we do allow here even if one must fight for it, is the ultimate prerequisite for human well-being and flowering. Marxism, at its best, also shares this ideal, whether or not it permits it in actual practice.

I do not want JNU to be destroyed. It is so hard to build an institution, but so easy to destroy it; a tree which takes a hundred years to grow to its full magnificence may be cut down in a day. This university is a place where so many aspirations have been fulfilled, so many careers launched. *Yahan hazaron khwaishein puri hoti hain*. But above all, it is a place where so many young women and men learn to think for themselves. Therefore, whether we wish to practise the hermeneutics of intermediality and diatopicality or not, I urge you not to reduce all politics to unthinking sloganeering or reactive agitation. I urge you, instead, to interrogate your own positions and critique yourselves too.

Thank you and Jai Hind![25]

*

Notes/References/Bibliography

1. This is a substantially revised version of the lecture I delivered at the JNU 'Teach-In' on 7 March. The original may be viewed on https://www.youtube.com/watch?v=tBAuVr36b1A; transcripts are also available online on various websites, including *Scroll.in* (http://scroll.in/article/804802/did-you-check-your-facts-makarand-paranjape-has-some-questions-for-kanhaiya-leftists-and-jnu). I am grateful to the organizing team of JNUTA for inviting me to speak in the series and the editorial collective for their patience, persistence and inputs.
2. Makarand R. Paranjape. *Making India: Colonialism, National Culture, and the Afterlife of Indian English Authority*. Dordrecht: Springer, 2014 and New Delhi: Amaryllis, 2015.
3. Which, in a slightly modified form, *swasdee,* is the common Thai greeting.
4. He derives it, in turn, from the work of the Indo-Catalan theologist, Raimundo Paniker. Boaventura de Sousa Santos, 'Public Sphere and Epistemologies of the South', *Africa Development*, Vol. 37, No. 1, 2012, pp. 43-67, p. 47.
5. Ibid. p. 48.
6. Rabindranath Tagore, 1918, *Nationalism*, London: Macmillan, e-book.
7. E.P. Thompson, 'Introduction' to Rabindranath Tagore, *Nationalism*, London: Papermac, 1991: pp. 1-17.
8. I develop such an argument at greater length in my essay, 'Tagore's Nation: *Swadeshi Samaj* and the Political Novel', scheduled to be published by

Indian Institute of Advanced Study, Shimla in a volume on 'Tagore's Idea of the Nation'.

9. Sabyasachi Bhattacharya, 'Antinomies of Nationalism and Rabindranath Tagore', *Economic and Political Weekly*, Vol. 51, No. 6, February 2016, pp. 39-45.
10. Rabindranath Tagore, 1919, *The Home and the World*, Trans. Surendranath Tagore, Project Gutenberg, e-book; Tagore, 'Society and State', *The English Writings of Rabindranath Tagore*. Vol. 2, New Delhi: Sahitya Akademi, 1996; Tagore, *Gora*, Trans. Sujit Mukherjee, New Delhi: Sahitya Akademi, 2001; and Fakrul Alam and Radha Chakravarty, eds, *The Essential Tagore*, Cambridge, MA: Harvard University Press, 2011.
11. Quoted in Uma Dasgupta (ed.), 2003, *A Difficult Friendship: Letters of Edward Thompson and Rabindranath Tagore 1913-1940*, New Delhi: Oxford University Press, p. 31.
12. http://www.online-literature.com/tagore-rabindranath/creative-unity/2/
13. Gandhi and Tagore were in London at the same time in 1890, but their paths did not cross. Gandhi was in England qualifying for the Bar, while Tagore spent a few months in England in 1890. Neither of them had any international acclaim then. Gandhi of this period was also more interested in trying to be quite the English gentleman than in India's freedom.
14. The divisions between the left and the right were then not as marked and antagonistic. The founder of the Ghadar Party, Lala Har Dayal, who was an Arya Samaji, wrote a fascinating book called *Karl Marx – the Rishi*. Savarkar was from the ideological right, while India's most celebrated revolutionary, Bhagat Singh, was clearly a communist. But all these revolutionaries saw themselves working for the same anti-imperialistic cause. Today, we have almost forgotten those historical conjunctures.
15. The British Empire was an efficiently run police state designed to exploit the colonies economically and suppress them politically. Every single major opponent of the Raj was neutralized – Tilak was sent to Mandalay, Aurobindo jailed in Alipur, Savarkar transported to Andamans, and Bose forced to flee under disguise. Several thousand less prominent opponents were hanged or incarcerated.
16. Karl Marx, 'The British Rule in India', *The Daily Tribune*, 25 June 1853, at https://www.marxists.org/archive/marx/1853/06/25.htm, accessed on 12 September 2016.

17. Paranjape, 2014, *The Death and Afterlife of Mahatma Gandhi*, Abingdon and New York: Routledge, and New Delhi: Penguin Random House, 2015.
18. Quotations that follow are from Volume 99 of Mahatma Gandhi, *The Collected Works of Mahatma Gandhi,* 100 vols, New Delhi: Publications Division, 1999, e-book version.
19. This refers to the story of Gajendra Moksha from the Bhagavat Purana, which features in many compositions such as Meerabai's, as a paradigm of God's grace that follows a devotee's complete and unconditional surrender.
20. M. (Madhav) S. (Sadashiv) Golwalkar (1906–1973) was second *sarsanghchalak* (chief) of the RSS, a position he occupied for over thirty years. The book, *We or Our Nationhood Defined,* published under his name, was actually an abridged translation of Savarkar's *Rashtra Mimansa.*
21. See, for instance, Stephen G. Wheatcroft's 'Victims of Stalinism and the Soviet Secret Police: The Comparability and Reliability of the Archival Data. Not the Last Word', *Europe-Asia Studies*, Vol. 51, No. 2 (1999): pp. 315–345. The Chinese record has been examined with devastating detail in Frank Dikötter's tetralogy: *The Age of Openness: China Before Mao*, Hong Kong: University of Hong Kong Press, 2008; *Mao's Great Famine: The History of China's Most Devastating Catastrophe, 1958–62*, Bloomsbury, 2010; *The Tragedy of Liberation: A History of the Communist Revolution, 1945–1957*, Bloomsbury, 2013; and most recently, *The Cultural Revolution: A People's History, 1962–1976*, Bloomsbury, 2016.
22. Apologists claim that Lenin was the 'good', while Stalin the 'bad', Communist. But Emma Goodman's account of her visit to the early Soviet Union, *My Disillusionment in Russia* (New York: Doubleday, 1923), suggests otherwise. In Petrograd she heard that free speech was a 'bourgeois superstition' (https://theanarchistlibrary.org/library/emma-goldman-my-disillusionment-in-russia); Sergei Zorin quipped, 'There can be no free speech in a revolutionary period'. At that time, Goldman modestly concedes, 'I had no right to judge.' But even after the so-called revolutionary period, was freedom restored?
23. Not surprisingly, the setting up of faculties in 'scientific socialism' has been smuggled in the JNU Vision statement (http://www.jnu.ac.in/AboutJNU/vision.asp) though there is no such thing in the JNU Act. The myth of scientific socialism, though exploded a long time back, still 'officially' persists in JNU.

24. I was branded even before I joined JNU. During this very crisis, there have been several 'Open Letters' against me. In fact, even my lecture was interrupted, with placards going around alleging that I had signed some petition in Hindi (which I don't recall ever signing). There were attempts to upstage my 'teach-in', with the sudden arrival of Soni Suri while I was speaking, who was introduced and installed right beside me. Kanhaiya Kumar announced himself to be my 'Chair' and, after I'd finished, proceeded to interrogate me himself, without allowing sufficient time to respond.
25. Today is Shivaratri. When the *samudra manthan*, the primal churning of the Milky Way took place, only Shiva of the contesting devas and asuras agreed to swallow the poison that was spewed out. The rest wanted amrita, the nectar of immortality. *Aaj bhi manthan ho raha hai. Is mein se bhi vish aur amrit niklega.* Today, too, no one wants the 'poison' of patriotism, responsibility, tolerance, or service – all that used to go under the notion of 'nation-building'. Instead, it seems we only want our own selfish 'nectar', whether it be less accountability, more entitlements, more unearned privileges. Under such circumstances, only he or she will be considered 'Shiva', the good, the auspicious, the propitious, who worries about the common good, the collective well-being, the welfare of all, even risking individual or group interests, not just to lead, to take others along. The 'poison' of such a nationalism, like *halahala,* may burn our throats, but it will gladden our hearts. I invite you to sample it.

I hadn't ended my lecture with 'Jai Hind,' but it seems not out of place to insert it now, given my stance.

Picture credit: Sorit Gupto, *Down to Earth*

Two Concepts of Nationalism

Prabhat Patnaik

(9 MARCH 2016)

I HAVE BEEN TRAVELLING MUCH OF late, and wherever I go, a mention of the fact that I am from JNU makes people sit up and take notice of me. That is because of the kind of resistance that JNU has been putting up against the NDA government's assault on thought. The present meeting is an instance of this resistance and I am grateful that I have been included among the lecturers invited for exploring the theme of nationalism. I have been in JNU for long and at a rough reckoning may have given close to four thousand classroom lectures; but this lecture is a unique experience for me.

Typically, the term 'nationalism' is always used as if it is a homogeneous category; this, however, is wrong. All of us would draw a distinction between the nationalism invoked by Hitler and the nationalism invoked by Gandhi. But even though we do that, in a good deal of the literature, this distinction is simply not drawn.

As a matter of fact, the entire trajectory of nationalism in Europe was very different from that of the nationalism that came to prevail in the Third World, in the course of the anti-colonial struggle. In Europe, the terms 'nation', 'nation state', and 'nationalism' came into vogue in the seventeenth century, after the Treaty of Westphalia which brought an end to the Eighty Years' War between Spain and the Dutch and the

German phase of the Thirty Years' War. This 'nationalism' had, I believe, at least three important characteristics.

The first characteristic was that it always looked at an enemy within: the Jews everywhere, the Catholics in northern Europe which was Protestant, and the Protestants in southern Europe which was Catholic. It was a nationalism which always picked out an enemy within. It was not an inclusive nationalism, but one directed against this enemy within.

The second feature was that it was a nationalism which was imperialist from the very beginning. Oliver Cromwell, almost within days of the Treat of Westphalia, invaded Ireland, which was the first colony of conquest in the world. And there was an intense struggle over acquiring imperial possessions. Even when the European powers were living in peaceful coexistence of sorts within Europe itself, they were engaged in struggles amongst themselves all over the world – in south India, for instance, where the Carnatic wars were being fought between the English and the French. This struggle for empire was a part of that nationalism which was associated with imperialism from its very inception.

The third feature of that nationalism, to my mind, was that it apotheosized the nation above the people. It was not the people's living standards, the people's conditions of life which were important, but the power, the prestige and the wealth of the nation. This conception underlay not only the ideas of the mercantilists who anyway believed in grabbing as much as possible from the rest of the world to raise their nation's wealth, but also classical political economy. It was, in short, true of all the different strands of bourgeois thought.

Adam Smith's opus was called *An Inquiry into the Nature and Causes of the Wealth of Nations*. The wealth of the nation, it emphasized, had to be increased, even though nowhere in this work was there any suggestion that this increase was going to benefit the people at large, the working people. So the nation was apotheosized above the people. Smith differed from the mercantilists in his conception of what constituted 'wealth', but not of what constituted the 'nation'. 'Wealth', he argued, did not consist in the accumulation of gold and silver as the mercantilists had believed; it consisted in the capital stock of the nation, and capital accumulation was the means of raising the wealth of the nation. But such accumulation was at no point claimed to be of any benefit to the living standard of the people. In the theory of David Ricardo, the other great classical economist, the workers always remained at a subsistence level of wages, no matter how large the capital stock the nation possessed; and yet, an augmentation of this stock was considered eminently desirable.

These features made European nationalism essentially an aggrandizing nationalism. In fact, countries which acquired nationhood rather late in history, Germany being the classical example, felt excluded from this universal aggrandizement, because, by the time they came into their own, the world had been more or less divided up into possessions of the English, the French, the Dutch, and so on. They, therefore, pursued a particularly aggressive form of nationalism. That aggressive form of nationalism at the time when Germany became a nation was associated with financial interests, with finance capital, presided over by financial oligarchies, which had become prominent within capitalism. The outcome of this aggressive rivalry between financial oligarchies belonging to the different European nations was the First World War.

A well-known social democratic writer, Rudolf Hilferding, who wrote a book on finance capital, had said that the ideology of finance capital was the glorification of the national idea. This glorification of the national idea was captured in Erich Maria Remarque's novel *All Quiet on the Western Front*, which many of you might have read. This national idea really got intensified through the war and reached its apogee under fascism. Fascism was the apogee of an aggrandizing nationalism.

The aggrandizing nationalism itself, however, was essentially bourgeois in character (Oliver Cromwell, we must not forget, was the leader of the English bourgeois revolution). It was associated with mercantile capitalism in its early years, with industrial capitalism subsequently, and with financial capitalism in the twentieth century, when it reached its apogee under fascism.

The twentieth-century experience with nationalism in Europe has had a deep impact on progressive opinion there. It is the main reason why progressive opinion in that continent in the aftermath of the Second World War has been so opposed to nationalism, and has supported, and does so to this day, the European Union as a supra-national institution, even though that institution has been dominated by finance capital insistent upon imposing 'austerity' all over Europe, to the detriment of its working people. It has taken it for granted that all 'nationalism' must be synonymous with an aggrandizing nationalism, and hence a replica of European nationalism.

This presumption, however, is wrong. When you look at countries like India where nationalism developed as a part of the anti-colonial struggle, it had to be inclusive because it was taking on the might of an imperial power. This might could be taken on only if the people were united; and, consequently, it had to be an inclusive nationalism. It strived to bring about a situation in which everybody was a part of this nationalism, as opposed to the 'enemy within' which had characterized European nationalism. Because of this, while in progressive circles in Europe after Second World War, as I just said, nationalism was a dirty word associated only with the right, such is not the case in countries like ours. Our nationalism, being a nationalism that was anti-colonial, had to be inclusive.

At the same time, this nationalism also had an enormous sympathy for other nationalisms of an anti-colonial kind that were developing in other parts of the world. It had to have solidarity with the struggles of other people against colonialism and consequently, it was a nationalism that recognized the validity, the legitimacy, of other nationalisms, rather than excluding them. It saw them as part of a common anti-colonial struggle.

The third, and the most important, feature of this nationalism to my mind is that it did not glorify the nation above the people, and the classic quote in this respect is from Gandhi, who saw the essence of freedom as wiping away the tears from the eyes of every Indian. In other words, the focus was on the people. The nation was not above the people; it was constituted by the people.

These were some of the ways in which our anti-colonial nationalism was fundamentally different from the aggrandizing nationalism that developed in Europe and reached, as I said, its zenith in the period of fascism. But all this nationalism of the Third World, not only India but also elsewhere in the Third World, had another feature, which was very important. In order to be inclusive, in order to bring people into the anti-colonial struggle, it had to produce a kind of social contract. You look at the Freedom Charter in South Africa; you look at the Karachi Congress resolution in India; these are all instances of such social contracts. And such instances were replicated explicitly or implicitly elsewhere too where there was resistance to colonial-style oppression.

This kind of nationalism, in short, was based on an agenda, which was an agenda of inclusion, an agenda of democracy and an agenda of egalitarianism. The Karachi Congress resolution of 1931, for example, for the first time talked about universal adult suffrage being the basis for the formation of governments in post-Independence India. It talked about many other things: it talked about juridical equality or equality before law; it talked about secularism in its own way, that the state will have no religion; it even talked about the abolition of capital punishment, which we have not achieved to this day and which is very important to remember on this occasion because the attack on JNU is being sought to be justified on the grounds that the students here are opposed to the hanging of Afzal Guru and Yakub Memon. The Karachi Congress resolution also stated that there would be free and compulsory primary education, which we still don't have. So, it was really a charter, and that charter formed a social contract on the basis of which our nationhood was constituted and which found its way into our Constitution.

What we had in short was a people coming into nationhood, forming, or attempting to form, a nation state, to replace the colonial state. This was very different, as I said, from the aggrandizing nationalism of the European kind.

I do not wish to glorify this nationalism or to pretend that it arose fully formed like Minerva from the head of Zeus. The fact that the bourgeoisie was a leading element of the multi-class, anti-colonial struggle meant that elements of an aggrandizing nationalism, which typically form part of the bourgeois world view, kept intruding into it. Nonetheless, this inclusive anti-colonial nationalism was indubitably conceptually different from the aggrandizing European nationalism.

From its very inception, however, this inclusive nationalism had a lot of internal enemies. If you are talking about equality, if you are talking about equality before law, if you are talking about universal adult franchise, you are really dealing an incredibly powerful blow to the millennia-old caste structure. In a situation of institutionalized inequality that had prevailed in our country for millennia, to say that a Dalit would have the same political rights as a Brahmin, would have a vote having the same value as that of the Brahmin, was a revolutionary statement. Remarkably, it was made in 1931. Let us not forget that even in France, universal adult franchise came only in 1945; in India it came in 1952, but was visualized in 1931 itself. Britain had moved towards universal adult franchise only in 1928 when women got the vote, though some restrictions on franchise had still remained at that time.

The idea of everybody having an equal vote and therefore choosing the government together, was, for traditional India, a truly revolutionary concept. I come from a village in Odisha, which was dominated by Brahmin landlords and I remember how scandalized they were during the 1952 elections that their vote would have the same value as that of the village Dalits. So it was really a substantial change, which obviously had its own enemies to start with, namely, the dominant forces of the traditional Hindu society.

One of our JNU colleagues, Professor Suvira Jaiswal from the history department, has argued, very persuasively to my mind, that the essence of Hinduism is the caste system. No matter what else changed about it, the caste system continued to remain at the core of Hinduism. And the fact that a modern India was coming up that dealt a conceptual blow against the caste system, was, from the very beginning, anathema for the dominant forces of the traditional society.

Many people have talked of an egalitarian tradition in Indian society. Of course there was a subterranean egalitarian tradition, but the dominant tradition, which was that of a society based on caste system, was inegalitarian. So, looking at modern India as in some sense a continuation of traditional India, is a view I don't share. Modern India should rather be seen as one in which people lift themselves up with their own bootstraps in order to constitute a nation; and it comes into being in the course of the anti-colonial struggle.

Enmity towards this inclusive, egalitarian nationalism also came from a second source, namely, capital. Capitalism, because of its inherently inequalizing tendencies, is really incompatible with the coming into being of such a nation. If the ideal is egalitarian, capitalism is obviously not the means towards it. In fact, whether you look at Gandhi or Ambedkar or Nehru, they all believe that capitalism is not the solution to India's problems: each of them, no doubt, had a different idea of what the solution was in terms of the economic regime, but all of them were united on this point. They could see that capitalism with its inequalizing tendencies was incompatible with the social contract underlying the nation that was coming into being.

For a while what we tried to develop in the Nehruvian era was a controlled capitalism, a regulated capitalism, in which even though capitalists would be there, they would be so restrained by controls and regulations that they could not do much damage, that the inequalizing tendencies of capitalism could be reined in.

But that presumption itself was false to start with; and with neo-liberalism, even those controls have all gone. In the last few years, as we know, inequalities have risen dramatically and a corporate financial oligarchy has come into being which is much more aligned to global finance. The Indian economy as an integrated unit is of little interest to it. Our corporate groups buy companies elsewhere, just as advanced countries' companies take over companies here and in the rest of the Third World. The new corporate financial oligarchy becomes a major opponent of the inclusive nationalism engendered by the anti-colonial struggle, because this inclusive nationalism is fundamentally opposed to all that neo-liberalism stands for.

These two elements opposed to inclusive nationalism, namely, on the one side the dominant forces of the traditional Hindu society, who, whether they admit it or not, are defenders of the caste system, and on the other side the modern corporate oligarchy, come together to attack this nationalism. And they do so through a simple conceptual trick, of obliterating it altogether. The trick consists, in other words, in the fact that they substitute an aggrandizing nationalism for the democratic, egalitarian, inclusive nationalism and deny the very existence of the latter as a sui generis entity. This is the reason why I say that it is very important to draw distinctions, to distinguish between alternative concepts of nationalism.

Yesterday, I saw in the papers that Arun Jaitley has accused Rahul Gandhi of betraying his father, grandmother and great-grandfather, saying that while they had stood for nationalism, Rahul Gandhi was hobnobbing with the 'anti-nationals' of JNU. The real point, however, is that the 'nationalism' Nehru had talked about and the 'nationalism' in terms of which those with whom Rahul Gandhi is hobnobbing are considered 'anti-national', are not identical terms.

In other words, there is a deception whereby the concept of nationalism as an inclusive, egalitarian, democratic concept is substituted by an aggrandizing nationalism; and the moral high ground that the former has historically occupied in the eyes of the people is then sought to be appropriated by the latter. The claim is that the nationalism the government stands for is the same as what Gandhi had stood for, but that the JNU students stand for something altogether different.

In fact, you may recall, Gandhi had been insistent that fifty-five crore of rupees which were due to Pakistan should be handed over to that country, against a lot of pressure at that time, including from within the Congress. So, what Gandhi had stood for as 'nationalism' is very different from what this government is calling 'nationalism'. But this verbal trick is playing a very important role in misleading people and we should be sensitive to that.

The second thing which I want to draw your attention to is the following. If it is a nationalism based on a social contract, how can it be ensured that this contract is going to be honoured? How can it be ensured that there is no violation of this contract by the dominant segments of society, by the dominant groups of society, by the dominant regions inside the country? There was a very simple answer that Lenin had provided to this question, namely that in big, heterogeneous countries which consist of large numbers of different ethnic, linguistic or other groups, the right to secession must be allowed. If anybody feels that the contract is being violated, such an entity must have the right to secede; and the very fact that this right to secede is recognized would also prevent the dominant segments from doing things that would make people secede.

Now, in India of course the right to secede was never a part of the Constitution. Kashmir was given a special status, but the right to secede was never written into the Constitution. Precisely because of this fact, however, it is very important that whenever questions are raised about the violation of the social contract, they must be discussed. In other words, there must be an openness, through which people can raise issues of the violation of the social contract upon which the modern Indian nation is based.

And if that is the case, calling somebody 'anti-national' for raising such issues is against the spirit of this inclusive nationalism. In other words, one of the features of this inclusive nationalism is that people should not be called 'anti-national' for raising issues regarding exclusion or oppression of marginalized segments or regions. No expression of an opinion on such issues, as distinct from actual armed action or materially aiding and abetting such action, can possibly be construed an offence according to this inclusive nationalism.

This is not just an empty ideal. Notwithstanding many transgressions, of which in my view the arrest of Sheikh Muhammad Abdullah was one obvious example, there has actually been in the past a degree of tolerance towards the expression of such opinions. For instance, for a very long time, the CPI (M), the biggest communist party in the country, actually had in its programme a recognition of the right to secession. This was changed much later, in the 1970s; and it was changed on the grounds that this might be used by imperialism, not on the grounds that this was an 'anti-national' demand. Hence, when Jyoti Basu became the deputy chief minister of West Bengal in 1967 and 1969, the party he belonged to actually recognized the right to secession. Yet, nobody said that his party was anti-national; nobody said he could not be the deputy chief minister of West Bengal because he belonged to an anti-national party.

The fact that in the course of a people becoming a nation on the basis of a social contract, many would raise voices that the social contract is being violated, is something which is to be accepted, which is to be recognized, and which is to be tolerated. And typically, the ideal in India was to tolerate all of this. The fact that we are not doing so today is because, as I said, we are moving away from one notion of nationalism to another notion of nationalism, from the inclusive, anti-colonial notion of nationalism to an alternative, aggrandizing notion of nationalism.

This aggrandizing notion of nationalism to my mind is the ideology of the corporate–communal alliance which currently rules the country. It is a useful ideology for this alliance because once the term 'nation' is defined in this aggrandizing sense, as a metaphysical concept placed above the people, what exactly constitutes being 'national' becomes subject to interpretation by the government. It may be laid down, for instance, that observing karva chauth is national and not doing so is anti-national, that eating beef is anti-national, and so on. The discourse, in short, can be so manipulated that 'national' gets identified with the practices of the Hindu religion. Likewise, it may be laid down that anybody who opposes the 'Make in India' campaign (supposed to make the 'nation' great) is ipso facto anti-national, in which case objections to concessions to the corporate oligarchy under this campaign may be deemed anti-national. In short, a concept of nationalism which identifies it with aggrandizing nationalism and places the nation above the people is useful both to the Hindutva elements and to the corporate interests, which is why it becomes increasingly the ideology of the corporate–communal alliance.

What it leads to is a destruction of thought. Any thinking must be associated with raising questions, and to these questions there will always be at any time a multiplicity of answers. Hence, in any society at any given time, there will always be people holding all kinds of divergent views. If views different from what the government considers 'acceptable' are suppressed on the plea of their being anti-national, you are in effect destroying thought, putting pebbles into peoples' minds and preventing them from thinking for themselves.

This attempt at destruction of thought is a very serious phenomenon and it is not surprising that the most outstanding institutions in the country, whether it is the Film and Television Institute of India, or the fine arts department of M.S. University, Baroda, or JNU, or the Hyderabad Central University, or the Jadavpur University, are the ones currently under attack.

There is another feature of these institutions that I would like to draw your attention to, namely that they are all publicly funded institutions. You don't find any opposition arising in private universities or private institutions. I'm not blaming the students of private universities or institutions, but because they are constrained willy-nilly to get commoditized, a process of destruction of thought which necessarily comes with the commoditization of education, has already become institutionalized there. It is the few places which, because of their character of being publicly funded, have avoided getting commoditized until now, and which therefore still constitute sites of critique, of discussion, and of intellectual vibrancy and excellence, that are now being targeted.

A government that destroys the best institutions of the country, that destroys thought, is effectively making the country parasitic on foreign countries for ideas. It is a matter of supreme irony that this very government (and the Hindutva forces behind it) talks of nationalism! Indeed it justifies its act of promoting parasitism on advanced countries for ideas in the name of nationalism! Making the country completely dependent on imperialism for ideas is sought to be justified in the name of nationalism!

So, the struggle in which you are engaged at JNU is for exposing this aggrandizing nationalism, for defending thought, for defending the critical tradition that has been built up here, and for striving for excellence. These constitute a necessary condition for us to be able to respect the social contract on the basis of which this nation was formed. I wish you all success.

*

Notes/References/Bibliography

Akeel Bilgrami, 2014, *Secularism, Identity and Enchantment*, Cambridge, Mass.: Harvard University Press.

Prabhat Patnaik, 'Nationalism, Hindutva, and the Assault on Thought', *The Marxist,* Vol. XXXII, No. 1, January-March, 2016.

Picture credit: Gayatri Balusha

राष्ट्रवाद की कल्पनाः स्मृति, मिथक और उग्र हिन्दुत्व

बद्री नारायण

(10 मार्च 2016)

मैं आभारी हूँ आप सब का, विशेषकर जे.एन.यू छात्रसंघ का और जे.एन.यू के अध्यापक संघ का, कि मुझे आपने मौका दिया इस विषय पर अपनी बात कहने के लिए। बात जो कहनी है, वो तो कहनी है। लेकिन उसकी शुरूआत मैं करना चाहता हूँ कुछ ऐसे दो–तीन वृत्तांतों से, जिससे आपको मालूम होगा कि दलितों के स्वप्न में या मन में राष्ट्रवाद की क्या संकल्पना थी या वो कैसा राष्ट्र चाह रहे थे। उनके मन में किस तरह की राष्ट्रीय कल्पना थी और कैसा राष्ट्र बना कर उनको दिया जा रहा है या बनाने की बात की जा रही है। या जिस तरह से देशप्रेम और देशविरोध के लिए जो राष्ट्र खड़ा किया जा रहा है, उस राष्ट्र का उन दलितों के मन के राष्ट्र से क्या संबंध है? इस पर मैं बात करुंगा। और मैं आपको याद दिलाना चाहता हूँ 1950 के बाद का समय जब जवाहरलाल नेहरू इलाहाबाद के फूलपुर से चुनाव लड़ते थे। उस समय उनके चुनाव प्रचार में जो मंच होता था, उस मंच पर कई बार दलित गायक और लोक गायक गीत गाया करते थे। उन गीतों में राष्ट्रवाद का स्वप्न झलकता था। और कई बार तो यह होता था कि नेहरू के भाषण के बाद भी गीत चलता रहता था। लोग नेहरू जी को सुनने आते थे, उनसे ज़्यादा या कम तो मैं नहीं कहूँगा, लेकिन लोग उन गायकों को सुनने आते थे। वे उन गायकों को सुनने आते थे जो

(Editors' Note: This lecture was based on the author's published writings, as listed in the references, and on ongoing field research.)

दलित समाज के थे और वे अपने गीत गाया करते थे। तो यह जो संदेश होता था, वह सिर्फ नेहरू का नहीं होता था, वो उन दलित गायकों का भी होता था। और वो संयुक्त संदेश होता था जो दलित गायक या दलित मन और नेहरू के मन का स्वप्न उन दिनों हुआ करता था। उसमें बाद में बिखराव आया। उसके अलग कारण हैं, उस पर बाद में बात की जा सकती है। तो जो गीत था, वह नवाबगंज, फूलपुर के पास के रामराज नाम के गायक के थे जो अवधी–भोजपुरी मिली हुई भाषा में गाया करते थे। नेहरू जी की सभा चल रही थी और वो गीत था...

भारत स्वर्गलोक होइ जइहैं
धीर धरा सजनी
धीर धरा सजनी
छुआ–छूत के भेद मिटिहैं
ई देखा बुधिमानी
पंडित धोबी के घर खइहैं
धीर धरा सजनी
भारत स्वर्गलोक होइ जइहैं
धीर धरा सजनी
बिद्या के प्रचार हय भारी
अब खुल गए मदरसा
बिजली टेबुल नहर गरे में
नाही बांटे अरसा
नदिया दूधन से भर जइहैं
धीर धरा सजनी
इसके आगे रामराज कहते हैं–
लेना देना सब छुट जइहैं
पूंजीपति माथ पकड़ के रोइहें
धीर धरा सजनी[1]
फिर इसमें वे आगे कहते हैं–
मनई हवाई जहाज से उड़िहें

धीर धरा सजनी

फिर वे आगे कहते हैं–

खाए के चावल मिलिहैं

धीर धरा सजनी

आप कल्पना करिए कि उन्नीस सौ पचपन के आसपास जो स्वप्न था उसमें खाने के चावल का भी स्वप्न था और हवाई–जहाज़ पर उड़ने का भी स्वप्न था और पूंजीपति माथ पकड़ के रोए, इसका भी स्वप्न था। तो इस इस गीत की जो क्रिटिकल लाइन है, वह है कि पूंजीपति माथ पकड़ के रोइहें धीर धरा सजनी। प्रश्न है कि क्या पूंजीपति माथ पकड़ के रो रहा है या नहीं रो रहा है। अगर नहीं रो रहा है तो क्यों नहीं रो रहा है? तो इसका उत्तर आपके पास है कि आज जो व्यवस्था है, वह किस तरह की है?

जब राम जन्मभूमि का आंदोलन चल रहा था और हम लोग उत्तर प्रदेश के गाँवों में काम कर रहे थे। इसके द्वारा मैं एक दूसरी स्थिति की ओर आपको इशारा करना चाहता हूँ– एक छोटी सी कथा के माध्यम से। यह कथा एक दलित व्यक्ति ने मुझे स्वयं सुनाई थी जब हम लोग अयोध्या के पास के एक गाँव में फील्डवर्क कर रहे थे। हमने एक उत्तरदाता दलित साथी से पूछा कि राम जी का तो बड़ा आंदोलन चल रहा है, इतना बड़ा आंदोलन चल रहा है, और आप लोग क्या कर रहे हैं इस समय? आप लोग क्या इसमें शामिल नहीं हैं या शामिल हैं? तो उसने बड़े उदास मन से कहा कि भैया हम लोग तो बस देखने वाले लोग हैं। हमने कहा क्यों देख रहे हैं आप, इतनी कोशिश हो रही है, आडवाणी जी अभी–अभी गुज़रे हैं, और बहुत सारी घटनाएं हो रही हैं। तो वह बोला कि नहीं बस रहने दीजिए। मैं नहीं बोलूंगा। हमने कहा, नहीं कुछ तो बताइए, फिर मैंने बहुत खोदा–बहुत खोदा तो उसने एक कहानी सुनाई। और अब मैं आपको वह कहानी सुनाता हूँ।

कहानी कुछ यों है कि राजा दशरथ के चार बेटे थे– राम, लक्ष्मण, भरत और शत्रुघ्न। और एक बार राजा दशरथ बाहर घूमने जा रहे थे तो उन्होंने देखा कि एक सुंदर हिरणी का छौना खेल रहा है। तो राजा दशरथ को लगा कि इसको हम ले चलें घर में तो इससे राम, लक्ष्मण, भरत और शत्रुघ्न खेलेंगे। तो वो उसको पकड़ना चाह रहे थे और छौना पकड़ में नहीं आ रहा था। तो राजा दशरथ ने अपने धनुष पे तीर चढ़ाया और उसको उसको बींध दिया, हिरन का बच्चा मर गया। वो उसको मरी हुई दशा में घर ले गए। घर ले जाकर उन्होंने रानी कौशल्या को दिया कि इससे बच्चा खेलेगा। और उधर उस हिरण के छौने की माँ घर में इंतज़ार कर रही थी। देर हो गई, रात हो गई, फिर वो निकली बाहर खोजने उस बच्चे को तो

किसी ने बताया कि राजा दशरथ ने उसे मार दिया है। तो वो पहुँची रानी कौशल्या के पास और रानी से कहा कि रानी ये हमारा जो बच्चा है, वो दे दीजिए। तो उन्होंने कहा कि अब तो यह मर गया है, तुम इसे लेकर क्या करोगी? इससे राम खेलेगा, लक्ष्मण खेलेंगे। तो उसने बोला कि नहीं इसको दे दीजिए मुझे। मैं इसको अपने घर ले जाऊँगी, और इसकी खाल में भूसा भरवाकर रखूंगी। एक तो इसको देख–देख कर मैं अपने मन को सांत्वना दूंगी कि मेरा बेटा अभी भी जीवित है। और दूसरा इससे मेरा दूध निकलेगा। जब तक बच्चा नहीं होता है, तब तक माँ का दूध नहीं निकलता है। तो उस हिरणी ने कहा कि यह बच्चा हमें दे दीजिए। रानी ने कहा कि नहीं, इसकी खाल से खंजड़ी बनेगी, और इस खंजड़ी से राम खेलेगा। और उन्होंने उसे नहीं दिया। तो उस दलित उत्तरदाता ने कहा कि हम उस वंश के लोग हैं, हिरणी के वंश के लोग। हम लोग दूर से इस खंजड़ी को बजते देख रहे हैं, जो अयोध्या में बज रही है। आप समझ सकते हैं कि किस तरह की एक प्रति–संस्कृति दलितों के मन में, इस पूरे जो जो राममय राष्ट्रवाद है, जो राम–केंद्रित राष्ट्रवाद है, के प्रति है। मैं राम की आलोचना नहीं करता, राम के साथ हम सबका अपनी तरह का जुड़ाव हो सकता है। मैं आपको बताना चाहता हूँ कि राम की राजनीति पर केंद्रित जो राष्ट्रवाद था, उस राष्ट्रवाद की कैसी कटु आलोचना एक दलित के मन में पल रही थी। उसके बाद एक तीसरी बात मैं आपको बताना चाहता हूँ । उसके बाद मैं फिर विस्तार से बताऊँगा आपको। वह तीसरी बात भी एक कथा के माध्यम से ही बताना चाहता हूँ।

कथा राष्ट्रीय स्वयंसेवक संघ के बारे में है। जब भी मैं शब्द आरएसएस कहूँगा, संघ परिवार कहूँगा, उसमें तीनों पार्टियां, तीनों तरह के विश्व हिन्दू परिषद, आरएसएस और भारतीय जनता पार्टी शामिल होंगे। अलग–अलग संबोधन करने में थोड़ी दिक्कत होगी। तो इस आरएसएस ने उत्तर प्रदेश के गाँवों में शाखा के विस्तार की जो राजनीति शुरू की उसका निर्णय गोरखपुर के अपने कनवेंशन में लिया कि अब उत्तर प्रदेश के गाँव–गाँव में आरएसएस की शाखा खोली जाए और धीरे–धीरे पूरे देश के गाँवों में फैला जाए क्योंकि पहले संघ शहरों पर केंद्रित हुआ करता था, धीरे–धीरे उसे गाँवों में फैलाना है। और उसके तहत वो गाँवों में जो रामलीला हुआ करती थी, उन रामलीला मंडलियों के साथ संघ के लोगों ने काम करना शुरू किया। और उनके साथ मिलके रामलीला आयोजित करनी शुरू की। और इस रामलीला के काम को एक–एक जगह हम लोग दर्ज कर रहे थे। रामलीला की तैयारी चल रही थी और इस रामलीला में पात्रों के रोल बांटे जा रहे थे, हम लोग एक–एक चीज़ दर्ज कर रहे थे हर उस प्रक्रिया का कि कैसे ये लोग कर रहे हैं और उसमें रामलीला खेलने वाले तो गाँव के थे लेकिन जो आयोजक थे वो स्थानीय प्रचारक थे जो आरएसएस के थे। उसमें दलितों को छोटे–छोटे कैरेक्टर्स दिए गए। जामवंत के, कुछ भालुओं के, कुछ बंदरों के, तो थोड़ी देर बाद उन लोगों ने नाराज़गी व्यक्त की और कहा कि

हम लोगों को राम का कैरेक्टर दो, हम लोगों को लक्ष्मण का रोल दो। हम लोगों को क्यों ये वानर–भालू का रोल दिए हुए हो? उसमें एक विवाद शुरू हो गया। और ये बड़ी मुश्किल हो गई हमारे संघ के जो प्रचारक थे उस समय जो आयोजन कर रहे थे कि कैसे उस अंतर्विरोध को सम्हाला जाए। इस राम के रोल की जो कामना है, ये कामना दो बात बताती है। एक बात तो ये बताती है कि कि हमें केंद्रीय भूमिका चाहिए। हमें जो तुम किनारे बैठाकर एक निम्न स्तर पर रखना चाहते हो, यह अब हमें मंज़ूर नहीं है। दूसरी यही चाहत रमाशंकर कठेरिया जैसे लोगों के वृत्तांतों को भी गढ़ती है। क्योंकि जिनको लगता है कि वो राम के वृत्तांत से राम के कैरेक्टर के साथ जुड़ते हैं, तो वो कठेरिया जैसे बयान देना शुरू कर देते हैं। तो ये दोनों ही अर्थ उसके हैं। मैं आपको बताता हूँ कि कैसे आरएसएस ने राष्ट्रवाद के अपने मॉडल से गाँवों में इस राष्ट्रवादी चेतना का प्रचार किया है। और इस राष्ट्रवादी चेतना के प्रसार के लिए गाँव की मैपिंग की जाए। गाँव कैसा हो, भारत का गाँव कैसा हो, इसके बारे में सोचा जाए, और समझा जाए। एक सज्जन हैं और अब वे नहीं रहे, दिवंगत हो गए। लेकिन इसके पहले उन्होंने अपनी आत्मकथा लिखी। वीएचपी के राष्ट्रीय सचिव, रामजी सिंह रामफल भाई उनका नाम था। और रामफल भाई ने अपनी आत्मकथा में ये लिखा है। उन्होंने याद करना शुरू किया कि हमारे समय में गाँव कैसा होता था। वे साठ–सत्तर साल के व्यक्ति थे और जब याद कर रहे हैं तो 1929–30 का गाँव याद कर रहे हैं। और वो मुरादाबाद के पास के गाँव के रहने वाले थे। तो वे बता रहे हैं कि हमारे समय में गाँव में जब भी मुसलमान बदमाशी करते थे, तो दलित और ऊँची जाति मिल के उनको बहुत मारते थे, बहुत पीटते थे। और दलित उस समय लाठी लेकर के खड़े रहते थे ऊँची जाति के साथ, उनको दुरुस्त करने के लिए। और भारत का गाँव ऐसा ही होना चाहिए जिसमें दलित हमारे साथ खड़ा हो करके हमारे साथ, मतलब ऊँची जाति के साथ; और वो दलित मुसलमानों को पीट सकें, मार सकें, उनको दुरुस्त कर सकें। उनका कहना था कि हमारे समय में गाँव ऐसे होते थे, अब गाँव बहुत विकृत होते जा रहे हैं, गाँवों में एकता टूटती जा रही है। ख़ासकर के दलितों और ऊंची जातियों में एकता टूटती जा रही है। तो कैसे इस एकता को बनाए रखा जाए ये उनकी चिंता है। तो आरएसएस ने अपनी विलेज मेकिंग जो अभियान शुरू किया, गाँव को बनाने का जो अभियान शुरू किया, उसका केंद्रीय सूत्र है कि कैसे एक मुस्लिम वर्सेस हिंदू की एक घृणा की पूरी पॉलिटिक्स के साथ एक गाँव बनाया जाए। एक गाँव नहीं सारे गाँव बनाए जाएं भारत के जहाँ–जहाँ मुस्लिम आबादी है, वहाँ–वहाँ उनको दुरुस्त किया जाए।

तो इस पूरी परिकल्पना में आप देखेंगे तो मुसलमानो से दलितों को एक सैनिक के रूप में ऊँची जातियों के नेतृत्व में लड़ना चाहिए। या ऊँची जाति के लोग उनके

साथ मिल के लड़ें और इसमें दलित लड़ें, मरे, कटें। लेकिन जो शासन है, जो जीत है, वह ब्राह्मिनिकल कल्चर की हो, जो हिंदुत्ववादी संस्कृति है, उसकी हो। तो ये प्रत्यक्ष में बात मैं बता रहा हूँ जो पहले ही लिखा हुआ है और उनकी पॉलिटिक्स का हिस्सा है। यह इस बात से ज़ाहिर होता है कि जो मूल परिकल्पना है, हिंदुत्वादी राष्ट्रवाद के एजेंडे की वो एक हेट्रेड पर, एक घृणा पर टिकी हुई है। इस घृणा में जो बनाम है, वह मुसलिम है और उसके बरक्स एक ऐसी एकता बनाने की बात की जा रही है जिसमें दलित मार्शल रेस की तरह उनके साथ लड़ें–मरें–कटें, और इस तरह का गाँव बनाया जाए। और इस तरह का गाँव बनाने के लिए राजनीति कैसे की जाए, उसका आधार क्या हो, कैसे उसको गढ़ा जाए, कैसे उसको रचा जाए, इसकी जो पूरी परिकल्पना है, मैं उसके बारे में आपको बता रहा हूँ। सामाजिक समरसता एक बहुत रोचक प्रक्रिया है जो गाँवों में आरएसएस ने शुरू की है। नाम तो सामाजिक समरसता है, लेकिन अगर आप सामाजिक समरसता अभियान की सभाओं में जाएं, तो आप देखेंगे कि वह सामाजिक घृणा का अभियान है। उसमें एक तरह से घृणा पैदा की जा रही है। ये शुरू हुआ महाराष्ट्र में, फिर ये उत्तर प्रदेश में आया, फिर बिहार, फिर सारे राज्यों में फैलाया गया। इसमें बाला साहब देवरस जो आरएसएस के थे, या और भी जो उनके लीडर्स हैं, वो सारे जाते थे और दलित बस्तियों में बैठ करके दलितों के साथ खिचड़ी खाने का अभियान शुरू किया गया। और खिचड़ी खाने के पहले एक बातचीत होती थी, एक डिस्कशन होता था, जो आज भी होता है। जहाँ भी होता है सामाजिक समरसता अभियान वहाँ पर ये भाषण होगा। अगर उस भाषण को दर्ज कर लें, उन बातों को सुनें तब आपको लगेगा कि कैसे घृणा पैदा की जा रही है। उसमें एक बहुत रोचक, एक सामाजिक समरसता अभियान में एक गीत बनाया गया। और वो गीत उत्तर प्रदेश की एक महिला प्रचारक ने गढ़ा जो दुर्गावाहिनी की है। यह उनकी महिला शाखा है। और उसमें भी मैं इसलिए बता रहा हूँ कि यह पूरा केंद्रीयकरण जो इस राष्ट्रवाद का है, वह कैसे एक अल्पसंख्यक विरोध और एक बनाम पर टिका हुआ है। और उस बनाम में दलितों की भूमिका कहाँ है, वो आपको मैं बताना चाहता हूँ। उन्हें कहाँ पर रखा जाता है, और कैसे दलित उसके ख़िलाफ़ प्रतिरोध करते हैं और कैसे बदलते हैं उस पूरी कहानी को। तो उसमें एक गीत बनाया गया जो सामाजिक समरसता अभियान में गाया जाता था। उस गीत में एक राजा की बेटी है जो जा रही है डोली पर, उसको एक मुस्लिम शासक आकर उसका हरण करना चाहता है, और उसपर आक्रमण करता है तो एक उसमें फिर बताया जाता है कि एक दलित लड़का आता है, जो वहाँ गाय चरा रहा होता है तो वो आकर के वहाँ उस लड़की को बचाता है। और उस मुस्लिम शासक को मारता है। मुस्लिम जो आक्रांता है, उसको मारता है। आप देखिए कि लोकगीत में जो लोक संस्कृति है, पॉपुलर कल्चर है वहाँ भी कैसे कम्युनल इंटरवेंशन किए जाते हैं। और कम्युनल इंटरवेंशंस के साथ एक वर्सेस खड़ा

करना और हेट्रेड की भाषा खड़ा करना, वो सामाजिक समरसता अभियान के माध्यम से चलाया जा रहा है, और वो उनका सबसे बड़ा अभियान है जो दलितों को जोड़ने के लिए किया जाता है। और इसी अभियान के तहत जो इसमें सबसे रोचक है कि अगर आपको किसी को जीतना है तो आप दो काम करिए। आप उनसे इतिहास को जीतिए, और आप उनकी स्मृति को जीतिए। इतिहास और स्मृति ऐसी चीज़ है, मैमोरी एंड हिस्ट्री, जिनके माध्यम से आप उनके मन में प्रवेश करते हैं। और उसी प्रक्रिया में, वैसा ही करने के लिए अगर आप देखेंगे तो संघ परिवार ने दलित समूहों के तमाम नायकों की कल्पना को इन्वेंट किया। अनेक नायकों को खोजा। ये जो जातीय नायक हैं, उनको खोजा गया। ऐसा नहीं कि वे नहीं थे, वे उनकी लोक संस्कृति में थे, उनकी लोक संस्कृति में उनका गायन होता था, लेकिन इन्होंने उसको भगवा रंग देने की कोशिश की।[2] और उसको पुनर्सृजित करके अपनी सांप्रदायिक राजनीति से उसको जोड़ने की कोशिश की। और मैं उसके बारे में आपको तीन–चार उदाहरण दूँगा, फिर हम आएंगे समकालीन राजनीति पर कि कैसे सांप्रदायिक राजनीति में यह चेतना बदल जाती है।

लखनऊ का नाम आप लोगों ने सुना है। लखनऊ के बारे में, दलितों के बीच चर्चा है कि लाखन पासी के नाम पर लखनऊ बना है। लाखन पासी वहाँ के राजा थे। जबकि भाजपा और संघ परिवार के वृत्तान्त का मानना है कि लखनऊ लक्ष्मण के नाम पर बना है। अयोध्या के राजा राम थे और लखनऊ के राजा लक्ष्मण थे। लेकिन जब उत्तर प्रदेश में बसपा सक्रिय हुई तो उसने बहुत रोचक ढंग से इस वृत्तान्त को अपने अनुसार खड़ा किया। उसने हिन्दुत्व की राजनीति को काउंटर करते हुए इसकी अपने ढंग से व्याख्या की। यह वास्तव में वृत्तांतों और व्याख्याओं का बहुत रोचक युद्ध है। बसपा के उभार के समय लखन पासी का वृत्तान्त विमर्श के रूप में पेश किया गया और लखन पासी से लखनऊ का नाम जोड़ा गया। तब संघ के लोगों ने यह कहना शुरू किया कि लक्ष्मण का नया अवतार लखन पासी थे। इस प्रकार विश्व हिन्दू परिषद और संघ परिवार के लोगों ने इस वृत्तान्त को अपने वृत्तान्त में समेट लिया। यही उनकी रणनीति और राजनीति है कि भले ही कुछ खोना पड़े लेकिन वे ब्राह्मणवाद की उच्च अवस्था के अनुसार अन्य चीज़ों और कथाओं को पुनर्व्याख्यायित करते हैं। इसलिए उन्होंने शुरू किया कि लखन पासी लक्ष्मण के ही अवतार थे। इस तरह के अनेक वृत्तान्त नागपुर, इलाहाबाद, बनारस से छपने वाली अनेक किताबों में मिल जाऐंगे। अलग–अलग सामाजिक समरसता अभियान की पुस्तकों में अलग–अलग वृत्तान्त मिल जाऐंगे। इसके सब लिखित प्रमाण मौजूद हैं।

ऐसे ही सैयद सालार मसूद शाह गाज़ीमियाँ का वृत्तांत है। उसे मुस्लिम आक्रांता बताया जाता है और वो जब यहाँ से जा रहा था तो लाखन पासी ने उसका विरोध किया। सात दिन लड़ाई चली लखनऊ के पास। और सातवें दिन लाखन पासी का

गला गाज़ीमियाँ ने काटा। और फिर वो एक नाली है उस नाली में उसका गर्दन गिरा, इसलिए उसका नाम सिरकटवा नाली पड़ गया।

तो इस तरह से उन्होंने बाकायदा चीज़ों को गढ़ा है। और आपको पता होगा कि इतिहासकार संकलन समिति जो है, इनका जो ऑर्गनाइज़ेशन है, इसने टीलों की खुदाई करके, वृत्तान्तों के माध्यम से एक सांप्रदायिक इतिहास खड़ा करने की कोशिश की है। तो लाखन पासी तक तो ठीक है, लखनऊ तक। पर जैसे ही वो वो गाज़ीमियाँ के ख़िलाफ़ खड़ा किया जाता है, तो वहाँ पर समस्या शुरू होती है। और फिर कहा जाता है कि देखिए हमारी दलित कौम मुसलमानों के कारण सत्ता से च्युत हुई, नहीं तो वे तो राजा थे। दलित लोग राजा थे इस क्षेत्र के। लाखन पासी, डालदेव पासी, बालदेव पासी, बिजली पासी–ये सारे राजा थे इस क्षेत्र के। और ये इन्होंने अपनी सत्ता खोई, मुसलमानों के षड्यंत्र के कारण और इनके कारण हम लोगों का इनका बड़ा नाश हुआ, इसलिए इनको आप यहाँ से हटाइए। ये यहाँ इस देश के लिए समस्या हैं क्योंकि इन्होंने पहले भी आपको सत्ता से च्युत किया है और आज भी आपकी सारी समस्याओं के कारण हैं।

यह हिंदुत्ववादी राष्ट्रवाद का मूल मूल केंद्र है जो जो बहुत साधारण है लेकिन प्रक्रिया में समझने में के लिए मैं आपको इतना वृत्तांत दे रहा हूँ । तो वहाँ तक तो हो गया, उसके बाद फिर कितने ही दलित नायकों को इन्होंने खड़ा किया। इनके नैरेटिव आप पढ़ेंगे नागपुर से छपी हुई पुस्तिकाओं में। उन सबमें आपको इस तरह के मुस्लिम राजा, मुस्लिम शासक आएगा, मुस्लिम शेख आएगा, मुस्लिम नवाब आएगा और उसके ख़िलाफ़ ये दिखाया जाएगा कि उसने दलित नायक की हत्या की या उस दलित नायक को उसने सत्ता से च्युत किया।

इसी में एक जो सबसे रोचक वृत्तांत है जिसके बारे में मैं बताना चाहता हूँ वो है सुहेलदेव का वृत्तांत। बहराइच में सुहेलदेव का मेला हर साल जेठ महीने के पहले रविवार को लगता है। इस मेले में दसियों हजार लोग आते हैं।[3] सुहेलदेव की कहानी सैयद सालार मसूद शाह से जुड़ी है। सैयद सालार मसूद शाह महमूद गजनवी के भांजे बताया जाता है जो इस्लाम की विजय पताका फहराने उत्तर भारत आया। उन्नीस साल के इस नौजवान की बहराइच में इस इलाके के राजा सुहेलदेव से लड़ाई हुई। इसमें सालार मसूद शहीद हो गया। उसे गाजी कहा गया। लोक स्मृति इसी सैयद सालार मसूद शाह को गाज़ीमियाँ कहती है। अभी शाहिद अमीन की किताब उनके ऊपर आई है। लेकिन उसमें सुहेलदेव के मिथ को नहीं समझा गया है, जो कि उसकी काउंटर हिस्ट्री है, काउंटर स्टोरी है और बहुत रोचक स्टोरी है। हम लोगों ने 2004–05 के दौरान उस पूरी प्रक्रिया को, उस मिथ को दर्ज किया था। हिंदू और मुस्लिम जनता गाज़ीमियाँ की मज़ार पर आती है और विभिन्न तरीके से पूजा करती है। यही नहीं गाज़ीमियाँ वहाँ के पांच पीरों के साथ पूजे जाते हैं। इसमें ओबीसी,

दलित, हिंदू, दलित सभी शामिल हैं। वे केवल मुसलमानों के देवता नहीं हैं। मुसलमान भी उन्हें पूजते हैं उन्हें, लेकिन वो मूलतः दलित और ओबीसी के देवता हैं। बड़े पैमाने पर उत्तर प्रदेश के और उत्तर भारत के विभिन्न भागों के लोग वहाँ जाते हैं। लोग अपनी मनोकामनाएँ लेकर जाते हैं और उनकी मनोकामनाएँ पूरी होती हैं।

लेकिन सैयद सालार मसूद गाज़ी भी आक्रांता के रूप में वहाँ पर है। अभी जो मैंने लाखन पासी वाली कहानी में आपको बतायी, वहाँ भी वही है। हर जगह, जहाँ भी मुस्लिम हैं, वहाँ दलित नायक खड़ा हो रहा है। उस दलित नायक को सैयद सालार मसूद गाज़ी के बरक्स, उसके समानांतर, उसके काउंटर के रूप में खड़ा किया जाता है। सैयद सालार मसूद गाज़ी को सुहेलदेव ने मारा था। ये तथ्य कहाँ से आया, कैसे आया, नहीं पता। लेकिन ये तथ्य है कि कैसे उसने उनको मारा और सबको तो सैयद सालार मसूद ने मार दिया। यह एक ऐसा नायक था जिसने गाज़ीमियाँ को मारा। और वो जो नायक था वो जाति का, कहीं से इनवेंट किया गया भर जाति का । भर तक तो ठीक था फिर कह दिया गया भर पासी, भर भी और पासी भी। भर और पासी के बीच के रिश्ते को ढूंढा गया। लेकिन अगर आज हम कहते हैं कि नहीं वो पासी था तो भर लोग कहने लगते हैं कि नहीं नहीं, आप गलत कह रहे हैं। वो तो भर था, पासी तो था नहीं। लेकिन ये जो आरएसएस का वृत्तांत है, उसमें वो भर–पासी के रूप में उनको प्रोजेक्ट किया गया है। और ये आज नहीं किया गया है। ये 1947 से 1950 के आस–पास ही रामराज्य परिषद वगैरह ने इसके लिए आंदोलन शुरू कर दिया था। और उन्होंने सुहेलदेव का मंदिर, सुहेलदेव की मूर्ति की स्थापना के ये सारे अभियान शुरू किये और ये था कि गाज़ीमियाँ को हटाओ यहाँ से। उनका वो ये जो है स्थान बंद करो। जब आरएसएस ने ख़ासकर के बहराइच, बिहार, उत्तर प्रदेश–नेपाल बॉर्डर मे काम करना शुरू किया, जो सबसे तीव्र प्रभाव का क्षेत्र है हिंदुत्व पॉलिटिक्स का। तो उन्होंने बहराइच को सबसे बड़ा केंद्र बनाया अपना। और गोरखपुर से लेकर के बहराइच तक का जोन है, पॉलिटिकली बहुत सेंसिटिव है। और क्योंकि इसमें मुस्लिम पॉपुलेशन भी है, मुस्लिम मदरसे हैं, बहुत सारे, इसलिये इस तरह के वर्सेस या बनाम की मोबलाइज़ेशन के लिए स्पेस ज़्यादा है। और उसमें तो वहाँ जो विश्व हिंदू परिषद से जुड़े राजा थे उन्होंने ज़मीन दी वहाँ सुहेलदेव के मंदिर के लिए। फिर सुहेलदेव का एक मंदिर बनाया। सुहेलदेव के मंदिर के साथ एक तालाब खोदा गया। ये सारा गाजीमियाँ के यहाँ भी है। और सिमिलर काइंड ऑफ जो कॉपीइंग होता है कल्चरल पॉलिटिक्स का वो यहाँ भी किया गया। वहाँ कहानी है कि वहाँ अगर आप तालाब में नहाएंगे, तो आपकी त्वचा की दिक्कतें ठीक हो जाएंगी, गाज़ीमियाँ के यहाँ। वैसे ही यहाँ भी कहा गया कि आप यहाँ नहाएंगे, सुहेलदेव के यहाँ, तो आपके तमाम कष्ट दूर हो जाएंगे जो भी एलमेंट्स हैं ख़त्म हो जाएंगे। सिमिलर काइंड्स ऑफ स्टोरीज यहाँ खड़ी की गईं। और आज वहाँ उस मेले को आरएसएस लगाती है। वहाँ का

सारा आयोजन आरएसएस करती है। और एक ही शहर में उन्होंने उसको एक हिंदुत्व पॉलिटिक्स के मोबलाइज़ेशन के केंद्र के रूप में विकसित किया है। तो आप देखिए कि कैसे एक वर्सेस खड़ा किया जाता है, उसमें एक खींचतान पैदाकर सांप्रदायिक रा. जनीति का मामला तैयार कर दिया जाता है। यह जो सारी दलित अस्मिता है, मेमोरी है, उसको कम्युनलाइज़ करने की कोशिश की जाती है। यह सब लगातार किया गया और अब भी किया जा रहा है। हालाँकि बसपा ने इसका एंटीडोट विकसित किया। बसपा ने इन सारे नैरेटिव को चेंज किया अपने, चेंज क्या किया रीक्रिएट किया।

साम्प्रदायिक दंगों के सारे तथ्य इस बात की गवाही देते हैं कि कैसे उनमें दलित जातियों का इस्तेमाल किया जाता है। कानपुर साम्प्रदायिक दंगों पर हम लोग काम कर रहे थे तो सोनकर और भंगी बस्तियों में जाकर हम लोगों ने बात की। वहाँ समझ में आया कि साम्प्रदायिकता के इतिहास की इन दंगों में कितनी बड़ी भूमिका है। इन बस्तियों के अखाड़े या रेसलिंग के केन्द्र हुआ करते हैं। उन अखाड़ों में तलवार, भाले, छुरियाँ, चाकू पटे पड़े हैं। इन अखाड़ों के संचालक प्रायः 'भइया जी' हुआ करते हैं। भइया जी मतलब संघ प्रचारक। भइया जी, प्यारे जी, रामजी जैसे 'जी' लोग अखाड़ों को संचालित करते हैं। जब हम लोगों ने उनसे पूछा कि ये अस्त्र यहाँ क्यों रखे हैं। पहले वे दलित चुप रहे लेकिन फिर बोले कि जब मुसलमान आक्रमण करते हैं तो इन हथियारों से हम अपनी बस्तियों की रक्षा करते हैं। इस प्रकार हम देखते हैं कि संघ की यह सह–बिरादाराना संबंध बनाने की संस्कृति थी जिसे साम्प्रदायिक दंगों के अखाड़ों के रूप में तब्दील किया जा रहा था। इन अखाडों में जाकर कभी अध्ययन कीजिए। इनमें भाले, तलवार रखे मिल जायेंगे। यह इतिहास और स्मृति पर क़ब्ज़ा करके उसे युद्ध की शक्ल में तब्दील करने की साज़िश है। उसे एक हिंसक और घृणित भाषा में बदलने की कोशिश है। केवल उत्तर प्रदेश में ही नहीं बल्कि यह बिहार में भी है।

बिहार में दीना और भद्री नाम के मुसहर जाति के नायक हैं। मुसहर जाति में यह बहुत पूजे जाते हैं और गाए जाते हैं। ये ज़मीनी संघर्ष के नायक हैं। ये तालाब खोदने का काम करते थे। दरअसल तालाब खोदने का काम मुसहर जाति के लोगों से कराया जाता था। बाद में जब राजाओं और ज़मींदारों ने तालाब खोदने का काम दूसरे लोगों को कॉन्ट्रैक्ट पर देना शुरू किया तो मुसहर जाति के लोगों ने विद्रोह किया। दीना और भद्री इस विद्रोह के नायक थे। लेकिन बिहार में उनको साम्प्रदायिक मेमोरी में तब्दील कर दिया गया। दीना और भद्री को राम–लक्ष्मण का नया अवतार बताया गया। इन दलित नायकों को कथित मुस्लिम आक्रान्ताओं के साथ लड़ते हुए, मरते या मारते प्रचारित किया गया। इस प्रकार दो तरफ़ से दलित मनोविज्ञान को एप्रोप्रिएट करने की कोशिश की जा रही है। पहले दलितों में आत्मसम्मान भरने के लिए और उन्हें संतुष्ट करने के लिए उन्हें राम–लक्ष्मण के साथ जोड़ना ओर दूसरे मुस्लिम आक्रांताओं के ख़िलाफ़ उन्हें खड़ा करना। ये दोनों रास्ते एक ही जगह जाते

हैं। इस तरह प्रतीकों के माध्यम से साम्प्रदायिक हिन्दुत्व का राष्ट्रवादी एजेंडा उनके सामने रखा जाता है। मैं ये नहीं कह रहा हूँ कि क्या अच्छा है और क्या बुरा है। मैं पूछना चाहता हूँ कि दलितों की स्थिति क्या है, उन्हें आप कहाँ रखना चाहते हैं। क्या उन्हें सिर्फ वानर, भालू का ही रोल देंगे। पांचजन्य के विशेषाँकों के ज़्यादातर लेखों में कहा गया है कि सारे दलित राम की सेना में लड़ने वाले सैनिक थे। ये वानर, भालू थे जिन्होंने लड़कर रावण के ख़िलाफ़ युद्ध में विजय प्राप्त की। यह भी आरएसएस के वृत्तान्त का हिस्सा है। क्या आप हमारे दलित साथियों को निचली अवस्था में ही रखना चाहते हैं? इसीलिए दलितों ने रामलीला में विद्रोह किया कि हमें राम या लक्ष्मण का केन्द्रीय अभिनय करने दीजिए।

दूसरी तरफ़ ब्राह्मणवादी हिन्दुत्व है जो उनके लिए सिर्फ लड़ने और मरने वाले सैनिक के रूप में प्रोजेक्ट करता है। संघ दलितों को वह स्थान नहीं देना चाहता जहाँ वे अपनी राजनीति खुद बना लें। दलितों का सैनिकों के रूप में इस्तेमाल करना संघ की राजनीति का हिस्सा है। आप जानते ही हैं कि अम्बेडकर को हथियाने/अपनाने की कितनी कोशिश हुई है। लगातार अम्बेडकर के प्रतीकों पर हमले हो रहे हैं। हर व्यक्ति और राजनीतिक दल अम्बेडकर को अपनाने में लगे हैं। बिहार में अम्बेडकर के मन्दिर बनाए जा रहे हैं। कहीं अम्बेडकर के मेमोरियल बनाए जा रहे हैं। पांचजन्य के वृत्तान्तों को देखिए। बहुत मज़ेदार निष्कर्ष निकलते हैं। हिन्दुत्ववादी राष्ट्रवाद की जो राजनीति है या जो उनका नेरेशन है, लगता है वे बहुत कुछ भूले हुए हैं। मैं उन्हें ग्राम्शी की एक बात याद दिलाना चाहता हूँ कि सबाल्टर्न नैरेटिव के दाँत बहुत तीखे होते हैं। अगर आप उसे निगलेंगे तो ये पेट फाड़कर बाहर निकल आयेगा। अम्बेडकरवादी वृत्तांतों की शक्ति है कि उसे पचाना बहुत मुश्किल है। आप उसे निगल तो सकते हैं लेकिन वह पेट फाड़कर बाहर निकल आएगा। आईआईटी मद्रास और हैदराबाद विश्वविद्यालय में अम्बेडकरवादी विचारधारा और परिष्कृत हिन्दूवादी राष्ट्रवाद की राजनीति के यही अन्तर्विरोध हैं। इसी की तरफ ग्राम्शी ने इशारा किया था कि अगर आप उसे निगलने की कोशिश करेंगे तो वह आपको ही खा जाएगा। क्योंकि दोनों का विरोधी संबंध है। हिन्दुत्ववादी राष्ट्रवाद की राजनीति अम्बेडकर को सन्दर्भ से काटकर निगलना चाहती है। वस्तुतः अम्बेडकर का वह दाँत टूट जाए और वे उन्हें पूरी तरह से निगल जाए। जरूरत है, हिन्दुत्ववादी राजनीति के उस एजेंडे को समझने की। जरूरत है अम्बेडकर के उस दाँत को बचाए रखने की। अगर अम्बेडकर को निगल लिया गया तो अधिनायकवाद को आने से कोई नहीं रोक सकता। हिन्दुत्व के राष्ट्रवादी एजेंडे की राजनीति को अम्बेडकरवादी और प्रगतिशील वामपंथी विचारधारा जैसी शक्तियाँ मिलकर के ही रोक सकती हैं। इस पूरे अभियान में सबसे खतरनाक बात यह है कि पहले शहरों में केन्द्रित संघ परिवार की राजनीति अब गाँवों तक पहुँच गयी है। गाँवों के स्कूलों और बगीचों में आरएसएस की शाखाएं लगायी जा रही हैं।

उत्तर प्रदेश के तमाम गाँवों में संघ की शाखाएँ लग रही हैं। अगर यह राजनीति गाँवों में फैल गई और लोगों की चेतना में साम्प्रदायिक भाव भर दिया गया तो क्या होगा आप खुद समझ सकते हैं।

संघ गाँवों में कैसे काम कर सकता है? संघ के लोग मल्लयुद्ध प्रतियोगिता कराते हैं। उसमें अवॉर्ड दिए जाते हैं। कुश्ती लड़ने से पहले एक दीक्षा कार्यक्रम होता है। उसमें कुछ उपदेश दिए जाते हैं। उसमें कहा जाता है कि आप लोग 'हिन्दू धर्म रक्षक और राष्ट्र रक्षक' हैं। इस देश को आप ही बचा सकते हैं। इस विशेषण का प्रयोग सुहेलदेव के लिए भी होता है। बहराइच में उनके मन्दिर पर 'हिन्दू धर्म रक्षक, राष्ट्र रक्षक' लिखा हुआ दिखाई देता है। ऐसा ही एक और विशेषण हिन्दू हृदय सम्राट योगी आदित्यनाथ के लिए आ गया है। तो दलित नायकों को वे 'हिन्दू धर्म रक्षक, राष्ट्र रक्षक' कहते हैं। यानी राष्ट्र धर्म के बिना नहीं और धर्म राष्ट्र के बिना नहीं। तो आज इस तरह से देश प्रेम को खड़ा किया गया है कि या तो आप देशप्रेमी हैं या देश के गद्दार हैं। वो कौन सा देश है? वो ये देश है, जिस देश में आपको मुसलमानों को मारना है, जिस देश में आपको तलवार लेकर लड़ना है। जिस देश में आपको धर्म–रक्षक बनना है। तभी आपको राष्ट्र–रक्षक कहा जाएगा। अगर आप धर्म–रक्षक नहीं हैं तो गद्दार हैं। दूसरी तरफ़ इनकी राष्ट्रवाद की कल्पना में या तो हमारा स्थान बहुत नीचे है या हम इनके विरोधी हैं। दलितों के लिए जगह है तो नीचे है, जहाँ से आपको युद्ध लड़ना है। जहाँ आपको सेवा करनी है। जहाँ आपको निगले जाने के लिए तैयार रहना है। जहाँ विरोध नहीं करना है। जहाँ जाति आधारित हिन्दुत्ववादी और ब्राह्मणवादी संस्कृति में आपको शामिल रहना है। यही सामाजिक समरसता है। अगर आप ऐसा नहीं करते हैं, तो आप सामाजिक समरसता को तोड़ रहे हैं। और इसका सीधा मतलब है कि आप देश के गद्दार हैं।

ब्राह्मणवादी और हिन्दुत्ववादी जाति आधारित संस्कृति को संरक्षित रखना ही सामाजिक समरसता है। इसमें कौन ऊँचा है? कौन नीचा है? यह समझ लेना जरूरी है। शायद हम लोग समझते भी हैं। कुल मिलाकर धर्मरक्षक, राष्ट्र–रक्षक की परिकल्पना में धर्म के साथ राष्ट्र को जोड़ने की जो कोशिश है, वह भारत के विचार (आइडिया ऑफ इंडिया) को तोड़ता है। इस प्रकार की राजनीति सिर्फ सड़कों पर ही नहीं हो रही है बल्कि गाँवों में लोगों के बीच हो रही है। वैश्वीकरण के चलते जो पूँजी आ रही है उसका बहुत चालाकी के साथ इस प्रक्रिया में/राजनीति में निवेश हो रहा है। संघ–प्रचारकों को पैसे दिए जाते हैं, जिससे वे सारे आयोजन करते हैं। यह पूँजी वैश्वीकृत है। यह प्रवासी भारतीयों का निवेश है। हमने तमाम तथ्यों का आकलन किया है। पहले पैदल या साइकिल से चलने वाले संघ–प्रचारक अब कारों में घूमते हैं। महंगे मोबाइल–फ़ोन का इस्तेमाल करते हैं। उनकी पूरी जीवन–संस्कृति

में परिवर्तन आया है। हो सकता है कि ये परिवर्तन उनको बर्बाद भी कर दे। लेकिन फिलहाल तो बहुत चालाकी के साथ इस पूँजी का इस्तेमाल पूरे भारतीय परिदृश्य को बदलने के लिए हो रहा है। इस राष्ट्रवादी राजनीति से देश और समाज को बदलने की कोशिश हो रही है। घृणा और हिंसा की भाषा से संघर्ष और टकराव की स्थिति पैदा करके धर्म–रक्षक राष्ट्र बनाने की कोशिश की जा रही है।

*

नोट्स / संदर्भ–ग्रंथ

1. बद्री नारायण, 2011, *द मेकिंग आफ द दलित पब्लिक इन नार्थ इण्डियाः उत्तर प्रदेश, 1950–प्रजेंट, आक्सफोर्ड यूनिवर्सिटी प्रेस, नई दिल्लीः 21–22*
2. बद्री नारायण, 2014, *हिन्दुत्व का मोहिनी मंत्र*, राजकमल प्रकाशन, नई दिल्ली
3. *उत्तर प्रदेश डिस्ट्रिक्ट गजेटियर – बहराइच,* 1988, कैलाश नारायण पांडेय, स्टेट एडीटर, गवर्नमेंट प्रेस, ऐशबाग, लखनऊः 79

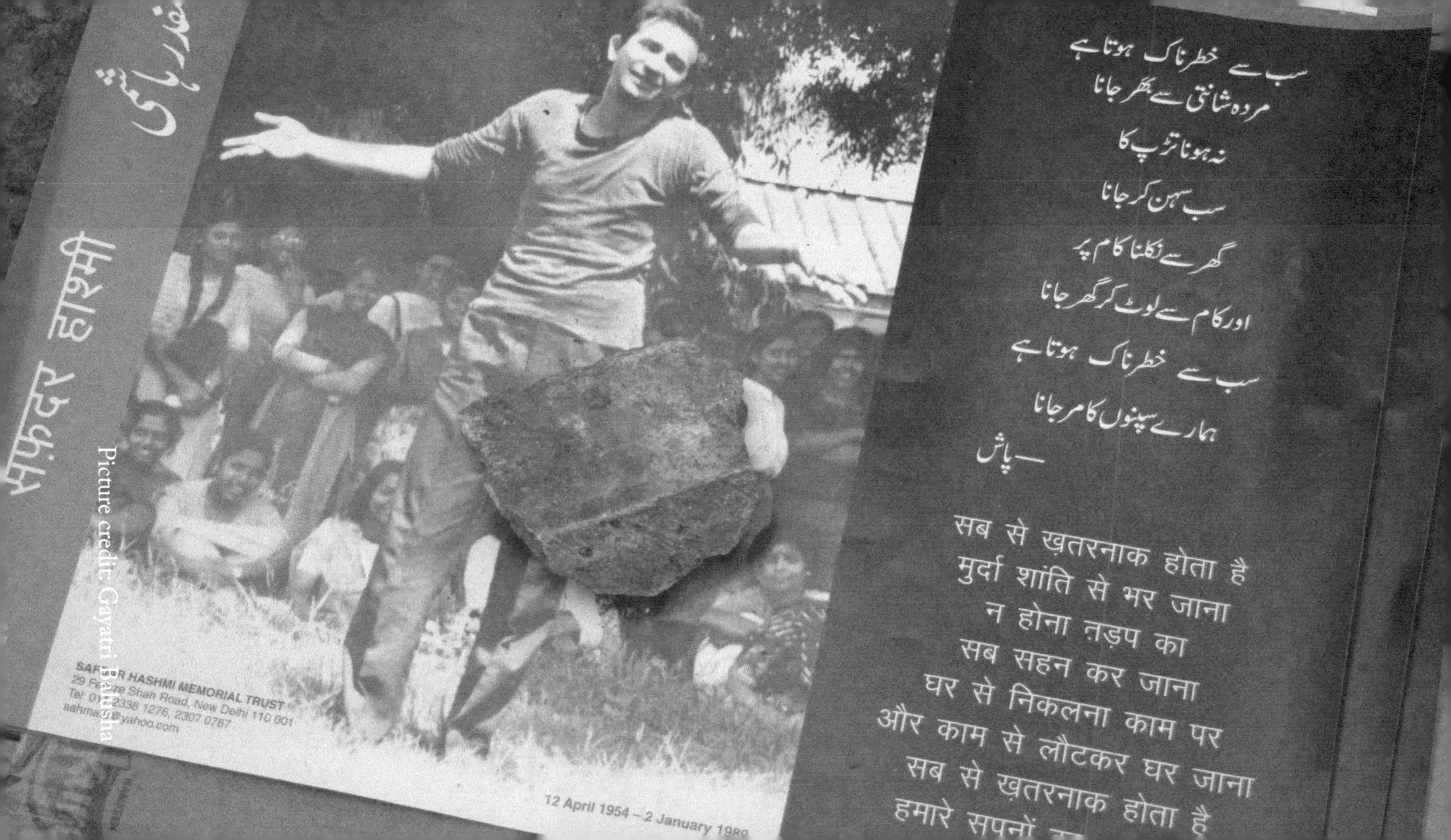

Picture credit: Gayatri Balusha

The Political Culture of Fascism

Jairus Banaji

(11 MARCH 2016)

WHAT I WANT TO DO IS talk about fascism in a strictly historical context. I will leave you to draw the kinds of analogies, connections and overlaps that what I'm going to say suggests to you in terms of whether it resonates with our situation in India today, okay? I am going to leave that to you. The three themes I want to talk to you about, which I think are key elements of the political culture of fascism, are as follows: the first is about the *constructed nature of nationalism*, you can also call this general theme 'fascism and the myth of the nation'. The second theme is associated with Wilhelm Reich, who was a psychoanalyst who worked in Berlin and had a considerable influence on sectors of post-war feminism. Reich's thesis was that *patriarchy and the authoritarian family* are the mainstay of the state's power in a capitalist society. This formulation enables us to integrate feminism and revolutionary Marxism in a way in which they are not often seen as being integrated with each other. I'll repeat that because it's such an important formulation: Reich's thesis is that the authoritarian family is a veritable 'factory' of reactionary ideology and structure and as such it is the mainstay of the state's power in a capitalist society. But particularly so under fascism, where this relationship between the two becomes overtly posited. The third thesis I want to present to you by way of describing a third element of the culture of fascism is Sartre's conception of – it will sound pretty dense but it's his conception – of *manipulated seriality*. I will explain later what I mean by that. At the heart of fascist politics is what he calls manipulated seriality. We need to understand this term 'seriality' to understand the dynamics of politics in any capitalist state.

So, these are the three broad planks or strands of argument I want to briefly speak about. The first one, the constructed nature of nationalism or what I've called 'fascism and the myth of the nation' is something that emerges very clearly in a short book that the German Marxist Arthur Rosenberg published in 1934, barely a year after he fled from Germany. Rosenberg was a Reichstag deputy for the Communist Party, that is to say, in Indian terms, he was a member of their Lok Sabha, because Germany had a similar political structure to ours, federal as well as central. He was not just a communist, he was on the left wing of the German Communist Party or the KPD, one of the leading figures of what was called the 'Berlin Left', along with the philosopher Karl Korsch. He resigned from the KPD in 1927 because he resented the excessive Russian interference in the affairs of the German party. Now, the very title of the Rosenberg's essay shows you how original his contribution was to the left-wing understanding of fascism, because it was called 'Fascism as a Mass Movement'. The Comintern really didn't believe that fascism would last long. It didn't believe it had deep roots. The Comintern saw fascism as a conspiracy hatched by finance capital, as if a collection of German bankers could sit somewhere and make fascism happen; as if Hitler was *simply* a puppet of finance capital; and as if the kind of mass appeal that the Nazi party generated in the late 1920s and early 1930s had no roots deeper than finance capital, which is a ridiculous view because it is so reductive, it completely misses what is so unique to these kinds of right-wing movements. So 'Fascism as a Mass Movement' was a direct challenge – the very title that Rosenberg gave his essay was a direct challenge to the Comintern's understanding of fascism, in other words, to the official Soviet line on fascism, that it doesn't have deep roots and that it has nothing to do with culture and with mass mobilization. What did Rosenberg argue? There are interesting overlaps between the three theses that I'm talking about – between Rosenberg, Reich, and Sartre, the three best thinkers of the left on the issue of fascism, there are interesting connections between the way they argued about fascism, which I'll try and draw out a bit later.

In Rosenberg, the argument is essentially as follows: Fascism only succeeds as a *mass* movement; it might exist in a society politically, within the political spectrum, but it will remain marginal as long as it has not mobilized a *mass base*. (I said I would not talk about India but look at the watershed of the 1980s in India to see this. The state-sanctioned pogroms of 1984 gave renewed legitimacy to mass violence and for the first time fuelled the expansion of communal forces further to the right.) So fascism only succeeds as a mass movement – that was the central argument of Rosenberg's essay. But then the question becomes – how does fascism, or how do right-wing movements generally, *construct a mass base*? That is the vital question we have to try and understand in our context here in India. His answer, it's a very interesting answer, was that the ideology which people call 'fascist' was *already widespread in Europe by 1914*. Now remember that the Nazi party wasn't formed till the 1920s, and Hitler and the Nazi party didn't become important until the very end of the 1920s, when the economic crisis hit Germany full blast. So what is Rosenberg saying when he says that the ideology we call 'fascist' was already widespread in European society by 1914? He is reversing the relationship between politics and ideology, he is saying the ideology is not a creation of the political party, the political party or movement is a creation of the ideology. So he is pointing to some slow-moving process within European politics and society which can be traced back to the 1870s and 1880s, and what is that? As and when parliamentary democracy began to spread in Europe, the traditional elites of European society were faced with a dilemma, namely, how do they win elections? I mean, these traditional elites had absolutely no appeal to the masses, absolutely none. They represented the interests of big business and big landed property; why on earth would they have any appeal to the masses, because they were in fact the oppressors of the working people. But this is in fact where the oppressor's ideology becomes important, because the kind of politics that emerged in Europe in the 1870s and 1880s is what Rosenberg called a 'new authoritarian conservatism'. The 'new authoritarian conservatism' was the nineteenth-century *precursor* of fascist ideology, of the fascisms that became more dominant later on.

Now, fascist ideology is actually only a pastiche of motifs, it is a pastiche of different ideological currents, it has very little coherence on its own. It's important to say this because it means you have to try and look at the individual components of a fascist ideology; and these should be obvious to us by today, for example, anti-Semitism and other forms of racism, support for a strong state that can act externally. They wanted German capital to become German imperialism so that it could compete effectively on the world market – hence, support for imperialism, for an aggressive external thrust; hostility to labour, incredible hostility to labour and to the organized working class; authoritarianism and, connected with that, patriarchy; and the last and most important of these components, of the kind of ideological pastiche that makes up fascism, is nationalism. The key to the success of the right-wing in European politics from the 1870s onwards lies in the emergence of a *new kind of nationalism*, which European politics hadn't known before the 1870s. That kind of aggressive, xenophobic nationalism was not there on the European scene in 1848, it wasn't really there even in the 1860s when Marx was writing *Capital*. It became dominant and much more aggressive, overtly aggressive, from the 1870s onwards. And that's partly linked to the rush for colonies, the whole frantic rush to divide up Africa, to grab pieces of territory and so on. But it's not only linked to that. I don't want to have a kind of economic-reductive explanation of nationalism itself.

So, what do I mean by the *constructed* nature of nationalism, why call it fascism and the *myth* of the nation? Do nations exist? Simple question, do nations exist the way that classes exist? Let me ask you that. I know what a class is when I see it. I know what the middle class is in a city like Mumbai and I know what kind of culture is epitomized by the middle class in India today. So I can see the middle class, I see its culture, I see its politics, and if I were living somewhere else, for example in rural India, I would confront other classes. I know what the working class looks like, I know where the working class is employed and there are other working classes who are not employed in large-scale units of production, they are employed in the home and so on and so forth. But the point about class is that these are real communities, these are real existing entities, even when they have no sense of themselves as such. *Who on earth would want to argue that a nation has the same ontology as a class, that a nation exists in the same sense that classes exist?*

Since nationalism is one of the main themes in these lectures, let me just sum up my own position vis-à-vis the two dominant interpretations or models of nationalism accepted currently. The first is associated with Ernest Gellner. Gellner's position was totally supported by E.J. Hobsbawm. The other position, which in some ways became more popular from the 1980s, is the one Benedict Anderson argued in *Imagined Communities*. Anderson describes the nation as an imagined community, but he wants to give a sort of positive spin to the word 'imagined', which is very, very different from the way Gellner understood nations and nationalism. Hobsbawm has this to say on the constructed nature of nationalism: 'With Gellner, I would stress the element of artefact, invention and social engineering which enters into the making of nations.' Then he quotes Gellner, 'Nations as a natural, God-given way of classifying people, as an inherent political destiny is a myth.' That's why I said fascism and the myth of the nation. 'Nationalism, which sometimes takes pre-existing cultures and turns them into nations, sometimes invents them and often obliterates pre-existing cultures, that is a reality,' and that's the dissymmetry here, nations are a myth, nationalism is a reality, and then Hobsbawm, by way of agreeing with this, says, 'In short, for the purposes of analysis, nationalism comes before nations. *Nations do not make states and nationalisms but the other way around*,' that's the argument made by Gellner and Hobsbawm, which I completely agree with. Now, in contrast to that, Anderson says, 'Gellner makes a comparable point when he rules that nationalism is not the awakening of nations to self-consciousness...' (Why not? Because nations don't pre-exist nationalism.) 'He [Gellner] invents nations where they do not exist. The drawback to this formulation,' says Anderson, 'is that Gellner is so anxious to show that nationalism masquerades under false pretences, that he assimilates invention to fabrication and to falsity rather than to imagining and creation.' Now look at the dividing-line here: one of them is saying – nations are fabricated, nations are fabrications; the other guy is saying – No, no, not quite, they are imaginings. So Anderson prefers to put it like that, imaginings and creations. In this way, Anderson is implying that for

Gellner true communities exist which can be juxtaposed to nations. What does Anderson have in mind? Very clearly, *class*. It's very clear that he has class in mind, for him class is as imagined a community as the nation is. What does he mean by imagining? The nation is imagined as a community, because it is always conceived as a 'deep horizontal comradeship'. Amazing! The obvious question, the big elephant in the room facing Anderson here is, who *does* the imagining? Even if you suppose that nations are imagined communities, who on earth is doing the imagining? As far as I'm concerned he hasn't answered that. And what sense does 'comradeship' have with the kind of profoundly unequal divisions that make up any country? What sense does it make to talk about a nation as a 'deep horizontal comradeship'? I can understand class being conceived and discussed in those terms, but not the nation.

There's one more thinker I want to bring into the picture, her name is Liah Greenfeld. She wrote a book titled *Nationalism: Five Roads to Modernity*, in which she examines nationalism in the contexts of France, Russia, Germany, etc. Now, she makes an interesting point which has a direct bearing on India. 'Much more often a nation is defined not as a composite entity', that means as something made up of individuals, 'but as a *collective individual* (This is creepy! It reminds me of Arnab Goswami…) endowed with a will and interest of its own, which are independent of and take priority over the wills and interests of human individuals within the nation.' Those human individuals are you and I, real people, real existential entities, we meet with each other, we talk to each other, and so on. But no, Arnab will have none of this, for him the supreme individual, the only one that matters is 'the nation': 'the nation demands to know!' Arnab keeps screeching at us every evening. So what does Greenfeld say about this conception of nationalism? 'Such a definition of the nation results in collectivistic nationalism.' *Collectivistic nationalism* is a good term for what we are up against in India today. 'Collectivistic nationalisms tend to be authoritarian and imply a fundamental inequality between a small group of self-appointed interpreters of the will of the nation – the leaders – and the masses, who have to adapt to the elite's interpretations.' Self-appointed interpreters of the will of the nation is *precisely* what we are up against in India today! As Greenfeld says, this nationalism is intrinsically authoritarian. In India a collectivistic, authoritarian nationalism is exactly what is being pushed down our throats today and used against the students in JNU.

That's one part of Rosenberg's argument, the argument about the constructed or mythical character of the nation. There is another part which is worth drawing attention to. Remember he said that the ideology which is called fascist was already widespread by 1914; so in a sense, Nazism was a product of that ideology, not the other way around. But Rosenberg went on to make another important point. He said what was peculiar to modern fascism was the 'stormtrooper tactic', as he called it. What's peculiar to modern fascism are the stormtroopers. Now, we've had a lot of experience with stormtroopers here in India recently, but I had promised I'd not talk about India, so I'll leave it to you to make the connection. 'Stormtroopers', the term basically comes from warfare. These are those elite squads that storm the trenches of the enemy. In trench warfare, which was the dominant method of warfare in the First World War. If you've seen this brilliant film called *War Horse*, it's all about trench warfare, which is one of the bloodiest, most manual forms of warfare imaginable. True, they had already started having aircraft and so on but the bulk of the killing took place in the fields, and it took place across trenches and between trenches, and trench warfare was essentially about storming the trenches. Now transposed to politics, this is what the stormtrooper does. The left did not invent the concept of the political stormtrooper, it was the right that invented it. The stormtroopers were those squads, in Italy they were called *squadristi*, that helped the Italian landowners in the south break strikes by sharecroppers, break those strikes, eliminate, murder the leaders of their unions in southern Italy. When the industrialists in the north saw what the stormtroopers were doing in the south, they invited them to the north, because they were confronted by working-class insurgency in the north. Now, the important point about the stormtroopers is what Rosenberg says – and I want to quote from his essay because it so accurately captures the political scenario of the last six weeks. This is what he says about the stormtroopers: 'The activities of the stormtroopers of the fascist type are in complete violation of the laws. Legally, the stormtroopers should be tried and sentenced to prison, but in fact nothing of the sort happens. *Their conviction in the courts is pure show, either they do not serve their sentence or they are soon pardoned.* In this way the ruling class shows its stormtrooper heroes how grateful and sympathetic it is.' Basically, the argument here is that fascism begins to flourish in a bourgeois democracy only with the active complicity and the connivance of the state. We've experienced this recently in the last six weeks, we've seen how entities of the state have reacted, how events have unfolded. *The complicity, the connivance of the state in allowing a free hand to the stormtroopers is a crucial part of the story of why fascist organizations do not simply disappear from the scene*, they are covertly patronized by the existing state even when that state, formally speaking, represents a constitutional democracy such as, for example, the Weimar Republic in Germany or our own democracy in India. So much for Rosenberg. I think those two or three insights are quite valuable.

Now, I want to move on to Wilhelm Reich, to an entirely different level of mediation from Rosenberg's picture of the kind of aggressive xenophobic nationalism that emerged in Europe in the late nineteenth century. Reich's key thesis is that patriarchy and the authoritarian family are the mainstay of the state's power. And in a sense Reich is not moving away from the theme of nationalism, he is addressing the same theme, what he is suggesting is a mechanism for the inculcation of nationalism from a young age. Reich published *The Mass Psychology of Fascism* in 1933, a year before Rosenberg's booklet. He had started drafting the book in 1931, and the problem he confronted was why the working masses allow themselves to be mobilized into movements that are manifestly opposed to their economic interest. This is a riddle. Why do the working people allow themselves to be galvanized behind right-wing chariots? Why? It's a real riddle, because those movements have *nothing* to offer to the working masses. This riddle, Reich argues, cannot be solved economically. He rejected reductionism of any sort, there was no economic solution to the riddle, there was no economic explanation for it. On the other hand, if the solution to the riddle lay in ideology, we would have to explain what it means to say this, and that is what Reich sets out to do *by making the family central to the kind of subjectivity presupposed in fascism.* The word 'subjectivity' now comes into the picture. There *is* a fascist subjectivity. There is a subjectivity presupposed in fascism and in the way it works, and the great themes that Reich develops in

The Mass Psychology of Fascism can be summed up in the three vectors that run through the first two chapters of his book. (There's an excellent translation of *Mass Psychology* by Theodore Wolfe, it's easily available on the net.) The crucial part of Reich's book is his conception of ideology as a *material* force. In other words, ideology has nothing to do with ideas in some abstract sense, it is not a mental phenomenon, it is very much rooted, bio-psychologically grounded, in structures that are *moulded by the family, by 'tradition', and by a repressed and often brutalized sexuality*. In other words, ideology is a material force, it is grounded in the family. The second vector that runs through Reich's argument is his conception of patriarchy as the mainstay of the state's power. I mentioned this earlier. And thirdly, Reich claims, there is a *resonance* between the authoritarian character-structures that are moulded inside the patriarchal family and the Führer ideology which is characteristic of all right-wing mass movements. Now, this Führer ideology revolves around a mass leader, someone with a strong, commanding will and ability to dominate the masses. Was Indira Gandhi a Führer in this sense? Not quite, she was an authoritarian leader, a strong-willed authoritarian political figure. She was quite capable of imposing a state of emergency on the whole country, but what political figure can you think of in India's recent political experience that strikes you as coming close to the figure of a Führer? A mass leader with a commanding will, a massive chest and so on? But who is it that creates the Führer? The people who support the Führer; the Führer would be nothing without those people. So that's what Reich is driving at, that to explain this dialectic between leader and mass we have to invoke character-structures of a certain type, the authoritarian, repressed character-structure and the resonance this finds in the structure of the Führer; one creates or at least allows for the other.

Again, there is a reversal of causality, a reversal of the direction in which the influence moves. Again, it is the 'mass' that comes first, the mass *culture* that comes first, and the politics that comes second. Politics in some sense is a reflection of that mass culture. So I won't say anything more about Reich, I think the whole idea of the family as a 'factory' of reactionary ideologies – not all families, but traditional, authoritarian families, patriarchal families – is fundamental. And the family as a battleground where the child will either survive as an independent individual later on in life, or be permanently scarred by childhood, defeated on the battlefield of childhood, defeated in the family. There's a brilliant movie by Theodor Kotulla titled *Aus einem deutschen Leben* (From a German Life), about the commander of a concentration camp, which traces the biography of this individual. The man ends up on an assembly line, processing death in the concentration camps in the 1940s, so the director is effectively asking, how could such an individual be formed? What is the process that allows for such an individual to emerge? Biographically, existentially, how can someone end up manning concentration camps, working on assembly lines of death? So the film starts with childhood, and it's a violent childhood, in a typically lower-middle-class, rural Prussian family, with a violent authority figure in the family, namely, the father. Now, this is the first sense in which the child confronts the state. In childhood, if you cannot stand up *for* your mother against your father, if you cannot resist the violence of your father, there is a definite sense in which you have already lost the battle. When you grow up, become an adult, you are not *going to be able to survive the battles of authority*, you will go on to be submissive to your employer, worship the state, you will worship state authorities and cringe before the power they embody. The mechanism involved here is identification, it's a kind of compensation mechanism, you lost in childhood, now as a grown-up you identify with authority, there you are, you have won. Now, carry this one step further into the realm of fascist politics and you'll see where the Führer figure is coming from. There is a brilliant passage in *Mass Psychology* where Reich talks about the individuals who support and worship the Führer as people who felt completely helpless in childhood. He stresses this helplessness, because when such children grow up, they seek compensation in this particular form. They lack any kind of independence of their own. They cannot think critically, they have been dominated emotionally, been scarred by childhood, and so on. So think about this. Think about the importance of character-structures, the kind of structures that are being moulded in the 'traditional' family in India and elsewhere. And again, feminism has a major role to play; here is one of those bridges between feminism and left politics. To talk about the family as the site of the first class struggle, the first battle, the first battle with authority.

Now, to Sartre, finally Sartre and his conception of *manipulated seriality* as the heart of fascist politics. There are classes in society, Sartre doesn't dispute that, but he divides society into those who are organized (that is, groups) and those who are not (series). It's a straightforward sociology; if you are organized you can do things, you have some degree of power; if you're not, you can't do a thing and you can have everything *done to you.* Take this away as the main lesson of this particular lecture, the division between organized groups and the unorganized mass which he calls 'seriality'. When you wait at a bus stop for a bus, you have no intrinsic connection with the other people who are waiting for the bus except the bus itself. The bus is what unifies you, the bus is your external kind of unity, but otherwise you have no internal relationship with the people you're waiting for the bus with. So he takes the example of the bus queue and develops it further and further. The type of ensemble we are talking about here is the *series*, and seriality is the condition of being part of the series. Groups dominate series *because* they are organized and have the capacity to act collectively. The vast mass of any modern society forms part of the inert structures that Sartre calls the series. Here 'inert' simply means unable to act, powerless. The state, for Sartre, is an ensemble of organized groups most of which have long ago evolved into institutions. We talk about the bureaucracy, the army, the media, political parties, and so on, but have you wondered about the kind of dense institutional realities these entities represent? They are profoundly institutionalized and have become part of automatically functioning machines. The important point is that these 'machines' would be literally unintelligible to us unless we assumed that they all emerged out of organized groups, just as the groups themselves emerged out of series/seriality, as every group does when people organize. The ruling class can rule because at its heart lies an ensemble of organized groups that have the capacity to control and dominate the masses. That's why trade unions are so important for workers. The union is their first experience of collective strength and solidarity. As an organized group it has the capacity to confront other organized groups. Employers are of course extremely well organized. So are the media. The organized groups that form the backbone of the media and of employers as a class are part of the vast ensemble of groups that make up the power of the state.

So what does 'manipulated seriality' mean? Well, this is Sartre's argument: organized groups are constantly working serialities. He says working serialities, meaning working *on* serialities or working *on* series, by a process which he calls 'extero-conditioning'. He takes that term from an American sociologist called Riesman in *The Lonely Crowd*. The millions of news consumers who watch the same TV channels with no connection between themselves except the anchor and the news they watch, believing what the others believe as if there really are 'others' who believe all this, are a perfect example of manipulated seriality. As long as 'social media' is organized differently, this danger is much less there. The process of domination of organized groups over series is the essential process by which rule occurs. How does the ruling class rule? It rules in this particular way, as the domination of groups over series. Under the pressure of extero-conditioning, series become 'worked matter'. As serial behaviour (pogroms, lynchings, 'riots', etc.) *violence is worked matter*, the product of organized groups acting on series in particular ways.

When Sartre says that manipulated seriality is the heart of fascist politics, it is this group–series relation he has in mind. The pogrom is the sovereign group (the state) or a non-state organized group *directing serialities in such a way that it is actually extracting actions from series*. There is nothing spontaneous about pogroms. The series is manipulated from the outside to act as if this was the organic action of a group and not the passive activity of a series. (A criminal jurisdiction that prosecutes only those who engaged in acts of violence and discounts the responsibility of the real commanders behind the scenes reflects a primitive judicial culture, out of line with international best practice.) The climate of violence that has been created in India today with black-coated stormtroopers attacking student leaders *with the full complicity of the state* is driven by a 'patriotic rage' that has been 'manufactured' (Rosenberg's expression). Nationalism is mobilized to intensify the climate of violence with slogans like 'you have insulted my country', 'you are anti-national', and so on. I wanted to go on to talk about other things, but I think I'll leave it at that.

*

Notes/References/Bibliography

Banaji, Jairus, 'Nationalism is the bedrock upon which all fascist movements have built themselves', https://www.sabrangindia.in/article/nationalism-bedrock-upon-which-all-fascist-movements-have-built-themselves, accessed on 20 March 2016.

Gellner, Ernest, 2009, *Nations and Nationalism*, New York: Cornell University Press, (second edition).

Goyal, Des Raj, 1979, *Rashtriya Swayamsevak Sangh*, Delhi: Radha Krishna Prakashan.

Greenfeld, Liah, 1993, *Nationalism: Five Roads to Modernity*, Massachusetts: Harvard University Press.

Hobsbawm, Eric, *Nations and Nationalism since 1780*, Cambridge: Cambridge University Press, (second edition).

Reich, Wilhelm, 1946, *The Mass Psychology of Fascism*, translated by Theodore Wolfe, accessible here: http://www.whale.to/b/reich.pdf.

Rosenberg, Arthur, 'Fascism as a Mass Movement', *Historical Materialism*, Vol. 20, No. 1, 2012, pp. 133–89; reprinted in Jairus Banaji, ed., 2016, *Fascism: Essays on Europe and India*, New Delhi: Three Essays Collective, second edition.

Picture credit: Samim Asgor Ali

विश्वदृष्टि, विश्वविद्यालय और राष्ट्र

सतीश देशपाँडे

(12 मार्च 2016)

आज मैं जिस विषय पर बोलना चाहता हूँ वह है – विश्वदृष्टि, विश्वविद्यालय और राष्ट्र। आप जानते ही हैं कि इन सभी शब्दों को लेकर लम्बी बहसें हुई हैं। फ़िलहाल इन बहसों को किनारे करते हुए मैं अपनी बात को सीधे और स्पष्ट शब्दों में कहने की कोशिश करूँगा।

आधुनिक समाज में विश्वविद्यालय इसलिए जरूरी हैं क्योंकि हम सबके लिए केवल व्यक्तिगत दृष्टि नहीं बल्कि एक विश्वदृष्टि – वर्ल्ड–व्यू – की ज़रूरत होती है। यह विश्वदृष्टि कोई कुदरती चीज़ नहीं है, और न ही यह कोई जादुई चश्मा या करिश्माई नज़रिया है जिससे अचानक सारे ब्रह्माण्ड की हर चीज़ नज़र आने लगे। विश्वदृष्टि आँखों की दृश्य–शक्ति या कानों की श्रव्य–शक्ति जैसे इश्वरीय वरदानों में नहीं है, बल्कि यह तालीम और रियाज़ से हासिल किया गया हुनर है। विश्वदृष्टि का मतलब है एक ऐसी व्यापक दृष्टि जो एक व्यक्ति को इस काबिल बनाये कि वह अपने व्यक्तिगत अनुभवों को, अपनी निजी अवस्था या परिस्थिति को, अपने इर्द–गिर्द घटित हो रहे व्यापक सामाजिक मुद्दों से जोड़कर देख सके। सुप्रसिद्ध अमेरिकी समाजशास्त्री सीसिल राइट मिल्स कहा करते थे कि समाजविज्ञान का ऐतिहासिक महत्व यही है कि वह हमें अपनी निजी परेशानियों (पर्सनल ट्रबल्स) को व्यापक सामाजिक मुद्दों (पब्लिक इशूज़) से जोड़ कर देख सकने की दृष्टि देता है। तो विश्वविद्यालय का सबसे मौलिक काम यही है कि वह हमें ऐसी विश्वदृष्टि तक पहुँचाए। लेकिन याद रहे कि हमें एक बनी–बनाई विश्वदृष्टि थमाने का काम नहीं है विश्वविद्यालय का। विश्वविद्यालय का असली काम ये है कि वह हर छात्र में वह विवेक जगाये जो अनेक

विश्वदृष्टियों को परख सके, उनका आकलन कर सके। इसी विवेक के सहारे हम अपनी पसन्द की विश्वदृष्टि अपनाने योग्य बनते हैं, और अपने निर्णय को तार्किक व सोचा–समझा आधार दे सकते हैं।

अगर विश्वविद्यालय का सबसे महत्वपूर्ण काम यही है तो विश्वविद्यालय अपने आप में क्या है? इस सवाल का जवाब यहीं हाज़िर है अपने इस अद्‌भुत जमावड़े में। यहाँ मौजूद हर व्यक्ति का अपना अलग व्यक्तित्व है, अपनी खास शख्सियत है। लेकिन हम सब जब यहाँ इकट्ठे होते हैं तो सामूहिक तौर पर हम एक अजीब, अद्‌भुत–सी चीज़ में अवतरित हो जाते हैं। यही सामूहिक हस्ती विश्वविद्यालय है, और हमारे पास जो है वो यही है। जैसा कि हम देख रहे हैं, उनके पास बहुत कुछ है। उनके पास इन इमारतों और भव्य भवनों पर जो ताले लगे हैं, उनकी चाबियाँ हैं। सारे अधिकारी उनके हैं, वाइस चांसलर, रजिस्ट्रार, तमाम अधिकारी उनके हैं। राजसत्ता उनकी है, पुलिस उनकी है, उनके टीवी चैनल भी तो हैं। इसके अलावा उनके पास भक्तों की सेना है। लेकिन हमारे पास विश्वविद्यालय है।

सच कहें तो विश्वविद्यालय हमारे पास नहीं है, हम खुद विश्वविद्यालय हैं। ईंट पत्थर की इमारतों से विश्वविद्यालय नहीं बनता। विश्वविद्यालय बनता है हम जैसे लोगों से जो सवाल पूछते हैं और ईमानदारी से उनका जवाब ढूँढ़ते हैं। एक ईमानदार विश्वदृष्टि की पहली शर्त होती है आत्मनिरीक्षण, क्योंकि विश्वदृष्टि केवल बाहर की ओर देखने वाली चीज़ नहीं है, इसके लिए खुद को भी देखना पड़ता है। किसी भी तरह की दृष्टि के लिए एक दृष्टिबिन्दु चाहिए। दृष्टिबिन्दु का मतलब स्टैंडप्वाँट, यानी आप जहाँ खड़े हैं, आपका जो भी अवस्थान (लोकेशन) है वही आपकी दृष्टि का कोण तय करता है। और उस अवस्थान से आपको वही दिखाई देगा जो उस कोण से दिख सकता है। और जरूरी नहीं कि बाकी लोग भी वहीं खड़े हों जहाँ आप खड़े हैं – दृष्टिबिन्दु एक नहीं अनेक होते हैं। इसलिए विश्वदृष्टि का मतलब केवल देखना नहीं है बल्कि इस दृश्यता के सन्दर्भ को समझना भी है। तो हमें अपने आप पर, अपने विश्वविद्यालय पर समीक्षात्मक नज़र डालनी होगी। यह सच है कि छात्रों और शिक्षकों का सामूहिक स्वरूप ही विश्वविद्यालय की अंतरात्मा है, लेकिन विश्वविद्यालय केवल आत्मा से नहीं बनता, उसका एक सांस्थानिक शरीर भी होता है। हमें यह पता करना है कि विश्वविद्यालयों के साथ आजकल जो हो रहा है इसके पीछे कौन से सामाजिक कारण हैं? विश्वविद्यालय की सामाजिक भूमिका क्या रही है? ये भूमिका कैसे बदल रही है? और इन बदलावों के कारण विश्वविद्यालयों पर तरह–तरह के प्रहार क्यों हो रहे हैं? अलग–अलग दिशाओं से, अलग–अलग तत्वों द्वारा, अलग–अलग कारण बताकर विश्वविद्यालय पर प्रहार हो रहे हैं। इन हमलों की पृष्ठभूमि को समझने के लिए जरूरी है कि हम विश्वविद्यालय की बदलती सामाजिक भूमिका को जानें।

चूँकी विश्वदृष्टि के निर्माण में आत्मीय और निजी को व्यापक और सामाजिक से जोड़ना पड़ता है, मैं अपनी बात को एक निजी अनुभव से शुरू करूँगा जो लगभग चालीस साल पुराना है। 1977 में मैं पहली बार किसी राजनीतिक विरोध प्रदर्शन या धरने में गया। संयोग से वह एक ऐसे व्यक्ति के लिए था जो देशद्रोह के अभियोग में जेलबन्द था। जॉर्ज फर्नांडिस उन दिनों जाने–माने समाजवादी मज़दूर नेता थे, रेलवे कर्मचारियों, मुम्बई के बन्दरगाह मज़दूरों और कई अन्य यूनियनों के मुखिया थे। उन्हें बरोडा डाईनामाइट नामक केस में देशद्रोह के अभियोग में कैद किया गया था। जनवरी 1977 में इमर्जेंसी के प्रावधानों को वापस लिया गया और तकरीबन 18 महीने बाद पहली बार आम प्रदर्शन की अनुमति मिली थी। तो जिस प्रदर्शन में हम गये थे वह दिल्ली में इमर्जेंसी के बाद का लगभग पहला प्रदर्शन था। इमर्जेंसी का ख़ौफ उस समय भी हावी था और उस छोटे से धरने में मुश्किल से कोई चालीस–पचास लोग थे, और हमारे इर्दगिर्द करीब दो सौ पुलिस के सिपाही। हमारे जुलूस को तिलक मार्ग पर तकरीबन 500 मीटर तक चलने दिया गया सुप्रीम कोर्ट की तरफ़, और फिर हम सबको पुलिस बस में भर दिया गया... थोड़े दिन बाद जब चुनाव की घोषणा हुई तो हमने – मैं और मुझ जैसे 20–30 कॉलेज छात्रों ने – घर–घर जाकर चुनाव प्रचार भी किया। जिस नेता के लिए हमने प्रचार किया वो थे अटल बिहारी वाजपेयी, जो कि नई दिल्ली निर्वाचन क्षेत्र के उम्मीदवार थे। उन दिनों मेरी राजनैतिक समझ बन ही रही थी, लेकिन उस समय भी हम अटल जी और राष्ट्रीय स्वयंसेवक संघ की विचारधारा का पुरजोर विरोध करते थे। किन्तु आपातकाल ने सबको सबक सिखाया था कि लोकतंत्र की रक्षा पहला काम है बाकी विचाराधारात्मक सवाल उसके बाद ही आते हैं। तो हमने आरएसएस और समाजवादी कार्यकर्ताओं के संग अटल जी के लिए चुनाव प्रचार किया।

मैं आपको यह किस्सा दो कारणों से सुना रहा हूँ। पहला कारण एक प्रकार का संयोग है। लगभग चालीस साल पहले का वह धरना भी एक कथित देशद्रोही के समर्थन में था, और आज के सन्दर्भ में भी देशद्रोह का अभियोग आप पर और आपके पूरे विश्वविद्यालय पर मँडरा रहा है। तो एक मायने में मेरा शीर्षक 'देशद्रोह से देशद्रोह तक' हो सकता था। उस समय के देशद्रोह और इसके वर्तमान अवतार में तुलना–भेद करते हुए और बहुत कुछ कहा जा सकता है, लेकिन मैं बढ़ना चाहता हूँ ज़्यादा महत्वपूर्ण दूसरे कारण की ओर जिसकी वजह से मैंने इस निजी इतिहास का जिक्र किया।

इमर्जेंसी के दौर की इन घटनाओं के मार्फ़त हम विश्वविद्यालय की सामाजिक भूमिका के केन्द्रीय विरोधाभास से आमने–सामने होते हैं। विश्वविद्यालय का प्रमुख उद्देश्य – हम इसे उसका प्रकार्य या फंक्शन भी कह सकते हैं – होता है वर्चस्व का समर्थन और वर्चस्ववादी तबकों के हितों की रक्षा। यह न केवल अतीत का

सच है बल्कि आधुनिक युग का सत्य भी यही है। लेकिन इसके बावजूद आधुनिक युग के विश्वविद्यालय की स्वाभाविक संरचना ऐसी है कि इसके सांस्थानिक ढाँचे में सत्ता–विरोधी या यथास्थिति–विरोधी सोच के लिए जगह बनी रहती है। यानी सत्तासमर्थन और सत्ताविरोध दोनों ही प्रवृत्तियों को विश्वविद्यालय सक्रिय प्रोत्साहन प्रदान करता है, भले ही इनका अनुपात समान नहीं होता। जिस कॉलेज और विश्वविद्यालय में मैं और मेरे साथी पढ़ते थे वे भी जेएनयू की तरह नामी संस्थान थे जहाँ के छात्र अच्छी सरकारी नौकरियों या बड़ी बहुराष्ट्रीय कम्पनियों में जाते थे। इमर्जेंसी का डर हममें भी कोई कम नहीं था, और यह सब जनवरी–फरवरी में हो रहा था जब कि हमारे इम्तहान मार्च के महीने में होने को थे। हमारे प्रोफ़ेसरान हमें बार–बार टोकते थे, समझाते थे – बन्द हो जाओगे, कैरियर बरबाद हो जायेगा, इस तरह के एक्टिविज़म से दूर रहो...। लेकिन हम जैसे मामूली मध्यम वर्गीय छात्रों में अगर इस ख़ौफ के ख़िलाफ़ खड़े होने का धैर्य पनपा तो केवल विश्वविद्यालय और उसके माहौल के कारण। हममें से लगभग सभी देर–सवेर अच्छी नौकरियाँ पाना चाहते थे, अपने परिवार के काम आना चाहते थे, और बाद में हमने कमोबेश यही किया भी। लेकिन वही विश्वविद्यालय जो हमारे मध्यवर्गीय स्वार्थों को साधने का ज़रिया था, उसी विश्वविद्यालय ने हमें अपने स्वार्थ से ऊपर उठने की प्रेरणा भी दी, हमें अपनों से अलग लोगों और उनके प्रश्नों की ओर ध्यान देने की सीख दी। आज आपके साथ भी कुछ ऐसा ही हो रहा होगा। आपसे भी यही कहा जाता होगा कि बेकार के धरने–जुलूस में मत फँसो, खूब पढ़ाई करो और अपना कैरियर बनाओ। और आगे चलकर आप भी बड़ी नौकरियाँ करोगे और अच्छे कैरियर बनाओगे – और मैं भी चाहता हूँ कि आपकी हर मनोकामना पूरी हो। लेकिन इस सब के बावजूद आज आप यहाँ खड़े हैं और इस लड़ाई को लड़ रहे हैं – यही विश्वविद्यालय का विरोधाभासी सच है, और इसी सच को जीवित रखने के लिए हम सब इस लड़ाई में हैं।

विश्वविद्यालय की सामाजिक भूमिका को दूसरे पहलू से देखें तो यह एक ख़ास किस्म की पूँजी का स्रोत है जिसे हम योग्यता पूँजी या प्रमाणक पूँजी कह सकते हैं। विश्वविद्यालयों और उच्च शैक्षणिक संस्थानों में छात्र उस प्रकार की योग्यता – और इस योग्यता के प्रमाणक, यानी डिग्री–सर्टिफिकेट इत्यादि – हासिल कर सकते हैं जिसकी समाज और ख़ासकर बाजार में माँग है। यही योग्यताएँ समकालीन मध्यवर्गीय जीवनशैली का आधार हैं क्योंकि यह न केवल आर्थिक हैसियत सुधारने के साधन हैं बल्कि सामाजिक हैसियत के द्योतक भी हैं। प्रमाणक पूँजी (क्रेडेन्शियल केपिटल) का स्रोत होने के कारण आजकल विश्वविद्यालय और उच्च शिक्षा का क्षेत्र संघर्ष और घर्षण से घिरा है। यह इसलिए कि हमारे इस "नियोलिबरल युग" में – कलियुग के

बाद आने वाला युग नियोलिबरल युग ही तो है! – सामाजिक गतिशीलता का एकमात्र ठोस साधन उच्चशिक्षा से मिलने वाली प्रमाणक पूँजी है।

व्यापक गरीबी और भयंकर विषमता से ग्रस्त हमारे समाज में आज हम न ज़मीन बाँटने की स्थिति में है न सम्पत्ति को। ऐसी हालत में गैरबराबरी को कम कर पाने के लिए एक ही व्यावहारिक उपाय बचता है और वह है उच्चशिक्षा बाँटना। गैरबराबरी को कम करना इसलिए जरूरी है कि ऐसा किए बिना हम अपने लोकतंत्र की हिफ़ाज़त नहीं कर सकते। इतिहास हमें सिखाता है कि भीषण विषमता और स्वस्थ लोकतंत्र का सहअस्तित्व ज़्यादा देर तक नहीं टिक सकता। दोनों एक साथ बढ़ नहीं सकते, लेकिन दोनों का स्वभाव ऐसा है कि एक बार जम गये तो स्थिर नहीं रहेंगे, बढ़ते–फैलते चले जायेंगे। जैसा सभी जानते हैं, पिछले तीन–चार दशकों में आर्थिक विषमता सारे विश्व में बेतहाशा बढ़ी है, और यही हाल हमारे जनतंत्र का है – यह लगातार गहराती जा रही है, नाना प्रकार के वंचितों को अपना हक माँगने को प्रेरित कर रही है। इसलिए अब हमारे सामने कोई विकल्प नहीं रहा। इन दोनों में हमें एक को चुनना होगा और दूसरे पर लगाम लगानी होगी। अगर विषमता को फलने–फूलने देना है तो लोकतंत्र की आहुति देनी होगी, या कम–से–कम उसे संकुचित करना होगा। और अगर लोकतंत्र का पक्ष लेना है तो ग़ैरबराबरी को ख़त्म करना होगा या कम–से–कम उस पर रोक तो लगानी ही होगी। आज ग़ैरबराबरी को कम करने के लिए हमारे पास कमोबेश एक ही उपाय रह गया है – उच्चशिक्षा। यही कारण है कि उच्चशिक्षा आज सामाजिक युद्धभूमि बन गयी है।

उच्च शैक्षणिक क्षेत्र में हैरान करने वाली तेज़ी से आये बदलावों को इसी पृष्ठभूमि के मद्देनजर आँकना है। पिछले तकरीबन दो दशकों में भारतीय उच्चशिक्षा जिस रफ़्तार से बढ़ी है वह शायद दुनिया के इतिहास में बेमिसाल है। 1991 से लेकर 2013 तक, यानी नियोलिबरल युग में, सरकारी आंकड़ों के अनुसार उच्चशैक्षणिक संस्थानों में कुल नामांकन साढ़े–छह गुना बढ़े हैं। आज हिन्दुस्तान में आप जैसे लगभग सवा तीन करोड़ नौजवान कॉलेजों और विश्वविद्यालयों में दाखिल हैं, और यह संख्या ऑस्ट्रेलिया की जनसंख्या से ज़्यादा है। केवल वृद्धि ही नहीं उच्चशिक्षा का चरित्र भी पूरी तरह बदल गया है। सभी जानते हैं कि तेज़ी से निजीकरण हो रहा है, और आज उच्चशिक्षा में लगभग 75 प्रतिशत संस्थाएँ निजी हैं। कुल दाख़िल छात्रों में से करीब 65 प्रतिशत इन निजी संस्थानों में पढ़ते हैं। इस बेतहाशा बढ़त के बावजूद सकल नामांकन दर (ग्रॉस इनरोलमेंट रेशियो) केवल 24 प्रतिशत है। यह आंकड़ा बताता है कि उच्चशिक्षा योग्य जनसंख्या (यानी 18 से 23 वर्ष तक का आयुवर्ग) का कितना प्रतिशत उच्चशैक्षणिक संस्थानों में दाख़िल है। इसका मतलब यह हुआ कि आपके आयुवर्ग का केवल एक चौथाई भाग उच्चशिक्षा में प्रवेश पाता है। आप में से हर एक व्यक्ति जो यहाँ बैठा है, उसके मुकाबले आप जैसे ही आपके तीन हमउम्र साथी उच्चशिक्षा से बाहर हैं।

अगर गैरबराबरी को कम करने की बात है तो हमें केवल उच्चशिक्षा की वृद्धि पर नहीं बल्कि उसकी सामाजिक संरचना पर भी ध्यान देना होगा। आज़ादी के पहले तीन–चार दशकों में उच्चशिक्षा पर कथित उच्च जातियों का लगभग एकाधिकार था। ऐसा होना स्वाभाविक था क्योंकि उन दिनों उच्चशिक्षा तक पहुँच पाने के आर्थिक व सामाजिक संसाधन केवल इन जातियों के पास थे। लेकिन पिछले 20 वर्षों में, यानी मंडल आयोग द्वारा सुझाए गये अन्य पिछड़ा वर्ग आरक्षण नीति के लागू होने के बाद, काफ़ी कुछ बदला है। आज देशभर के कॉलेजों और विश्वविद्यालयों में दाख़िल हो रहे छात्रों का एक बड़ा हिस्सा अपने परिवार के उच्चशिक्षा में प्रवेश करने वाले पहले सदस्य हैं। लेकिन इतना सब हो जाने के बाद भी सामाजिक असमानता को कम करने में उच्चशिक्षा का अब तक का योगदान नाकाफ़ी रहा है। इसका एक बहुत बड़ा कारण है उच्चशैक्षणिक क्षेत्र की अपनी असमानताएँ। यह जानकारी आम है कि हाल में बने शैक्षणिक संस्थानों में अधिकांश निम्न गुणवत्ता के हैं जहाँ की पढ़ाई का स्तर नामी या अभिजात संस्थानों से बहुत बदतर है। वंचित तबकों से जो छात्र उच्चशिक्षा में आये हैं वे ज़्यादातर ऐसी ही गुमनाम संस्थानों में हैं। अभिजात संस्थानों पर अब भी कमोबेश सवर्ण जातियों और सम्पन्न वर्गों का कब्ज़ा है। आज की सबसे बड़ी लड़ाई इन संस्थानों में वंचितों के प्रवेश की लड़ाई है। इस सवाल को लेकर उच्चशिक्षा में अत्यधिक तनाव और घर्षण पैदा हो रहा है क्योंकि अब तक अभिजात संस्थानों पर अभिजात वर्ग का ही कब्जा रहा है, और ये वर्ग इस वर्चस्व को अपना जन्म–सिद्ध अधिकार मानते रहे हैं। एसे में सामाजिक समता की ओर बढ़ने के लिए अभिजात संस्थानों की सामाजिक संरचना को बदलने का काम अनिवार्य भी है और कठिन भी।

समकालीन भारतीय उच्चशिक्षा की इस केन्द्रीय चुनौती की पेचीदगी को मैंने बहुत करीब से देखा हैदराबाद विश्वविद्यालय में, जहाँ मैंने 1991 से 1996 तक पढ़ाया। 1990–92 का समय भारत के इतिहास में एक महत्वपूर्ण मोड़ साबित हुआ क्योंकि इसी दौरान बाबरी मस्जिद को ढहाया गया, मण्डल आयोग की सिफारिशों को मंज़ूरी दी गयी, और बाज़ार–केन्द्रित नवउदारवादी आर्थिक नीतियों को लागू किया गया। इन तीनों के मिले–जुले असर से देशभर में जो राजनैतिक–सामाजिक तूफान उमड़ा उसका असर हैदराबाद शहर और हमारे विश्वविद्यालय – हैदराबाद केन्द्रीय विश्वविद्यालय – पर भी पड़ा। विश्वविद्यालय परिसर में सबसे ज़्यादा प्रभाव दिखाया मण्डल विरोधी आन्दोलन ने। इस आन्दोलन के विरोध में जो प्रतिवादी–आन्दोलन उभरा उसी से निकला एक नया छात्र संगठन – अंबेडकर स्टूडेंट्स असोसिएशन, जिसका नाम आपने सुना होगा। मेरी जानकारी में यह देश का शायद सबसे पहला छात्र संगठन था जिसने जाति के सवाल को प्राथमिकता दी और सामाजिक समता की व्यापक लड़ाई को विश्वविद्यालय परिसर के अन्दर लड़ने का साहस दिखाया। अभिजात संस्थानों में जातिगत भेदभाव और उपेक्षा के ख़िलाफ़ लड़ना कितना कठिन है यह मैंने अम्बेडकर

स्टूडेंट्स असोसिएशन के शुरुआती दिनों में देखा। सबसे बड़ी दिक़्क़त यह होती है कि अभिजात संस्थान के छात्र और शिक्षक, दोनों यह मानने को तैयार नहीं होते कि उनके अपने विश्वविद्यालय या विभाग में ऐसी कोई समस्या है। अभिजात संस्थानों के छात्र व शिक्षक योग्यता तंत्र की सतही विचारधारा में पूरी तरह गिरफ्त होते हैं। उन्हें योग्यता को विकसित करने में आर्थिक–सामाजिक संसाधनों का योगदान दिखता ही नहीं और वे यह मान कर चलते हैं कि योग्यता मात्र कुदरती प्रतिभा और व्यक्तिगत मेहनत से बनती है। ऐसे में जातिगत भेदभाव को मुद्दा बनाना आसान नहीं होता। अम्बेडकर स्टूडेंट्स असोसिएशन के सदस्यों और उनके समर्थक छात्रों ने जब इस मुद्दे को उठाया तो उन्हें बहुत सालों तक संघर्ष करना पड़ा। हर रोज़ हॉस्टल में किसी न किसी के साथ कहा–सुनी, हर रोज़ अपने अध्यापकों के अपमानजनक बर्ताव को सहना। दूसरे छात्रों से गरमा–गरमी, तनाव, कभी झड़पें। और जो सबसे ज़्यादा दुख देने वाले मुद्दे थे वे आन्तरिक मतभेदों को लेकर उठे। वंचित वर्गों की अपनी आन्तरिक विषमताएँ, जेंडर को लेकर बहुत सारे अन्दरूनी संघर्ष...। वे दिन आसान नहीं थे, बहुत संघर्ष के दिन थे, कष्ट के दिन थे। लेकिन प्रतिबद्ध छात्रों का छोटा–सा समूह इस मोर्चे पर कई सालों तक डटा रहा और खुद को ज़िन्दा रखने के साथ साथ जातिगत समता के प्रश्न को भी जीवित रखा। यही कारण है कि आज अंबेडकर स्टूडेंट्स असोसिएशन देश के अग्रगामी छात्र संगठनों में गिना जाता है क्योंकि उसका मौलिक काम था। खुद बाबा साहेब अम्बेडकर दलित छात्रों को राजनीति में नहीं उतारना चाहते थे। वे चाहते थे कि दलित छात्र पढ़ाई करें, अच्छी नौकरी पाकर समाज में पैर जमा लें, और उसके बाद अपने और व्यापक समाज के लिए काम करें। यही रवैया अम्बेडकरवादी पार्टियों का भी रहा है, जैसे बहुजन समाज पार्टी। ऐसे माहौल में अम्बेडकर स्टूडेंट्स असोसिएशन ने देखा कि हालात बदल गये हैं, और लकीर के फ़कीर बन कर बाबा साहेब का अँधाधुँध अनुसरण करना ठीक नहीं होगा। इसीलिए उन्होंने विश्वविद्यालय के धरातल पर जाति की लड़ाई को लड़ना शुरू किया और तमाम दिक़्क़तों से गुज़रते–गुज़रते आज रोहित वेमुला जैसे सितारे को तैयार किया। रोहित अब नहीं रहा, इसका ग़म हम सबको है। आपके साथियों ने बार–बार कहा है कि जेएनयू में जो घटित हो रहा है उसका सीधा सम्बन्ध अम्बेडकर स्टूडेंट्स असोसिएशन से है, और हैदराबाद विश्वविद्यालय में जो घटित हुआ और जो घटित नहीं हो पाया, उसका भी जेएनयू से सीधा सम्बन्ध है।

मूल बात यह है कि विश्वविद्यालय को बराबरी की ज़मीन बनाना, ये अकस्मात या अनायास नहीं हुआ। इसके लिए बहुत लम्बी लड़ाई लड़नी पड़ी, बहुत मेहनत करनी पड़ी। लेकिन इस लम्बी लड़ाई का असर अब दिख रहा है, ख़ासकर हैदराबाद विश्वविद्यालय और जेएनयू और ऐसे कुछ और विश्वविद्यालयों में। हालाँकि मंज़िल अभी दूर है और लम्बा सफ़र बाकी है, फिर भी आज हम दावे के साथ कह सकते

हैं कि हमारे समाज में अगर कोई संस्थान व्यापक रूप से समावेशी है, और जहाँ कमोबेश सामाजिक समता है, तो वह विश्वविद्यालय ही है। मेरी बात पर विश्वास न हो तो आप खुद सोचिए, गिनाइए मुझे कोई ऐसा संस्थान जहाँ सभी सामाजिक तबकों व समुदायों के लोग भी हों और उनमें आपस में बराबरी भी हो। भारत की संसद को ही देख लीजिए, संसद में महिलाएँ नहीं के बराबर हैं। कामकाजी दुनिया को देख लीजिए, यहाँ सब तरह के लोग तो हैं लेकिन श्रेणीबद्ध ढाँचे में कैद हैं जहाँ बराबरी का नामोनिशान नहीं है। जहाँ बराबरी है वहाँ समावेशिता नहीं, समावेशिता है तो बराबरी नहीं – इस नियम का एकमात्र अपवाद विश्वविद्यालय ही है।

आज हमारे विश्वविद्यालय एक नये तरह के सामाजिक अनुभव की सम्भावना को साकार कर रहे हैं जो और किसी भी संस्थान में उपलब्ध नहीं है, धार्मिक संस्थानों में भी नहीं। यह नया अनुभव है सामाजिक समता। सामाजिक समता की अप्रत्याशित जन्मभूमि हमारे विश्वविद्यालय ही हैं। आपका अपने विश्वविद्यालय में जो भी अनुभव रहा है, इसे केवल व्यक्तिगत या निजी चीज़ मत समझिए। आपका अनुभव हमारे समाज के लिए बहुत बड़ी चीज़ है, बहुत बड़ी उपलब्धि है, जिसे हासिल करने में तीन पीढ़ियाँ और छः दशक लग गये...

जिस अभूतपूर्व समता और समावेशिता की सम्भावना को हमारे विश्वविद्यालय साकार कर रहे हैं वह सबको नहीं भाता। चूँकि समता और समावेशिता के दुश्मन विश्वविद्यालय के अन्दर भी हैं और बाहर भी, हमारे विश्वविद्यालयों में, और ख़ासकर अभिजात विश्वविद्यालयों में, अन्दरूनी घर्षण के साथ–साथ बाहरी हमले भी होने लग गये हैं। विश्वविद्यालयों पर बाहर से किये जा रहे प्रहार मूलतः तीन प्रकार के हैं। पहले तरह के हमले सीधे राजनीतिक दलों द्वारा किये जा रहे हैं, जैसे अखिल भारतीय विद्यार्थी परिषद और उनके साथ की संस्थाओं द्वारा उदयपुर, ग्वालियर, लखनऊ और कई विश्वविद्यालयों में किये गये हमले। इन हमलों को जायज़ ठहराने के लिए आम तौर पर यही बहाना बनाया जाता रहा है कि भारतीय संस्कृति या हिन्दू धर्म का किसी तरह का अपमान हुआ है, और ऐसे आरोप के दम पर किसी व्यक्ति, संगठन या संस्था पर धावा बोला जाता है। दूसरी तरह के हमले इन्ही दलों व संस्थाओं से प्रेरित हैं, लेकिन यहाँ उनकी भूमिका प्रत्यक्ष नहीं परोक्ष होती है, और इस प्रकार के हमले में राजसत्ता का सीधे इस्तेमाल किया जाता है पुलिस के जरिए। इसके उदाहरण हैं हैदराबाद विश्वविद्यालय और आपका विश्वविद्यालय, जहाँ किन्ही राजनैतिक दलों की शह पर पुलिस कार्रवाई कर रही है। तीसरे तरह के हमले पहले दोनों से बिल्कुल अलग हैं और और हमें पूरी संजीदगी से इनके बारे में सोचना होगा क्योंकि ये हमले आम जनता की तरफ़ से आ रहे हैं। आप सब जानते हैं कि जे.एन.यू. और मुनिरका के बीच एक संकरी सड़क है। लेकिन आज हमें इस हक़ीक़त का सामना करना पड़ रहा है कि वह संकरी–सी सड़क अचानक एक बड़ी खाई बन गयी है।

आम जनता से आ रहे हमलों को हम दो भागों में बाँट सकते हैं – एक जो सम्पन्न मध्यवर्ग से आ रहे हैं, और दूसरा जो निम्नमध्यवर्ग या श्रमिक वर्ग की तरफ़ से आ रहे हैं। सम्पन्न वर्ग के विश्वविद्यालय–विरोध में कुछ नासमझी है और कुछ द्वेष भाव है। नासमझी इसलिए कि इस वर्ग की सामाजिक–राजनैतिक सोच रूढ़ीवादी रही है और यह वर्ग बुद्धिजीवियों को शक़ की नज़र से देखता रहा है। इसके अलावा, आजकल यह वर्ग अभिजात शैक्षणिक संस्थानों से चिढ़ने लगा है क्योंकि इन संस्थानों में अब साधन–सम्पन्न छात्रों को भी आसानी से दाख़िला नहीं मिल पाता, चाहे वह हैदराबाद विश्वविद्यालय हो या जेएनयू। जब आपके बच्चों को दाख़िला नहीं मिल पाता, और इस दाख़िले को आप अब तक अपना जन्मसिद्ध अधिकार मानते थे, तो थोड़ी तकलीफ़ तो होगी ही!

लेकिन साधारण लोगों का जेएनयू जैसे विश्वविद्यालयों के प्रति जो गुस्सा और आक्रोश देखने को मिला है, वह हमारे लिए बेहद चिन्ता का विषय है। आपने भी अख़बारों में पढ़ा होगा उन घटनाओं के बारे में जहाँ ऑटोरिक्शा वाले या राह चलते साधारण लोग जेएनयू का नाम सुनते ही गुस्से से बरस पड़े हैं। ऐसा क्यों हो रहा है? मेरे ख्याल से इस प्रकार के आक्रोश के दो कारण हैं जिनका सामना हमे करना ही होगा। दोनों ही कारणों का मीडिया और फेसबुक आदि माध्यमों में जानबूझ कर व्यापक प्रचार किया जा रहा है। इसमें एक धारणा यह है कि जेएनयू जैसे विश्वविद्यालयों में छात्र और शिक्षक सरकारी पैसों से ऐश करते हैं और इन संस्थानों पर सरकार बहुत बड़ी रकम खर्च करती है। दूसरी धारणा यह है कि इन विश्वविद्यालयों में देशद्रोही और गद्दार लोगों का जमावड़ा है। दुनिया जानती है कि इस बात का ज़ोरशोर से प्रचार हुआ है हो रहा है।

सरकारी पैसों के दुरुपयोग के तर्क को 'करदाता' (टैक्सपेयर) की भाषा में प्रचारित किया जाता है, कि आम लोगों की मेहनत की कमाई जिससे वे सरकारी कर या टैक्स भरते हैं उसी पैसे से विश्वविद्यालयों में लोग गुलछर्रे उड़ा रहे हैं। इस तर्क का सामना हम कुछ आंकडों से कर सकते हैं। आपके विश्वविद्यालय यानी जे.एन.यू. का सालाना बजट कुल मिलाकर लगभग 300 करोड़ रुपयों का है। इस 300 करोड़ की औक़ात का पता दूसरे आंकड़ों से तुलना करने पर होता है। आपने अख़बारों में पढ़ा होगा कि भारतमाता के एक सुपूत हैं श्री विजय मल्या जी जो हाल में किसी वजह से दुखी होकर विदेश चले गये। उनकी तरफ़ से बकाया रकम 9000 करोड़ बताई जाती है। अगर मल्या साहब से किसी तरह वसूली कर ली जाये, तो उस 9000 करोड़ में आपका विश्वविद्यालय, जिसका वार्षिक ख़र्च मात्र 300 करोड़ है, लगभग तीस साल तक चल सकता है, और अगर यह खर्च महंगाई के कारण बढ़ भी गया तो भी बीस साल तो बड़े आराम से निकल सकते हैं। इसके अलावा आपने सुना होगा कि इससे भी बड़ी एक रकम है 114 लाख करोड़ की, जो अलग–अलग कॉर्पोरेट कम्पनियों

का कुल कर्ज़ है जिसे सरकारी बैंकों ने उठाया है और जिसे अर्थशास्त्रियों की भाषा में एनपीए कहा जाता है, नॉन पर्फार्मिंग एसेट्स, यानी की भई पैसे डूब गये। आप खुद हिसाब लगा लीजिए कि अगर ये 1,14,000 करोड़ रुपये वसूल हो जाते तो कितने विश्वविद्यालय कितने साल तक चल सकते थे। यानी फ़िज़ूलखर्ची का आरोप निराधार है, हालाँकि हमें सार्वजनिक पैसे का पूरा पूरा ख्याल रखना चाहिए और इसका हिसाब देने के लिए तैयार रहना चाहिए।

रही बात देशभक्ति की तो दो मिनट इसकी भी बात कर लें ताकि बाद में न कहा जाये कि हमने इसकी बात ही नहीं की। आपने सुना होगा कि तरह तरह के महानुभाव हमारे कन्हैया कुमार से मिलने के लिए बड़े उतावले हैं क्योंकि वे कन्हैया से देशभक्ति के नारे लगवाना चाहते हैं। आप यह भी जानते होंगे कि इन महापुरुषों को कन्हैया ने कैसे मुँहतोड़ जवाब दिया है। इस बात पर मुझे जो चिन्ता सताती रही है वह है अतिरेकी भाषा का प्रयोग और प्रतीकों के साथ की जा रही नूरा–कुश्ती। आप सबकी जैसी होगी वैसी मेरी भी माँ है। मेरी माँ 81 साल की है, ज़्यादा पढ़ी लिखी नहीं हैं, थोड़ी बहुत हिन्दी और अंग्रेजी बोल लेती हैं लेकिन बात ढंग से सिर्फ कन्नड़ में होती है। मैं ये कल्पना कर रहा था कि अगर अपनी माँ से कहता कि, 'हे मातृश्री, तुम्हारे लिए मेरे पास अपार प्रेम है। मेरे नस–नस में तुम्हारे लिए भक्ति भाव कूट–कूट कर भरा है।' इस तरह से मैं उनसे बात करने लगूँ, तो वो तुरन्त मुझे पागलख़ाने भेजने की तैयारी करेंगी। ऐसा नहीं है कि मेरी माँ अजीब हैं, आप सब की माँओं से अलग हैं। मुझे पूरा विश्वास है कि आप ऐसी हरकतें अपनी माँ के सामने करोगे, तो आपकी माँ भी यही कहेंगी, कि बेटा या बेटी क्या हो गया है तुम्हें? ठीक कराओ इसे, दवा दिलाओ। तो क्या भारत माता हमारी अपनी माँओं से इतनी अलग है कि वह चाहती है कि बार–बार हम उसकी दुहाई दें, उसकी पूजा करें और बार–बार बखान करें कि माँ हमें तुमसे प्रेम है, हमें तुमसे प्रेम है। देशभक्ति के मामले में करनी की चलनी चाहिए, कथनी की नहीं। देशभक्ति की सही परीक्षा आपके काम से होती है, कि आप किस तरह का काम कर रहे हैं, किसके लिए काम कर रहे हैं? यही वाजिब परीक्षा है देशभक्ति की, नारे चाहे जो भी बुलन्द करें। आख़िर हमारे श्री माल्या साहब ने भी कई बार देशभक्ति के नारे लगाये होंगे। नारे लगाने भर से कुछ नहीं होता। नारे महत्वपूर्ण होते हैं, वो हमारे जज़्बातों को केन्द्रित करते हैं, उन्हें दिशा देते हैं। नारे राजनीति में बहुत काम आते हैं। लेकिन केवल नारे लगाने से कुछ नहीं होता। अगर आप सिर्फ जय भीम, जय भीम करते रहोगे, या लाल सलाम–लाल सलाम करते रहोगे तो कुछ नहीं होने वाला। नारों से आगे बढ़कर भी बहुत कुछ करना पड़ता है, ज़मीनी काम करना होता है। आपकी देशभक्ति का मूल्यांकन उस काम के आधार पर होना चाहिए। उस परीक्षा के लिए सारे विश्वविद्यालय तैयार हैं। लीजिए हमारी परीक्षा, पता कीजिए कि हम किन विषयों पर रिसर्च कर रहे हैं, किस के लिए काम कर रहे हैं?

लोग हमें जानेंगे, हमारे काम को जानेंगे, तो अपनेआप पता चल जाएगा कि देशद्रोह का आरोप कितना उचित है।

मैंने अबतक आपसे यही कहा है कि विश्वदृष्टि बनाने के लिए, विवेक पनपाने के लिए, विश्वविद्यालय को बहुत कुछ करना पड़ता है। विश्वविद्यालय मात्र कारख़ाना नहीं है जो किसी मशीन के कल–पुर्जों की तरह नौकरी–योग्य छात्रों को तैयार करे और अर्थव्यवस्था में खप जाने दे। मुझे गलत मत समझिए, मेरी प्रार्थना है कि आप सबको अच्छी नौकरी मिले। लेकिन नौकरी–शुदा बनने के साथ–साथ आप कुछ और भी बनें, ऐसी मेरी और आपके शिक्षकों कि तमन्ना है। कई साल पहले मैं जब जेएनयू में पढ़ता था, उस समय बंगलौर के कुछ साथियों ने हमें एक नया नारा सिखाया था। नारा कन्नड़ में था और हम उसे कन्नड़ और हिन्दी दोनों में लगाते थे। मेरे ख़याल से यह नारा बिलकुल जेएनयू का नारा है, इसकी किसी और परिसर में लगने की सम्भावनाएँ कम हैं। ये नारा उस समय के रेक्टर साहब को सम्बोधित कर कहता था कि 'रेक्टर अवरे, मनुष्यर आगी यानी रेक्टर साहब, मनुष्य बनो!'। आन्दोलनकारी छात्र नारा लगा रहे हैं विश्वविद्यालय के अफ़सर से दरख़्वास्त करते हुए, निवेदन करते हुए कि आप मनुष्य बनिए।

हमारे विश्वविद्यालय मनुष्य बनाने के लिए हैं, नौकरशाह बनाने के लिए नहीं। जैसा मैंने कहा कि आप सब खुद विश्वविद्यालय हैं, विश्वविद्यालय के जीते–जागते अवतार हैं, और केवल एक विश्वविद्यालय के नहीं सभी विश्वविद्यालयों के प्रतिनिधि हैं। और इस तरह का अवतार व प्रतिनिधि होने की कीमत भी आपको चुकानी होगी। कीमत यह है कि आप कभी भी आत्मनिरीक्षण को आत्ममुग्धता में बदलने न दें। आप ये न सोचने लगें कि देखो हम कितने महान हैं, हमारा विश्वविद्यालय कितना अनूठा है। प्रतिनिधि होने के नाते आपकी, हमारी, हम सब की, बहुत सारी ज़िम्मेदारियाँ हैं। हमें उन सभी विश्वविद्यालयों को याद रखना है जहाँ इस तरह की महफ़िल भी नसीब नहीं हो पाती। हमें ख़ास–तौर पर हैदराबाद विश्वविद्यालय और रोहित वेमुला को याद रखना है, सामाजिक समता के मुद्दे को याद रखना है। और तमाम उन ग़ैरबराबरियों को याद रखना है, जिनको हम विश्वविद्यालय के धरातल पर कुछ हद तक कम कर पाये हैं। हम एक नये परिवेश को सहेज पाये हैं जहाँ समता और समावेशिता दोनों हैं, और इसी वजह से हम पर हमले हो रहे हैं। हम पर हल्ला बोला जा रहा है उन ताकतों द्वारा जो नहीं चाहते कि इस तरह की नयी दुनिया छोटे से पैमाने पर भी रची जाय। हम पर हमले इसलिए हो रहे हैं कि हम विश्वविद्यालय के विरोधाभासी चरित्र को ज़िन्दा रखने की जंग लड़ रहे हैं। हम विश्वविद्यालय को केवल वर्चस्ववादी या सत्तानुकूल संस्थान बनने नहीं दे रहे हैं। और धीरे–धीरे ही सही हम अपनी लड़ाई जीत रहे हैं – क्योंकि अगर ऐसा नहीं होता तो इस तरह का बवाल नहीं खड़ा होता, कोई समस्या नहीं होती। हमारा संघर्ष कुछ और नहीं मनुष्य बनने और बनाने का संघर्ष है।

Picture credit: Samim Asgor Ali

विविधता और एकता का वैज्ञानिक पहलू

सत्यजित रथ

(13 मार्च 2016)

एक सवाल पूछ रहे हैं, हिंदी में बोलें, अंग्रेजी में बोलें?... अच्छा बाम्बे मिक्सचर में बोलते हैं। पहली बात तो ये है कि एक मित्रवर ने पूछा जो टीच–इन को फ़ोलो कर रहे हैं यूट्यूब पर कि, यार तुम कितना टाइम लोगे? मैंने कहा क्यों? यार लोग बड़ा अच्छा बोलते हैं मगर टाइम बहुत लेते हैं। यार घंटे भर बोले जाते हैं। और आख़िरकार समझ में आता है कि क्या कह रहे हैं ये, पहले क्यों नहीं बताते? तो अब हम जैव वैज्ञानिक हैं, बायोलोजिस्ट हैं, तो... टाइम आउट

Let me ask a question: Dhruv said, science has come up here, but everyone who has spoken here is from social sciences, तो वो science or यह science क्या अलग हैं? I have serious difficulties about this. And we will come back to this as we go along, but to go back to my friend, this is for him. So I'm going to do a little three sentence summary, कि क्या कहने जा रहा हूँ। और घंटे भर नहीं बोलूँगा चिंता नहीं कीजियेगा। लेकिन आधे घंटे में क्या कहने जा रहा हूँ। मैं ये कहने जा रहा हूँ कि जब हम सामाजिक प्लैटफॉर्म्स पर बात करते हैं, जब सामाजिक चर्चे–बहस होते हैं। तो कई बार ये सामने आता है कि हम जैव वैज्ञानिक सिद्धातों का आधार लेते हैं, और उन्हें आगे करते हैं कि हम ऐसे हैं, हमारा समाज ऐसा है। हमारे व्यक्तित्व ऐसे हैं क्योंकि हमारी बायोलजी ही वैसी है। क्या करें, उसके मुताबिक तो चलना ही पडेगा ना, निसर्ग नियम है। कई मुद्दों पर ये बात बार–बार सामने आती है।

And I think that it is important for us to decide how we are going to address this position. There are two ways of addressing this position, one way which is taken by very many of my friends and colleagues in social sciences and humanities is to say natural science is elitist. It is built into and pervaded by power structures and exploitation and therefore we are simply going to ignore natural science. And I suggest to you, perhaps with my biases and prejudices, that is not necessarily the most sensible thing for us to do in progressive movements and so let me offer you an alternative and that alternative is to question these easy, generalizing mythologies that are being perpetrated in the name of, 'साइंस कहता है'। तनिक पूछें तो कि साइंस सचमुच क्या कहता है। So in pursuit of this argument, I am going to do something that most of my friends have expected me not to do. तो मैंने जब पूछा कि भैया क्या बोलें, तो किसी ने कहा कि talk about the history of science and the trajectory of science. किसी ने कहा कि जेनेटिक्स और कास्ट जेनेटिक्स के बारे में जिसके बारे में मैंने और कई जगहों पर कुछ न कुछ कहा हुआ है। मेरी परेशानी ये है कि जब टीच–इन की बात है, तो यहाँ जो खड़ा है, खड़ी हैं, उन्हें आपके सामने रखने के लिए जिस विषय पर बात कर रहे हैं वह उसमें तनिक सी, थोड़ी सी, इस समझ की बारीकी होनी चाहिए ना। तो भैया अपने विषय में बात करो। दूसरे के विषय में नहीं करो। जब सिखाने को चाह रहे हो। So what I'm going to do is try and use examples that are not from the common positions and arguments and mythologies of biology that are used in these kinds of social contexts and circumstances. I'm going to use somewhat unusual ones and I'm going to make points about what biological systems do with notions of unity and diversity. What does unity mean in biological terms and what does diversity mean in biological terms and what I'm going to argue to you are the meanings of these terms and of the implicit value judgements, if you will, in them are extraordinarily diverse within biology itself and I suggest to you that it is important for us to take this into our understanding of what people are talking about. The bottom line of what I'm going to say is that when people tell you what biologists say, what they are really telling you is what they would like biologists to say which is not necessarily the same thing. So this is the summary. लेकिन भैया हिंदुस्तानी हैं, परंपराएं हैं, यूं ख़याल–वयाल की परंपरा है, विलंबित ताल तो होना ही चाहिए। तो अम् उसमें... जब ये पूछें कि ऐसी कोई परंपरा है कि बिलकुल थोड़े में कह दो? तो it turns out कि है। Since I'm doing this off the top of my head, I will make mistakes and please feel free to correct me. How should a speech be? *Vaakya*, as in that which ought to be said or that which can be said. तो वाक्य कैसा होना

चाहिए? And a really nice description comes to mind: सार्थम् तथ्यम् हितम् वाक्यम् लघु युक्तम् अनुत्तरम। सार्थ होना चाहिए, तथ्य होना चाहिए, हितकर होना चाहिए, ऐसा वाक्य लघु होना चाहिए। और अनुत्तरणीय होना चाहिए, कि उसका जवाब नहीं। This is one tradition, but keep in mind that we in the subcontinent have an extraordinary diversity of traditions. So making an unanswerable argument in and of itself is not necessarily safe for you. I will remind you, in the Brihadarankya Upanishad there is one, well, more than one, but there is a याज्ञवल्क्य गार्गी संवाद। तो गार्गी जी ने सवाल पूछे, याज्ञवल्क्य जी जवाब दे रहे थे। फिर एक सवाल पे आ गए तो याज्ञवल्क्य जी या तो उत्तर जानते नहीं थे, या तो देना नहीं चाहते थे, जो कुछ भी हो। तो जो अनुत्तरणीय सवाल पूछा गार्गी जी ने, तो याज्ञवल्क्य जी ने कहा, क्या कहा? संस्कृत पढ़े बहुत दिन हो गए। 'गार्गी मातिप्राकृति' कनि कि do not overstep माते मोधा व्यपतत् तत यानि कि your head will fall off. तुम्हारा सर कट जाएगा। So the unanswerable question can also be addressed in our traditions with violence, ये भी एक विरासत है हमारी। ये भी एक परंपरा है। We have a multiplicity of traditions that we need to integrate them, as Amartya Sen, I think, said, in our multiple identities as human beings. Actually Yajnavalkya was a very interesting character. यहाँ गार्गी जी को तो सिर्फ ये धमकी दी कि सर कट जाएगा। और एक जनाब थे, क्या नाम था विदग्धशातल्य। तो उनसे कुछ सवाल जवाब हुए, बोलचाल हुई। फिर याज्ञवल्क्य जी ने विदग्धशातल्य जी से सवाल पूछा और जब जवाब दे नहीं पाए तो याज्ञवल्क्य जी ने न सिर्फ उनका सर उड़ा दिया, लोमड़ियों को उनका सर भेंट कर दिया। There are tragic consequences in our traditions for transiting from ordinary conversations into violence. Although, maybe Yajnavalkya was like one of the hopefully occasional faculty members one sees in universities. He was a character. जनक जी had kept a debate and the prize of the debate was some x cows and y gold and so on and so forth, so what did Yajnavalkya do? चेले को बुलाया और कहा, ले जाओ घर, without participating in the debate. This is not entirely unheard of amongst university faculty members as characters. Anyway, to go back to the issue of questioning, even though there are consequences to questioning we are still talking about questioning being a tradition to respect no matter what sort of answers you get to the questioning. After all, one of the great sources of so-called traditions says that when somebody very earnestly asks कि भैया, I don't understand why we are fighting in this war. What was the answer given to him? क्लैव्यं मा स्म गमः पार्थ नैतत्वरयुपपद्यते,

क्षुद्रम् हृदयदौर्बल्यम् त्यकत्वोतिष्ठ परंतप। In other words, this is unmanly, शोभा नहीं देता तुम्हें ऐसे सब सवाल पूछना। Let us go back to the issue of questions and when we begin to ask questions about the state of society, what we really come up against, is what has come up in this particular debate again and again, which is यार पॉलिटिक्स क्यों कर रहे हो? सबने सुना है? यूनिवर्सिटी है, पॉलिटिक्स क्यों कर रहे हो? So, the reality is that कहाँ नहीं है? हांय? अरे भैया हर घर में है। तो करने न करने की बात नहीं है, मानने न मानने की बात है। So, and this is where, people begin to make these implicit distinctions, that even Dhruv made, which is कि साइंस का ज़िक्र अभी तक नहीं हुआ। यानि कि सोशल साइंस का ज़िक्र हुआ, लेकिन सोशल साइंस कोई असली साइंस नहीं है। तो अब पलायनवाद को स्वीकर कर रहे हैं। सो, सोचते तो हम हैं, सोशल साइंस और नेचुरल साइंस के बारे में हम अलग–अलग सोचते हैं। एक कहीं न कहीं दिमाग में अलग सी सोच रखते हैं। क्यों रखते हैं? वजह क्या है, उसका मूल क्या है? so, maybe think about it this way मैं कोई उत्तर देने नहीं आया हूँ, मैं सिर्फ बहस छेड़ने आया हूँ। Maybe think about it this way कि जब हम नेचुरल साइंस की बात करते हैं, we see natural science as being outside social interactions, we see social science as being imbued with social interactions so we therefore think that somehow these two are different और जहां तक हमारी अपनी बात है, तो उसमें पॉलिटिक्स बहुत ज़्यादा आएगा सोशल साइंस में, और नेचुरल साइंस में तो पॉलिटिक्स है ही नहीं। Some version of this notion is what we all carry and my problem with that notion is at many levels but for the purpose of this conversation, I suggest to you that a major outcome of this, perhaps unlooked, is that we begin to use tentative, small, explanatory models from the natural sciences and particularly from the life sciences, as universal truths to be imported by analogy into discourses of society. All said and done, argument by analogy is one of our major philosophical traditions, right? पिंड ब्रह्मांड बना है। So there's all of this and what that does is, it creates, reinforces and writes into stone the idea of myths as scientific truths, and I'm arguing, therefore, that if at all we want to contest this, we are going to have to examine the details, without which it cannot be done and that's why, a couple of examples. The issue of, as soon as you say science, particularly life science, and in the context of society, many of my friends said, यार तुम वो कास्ट जेनेटिक्स पे बात करो। Simply in the spirit of perversity, let me not talk about that, let me talk about something going a little further back a few tens of thousands of years further back, and let us talk about what biologically for our broad species group ideas of diversity and unity have meant. So think about the human genome sequencing. What the world community of life scientists did almost twenty years ago from now is that they sequenced the human genome. But there is no such thing as the human genome, because if you say *the* human genome, that's a singularity, that's a unity, that's one thing. And if you look at ourselves, we are clearly not one thing, we're not copies. So what are the sources of this immense diversity simply in appearances that we have. So there are arguments about nature and nurture, which we will talk about if time permits, but the problem with the human genome as an idea at its core is this: there is no such thing. There is an approximation. Somebody has put together a group of sequences of DNA from one person, actually from, if there are biologists here, they will remind me of three people or four people, but a mixture of three or four people, a DNA of three or four people was sequenced. And what we are looking at as a human genome is actually an approximate guess at best. We've done better simply by virtue of technology and the approximation has become less and less and less. But it's still an approximation. One of the consequences of that sequencing and of other ways of identifying genetic differences between individuals that have grown up out of that process has been a fair amount of support for the 'out of Africa' hypothesis that has been in the limelight for many years now as the explanation for the origins of humanity. And the argument there is that as a species we came out of Africa – whether before the Sumatran volcano erupted or little before or little bit after is still open to question and debate but we did indeed. We came out of Africa and we migrated here, there and everywhere, and our argument, therefore, has been most dramatically posited in old hyperbole in the pages of scientific journals about identifying Eve, identifying Adam और हम सब हैं ही आदम हव्वा की संतान, so there's all of that. And then people began saying really? Is that quite correct? Has anybody taken a careful look at the data? And people began taking a careful look at the data. Parallely, people began doing genetic sequencing, gene sequencing from non-human species. This is as different as you can get, completely different. Something like, we are homo-sapiens in formal nomenclature terms, the Neanderthals are homo neanderthalensis, so Neanderthal DNA was sequenced. And then somebody went and said if you look at genome sequences, more than ninety per cent of the genome sequences shows evidence of having come out of Africa and therefore, we are all one lineage that has come out of Africa and that is when people began looking at sequences a little more carefully and it turns out कि हममें निंडरथाल जींस भी हैं। Consider the kind of problems to the idea of species unity, species homogeneity that it creates. Because it says effectively as one interpretative explanation that we as one species have cross-bred at some point in our ancient evolutionary history with another species. What happened to unity? What happened to homogeneity? And what happened to these great biological myths that are written in stone in public discourse. This is not simply true of the Neanderthals, this is true of other non-human homo lineages such as the Denisovans, for example, who, as far as anybody can tell, were far close relatives of the Neanderthals than of the homo-sapiens. The bottom line in all of this is the clear divisions of species diversity between species and unity and homogeneity within species is not as clear cut as that. And clearly, the old gentleman with a much longer beard than mine, Darwin, knew this perfectly well, because he suggested, or well, the explanation that he suggested has grown to a very interesting perspective of what diversity and unity might mean in biological terms, which is that we generate random diversity amongst ourselves and then from random diversity there is, and I am going to use a phrase I absolutely hate, 'survival of the fittest'. Please see quotation marks around the phrase, 'Survival of the fittest'. Very, very good people come to populate the Earth. This is a fairly common notion around here. तो पहली बात ये है कि डार्विन ने ऐसा कुछ नहीं कहा। लेकिन भैया डार्विन साहब को मर के does anybody remember कितने साल हो गए, काफी साल हो गए, तो पुरानी बातें क्यों निकालें, let us simply say that the reality is that we have no idea of what fitness means. We really don't. As a matter of fact, what we think of as fitness is simply a matter of local contingent circumstances. उस वक्त क्या है, उस वक्त कैसे है? तो उसके लिए एक उदाहरण देता हूँ। मैं तो यूनिवर्सिटी में नहीं पढ़ा। मैं मेडिकल कॉलेज में गया। तो जब मेडिकल कॉलेज में हम गए तो मेडिकल कॉलेज में कोई बहस नहीं सिखाता। मेडिकल कॉलेज में याद करना पड़ता है। तो वो बात छोड़िए। When I was in medical college which is now you know, like forty years back, pretty much Darwin's time, there was a major problem with typhoid fever. Everybody had typhoid fever. There was a major problem with typhoid fever, एक एंटी–बायोटिक था, जो हमारे सीनियर्स के जमाने में काफ़ी अच्छा काम करता था। कहते थे क्लोरेम्फेनिकल। क्लोरोमाइसिटिन दे दो, बस काम कर जाएगा। और वो काम कर सकता था। जहां तक हो सकता है, काम करता था। But by the time we were senior medical students, it became very apparent that the new strains of the bacterium जो माइक्रोब है, टाइफॉइड फीवर का, what am I missing in Hindi, which generates typhoid fever, that microbe had become resistant to chloromycetin. Everybody's heard of antibiotic resistance? So the microbe had become resistant to chloromycetin. So there was a general opinion amongst physician कि अब क्लोरोमाइसिटिन नहीं दो भैया क्योंकि काम नहीं करता। As a result what happened? Slowly, but over the years, people stopped using chloromycetin. No surprise here. Now you would think that if an organism, if a bacterium has become resistant to chloromycetin, that is why in a community which is getting typhoid fever and is transmitting typhoid fever – you know our waste disposal systems are what they are, and, therefore, we tend to spread this stuff, because we don't deal with public health in the effective fashion – the organism has become resistant to chloromycetin. उसकी फिटनेस बढ़ गई। ठीक है न? सब माने, कि उसकी फिटनेस बढ़ गई? Because it has competed and survived. जब बाकी सब मर गए, इसकी फिटनेस बढ़ी। तो इसकी फिटनेस बढ़ी तो अनादिकाल तक इसकी फिटनेस बढ़ी रहनी चाहिए थी न? दस साल पहले जब लोग देखने लगे कि एंटीबायोटिक रेज़िस्टेंस की प्रोफाइल क्या है? आज कल के जो टायफॉइड फीवर के बैक्टीरिया हैं, उनकी? तो उनमें से कई सारे क्लोरोमाइसिटिन को सेंसिटिव हैं। ये कैसे हो गया? If fitness increases as an absolute value, remember what we keep doing, this is why I'm saying, we make these transitions from tentative ideas that are contingent in the natural sciences into broad brushed mythologies in public discourse. So has fitness increased in some global value? Not at all. All that happened was, उस वक्त काफ़ी एंटी–बायोटिक इधर–उधर था, तो जो रेज़िस्टेंट था वो बढ़ा। But in order to be resistant to the antibiotic तो उस बेचारे बेक्टीरिया को भी कुछ काम करना पड़ा न? It had to make something that would allow it to become resistant. वो जो कुछ बना रहा था whatever protein the bacterium was making, whatever he (he is a good term to use for bacteria) was making, whatever the species, whatever the population was making, for protecting itself against an antibiotic was a great advantage when the antibiotic was there but it became a great drag when the antibiotic was not there. क्योंकि तो बनाए जा रहा है, बनाए जा रहा है, बनाए जा रहा है। बाहर एंटीबायोटिक है ही नहीं बिटवा। है न? तो उसके जो प्रतिस्पर्धी हैं उनका काम पचास प्रोटीन बना के चल जा रहा है। ये इक्यावनवां भी बना रहा है। तो जब ज़्यादा बना रहा है तो ज़्यादा खाना पड़ेगा। और जब ये होता है, then in competitive terms, you now have the situation that the resistant bacterium is less fit. The ideas of 'survival of the fittest' are this extraordinarily plastic and contingent on circumstances. This is a major issue and as I said, I am purely for perverse reasons not going to use ordinary, regular examples of diversity, I am going to use other examples. कहते हैं, especially in my field, मैं इम्युनॉलजी में काम करता हूँ, यानि कि प्रतिरक्षा विज्ञान में काम करता हूँ, I and my colleagues work on how the body protects itself, right? Straight forward. And every time, and this is absolutely classic, every time people in my field, my discipline, begin to talk about immune response, the analogy drawn is of a war. It's like just war doctrine kind of argument made by this analogy. The argument is the body fights a defensive war because the body is attempting to protect its 'unity and integrity' – everyone has heard this terminology. And since all of us are here, each one of us at this point in time, has at least won the battle. That's the interpretation, or at least it should be the interpretation ये तो मंज़ूर है आपको? तो ये सवाल पूछें कि एक मानव शरीर ले लें, एक ऐसे मनुष्य का, जो मनुष्य कल्याण के लिए अपना शरीर देने के लिए तैयार हैं। ध्रुव भैया हाथ ऊपर कर रहे हैं। और everybody is familiar कि शरीर कोशिकाओं का बना हुआ है। The body is made up of cells, तो अपन ये करें, Never mind how we disassemble Prof Dhruv Raina's body into its composite cells पूरे जैसे हैं, वैसे ले लें, and collect cells. Your expectation is that every cell in that test tube full of formerly Dhruv Raina's cells will consist of Dhruv Raina's cells, correct? That's obvious. More than half of those cells aren't his cells at all, more than half of those cells are bacteria, because half the cell count in your body is actually bacteria. You can debate कि exactly हाफ है क्या? कोई कहता है 30% है, कोई कहता है 70% है या काफ़ी बैक्टीरिया हैं। ठीक है न? If we have been fighting this immune response war in order to protect the sovereign territorial 'unity and integrity' of our bodies, what is this bacteria doing in Dhruv Raina's test tube? So it turns out that immune responses don't actually function like that. Do they kill bacteria? Sure. Do they quite frequently not kill bacteria? Sure. How do they decide? That's trying to figure out how they decide. But ज़ाहिर है when half the cells in your body are not your own, there is something wrong with the simplified notion of immune response as a defensive war. And as I was saying this, I was wondering whether I need to underline the implications of this, but I clearly don't. So I will simply continue telling you this story for a few more minutes. आप पूछियेगा कि (...) this is a diversity, in your body this is a diversity. Is this simply a diversity that we tolerate? तो प्रयोग किया जा सकता है। प्रयोग क्या है? अब इंसान को लेना तो मुश्किल है, लेकिन चूहे को ले सकते हैं? तो चूहा ले लो और पूरी चूहे की नस्ल स्टेराइल बबल में रखो। So, effectively what you are doing is by virtue of engineering technology, you make a germ-free, microbe-free environment, you keep mice, you breed mice within that environment. Do they live? Yeah sure, खान पान होता है, सब कुछ होता है, they live, they breed, everything is okay. No, everything is not okay, so it turns out that in mice that have no exposure to germs, immune system का ये आप सोचेंगे कि कोई काम ही नहीं है, लेकिन their body parts don't all develop properly. If you look at their immune organs, if you look at their lymph nodes. So these lymph nodes are organs, तो अपने आप बनने चाहिए। ये बाहरी मदद क्यों लगती है? अपने आप नहीं बना सकते? And the answer is नहीं बना सकते। As a matter of fact, many organs in the body are developmentally dependent on signals that look remarkably like the signals the immune system uses when it responds to microbes. What it does in response to microbes, number one, is quite frequently what it also uses to build its own organs, and number two, some of that organ building exercise, it simply cannot complete if there are no microbes. That's one thing, the second thing which is wrong with these mice that are germ free, is that they are really not very well. Vitamin नही होता, some amino acids, some small hormones, lots of things they are deficient in. Why are they deficient? Because it is bacteria in your gut that is making all of this. तो आप कहोगे, कि यार the bacteria in your gut वो तो अंदर नहीं जाते न, मतलब अंदर हैं लेकिन अंदर से अंदर नहीं जाते न। तो इस वजह से उनके ख़िलाफ डिफेंस करने की कोई जरूरत नहीं पड़ती। सरासर झूठ है। सरासर झूठ क्यों है? मोहतरमा से पूछिए, वहाँ बैठी हैं, कि जब आपकी आंत में जितने बैक्टीरिया हैं, उनकी जांच तलाश करें, तो दो तिहाई से ज़्यादा बैक्टीरिया के ऊपर एंटीबॉडीज हैं। इसका मतलब ये कि आपका शरीर

उनके ख़िलाफ इम्यून रेस्पॉन्स बना चुका है। फिर भी वो वहीं के वहीं हैं, और वो जो कर रहे हैं उस से आपको भी फायदा हो रहा है। These are the contingent complexities of immune responses. The trivial, linear, foolish narrative of all-out war is simply not biological, it's human. So, one last point about diversity and the sheer value of diversity. You take cells in your body. In the first place every one of your cells has a somewhat different genome sequence. There are cells in your body which do not have your entire genetic complement and these are the cells in your body, for example, that make anti-bodies. And everybody has heard of anti-bodies. Let's not worry about what they are and so on and so forth, everybody has heard of anti-bodies. वैक्सिन्स दिए जाते हैं, एंटीबॉडीज बनती हैं, प्रोटेक्शन करती हैं, वगैरह, वगैरह, वगैरह। Now, if you take the cells that make anti-bodies, each one of those cells individually is different from every other cell. The diversity of your anti-body repertoire is immense. We're talking about diversity in the millions, right? Here is an example of a diversity in your body of your own cells, so you turn around and ask the same question, is this diversity simply being tolerated, ये इसका कोइ मतलब भी है? And repeatedly over the past fifteen years, and I will stop here, because I am now referring to relatively recent biological science, over the past fifteen years, it has steadily become more and more apparent that as we restrict the diversity of the anti-body repertoire, so we limit the ability of the body to make effective immune responses against microbial diseases. There is positive value in diversity even in biological systems. So last point, or more correctly an epilogue. What I'm trying to say is, when we find something that we think is problematic, we have options and choices. One option is पीठ फेर के चले जाना। और ये कहें कि इसका कोई मतलब नहीं। the other option is, खड़े होकर पूछें, अच्छा सचमुच? सबूत है? क्या है? समझाइए तो? Because ultimately everything that we are trying to do deals with trying to build more and more nuanced, more and more complex models of understanding. That's what scholarship is about, that's what university is all about. Many of my friends in the natural sciences have this tendency of saying यार ये सोशल साइंस अपन बिल्कुल नहीं समझते, वो क्या करते हैं। We are looking for objective truth. सुना है? तो अब सत्य के साथ मेरा बड़ा पेचीदा रिश्ता है क्योंकि सत्य के कई पहलू हैं। And I will remind you again of our own tradition in terms of the dimensions and perspectives of truth. Again, याद होना चाहिए, सलाह है तो सभा के बारे में कहें, न सा सभा यत्र न संति वृद्धा, that is not a sabha where there are no elders. न ते वृद्धा ये न वदंति धर्म, that those are not elders, who do not talk about the right way. ना असौ धर्मो यत्र न च अस्ति सत्यम्, that is not the right way which does not have the truth. And the last line, न तत् सत्यम् यत्छले नानुबिद्धम। वो सत्य नहीं है जो छल–छलावे से ओत–प्रोत और बंधा हुआ है।

Picture credit: Samim Asgor Ali

Crisis of Indian Nationalism

B.S. Butola

(14 MARCH 2016)

I SINCERELY THANK JNUTA, JNUSU AND particularly my colleagues and students for giving me an opportunity to debate on an issue like nationalism and sedition with an open mind, without any fear and prejudice. I was never a student of geography until I came to JNU. During those days, JNU was more interdisciplinary than it is today. Students were admitted to one discipline or a centre but they had the freedom to take courses in other centres. I had the liberty of attending classes across centres.

It is this exposure to different disciplines that helped me to shape the viewpoint that I am going to share with you this afternoon. But friends and students, my exposure to the north-east for nearly sixteen years with lots of students whom I had the opportunity to teach and guide, was the second most significant factor in crystallizing my views. I have supervised over twenty research scholars on various socio-economic and environmental aspects of the region, subject to their satisfying one necessary condition: 'I would not supervise a student unless I visit the area he/she is interested in specializing.' As a result of that, I am indebted to students of the North Eastern Hill University (NEHU), particularly students coming from Nagaland, Mizoram, Manipur, Arunachal Pradesh, Assam, Meghalaya, Tripura for first-hand knowledge about the nature of identity assertions and sub-nationalist contestations. As a result of that, when I talk about nation, it reminds me of a poem by 'Dhoomil' Sudama Pandey: 'If you really want to know the virtue of iron, please don't look at the power of the sword of Maharana Pratap, but think and look at the snaffle (rein, lagaam) that the horse has in his mouth because he only knows what the actual worth of the iron is.' When we talk about the nation and nationalism, the Nagas, the Mizos and others have an imagination of a larger Nagaland and Mizoram. Similarly, the worth of the true nation is part of the living memory of the people of the north-east. Suddenly, on 15 August 1947, their nation was bifurcated; without really knowing, one fine morning they became anti-national, because they had not participated in the making of the history and geography of this country. What I'm saying is that the method they may have adopted is wrong, but the issue they are raising is genuine. What they are saying is very simple: When a nation was being made they experienced Partition without their participation and consent. Their anguish is also that most narratives that were/are created only talk about the partition of Bengal and Punjab, what about the territories, societies, culture and communities of the north-east? We have so far refused to listen to the alternative voices and particularly the voices from the margins of the nation state.

It is against this backdrop that I present this talk for your critical scrutiny. Why crisis of the nation? The way the nation has been constructed has the answer within it. There are two ways in which the nation has been constructed so far. One is called the legal or political way of constructing a nation. The other is based on the civil or justice paradigm. The former is most common and a widely accepted paradigm. It is based on three founding pillars of the modern nation state.

The first is the Treaty of Westphalia,[1] where it was mentioned that a unitary centralizing power is indispensable for new political dispensations. The second one came from what is known as a popular article about *The Rights of Man* by Thomas Paine.[2] Who was Thomas Paine? He was the only person who had participated in all the three revolutions – the American Revolution, the French Revolution and the English Revolution. And the tragedy of this man was that when he wrote *The Rights of Man*, Edmund Burke had the audacity to abuse him in every possible term for being the propagator of this treaty, and justifying the

French Revolution. His only fault was that he was the first to talk about 'The Rights of Man'. The third pillar was the American Revolution itself, particularly its 'Right of Representation' from 1750 to 1770. The thrust of the Revolution was 'no taxation without representation...'

There was another significant contribution to such legal construction of a nation but it came much later from John Stuart Mill's *On Liberty* in 1859.[3] But how does it matter? It matters because all these things were epitomized in the French Revolution (1789–93) but with a difference. Thereafter, it was proclaimed that the nation will not be considered only as a political entity, as a legal entity, but it should be considered as a civil entity in which the laws, rules and regulation, rights were essential and may be only necessary conditions, but are not sufficient. On the contrary, these will have to be qualified with justice. It was advocated by none other than Rousseau. As a result of that, Voltaire had said that reason, literacy, education, should be qualifications of being a citizen. These views were fiercely contested by Rousseau who said no such condition should become the basis of citizenship; unless you take knowledge, wisdom, 'Social Contract'[4] and justice on. According to Rousseau, if a nation is not just, if a nation's rights are not just, if any law of the nation is not just, that nation does not deserve to be a nation. It is an irony that Voltaire, who was an epitome of individual rights, proclaimed, 'I don't agree with what you say but I will defend to the death your right to say it',[5] but had no patience to extend the same generosity towards Rousseau. As a consequence of these, when we talk about sedition, it needs to be taken a little more critically. Sedition may be legally right, but in terms of justice, may not be so. It is particularly relevant in the present situation where the charges of sedition are slapped against the JNUSU president and twenty other students, which is outrageous both from the point of view of legal and justice paradigms.

A lot has been said about the legal aspects of a nation and sedition from the legal perspective by the previous speakers. Therefore, today I want to discuss the same from the perspective of justice in the context of crises of the nation states. But before I take it up for discussion, let me just tell you why I choose to speak on this topic. And how nations become a reality. The first thing that was crucial for the rise of the nation was the transition from subject to citizen. Please remember that the law of sedition in India was promulgated soon (1870) after the first war of India's independence (1857). At that time Indians were not citizens, we were British subjects. Today, if you apply the same law to citizens, it is irrelevant. We are citizens. Citizenship can never be gifted to anybody. Human history tells us that it has been won and one can only enjoy it if one has the wherewithal to defend it.

The second important aspect essential to the rise of the nation state is the emergence of democracy, which is again a much contested domain. Somebody says that the right to get elected or to participate in the election process and choose your leader is democracy. These things are no guarantee of democracy. In fact some of the worst dictators also rose to power through elections. An electoral democracy becomes a proper democracy only when it is interlinked to citizenship. Now, the question is, who is a citizen? A citizen is one who has the right to produce and reproduce the material as well as cultural wealth and social relations. They have the right to invest, and also, the right to participate in making history. But that does not make it democracy ... without ... our consent. Democracy without consent is not a democracy. How do you really get the consent? After the French Revolution, when legitimacy shifted from the divine to the people, what the new ruling class did is that they started a ministry, an institutional process and mechanism where consent could be manufactured. It was all because of the imperatives of the political and legal notion of the nation state. The process was very simple, the state engaged people through various ways in the process of manufacturing consent. The whole process proved detrimental to justice or to the social contract aspects of the nation states. Meaning thereby, democracy becomes a misnomer unless one works towards democratizing the knowledge system itself, the basic social unit, i.e., the families, the classrooms, the political parties, even the entire system of socialization. Unless you build a movement in democratizing these components of our society, democracy will not be possible, nor will the goals of social justice be met. Therefore, you continuously renew new social ties or social contracts. Democracy is a system of renewing your social contract on a daily basis. Therefore, the first aspect is citizens, second aspect is that of democracy.

Democracy is also about activating people or motivating people to question the kind of patriarchy that exists, the undemocratic practices, the kind of knowledge we are fed in every sphere of our lives. In fact, T.S. Eliot once said, 'Where is life we have lost in living? Where is the wisdom we have lost in knowledge? Where is the knowledge we have lost in information?'[6] We must question everything and this alone can guarantee a successful democracy. Now what is actually happening is that in the name of the right to know, what you know is basically information, not knowledge. Democracy based on mass production and circulation of information without taking into consideration the institutional mechanism to filter knowledge from information and wisdom from a mass of information is destined to fail.

The third important aspect is that of territory, and when you create national territory, the boundaries become very important. What actually happened was that boundaries started becoming one of the criteria by which you construct the 'other'. Therefore, geography, or somebody may call it geo-bodification, is considered essential for the existence of a nation. Take, for example, in Germany, when the nation came into existence, the concept of 'Germania' formed the core of the nation state. Like Mother India in India there is also a 'Germania' in Germany and 'Mariana' in France. What that means is that you are imposing the political territory onto the female body and vice versa. Why 'Mother India'? The concept was taken from the novel *Anandamath* by Bankim Chandra Chatterjee.[7] It is very surprising that in *Anandamath*, the enemy was British to begin with, in its first edition, but since Bankim Chandra was a regulatory officer under the British, he apprehended some trouble, hence, subsequently replaced the British by Muslims in the second edition. Ever since, this became the most potent, the most useful document for the people who are trying to change the colour and the size of their trousers now. So far as the British were concerned there were no takers, but as far as the Muslims are concerned it helped in the geo-bodification of India. Now why mother? Because in patriarchy, mother is constructed as weak, fragile, emotional, compassionate, caring and always in need of protection; therefore, it is the duty of the son – the devout son, the proud son – to protect his mother. Contrary to this, if you have to protect your father, it is unbecoming of patriarchy. The patriarch can command everybody, nobody can command the patriarch. As a result, this mother concept becomes very useful, it continues to survive and reproduce the kind of weakness, the kind of emotional aspect that is very important for the existence of a nation.

The other important aspect of the nations and the crises is the concept of identities. E.J. Hobsbawm in his book, *Nations and Nationalism since 1780*,[8] says that in Europe, there were as many as 400 identities before 1780 but after 1880, when the nation state came into existence, only seventeen identities were left, and today the process goes on in other spheres of life. The days are not very far when things will get universalized by destroying the diverse and pluralistic universe. For example, at present there are 60,000 different languages and dialects people speak or use for communication; by 2051, only four languages may survive. With time the linguistic identities will go, national identities will disappear. Once you have a national identity, it is unitarian. In fact, if you are a nation you can have only one flag, one song, sometimes one uniform, or one currency, one legal system, etc.

What I'm trying to say is that I have seen people in Arunachal Pradesh, there is a community called the 'Monpas'. It is natural for the Monpas to get married by capture. As per their tradition, if someone captures the girl and keeps her confined for three days, he is entitled to marry her. Now, say for example, if he fails three times, throughout his life he is forbidden to marry.[9] We are today trying to judge various cultures and traditions through the common lens of the IPC, but please try to understand. I am not trying to reason that what the Monpas are doing is correct, but one must understand the practices to bring them into a discourse of citizenship. Do not 'Other' them, because Sartre says, the moment you 'Other' someone, you are bound to condemn him because 'Other' is someone who has no right to survive. This is just one of many instances by which the nation starts 'Othering'. As opposed to this, in social contract, there is no 'Other'. In social contract, you can always revive, you can always change. Change does not threaten, it only induces resilience.

It is in this context that I want to mention another important aspect of nationalism, that is, constitutionalism, which is about one law, one rule, one kind of thing. In the case of India, there is a Constitution.

It is called 'Samvidhan', which could mean 'samay ka vidhan', it is the need of the hour, at that point of time this was a necessity. With the passage of time are we able to change this Constitution? It is also 'Sambandho ka vidhan'. It is a document of different kinds of social contracts and also 'Sambidhan', meaning everybody is equal in the eyes of the Constitution. Now the thing is whether the people of the country need to be constructed according to the Constitution or whether the Constitution of the country needs to be changed according to the people. This was the question to which Dr Bhim Rao Ambedkar was trying to find an answer. He said in no uncertain terms, when you are fighting for your independence and citizenship, should the right to 'Self-Rule' be the important agenda, or the right to 'Self-Respect'? It is well known what happened thereafter. 'Self-Respect' is an agenda of social justice, while 'Self-Rule' is actually an agenda of your legality, the political discourse, and as a result of that, we must also say that the Constitution of our country must bring forth the justice aspect of it. If it does not ensure justice on questions of gender, ethnicity, language, reason, or the right to hold different viewpoints, is everybody who is not agreeing with you necessarily turning against you? The point is that, justice, plurality and diversity are the essence of the Constitution, not only the legality. The moment you talk of uniformity, it can only take place at the cost of justice, and at the prospect of injustice.

What actually is happening is that everything is being done, as Habermas said, through 'strategic action'. There are two types of languages being used by the state and the economy in their engagement with the people. They are using a type of language that is called the strategic language and what the people and society are talking of is communicative language; and there is a disconnect.

Nations have outlived their utility, so the earlier they go the better. Because human history never paid a bigger price for anything as they have paid for nation. So long as the nation continues, the process of 'Othering' will continue on different pretexts. Enemies will be created – enemies outside – and enemies within will be externalized. For example, if somebody is a communist possessing Western ideology, you externalize him. Similarly, a Muslim is also external because he is not loyal to the country. Somebody said that he is Muslim because his concept of janambhumi, punyabhumi, or pitribhumi is different and on the basis of that, you externalize him. Though the reality is: What is different between a Muslim and me, or for that matter, anybody else? In fact, what we should look at is how many commonalities are there; and that is truly more important. There is no doubt that diversity is full of hopes and opportunities. Therefore, it should be celebrated. But if there are no discernible indicators of diversity, we should not artificially create one and make it a basis of 'Othering', which is unfortunately the case with most of the Muslims in India.

The last thing I want to say about this, and then I will come to crises, is the way they have considered the geography and obviously the territorialization of it. The political territorialization needs serious reconsideration. In India, we are having problems with Bangladesh, Nepal, Bhutan, and sometimes with Pakistan. You can't rethink that political boundary or legalized political boundaries are not genuine. The Brahmaputra has its source in Tibet, but flows through India into Bangladesh. Why can't this be a unit of our political imagination, which can bring us all together, rather than this becoming a bone of contention? Similarly, the case of Nepal is also significant. If there are cultural similarities, relating to language for instance, why can't they be taken on board, rather than sticking to a political boundary, which is basically what I would call a colonial design? The colonial power really wanted India to be divided the way it is. Unfortunately for them in India, they could not do what they did in Africa, i.e., to cut this country too like a cake. But unfortunately, the ecological aspect, the cultural aspect, and many other aspects which provide a better alternative to reconfiguring the territory of this country were not given a serious consideration. We are sticking to these boundaries because a map is there. For most people, it is surprising that at one point of time 78 per cent of people in parliament could not even sing the national anthem and 98 per cent people did not even draw the map of India. We must understand that the map of India is not the India everyone knows, India lives in everybody's heart. India lives in the kind of social contract in which we continuously engage ourselves.

It is against this background that I would like to tell you what are the crises of the nation state and how even sedition, which is basically a political and legal kind of category, does not apply to a social contract category, and how we are really being misguided.

One, as I said earlier, there is a contradiction between political citizenship and civic citizenship. What the people of JNU really want is that while we are not against political citizenship, we also want a civic citizenship. Second, that we have a disagreement, and the moment I disagree with you, I become your enemy. The nation was supposed to strive on three basic principles – liberty, equality and fraternity, which was also the theme of the French Revolution. Today, what is actually happening is that neither liberty, nor freedom, nor equality is in the agenda of the nation state. In fact, what actually happens today in the age of economic liberalization is that we are losing a great deal of biodiversity, diversity in terms of food products, cultural and social capitals, ways of life, traditional and indigenous knowledge systems, etc.

The other important aspect of this is the threat posed to the nation by the ecological crisis. Nations are saying now, we are helpless. What do you need to do? Bring carbon emission down, bring down the emission of CFC gases. George Bush had the audacity of saying that Indians are rearing a large number of cattle, which is adding to the methane in the atmosphere. He said that Indian middle-class income has increased, therefore, Indians are eating more rice, food habits are changing, and therefore, rice is becoming costly. But the ecological crises which the nation states are not able to overcome are resulting in poor people being blamed. It is not their fault.

To understand this mechanism let me bring two more components into the discussion. It is being said that nations are also supposed to be a repository of culture or a container of culture. But today, what choice do we have? Our children have? Our children have the choice between Mickey Mouse/Donald Duck and Hanumanji. The former decontextualizes and the latter brings obscurantism. Now the problem is that I am against Mickey Mouse/Donald Duck but I am equally against Hanumanji. But as a result of this corporate entertainment, Mickey Mouse/Donald Duck, the better of the two competitors, is pushing all cultural symbols to the margins and, ultimately, extinction.

Take the Barbie doll, for example, which runs into a forty-four-billion-dollar business per year, and look at the fate of the 43,000 dolls that Shankar's International Dolls Museum has, representing different cultures! The Barbie doll has outpaced them all and no nation can protect these cultures. One must really understand whether nations are for the cultural right of the people or not, and this really reflects the crisis. If you fail to deliver what you are supposed to, that is the real crisis. Somebody who is invading your culture and plundering your cultural capital should be your concern.

The other important aspect that I really want to talk about is the crisis of the geo-body. Now what actually is happening is that not many people today want to stick to the map aspect of geography. Maps are really becoming a kind of trial. Maps are becoming a trap. What actually happens is that people really want to go beyond this map trap. I mean, if you can contact and interact with the people – not to talk to them of their nationality – but their way of life, the languages that they speak and calculate the degree of difference that may exist. That is essential for building the bonds of mutual respect and understanding.

There are no short cuts in history. Lenin said once upon a time: It is not that a ruling class can't be thrown out of power without a revolution, but revolution is a must because then they will also know how to use the power they get thereafter. This is a must. History is a very good teacher, not only the history that departments of the history can teach, but also the way you participate in history. That is also a very good teacher. History department teaches, there is no doubt about that, but the way you all participate in history-making is also a good teacher.

Now the nation state along with the corporate, liberal interests have declared a war against life in general and life processes in particular. Today, these forces have been actively working to recast certain organisms. What is the green revolution? The green revolution is nothing but your ability to change the rhythm of the agricultural product and synchronize this with market rhythms. What is the blue revolution, you have changed the rhythm of aquatic lives, particularly fish. What is the white revolution? It is a process of tempering the biological clock of the cattle for earning higher profit in the market. Now the greatest achievement of the white revolution is that India is the largest producer of milk, though per unit production is much lower. One of the highlights of this revolution is that different breeds of cows and buffaloes will be completely eliminated and only the Jersey cow will live.

Now come to health. We are told that India is becoming the health resort of the world. But it is a big misnomer. What is truly happening is that today India has become the source of the organ trade, the designer baby and the outsourced womb. The nation state is failing miserably to protect its people. On the contrary, it legitimizes this murky business. Now everybody knows that a certain homeopath succeeded in transplanting 5,000 kidneys in moving vans. It was a full-fledged illegal organ trade and there was no sedition charge against him.

One must really talk about the nation state and the stoic silence it maintains over such a catastrophe. Catastrophe here I mean in a Darwinian sense. Darwin wrote a book in 1857, *On the Origin of Species by Means of Natural Selection*. Now the nation state is writing a book, 'The End of the Species', because today all of the species including the human species are at the brink of total extinction and will be replaced by 'designer species' or 'Cyborg Species'.[10] What is actually happening is that people do not want a tailor-made world but they have no option. Now everybody wants a designer baby, a baby who will be very good at football, etc., so they go to the best sperm bank, etc. This has resulted in the violation of your human rights, because human rights have never been considered a matter of serious debate and discussion as far as the crisis of the nation state is concerned. This, I think, is an ontological war that nations are launching on human beings and on every living being. People do not have choices except for what is available in the market. It is the market which is deciding the social and it is the social which is deciding the human, the organic.

What is poverty in India today? Poverty in India today is not defined in terms of calories per capita, etc. No! This is again an outdated concept. A poor person is one who fails to be a good consumer! So the onus of being poor lies on the poor themselves, because they fail to be good consumers. Since you fail to consume, so you are poor. You are not a good consumer, therefore you are poor.

It is in this light that nation states are doing injustice to their own people. For most people, the nation stands forth as a legal category, not as a civil category. Nations should stand forth based on social contract. In the case of India today, we have a very narrow definition of nation which is being seen in terms of the political viability. Please consider whether it is justifiable in terms of justice or not. In the case of JNU today it is only two, three, four, five, six or eight people who have been charged with sedition. The time is not very far, if the political alone remains the central theme of the nation state, when everybody will be on the other side of the nation state. The reason is that one must really come forward to say that the nation must stand for the continuous renewal of social contract and that is the only future that matters. Thank you.

*

Notes/References/Bibliography

1. The Westphalian System was based on four basic principles: 1. Principle of Territoriality: a. well-defined territorial boundaries, b. absolute monopoly of power, c. legal system, d. taxing authority and, e. congruency of territory, state, people, nation, religion and all social systems. 2. Principle of Sovereignty: a. States are the only relevant actors, b. Outward sovereignty (no superior authority), c. representation of interest is based on self-help, d. inward sovereignty (free choice of political system), e. Not accountable about internal affairs. 3. Principle of Legal Equality: a. Sovereign states have equal rights (whatever their size, population, power, etc.), b. Relations among states governed by international law or treaties are based on voluntary acts, c. International cooperation takes place out of self-interest. 4: Principle of Balance of Power: a. Sovereign states form a state-system, b. The state-system is stable, if a balance of power exists, c. Weak states form alliances against strong states, d. Since 1713 (Peace of Utrecht), the 'Concert' of the five European Great Powers (Great Britain, France, Austria-Hungary, Russia, Prussia/Germany) formed; United States and Japan joined the Concert at the end of the nineteenth century.
2. Thomas Paine, 1984, *The Rights of Man*, Harmondsworth: Penguin Classics.
3. John Stuart Mill, 2001, *On Liberty*, Ontario: Batoche Books Limited.
4. Jean-Jacques Rousseau, 2006, *The Social Contract* (The Principles of Political Right), Harmondsworth: Penguin Books.
5. It has been reported that these words were never spoken by Voltaire. On the contrary these were attributed to him by one of his biographers Evelyn Beatrice Hall in 1906.

6. T.S. Eliot, 1934, 'Choruses From the Rock', Opening Stanza.
7. Bankim Chandra Chatterji, 2006, *Anandamath*, New Delhi: Orient Paperbacks.
8. E.J. Hobsbawm, 1992, *Nations and Nationalism since 1780: Programme, Myth, Reality,* Cambridge: Cambridge University Press.
9. This was revealed by the villagers and Lamas during the field survey of Kameng Himalayas, Arunachal Pradesh, 2004-05.
10. Donna J. Haraway, 1985, 'A Cyborg Manifesto: Science, Technology and Socialist-Feminism in the Late Twentieth Century', *Socialist Review*, no. 80, pp. 65–108; 1991, *Simians, Cyborgs, and Women: The Reinvention of Nature*, New York: Routledge, pp.128-49.

Picture credit: www.standwithjnu.org

Nation-building in India and Its Contemporary Challenges

Anand Kumar

(16 MARCH 2016)

FRIENDS, THIS IS A VERY SERIOUS process, which the nation is witnessing, courtesy JNU and greater courtesy Shri Narendra Modi, Rajnath Singh and Smriti Irani! They have made us interrogate our statecraft, they have made us check again the meaning of democracy, the meaning of freedom, rule of law and the threat of lumpenization of public sphere and I salute the genius of JNUSU and JNUTA in suggesting that a thought has to be challenged by a superior thought, not by lathi, not by gaali, not by fraud and lies. So, in the last three weeks, you have shown resilience and you have rallied, people of substance, the mind makers of modern India, who are respected for their depth of scholarship, their objectivity and their courage of conviction.

Nation-building is a very important challenge for a great civilization like India which has been humiliated, defeated, fractured and fragmented by 200 years of imperial rule, and which is trying to pick up the pieces through the process of democracy and through the wisdom of its people. The idea of India has gone through a paradigm shift. And people like us, who are successors to the theories of unity in diversity, continuity and change, dialogue between tradition and modernity, who are inheritors of a legacy of objective social analysis with a touch of optimism about social change in India, caste in India, communalism in India, injustices in India, have had to carry on the dialogue with reality. Nationalism and national unity are not two sides of the same coin. If we pursue the wrong kind of nationalism, exclusive nationalism, it can contribute to the destruction of the nation. And all patriots, in half pants and full pants, must not take the nation for granted, because the nation is built on 'we feeling'. 'We feeling' is hard to sustain. It has to be given institutional backup – institutions that can create 'we feeling' – and backed by the rule of law. It has to be supported by political, economic and social justice, so that the age-old habit of human beings, of converting hierarchies into frozen steps of inclusion and exclusion, can remain fluid and can be verified by the judicial system, by common citizens' common sense.

The case of India as a nation is a very complicated one. The challenge of nation-building has been a very serious challenge from the beginning because the models that were available to the people of India in the 1930s and '40s were coming out of European history. The Europeans, the Western nations generally, had the privilege and the courage to interrogate themselves again and again. If they found irrationality, they went for a social contract. So the political revolution of France, the Industrial Revolution of England, coupled with the American Civil War, and the Russian Revolution, all created a different kind of homogenizing experience. Europe had a civilizational advantage or disadvantage above India of being monolithic – one religion, one race. And when a few million migrants moved in as punishment for their colonial past, the Russians are saying no more multi-culturality, the land of Rousseau is saying no more social contract, get these blacks out, get these Muslims out! It's just a post-Second World War phenomenon for them. But their model of nation, their definition of nation, charmed some of us. We thought, oh, we have some advantage, only we need to cut the corners, and the advantage is that there is a major religious tradition – called Hinduism. So why can't we have, after colonials are gone, a Hindu Rashtra! And then some others thought, why not a Muslim nation.

And you will be surprised that this evening I will be recommending that you hold your study of Ambedkar – one of the architects of the Constitution; don't go to Nehru or rush to Gandhi, don't do that; or Rabindranath Tagore – a proponent of inclusive nationalism bordering humanism, who said it to the Japanese in their face, and Americans in their homeland, that what they were pursuing was a very brutalizing experience – don't do that at the moment. Instead, go and read immediately, and simultaneously, Shri Golwalkar's *Bunch of Thoughts* and Shri Muhammad Ali Jinnah. Both of them have such a historical understanding of Indian civilization, including two of its great religious orders – Hinduism and Islam. They treat them as bricks, which can be placed here or there, but cannot be put together. This mechanistic understanding of Indian civilization and its flow – living in denial about the diversities of Muslim samaj, Hindu samaj, their pathologies, their successes and failures – made them blind enough to play the ball with their colonial masters and their policy of divide and rule. It is a sad story for those who believed that Hindi, Hindu, Hindustan, could be a model because that model was very close to the European definition of a nation, cultural nationalism as a primary motive around linguistic homogeneity. But with the onward march of events and processes and the two world wars – which were fought around the idea of exclusive nationalism, in which nearly every home had a wailing woman and a killed man, in France, Germany, England, Holland, Belgium, Poland, Russia – they got tired of this idea of exclusive, pure and uniform nationalism.

In the sociology of identity formation, there are seven interconnected principles of identity formation in all parts of the modern world as they are also for us in India: 1. individuality, 2. locality, 3. community, 4. ethnicity, 5. nationality, 6. civilization, and 7. humanity. First, and foremost, we are all given the opportunity to have our own individuality – your name, your likes, your dislikes, individual preferences generally. Our individuality is a continuously evolving reality and we try to engage with other forms of our reality around this central value of our individuality. Then, immediately beyond individuality, there is something called locality that is ignored when you confront a larger reality called a foreign nation. But otherwise, locality is an important marker of our identity as it defines our group in the primary sense. When we grow up, we learn social and cultural skills in the locality. Locality is immediately supplemented by community, which then is followed by ethnicity, where you have certain broader, defining social and cultural principles, language, customs and norms. Ethnicity is an important marker of our identity but often, in our anxiety about protecting national unity, we try to bulldoze the idea of ethnicity. About the simultaneous existence of the difference markers of our identity, a very interesting proposition was made by one of the top leaders of Sindh, when he was confronted by the Pakistani regime which wanted to know who he was. He replied: How can I answer, because I have many people living inside me; I am a Sindhi for 5,000 years, I am a Muslim for 1,400 years, and I am a Pakistani for 40–45 years; so tell me which one has to be surrendered in order to prove my loyalty to the government of the day, which is there like the wink of an eye, here today, gone tomorrow. I cannot surrender any of them, they are all close to my heart, they all define me collectively, and I am proud of all three of them.

There was a time when there was a colonial challenge to our identity and the colonizer said: What is India? We came here, we conquered you; you people, thousands of castes, hundreds of languages, dozens of faith systems, can you stay united one day without us? We have come here to civilize you. And the Indians were really baffled, some of our forefathers and mothers. Even in that historical situation, the first flush of identity formation was around ethnicity. You remember the name of the major newspaper published by one of the greatest icons of Indian nationalism, Bal Gangadhar Tilak, it was *Mahratta*. And the name of the newspaper published by Lala Lajpat Rai, it was not Hind Kesari, it was *Punjab Kesari*! Then they realized that the challenge was much bigger and they soon made efforts towards national-level organization and mobilization. Above nationality comes civilizational formations. Every human being has a civilizational identity as well. Don't think that Africans don't have a civilizational imperative or the people in Latin America don't have civilizational cravings, or civilizational heritage, and of course we have it. Our civilizational heritage is spread all over India. And above civilizational heritage if you can rise to the occasion – as did Martin Luther King, as did Nelson Mandela, as did Mohandas Karamchand Gandhi – there is humanity, the largest possible envelope. Unfortunately, even after two dangerous and condemnable wars spread over years, the human family has evolved only up to the United Nations Organization. It has not developed the capacity and the courage to create the political architecture of a world government. But your generation is not going to be a prisoner of our failures, your generation has the right to interrogate, the beginning and the end of the journey of nationalism. And your generation has to address the deficits of nation-building left at your doorstep by our generation as we addressed some of the problems created by the previous generation, which had not recognized some of the imperatives of nation-building in terms of political geography.

So, friends, this is one reality that has to be addressed and each layer is interconnected with each other. If you don't have your individuality, your nationality is useless. If you don't allow ethnicity, diversity of ethnicity to flower within the frame of nationality, it will become very suffocating as it happened in Pakistan. What was the genesis of Bangladesh? Linguistic antagonism, linguistic fetish, linguistic animosity. Religion was common but language was different, and they wanted to pray to Allah in Bengali and they thought: Allah is all-knowing, he will understand our Bengali prayer. But the Pakistani part said, no way! Urdu is going to be our official language. Or as it happened in Sri Lanka, as the majority community insisted on Sinhala; and Tamilians said, what about Tamil. They said, go back to Tamil Nadu. They said, what are you saying? We built this country together, we stay here, and there was a huge trajectory spanning four decades and Sri Lanka doesn't know which way to turn. So those who think the idea of nationality and nationalism is their monopoly, they have a very dangerous project that is an outdated, nineteenth-century Western project.

* * *

हमारे मुल्क में नेशनलिज़म को बनाने और पहचानने के लिए जो बहसें चलीं उनमें से एक आइडिया तो ये वाला था कि बिना एक डोमिनेंट आइडेंटिटी के नेशन–बिल्डिंग कैसे होगी। जैसे कि गोलवलकर साहब ने लिखा है – और वो एक पूरी परिभाषा है – कि भारत की राष्ट्रीयता, हिंदू राष्ट्र के सपने के इर्द–गिर्द बनी है। और इसके तीन दुश्मन हैं। मुस्लिम, ईसाई और कम्युनिस्ट। ये उन्होंने लिखा है, 'बंच ऑफ थॉट्स' में। और मुसलमानों के बारे में जो उनकी समझ है, वो दर्जा दस का भी इम्तिहान पास करने लायक भी नहीं हैं। और हिंदुओं के बारे में उनकी समझ, दर्जा पांच भी पास करने लायक नहीं। बहुत ही नादान किस्म का विश्लेषण। क्योंकि इन धार्मिक परम्पराओं में जो डाइवर्सिटी है – भाषाओं की, परंपराओं की, आहार–विहार की, सपनों की – उसे वे नज़रंदाज करते हैं। जो धर्म और जातियां जितनी पुरानी होंगी,

उसमें विविधता उतनी होगी, क्योंकि काल उनके साथ संवाद करता है। और वही बात इस्लाम की भी है। और यही बात जिन्ना साहब ने भी कही। जिन्ना साहब को मैं माफ़ इसलिए करुंगा, कि जिन्ना साहब ने कानून की पढ़ाई की थी। जिन्ना साहब पर पहली पुस्तक सरोजिनी नायडू ने लिखी थी जिसका नाम था *मोहम्मद अली जिन्नाः द अंबेसडर ऑफ यूनिटी*। स्नेक्स के रूप में पोर्क खाते थे। नमाज़ पढ़ने की तमीज नहीं थी, मुसलमान वो ऐसे ही लगते थे, जैसे कोई आदमी कश्मीरी टोपी पहन ले शेरवानी वो पहनते थे, इसलिए अपनी पोशाक से मुसलमान लगते थे। बाकी उनका सारा का सारा गेटअप एक वेस्टर्नाइज़ड, मॉडर्नाइज़ड इंटलेक्चुअल का था। उन्होंने जो बातें अपने भाषण में कहीं, अलीगढ़ मुस्लिम यूनिवर्सिटी से मुस्लिम लीग कॉन्फ्रेंस तक, बेहद, ग़ैर–ऐतिहासिक बातें, लेकिन उस दौर का सिक्का था, चल गया। जैसे आजकल चल गया, कि जेएनयू एंटीनेशनलस का गढ़ है। जेएनयू टेररिस्ट्स का गढ़, जेएनयू सेपरेटिस्ट्स का गढ़। जब आप ज़ोर–ज़ोर से बोलेंगे, और एक ही बात बोलेंगे, तो कुछ समय के लिए नादान लोग, जो आपकी इज़्ज़त करते हैं, आपको सही मानेंगे। लेकिन जब भेद खुलेगा, जब झूठ आगे आएगा, तो आपसे जो जितनी मुहब्बत करते हैं, उतनी ही नफ़रत करने लगेंगे। इसलिए मैं नरेंद्र मोदी से कहना चाहता हूँ कि झूठ की हुकूमत मत चलाओ। सामना करो, ये कहो कि हिंदुस्तान का जो आने वाले समय का सपना है, तुम्हारे सपने और जेएनयू के लड़के–लड़कियों के सपनों में टकराहट हो रही है। ये कहो कि ये लड़के और इनके टीचर उन सवालों को उठाना चाहते हैं, जो सवाल हिंदुस्तान की सरज़मीं पर ज़िंदा हैं, और मरने का नाम नहीं लेते।

क्या आपको मालूम है कि मणिपुर में पिछले कई बरस से नाराज़गी इतनी है कि हिंदी की फिल्में नहीं दिखाई जातीं। क्या आपको मालूम है कि असम में वो हिंदू हैं, लेकिन उनकी जो आइडेंटिटी है, बँट गई है दो हिस्सों में। जो वहाँ के ब्राह्मण और कायस्थ हैं, उनके बारे में औसत असमिया कहता है, वो खुद भी कहते हैं कि हम तो कन्नौज से आए थे, या हम इलाहाबाद से आए थे, और अन्य कहते हैं कि हम थाइलैंड से आए थे। एक लड़का मिला, उसने हमारी एक स्टूडेंट के साथ शादी की थी। मुझसे मिलने आया था। कहा, सर हम लोग आठ सौ साल पहले हुनान से, मशहूर हुनान, माउत्से तुंग की हुनान रिपोर्ट वाला। जब वहाँ पर फैमिन आया था, आठ सौ साल पहले, तब हम वहाँ से यहाँ आए थे। मैंने कहा यार तुम्हारी याददाश्त बहुत तेज़ है! यही आइडेंटिटी का सवाल है। क्यों वह चीन से जुड़ना चाहता है। क्योंकि इस समय पूरी एसमीज़ आइडेंटिटी डीकंपोज़ हो रही है, डीकंस्ट्रक्ट हो रही है। तो वो ये भी कह सकता था कि डेढ़ सौ साल पहले हम किसी सूखा पीड़ित असमिया इलाके से आए थे। उसने चीन से अपने को जोड़ा क्योंकि आज चीन चढ़ा हुआ है। ऊँचाई पर है चीन। भारत की नेशन–बिल्डिंग प्रोसेस को भी ये देखना है कि जो लोग अपनी आइडेंटिटी को भारत की आइडेंटिटी से अलग रखना चाहते हैं, उनकी कुछ शिकायतें

हैं, जिनकी सुनवाई नहीं होने से नाराज़गी में वो कहते हैं कि हम तुम्हारे साथ नहीं हैं। हालांकि ज़मीन ने, आसमान ने, दरिया ने, जंगल ने उनको अगल–बगल का ही बनाया है। आप अपने पड़ोसी नहीं चुन सकते, आप अपना मुल्क नहीं चुन सकते। चुनने के लिए माइग्रेट करना पड़ता है। तो नेशन–बिल्डिंग का एक ये जो फॉर्मुला है, ये उन्नीसवीं सदी का है, उसको वो करेक्ट नहीं कर रहे हैं, और हमारी बदकिस्मती से उनके हाथ में हुकूमत आ गई। ये पुरानी दवाई है भाई साहब, ये डेटेड है, पॉइज़न हो चुकी है, इसका इस्तेमाल मत करना वरना जाट कबूल नहीं करेंगे, पटेल कबूल नहीं करेंगे। छोड़ दो हिंदू और मुसलमान को, सिख और ईसाई को। अब तो हिंदुओं के बीच में भी दरारें आ गई हैं।

हिंदुस्तान के सामने जो चेलेंजेस हैं, उसमें एक तो हिंदुत्ववादियों का डिस्कॉर्स है। एक और ग्रुप है जो इतनी ही एक्सट्रीम पोज़ीशन लेता है। एक ग्रुप को हिंदू के अलावा कुछ दिखाई नहीं देता। और हिंदू को वो समझते हैं कि वो मोनोलिथिक है। हम जैसे देखते हैं, वैसे हिंदू देखता है। हिंदू धर्म में ज़बरदस्त आत्ममंथन चल रहा है। एक छोर पर गांधी, दूसरे छोर पर कबीर। एक जगह जवाहरलाल और अंबेडकर, एक जगह सावरकर और गोलवलकर। और ये सब अपने–अपने तरीके से हिंदू होने का दावा करते हैं। बाबा साहब तो थक गए हिंदुओं को कहते–कहते कि सुधर जाओ, सुधर जाओ, सुधर जाओ। लेकिन बहुत सारे लोग जो बाबा साहब को मानते हैं वो फिर भी अपनी हिंदू आइडेंटिटी को नेगोशिएट करना चाहते हैं। ऐसे ही मुसलमानों का है। ये जो आपने समझ रखा है कि कोई एक बटन है जिसको दबाने से सब कुछ हरा–हरा हो जाता है, माइंडलेस कम्युनिटी है मुसलमानों की। यह सच नहीं है। इनकी जीनियस का लोहा यूरोप भी मानता है। वो आज तक कहते हैं, अलजबरा, वो उनको दूसरा वर्ड नहीं मिला, इतना एडवांस था मुस्लिम माइंड, अरब देश का, जिसकी कनेक्टिविटी थी ग्रीस के साथ, जिसकी कनेक्टिविटी थी इंडिया के साथ। लेकिन मुसलमानों में भी जाति है, और उसको लेके पसमांदा और सैयद साहबान के बीच में बहस चल रही है। औरतों मर्दों का सवाल खाली हिंदुओं का नहीं है, सिखों का नहीं है, मुसलमानों के बीच में भी है और वो डेमोक्रैटिक डिविडेंड है। लेकिन हमको सवाल पूछने तो दो भाई, जवाब तलाशने तो दो। आप तो कहते हो कि बस सन्नाटे में रहो, डर के रहो। हम जो चाहें वैसे चलने दो। इसीलिए आज... इस मुल्क में नेशन–बिल्डिंग के लिए अतीत से, कनेक्टिविटी तो रहेगी, जाएगी नहीं। लेकिन भविष्य में ही समाधान है, अतीत में नहीं। न तो अकबर बादशाह का दरबार फिर से लगाने में सोल्यूशन है, ना अशोक महान के राज में लौटने में सोल्यूशन है। ना मराठा साम्राज्य और सिख साम्राज्य, और ना पृथ्वीराज चौहान का राज लाने में ही सोल्यूशन है। दुनिया बहुत आगे निकल गई है। दुनिया मानवता की तरफ़ बढ़ रही है। दुनिया जाति की तरफ़ नहीं घिसट रही है। जाति जहां तक चलेगी, चलेगी। इसके आगे जाति का

भविष्य राष्ट्रीयता के साथ जुड़ने में है। राष्ट्रीयता और जातिवाद में जब–जब विरोध होगा, जाति हारेगी, इसमें अब कोई शक नहीं रह गया। और यही साम्प्रदायिकता के साथ भी है। साम्प्रदायिकता एक पॉलिटिकल कैपिटल है। उसकी पैथोलोजी को समझना पड़ेगा। डेमोक्रेसी यूनाइट्स एट ऐब्स्ट्रैक्ट लेवल, एज इन द प्रीएंबल ऑफ द कॉन्स्टीट्यूशन ऑफ इंडिया। बट डेमोक्रेसी डिवाइड्स ड्यूरिंग एव्री इलेक्टोरल कॉम्पीटिशन। (Democracy unites at abstract level, as in the Preamble of the Constitution of India. But democracy divides during every electoral competition.) और एक क्लीवेज ट्रेडीशनल आइडेंटिटीज़ की भी है जिसमें कास्ट की आइडेंटिटी पोलिटिसाइज़ हो जाती है, रिलीजन की आइडेंटिटी पोलिटिसाइज़ हो जाती है, और जब पार्टियाँ कमज़ोर होती हैं तो जातियाँ और संप्रदाय मज़बूत हो जाते हैं। और यही हमारी शिकायत थी कांग्रेस पार्टी से। उसको इतना बड़ा मौका मिला था। इन सपनों को साकार करने का। लेकिन वो सेल्फ गोल में ही फँस गए। उनका मिशन बदल गया। और आज बहुत कुछ जो हमारे पाँव में काँटे गड़ रहे हैं – नई फ़सलों के काँटे तो बाद में गड़ेंगे, पांच साल बाद, तीन साल बाद, या जेएनयू में अभी पांव में काँटे गड़ रहे हैं – मुल्क की बनावट में जो दिक्कतें आ रही हैं, उसके लिए साठ–पैंसठ साल की हमारी मिस्ड अपॉर्चुनिटीज़ हैं।

नेशन–बिल्डिंग की जो दूसरी एक्स्ट्रीम पोज़ीशन है, वह ये रिकगनाइज़ नहीं करती कि इंडिया हैज़ मूव्ड इनटू ए न्यू पैराडाइम। मैं उस बहस में नहीं जाऊँगा, जो मेरी क्लास में पिछले पच्चीस साल चलती रही है – सेमीकोलोनियल, सेमीफ्यूडल इंडिया। उनको लगता है कि ब्रिटिश पावर ट्रांसफर करके गए। हाँ एक किताब ज़रूर है *ट्रांसफर ऑफ पावर*, वो कैंब्रिज यूनिवर्सिटी ने छापी है। कई वॉल्यूम हैं। लेकिन ट्रांसफर ऑफ पावर ही नहीं हुआ है। उसके बाद बहुत कुछ हुआ है। कुछ एम्पावरमेंट भी हुआ है, सिटिजन भी आगे बढ़ा है, खाली स्टेट नहीं चल रहा है, ऑर्डिनरी लोगों की कैपिसिटी भी बढ़ी है। देअर कैपेसिटी टू वॉइस, देअर कैपेसिटी टू डिसेंट, देअर कैपेसिटी टू प्रोटेस्ट। लेकिन उस पोज़ीशन वाले अभी भी वहीं ठहरे हुए हैं। और इसीलिए उनको लगता है कि ट्रांज़ीशनल एफ़ीमेरल रियलिटी है ये इंडिया। सौ सूबे तो बन ही जाएंगे। मैं भी उसी ट्रेडीशन से आता हूँ जिसने भारतीय संविधान सभा को एक डर्टी कंप्रोमाइज़ माना था। आपमें से कुछ लोग जानते होंगे कि पूरी कांग्रेस सोशलिस्ट पार्टी ने गांधीवादियों की तरह से, कम्युनिस्टों की तरह से ये घोषित किया था कि इस संविधान सभा में नहीं जाना है। क्योंकि इस संविधान सभा में जाने के लिए ब्रिटिश क्राउन की लॉयलिटी की कसम खानी पड़ती है। हम नहीं खा सकते। जवाहर लाल गए, राजेंद्र प्रसाद गए, मौलाना आज़ाद गए, बाबा साहब अंबेडकर गए, उन्होंने कॉन्स्टीट्यूशन बनाया। आज उस कॉन्स्टीट्यूशन में सौ से ज़्यादा तरमीम हो चुकी हैं। और आज जो डेमोक्रेटिक सोशलिस्ट ट्रेडीशन है उसकी लेजिटिमेसी के

लिए भी इस कॉन्स्टीट्यूशन में बहुत स्पेस मिल गया। उसकी कई धाराओं को चैलेंज किया गया। जैसे आज आप 124 ए को चैलेंज कर रहे हैं। ऐसे कई धाराओं को 117 को, 144 को, हैबियस कॉर्पस मूव कर कर के, और फिर इमर्जेंसी वाला डर्टी प्रोविज़न जो 74 में चैलेंज किया गया। इस कॉन्स्टीट्यूशन को धीरे–धीरे जीने लायक, अपनाने लायक बना लिया गया। सेंस ऑफ हिस्ट्री होना चाहिए था, जो डॉक्टर अंबेडकर को था, लेकिन डॉक्टर लोहिया को नहीं था। मैं लोहियाइट होने के बावजूद आपसे कहना चाहता हूँ। और यही बात मैं औरों से कहना चाहता हूँ कि जो हिंदुस्तान को, भारत को, इंडिया को एक शानदार ह्यूमेन सोसाइटी अप्रोचिंग यूनिवर्सैलिटी, अप्रोचिंग ह्यूमनिज़म एंड ह्यूमेनिटी बनाना चाहते हैं, उनके लिए भी ज़रूरी है कि वो टाइम और स्पेस के कंजंक्शन को समझें। बहुत डरा रखा है इन्होंने कि देश टूटने वाला है। और ये सही बात है कि हिंदुस्तान की आर्मी एक तिहाई हिदुस्तान की रखवाली में परछाई की तरह पीछे खड़ी रहती है, और ये एक असफलता है देश की। डेमोक्रेटिक इंस्टीट्यूशंस की लिमिटेशंस हैं।

पार्लिआमेंट्री डेमोक्रेसी काउंटर प्रोडक्टिव हो चुकी है, हर चुनाव में काला पैसा और नंगा नाच करता है। हर चुनाव में कुछ और अपराधी पार्लिआमेंट में बढ़ जाते हैं और ये हम और आप नहीं कह रहे हैं। ये असोसियेशन ऑफ डेमोक्रेटिक रिफॉर्म ने कहा, इसके फाउंडर्स आइआइएम जैसी जगह के प्रोफ़ेसर लोग हैं, उन्होंने कहा है कि पार्लिआमेंट्री डेमोक्रेसी काउंटर प्रोडक्टिव हो रही है। देअर इज़ ए नीड टू मूव टुवर्ड्स डीसेंट्रलाइज़ेशन। इंडियन नेशन बिल्डिंग, बिकॉज़ ऑफ इट्स सिविलइज़ेशनल हेरिटेज रिक्वायर्स डीसेंट्रलाइज़ेशन। (There is a need to move towards decentralization. Indian nation-building, because of its civilizational heritage requires decentralization.) अभी मैं कुछ सरकारी कागज़ात देख रहा था, पंजाबी सूबे को लेकर इतना डरा हुआ था दिल्ली दरबार – फ़तेह सिंह साहब, तारा सिंह साहब। और क्या था पंजाब में? वो एक मांग कर रहे थे कि एक टैलिविज़न चैनल हो जिसमें गुरुबानी लगातार सुनाई जा सके। वो कहते थे इससे देश टूट जाएगा! वो कहते थे कि – एक अकाली दल वहाँ पर है जो किसानों की पार्टी है, उसका ट्रेडीशन है पुराना, एंटीकॉलोनियल। इमर्जेंसी मे सारा मुल्क डर गया था, सिवाय पंजाब के, रोज़ सत्याग्रह करते थे अकाली – अगर अकाली चंडीगढ़ में बैठ गए सरकार में तो हमारी सुनेंगे नहीं और पाकिस्तान से मिलकर पंजाब को अलग कर देंगे। कैसे कैसे भूत डराते हैं इनको। आज बार–बार दौड़ते हैं पंजाब। और आज पंजाब एक मज़बूत बाड़ की तरह से हिंदुस्तान की रक्षा के लिए हर तरह से तैयार है, हर तरह से योगदान कर रहा है। तमिलनाडु, मैं पढ़ रहा था, पेरियार रामास्वामी नायकर का एक पूरा लेख है जो तमिल में, मोस्ट ऑथेंटिक, *कम्युनिस्ट मेनिफेस्टो* की जैसी इज़्जत कम्युनिस्ट करते हैं, उस लेख की इज़्जत तमिलनाडु में,

पेरियार को मानने वाले करते थे, रैशनलिस्ट करते हैं जिसमें उन्होंने लिखा है, *फ्रॉड ऑफ़ रिलिजन*, धर्म का ढोंग। वो कहते थे कि देश के चार दुश्मन हैं: सबसे बड़ा दुश्मन ब्राह्मण, नंबर दो दुश्मन, हिंदी, नंबर तीन दुश्मन, कॉग्रेस, नंबर चार दुश्मन, गांधी! द्रविडिस्तान बनाना है। उसी तमिलनाडु की पॉलिटिक्स में एक दिन ऐसा आया व्हेन द पीपल ऑफ तमिलनाडु इनक्लूडिंग बोथ द मेजर पार्टीज़ द्रविड़ मुन्नेत्र कलग़म एंड ऑल इंडिया अन्ना द्रविड़ मुन्नेत्र कलग़म प्रेस्ड सेंट्रल गवर्नमेंट ऑफ इंडिया टू यूज़ मिलिट्री माइट टू डिफेंड द तमिल ब्रदर्स एंड सिस्टर्स इन जाफना। डाइनमिक्स ऑफ टाइम, सर्कमस्टांसेस चेंज, कॉन्टेक्स्ट चेंजज़। इट इज़ इंपोर्टेंट फ़ॉर एनीबडी हू इज़ इनवॉल्वड इन नेशन–बिल्डिंग टू हैव पेशेंस, पेशेंस टू अंडर्स्टेंड दी अदर्स पर्सपेक्टिव। और वो पेशेंस यहाँ पर नहीं है।

निष्कर्ष में यह कहा जा सकता है कि हिंदुस्तान में नेशन–बिल्डिंग से सम्बंधित जो बड़े सवाल रहे हैं जिनको अब हम सुलझाने के कगार पर आ गए हैं – इन सवालों में पहला है रिलीजियस प्लूरलिटी का सवाल। दुनिया में कई जगह एथनिक क्लींज़िंग हुई। यूगोस्लाविया इसी में बरबाद हो गया। टीटो का सपना चूर–चूर हो गया। लेकिन भारत में हम सेक्युलरिज़्म को आर्टिकल ऑफ फ़ेथ के तौर पर जीना सीख गए हैं। और जेएनयू में तो इफ़्तार का भी इंतज़ार रहता है और होली का भी इंतज़ार रहता है। इफ़्तार बढ़िया बिरियानी खाने के लिए और होली मज़े से भांग पीकर नाचने–गाने के लिए। और हमको उसमें कोई झगड़ा नहीं लगता। दोनों में गले ही तो मिलते हैं, कोई चाकू नहीं मारते एक दूसरे को। और ये पूरे मुल्क में फैल रहा है, धीरे–धीरे, दिस वे ऑफ़ लाइफ़। मल्टी रिलिजिओसिटी। इसी तरह से कास्ट का सवाल। यंगर इंडिया इज कनविंस्ड दैट आइदर वी आर डूम्ड विद कास्टिज़्म और वी गो बियोंड कास्ट एंड चेलेंज द ग्लोबल सिस्टम दैट वी आर सेकेंड टू नन इन टर्म्स ऑफ आवर ड्रीम्स, आवर स्किल्स एंड आवर कैपेसिटी। मंडल की वजह से एक बार हुई सिविल वार जैसी स्थिति बनी लेकिन जब मंडल–2 आया तो कुछ ख़ास नहीं हुआ। और ये जो रिजर्वेशन को लेकर बहस चल रही है, ये भी अपनी लास्ट डांस एंड सॉन्ग पर है। ये डेथ विश है। डॉमिनेंट कास्ट का डेमोक्रेसी में रिजर्वेशन मांगना मूर्खता की राजनीति का एक सुंदर उदाहरण है। अगर पटेल पिछड़ा है, जाट पिछड़ा है, ठाकुर पिछड़ा है, भूमिहार पिछड़ा है तो अगड़ा कौन रह गया भाई। यही तो किया था आपने मूर्खता का काम। जब आया था साइमन कमीशन, पता लगाने कि कौन कौन माइनॉरिटी है तो ब्राह्मणों ने मैमोरेंडम दिया कि हम माइनॉरिटी हैं, ठाकुरों ने मैमोरेंडम दिया कि हम माइनॉरिटी हैं। तो सिवाय इंडियन नेशनल कांग्रेस के कोई नहीं था जो कहे कि हम माइनॉरिटी नहीं हैं, क्योंकि उसमें एक करेंसी थी, एक वैल्यू थी, कुछ फ़ायदे थे। तो जात का सवाल। तीसरा जो नेशनल कॉन्सेंसस बन गया है, और सोशिओलॉजिकली हमको इंटर्नलाइज़ करना है और वो है जेंडर जस्टिस का सवाल। घर से लेकर बाहर

तक एक कैदख़ाने से दूसरे कैदख़ाने में गुज़रने की जो मजबूरी है, जिसको किसी ने कहा औरत होने की सज़ा, जिसको तमाम नेशन–बिल्डिंग के दावों के बावजूद औरतों के बीच से चीख निकलती है, 'अगले जनम मोहे बिटिया न कीजो'। ये कौन सा मुल्क बन रहा है और ये कौन सी नेशन–बिल्डिंग हो रही है। इसको ठीक किए बिना अब औरत तो आगे कदम बढ़ाएगी नहीं और आपको भी एक कदम आगे बढ़ने नहीं देगी वो लड़के रहेगी, लेके रहेगी, जीत के रहेगी।

और चौथा सवाल है रीजनल डिस्पैरिटी। आप उड़ीसा को, तैलंगाना को, झारखंड को, छत्तीसगढ़ को नक्सल अफ़ैक्टिड एरिया कहकर खारिज नहीं कर सकते। वो अपना हिसाब मांगते हैं और उनको हिसाब देना पड़ेगा। क्षेत्रिय विषमता, रीजनल डिस्पैरिटी भारत की नेशन–बिल्डिंग का बहुत बड़ा स्टंबलिंग ब्लॉक है। और बहुत दिन तक यूपी और बिहार के लोग महाराष्ट्र की सड़कों पर पिटने को तैयार नहीं होंगे। और बहुत दिन तक नॉर्थ–ईस्ट के लोग दिल्ली और बंगलौर में डर–डर के जीने को तैयार नहीं होंगे। ऐसा हमको नेशन नहीं चाहिए जिसमें हमको डर के जीने की मजबूरी हो। सिर उठा के चलना है, रवींद्रनाथ टैगोर का सपना। और अब आप इस सब को लेकर के कहते हो बहस कर रहे हो। एंटीनेशनल लोग हैं। इस देश से प्यार है तभी तो एंटीनेशनल नहीं हैं। और ये सब जो ये कहने वाले लोग हैं, मुझे थोड़ा बहुत पता है इन लोगों के बारे में, सबके खानदान की जो यंग जनरेशन है – असली हिंदुस्तान की यंग जेनरेशन तो इंडियन यूनिवर्सिटीज में पढ़ने के लिए लड़ रही है, ऑक्यूपाइ यू.जी.सी से लेकर के यूनिवर्सिटियाँ खोलो की लड़ाई लड़ रही है – और ये जो नकली देशभक्त हैं इनके सबके बच्चे, इनकी बहुएँ, इनके नाती–पोते अमेरिका में बस रहे हैं, योरप में बस रहे हैं। और चाहे तो एक बार, मैं मीडिया को कहुँगा इस रिसर्च को करने के लिए कि आप ज़रा देखिए कि हिंदुस्तान की मौजूदा कैबिनेट में, हिंदुस्तान के रूलिंग अलायंस में, इनमें से कितने लोग हैं जिनका एक पाँव भारत में और जिनका भविष्य विदेश में है। विदेशों में बसे हुए बच्चों से लेकर के, विदेशों में जमा खातों तक ये बिल्कुल आर्टिफिशियल फ़ेक और डेंजरस किस्म के देशभक्त हैं।

इन चैलेंजेज़ को हम आप पर छोड़ रहे हैं। भारत की नेशन–बिल्डिंग की प्रोसेस, लिंग्विस्टिक स्टेट रीऑर्गनाइज़ेशन के बाद एक बड़े हर्डल को पार कर सकी थी। नेशन–बिल्डिंग प्रोसेस, पॉलिटिकल ज्योग्राफी के रीऑर्गनाइज़ेशन से नॉर्थ–ईस्ट में, और सेंट्रल इंडिया में तीन राज्य बनाने से बहुत हद तक एंटागोनिज़म को कम कर सकी है। लेकिन जब कांस्टीट्यूशन के साथ छेड़छाड़ करोगे, रूल ऑफ़ लॉ नहीं रहेगा। मेजॉरिटेरियनिज़म आएगा। डॉमिनेंट कास्ट डेमोक्रेसी के पाँव पसारे जाएँगे तो जिनको तकलीफ़ है, वो पहले प्रोटेस्ट करेंगे, वॉइस करेंगे, फिर वो रेज़िस्ट करेंगे। और जब प्रोटेस्ट और रेज़िस्ट नहीं चलता तो फिर आप उनको एग्ज़िट करने को मजबूर करते हैं। फिर दोष मत देना कि तुम ये कर रहे हो, ये तुम्हारा बनाया हुआ

है कि लोगों के मन में अपनी जड़ों से कटने की मजबूरी आ रही है, अपनी रक्षा के लिए। क्योंकि साथियों, और ये मेरी आख़िरी बात है, दुनिया और भारत में सभी व्यक्ति पाँच बातें चाहते हैं, इनके लिए सपने देखते हैं, आन्दोलन करते हैं, होने पर संतोष मिलता है, न मिलने पर आक्रोश और भेदभाव की भावना जगती है। ये पांच ज़रूरतें हैं: 1. न्याय, 2. आत्म–सम्मान, 3. अस्मिता, 4. शांति, और 5. प्रगति।

हर किसी को ये पाँच चीज़ें चाहिए। और इसीलिए आज़ादी की लड़ाई थी, इसी के लिए लोग फंदों पर झूल गए थे कि इस ज़िंदगी से मौत बेहतर है। पहले चाहिए जस्टिस, आप में से कौन ऐसा है जो इनजस्टिस के साथ जीना कबूल करेगा या करेगी? नो वन, नाइदर कन्हैया, नॉर नरेंद्र मोदी। दे हैव अ कॉमन ड्राइव एंड डिज़ायर, टू लिव इन अ जस्ट सोसाइटी। दूसरी बात जो सबको प्यारी होती है, जैसे हमारी माँ प्यारी, वैसे हमारी डिग्निटी प्यारी। कोई भी सोने के पिंजरे में नहीं रह सकता – सीबीआई वाले खाली रह सकते हैं और कोई भी सोने के पिंजरे में नहीं रह सकता – दे वॉन्ट टू लिव अ लाइफ विद डिग्निटी। आधी रोटी खाएंगे। इसीलिए बिहार के, उड़ीसा के और उत्तर प्रदेश के गांवों से लोग भाग–भाग कर के शहरों में जाते हैं। जिस इलाके में मेरा रोज़ का आना जाना रहता है, सीलमपुर, सीमापुरी, मुस्तफ़ाबाद, पीने का पानी नहीं है, रहने का घर नहीं लेकिन इज़्ज़त है। डिग्निटी। तीसरी बात जो डिग्निटी के बाद हर किसी को चाहिए, वो है आइडेंटिटी। और जैसा मैंने कहा आइडेंटिटी मल्टीफ़ोल्ड होती है। कभी मुझे भोजपुरिया होने में मज़ा आता है, कभी मुझे बनारसी होने में मज़ा आता है, कभी मुझे सोशिओलजिस्ट होने में मज़ा आता है। क्यों रोकते हो भाई इनमें से किसी एक को? क्यों हाइरार्की बनाते हो आइडेंटिटी की? वो ज़माना अलग था, वो एक दूसरा, एक पोइटिक फ़ेज़ था, इंडियन फर्स्ट, इंडियन लास्ट। लाइफ़ इज़ मच मोर रिच। वी हैव मैनी मोर सोर्सेज़ ऑफ़ आइडेंटिटी। आइडेंटिटी। और चौथा जो सब चाहते हैं, लेकिन वो जस्टिस, डिग्निटी, आइडेंटिटी के बाद आता है, वो है पीसफुल प्रोग्रेस। कोई अपनी जगह पर बैठा नहीं रहना चाहता। वो पीस चाहते हैं और प्रोग्रेस चाहते हैं। यही तो पाँचो बातें आप सबके सपने हैं।

Picture credit: www.standwithjnu.org

At the Limits of Postcolonial Nationalism

Suvir Kaul

(17 MARCH 2016)

THANK YOU ALL FOR HAVING ME here. I want to begin with a simple expression of solidarity. JNU stands right now internationally, and I will elaborate on what that means, for the right to speak – speak loudly and forcefully, speak rationally and with clarity – of difficult ideas. All across the world, what you are performing here has galvanized university communities. I know this not only because I have been part of signature campaigns and consciousness-raising campaigns in the United States and other parts of Europe, but also because I was on a recent visit to Bangladesh and I was astonished at a party, not necessarily with academic guests, but with common citizens of Bangladesh – at the number of them who had actually listened to a great many of these lectures, and more importantly, who had listened to comrade Kanhaiya's speech when he was released. And they kept saying to me, to the point of embarrassment, that they were astonished that such political energy was feasible any longer anywhere in the subcontinent. I'm paying this compliment to you to remind you that what is going on here has ramifications not simply for JNU, not simply for Indian universities, but for universities across the subcontinent and across the world. I also want to say, this is – as you know so much better than I do – going to be a very long struggle. So my solidarity and those of people like me are with our two comrades who are still in jail and indeed with the many of you who face the threat of administrative action. You must not back down … I know you won't, and there will be a great many of us joining with you.

*

I should move now to my lecture … My title asks us to think a little more closely … about the term 'colonial' and indeed about the term 'postcolonial'. As all of you know, at a simple conversational level, the word 'post' is meant to mark a major breach: that *was* the colonial period, the period of empire, the period of imperialism. *Now* we live in a postcolonial period where an independent nation forges its own assumptions about what constitutes justice, what constitutes an appropriate future, what constitutes the participation of citizens in an inclusive democracy … or so that understanding of the term 'post' [makes clear to] us. But the term 'post' doesn't mark, as we well know, a breach. It also marks continuities. To that extent, the term 'post' derives a great deal of its force and its historical power from another term that is often used to describe the transition between the British empire and India as a part of that British empire and independent India, which is the *transfer of power*. No matter how much we celebrate the 'post' that nationalists achieved when they moved us as an entity towards freedom, we are always dealing with the uncomfortable fact that what we saw happening in 1947, in the prelude to 1947 and in the years after, is actually a systematic transfer of power between colonial elites and postcolonial elites. Now, nothing I'm saying here is news to you. All of you in your daily lives, as also in your academic reading, know that this is the case. All of you have been dealing with the fact that what begins this entire JNU 'problem', if I can call it that, or the entire JNU 'possibility', [is] the fact that an act of sedition was invoked to shut up a group of students who were doing what students in a campus should feel entitled to do – raise slogans, debate ideas, quarrel publicly about what they value in the nature of their public lives.

All of you, I'm sure, have heard more than once about the history of these Acts on sedition [Section 124A, Indian Penal Code 1860]. As you know it is a colonial Act that the postcolonial government, the independent Government of India, has refused to remove from its statute books, the IPC, regardless of the fact that judge after judge at the high court level and mostly at the Supreme Court level have basically suggested that the section on sedition ought to have no place in our rule books. But there is an even longer history that gets left out in this conception of a nineteenth-century colonial Act that is carried into independent India, and this takes us back to the year 1661 and the Restoration of Charles II. You will remember that in the middle of the seventeenth century – I will spend the next few minutes talking a little about British history – there was essentially a revolution that dethroned and then decapitated a king. Given the context of seventeenth-century insurrections, this was an astonishing and, in its own way, a world-creating idea at that point. But in 1661, with the Restoration of Charles II in 1660, what was promulgated was one of the first Acts by the British parliament that convened to welcome him to England ... what they promulgated was, and I'm going to quote the full title of this act, 'An Act for the Safety and Preservation of His Majesty's Person and Government Against Treasonable and Seditious Practices and Attempts'. This is the logic of a monarchy reasserting its absolutist authority that we have inherited via our British administrators. This is the Act that has been used against, as you know, not only your comrades from this campus but against a great many other Indians in vulnerable situations. I will also remind you that Hardik Patel, no matter what his politics, is also in jail on charges of sedition. So this is an act, an IPC section that is being used at will to go after not simply the vulnerable but anybody who might become potentially a threat or a challenge to state power. So one of the long-term struggles that all of us have to engage in – and this too is a part of my understanding of what it means to work towards a genuinely postcolonial judicial apparatus – is to try and get rid of this Act. I have no idea how long the courts will continue to, in their own small ways, support individuals against the state, but the only solution really is to get ourselves to a point where we no longer have to worry about the might of the state and its minions, including those in university administrations who seem to forget what their job is as *faculty*.

*

I am also particularly grateful to JNU for having allowed us to think once again about Kashmir. I know this is an extraordinarily complex idea. The importance of JNU is that you have allowed a conversation, initiated a conversation, however broken or put down. You have initiated a conversation about Kashmir that is not permissible anywhere in Kashmir. I hope all of you are aware – I'm sure you are – that anyone in Kashmir, especially in the universities, who has asked any questions about the administration and its use of power, the government and its use of power – and it doesn't matter who's in power there, which mainstream political party is in power there [for] they have all been quick to use the Public Safety Act to lock people up. The Public Safety Act and the Armed Forces Special Powers Act (AFSPA) drew their legitimacy and their historical legacy from colonial laws. You will remember – I'm sure some of you know this kind of legal history better than I do – that it was Lord Linlithgow who promulgated the first Armed Forces Special Powers Ordinance and he did so precisely because Gandhi and the national movement were becoming very difficult for him to handle. That is the AFSPA that the postcolonial government confirmed in order for it to send in the military to Nagaland, to Manipur, into various parts of the north-east, including Tripura until 2015, and that is certainly the Act that continues to allow all manner of military impunity in Kashmir. These are some of the ways in which our institutional structures inhabit the world of *colonial* and not of *postcolonial* thinking.

Indeed, for me, the even more challenging idea is that of the hold of empire on the modern political imagination. We all believe that the moment of decolonization has come and gone. We all hope for and sometimes we presume that our political imaginations have found a kind of emancipatory vocabulary that is no longer in the thrall of colonial conceptions, imperial conceptions of the importance of nation states, or indeed of the importance of particular forms of citizenship. You will all remember that in the empire we were *subjects* not *citizens*. That transition is an enormously difficult transition, as we see. It cannot be made simply at the level of form, simply at the level of language. Speaker after speaker has informed you that democracy, democratic thought, democratic practice is an ongoing process. It has to be reaffirmed in everyday choices, but it also has to be reaffirmed in the nature of the experiences you are allowed to have. It cannot be blunted and denied with the forceful ease with which government after government seems to want to do so. So, part of what I wanted to remind us about here is that a postcolonial nation is in a sense ... a nation always in the making, never perfect, never arrived at, because it is the product of an everyday tension between *democracy* and *nationalism*. This for me is one of the cardinal principles that guides my political optimism and my political hope. I keep imagining that all of us know those moments in everyday life, in the life of individuals or in the life of communities, where democratic aspiration rubs up against the instruments of nationalism and questions those nationalisms. Those are the moments where difficulty emerges; those are the moments where political possibility emerges. Now I'm doing this at a very abstract level, but I wanted to flesh it out a little by calling attention to my own experiences, as a Kashmiri, of life in Kashmir.

I didn't grow up there. I grew up in Bengal, though Kashmir was always home. These are issues I've developed at greater length in the book *Of Gardens and Graves*, which is my attempt to come to terms with what has been happening in Kashmir not only in the last twenty-five or twenty-six years but in the lead-up to what today we've come to think of as the problem of Jammu and Kashmir. I didn't grow up in Kashmir, I grew up in Bengal, but Kashmir was always home because my grandparents had homes there. In fact, they had identical homes next to each other. I would always visit over the summer. In 1989 ... in January 1990, as you know, in the face of an armed insurrection, there was a massive governmental crackdown. Kashmir changed, Srinagar changed in a way that it hadn't before. Nobody [but] my father went back to check up on our house for two or three years after, but then there was a long period, almost a decade, when nobody went home, to our homes in Srinagar. But in 2003, when political events there seemed calmer and the insurgency seemed to – and I'm using the vocabulary that is used by the state and the newspapers – when the insurgency seemed to have been checked we went back to try and revive our house there. All our neighbours – and here I will identify them as Muslim because they continued to live there where the largest number of the Pandits had left – every one of our neighbours said that things were so much better then. I remember walking around the city wondering how this constituted, how what I was seeing there constituted, being 'better'. It was armed encampment. Certain parts of Srinagar continue to be an armed encampment even today, but in 2003 you could not go anywhere in the city without seeing automatic-weapons-carrying BSF or CRPF or military police all across the city, every 150 yards. One of the reasons, oddly enough, our house was untouched was because at the two main entry points into this neighbourhood were enormous bunkers. So nobody came and went from that neighbourhood without fear of being questioned or worse.

That's the moment when I began to wonder, as somebody who easily, effortlessly thought of himself as both Indian and Kashmiri, about what it means to live in a situation where all my democratic beliefs in being Indian were up against what I was seeing, my experience of life, in Kashmir. I was enormously troubled, as you can imagine, by what I saw there, by what I heard and by the fact that every time I expressed my sympathy with what was the visible oppression of people around me, my neighbours would say, 'No, no you mustn't feel badly. We know what happened with you people.' But I was always in an anomalous situation. I was notionally a Pandit, one of those families that had left in 1990, but in fact I hadn't. I was always a visitor and it was out of my troubled feeling then that I began to try and read. It is easy enough to think when you're growing up in India or you're growing up in Kashmir, if you're growing up Indian *and* Kashmiri, to think you know enough about the history of Kashmir to recognize that something has gone enormously wrong. As a matter of fact, I knew nothing and I am certainly more educated than most. It took an enormous amount of work for me, and conversations, conversations – most importantly, *empathetic* conversations – with people around me. It took an enormous amount of work for me to read against my own sense and understand the history of Kashmir, not just what had happened in 1947 during Independence, including the instrument of accession signed by the raja, handing over the authority of Jammu and Kashmir, in the face of tribal invaders from Pakistan, to the Indian army which landed there. I discovered a far more complicated history. I also discovered a much worse picture of Indian parliamentary democracy or electoral democracy that I could've imagined.

Almost every one of the early elections in Jammu and Kashmir, especially in the seats in *Kashmir*, were rigged, by which I mean candidates were elected unopposed. If you as a candidate decided to turn in your papers to the Election Commission, unless you had been pre-approved there was no chance you would be allowed to even stand for elections. So, on the face of it, for three decades and more India could claim to the world, and in fact could claim to *itself*, that elections were being conducted in Kashmir with great regularity, and it was only a fringe group of people who were not acknowledging India's political and moral legitimacy. As it turns out, electoral democracy was precisely the façade under which Kashmiri political opinion, particularly Muslim political opinion, was being marginalized entirely. Now this complicates my understanding and I recommend that it should complicate our understanding of the ease with which we think of Kashmir as an *atoot ang* of this nation. That doesn't mean, even for a moment, that I have got to a comfortable position where I can say, 'Because I believe in the principle of self-determination I know what the future of Kashmir can be.' I don't have any longer the right to know that – and I recommend that for all of us as democrats – *we do not have the a priori right to decide how a people or a community should think about their political future.*

But it is our political responsibility, particularly our political responsibility as teachers and as students, to argue that that conversation about Kashmir – its future, its past, its present – must happen, and it must happen in places like this because this government will not let it happen anywhere else. So it becomes our *responsibility* and it becomes our *right* to have that conversation and that is partly what JNU has allowed to happen. Believe me, as I began by saying, these conversations are resonating across the globe. For all their pitfalls and their difficulties, there should not be a single line – and I know that JNU believes in the multiplicity of voices that should debate these questions. I'm not for a second arguing that JNU Students' Union or the faculty community at large should come out with a line on Kashmir, not at all. What is important is that these conversations, these difficult conversations, should happen and that they should become part and parcel of our understanding of a much broader national conception. That to me is what a genuinely postcolonial nationalism will make available to us: at least the possibility of political debates about the flashpoints in our democracy, not just in our nation but in our *democracy*.

*

I also want to ask us – and this I'm asking almost as a theoretical challenge to the students at JNU – because we, people like me who did not grow up as colonial subjects, who were born when India became independent, we grew up, we learned, we were proud of the very powerful legacy of anti-colonial nationalism. That legacy, unfortunately, blunted our awareness of those parts of this country where there were struggles that pre-dated Gandhian nationalism or the Gandhian national movement, and which continued to be marginalized in independent India. It took my generation a long time to recognize what we were not able to see because we were so much the beneficiaries or the legatees of this form of anti-colonial nationalism with all its celebratory overtones. Now I worry, as all of you do and as Professor Janaki Nair said, a great many of the speakers [also did], about the history of that nationalism because it turns out to be, if not a coercive history – and very often it is a coercive history –a history that marginalizes many communities. So, my challenge to you and your generation is: what kind of nationalism should we attempt to replace it with, or is the term nationalism, the idea of nationalism, the political mobilizatory power of nationalism, so necessarily tainted that there is no possibility of doing anything but refusing it at every point? There is a reason that I'm asking this question. It will be your challenge in the years ahead – it will be our challenge too – but it will be your challenge for longer, and perhaps you will be able to think about it more creatively.

Many years ago, when Mrs Thatcher, Prime Minister Thatcher, in England, went on to win two elections, a great many people wondered about one astonishing fact: the English labouring classes, the English working classes, seemed to have voted in enormously large numbers for her. Now, this seemed to be a contradiction in terms. Rather than voting for Labour they were voting for Margaret Thatcher and the Conservatives, for her version of the Conservative Party. Now, Stuart Hall, whose work some of you will know, the brilliant Jamaican cultural critic who lived his life in the United Kingdom, asked what seemed to be a deceptively simple question: Why did that happen? How do you explain the fact that large constituencies, particularly working-class constituencies, in Britain who should never have believed in Margaret Thatcher believed in her? There were at least two arguments that he developed. One was that Margaret Thatcher had tapped into, in its own ironic way, a *postcolonial* Britain, into a Britain that seemed diminished by the loss of its imperial territories and which seemed to have very little by way of ideological possibility to offer its citizens. What Margaret Thatcher made available was a particularly powerful, jingoistic, militarized nationalism. All of you will remember the war around the Las Malvinas (Falklands), the islands off the coast of Argentina, where Margaret Thatcher sent in the British Navy to make sure Argentina didn't effect its rightful claim to those islands. That form of jingoistic nationalism, *militarized* nationalism, is something that is on the rise in India too and we have to figure out ways in which to counter it.

But there was something else that Stuart Hall argued that has stuck with me all these years. He said the Left in England – the broad Left – had too easily evacuated the symbols of patriotism and nationalism, thus allowing Margaret Thatcher and the Tory party to claim them as their own. What were these symbols? The queen, the flag and the national anthem (the odious 'Rule Britannia' which promises that Britons will never be slaves and was written at the time when Britain was enslaving hundreds of thousands of, not only Africans, but people across the world). He pointed out that what the Left had not done was to find an equally persuasive set of symbols with which to counter these traditional imperial symbols of British nationality. That I suspect is our challenge too at this point. We have resurrected, I shouldn't say the word we – you people have resurrected – the term azadi ... That is a term that potentially has the power to resonate against the insistence on our worshipping Bharat Mata, our saluting the flag, our not even questioning the crores, the thousands of crores that are spent on our armies and our paramilitary apparatus. But it is only one term – not of recent provenance, but of a relatively recent currency. So it is our challenge, those of us who believe in democracy and progressive thought, to be able to articulate a set of ideas, images that will be powerful enough to resist the vulgar, militarized nationalism centred around particular slogans that is so favoured by politicians of all stripes, and indeed administrators of all kinds.

So I offer that to you as a challenge. Is there a possibility for us to be able to develop a political imaginary outside of the thrall of empire because, as far as I'm concerned, our suspicion of the flag and other national symbols like that is well founded. Symbols like these have historically always been used to mobilize majority populations in the service of elite interests. But figure out ways, persuasive ways, in which to counter them – because there is an enormous world of public opinion outside of JNU and outside of our worlds that needs to be educated into these conversations. That too is your challenge. My way of dealing with my own demons, the demons of somebody who wishes to be thought of as Indian and democratic while being thought of as Kashmiri, was to write a book about this whole process. That entire book really is the story of my struggle to come to terms with some ideas. Now I'm not recommending that all of you go off to write books along those lines. But I am recommending that you recognize that this is your challenge. Kashmir is the flashpoint where this entire JNU problem began. You have stumbled upon, you have articulated symptomatically, what is one of the powerful problems, one of the most powerful articulations of the problem, of postcolonial Indian nationalism. How and why and when will we get to a point when we can rid ourselves of the burden of the imperial nation state formation to a point when we can ask the kind of questions that can lead to a genuinely egalitarian, inclusive community at the end of it?

*

I'm going to stop talking about nationalism now, but I did want to end by taking us back to *The Country Without a Post Office*. That is where you will remember all of this began. I thought that I would read – not all of it because it is a comparatively long poem – but I would read several stanzas from a poem that is contained within the volume of poetry that is *The Country without a Post Office*. This is Agha Shahid Ali's wonderful poem 'A Pastoral'. It is a poem of loss, of longing, but also of political hope and that is why I read it to you. Not only to remind you of what Kashmiris have suffered and continue to suffer but of political possibility and solidarity. Agha Shahid Ali dedicated this poem to a Hindu friend of his. This is 'A Pastoral':

> We shall meet again, in Srinagar,
> by the gates of the Villa of Peace,

our hands blossoming into fists
till the soldiers return the keys
and disappear. Again we'll enter
our last world, the first that vanished
in our absence from the broken city.
We'll tear our shirts for tourniquets
and bind the open thorns, warm the ivy
into roses. Quick, by the pomegranate –
the bird will say – Humankind can bear
everything.

This is the both our problem and our possibility: 'Humankind can bear everything.'

No need to stop the ear
to stories rumored in branches:

This is the invitation: No need to stop our ears to the stories that have circulated to us from the margins of our nation.

Pluck the blood: My words will echo thus
at sunset, by the ivy, but to what purpose?
In the drawer of the cedar stand,
white in the verandah, we'll find letters:
When the post offices died, the mailman
knew we'd return to answer them. Better

if he'd let them speed to death,
blacked out by Autumn's Press Trust
not like this, taking away our breath,
holding it with love's anonymous
scripts: 'See how your world has cracked.
Why aren't you here? Where are you? Come back.

Is history deaf there, across the oceans?'

'Is history deaf there,' – I'm repeating a line that he doesn't repeat – 'Is history deaf there, across the oceans?' … or indeed across the Pir Panjal Pass?

Quick, the bird will say. And we'll try
the keys, with the first one open the door
into the drawing room. Mirror after mirror,
textiled by dust, will blind us to our return
as we light oil lamps. The glass map of our country,

still on the wall, will tear us to lace –
We'll go past our ancestors, up the staircase,
holding their wills against our hearts. Their wish
was we return – forever! – and inherit (Quick, the bird
will say) that to which we belong, not like this –
to get news of our death after the world's.

On that note, thank you for listening to me and good luck with your struggles ahead. All of us are with you. Thank you so much.

*

Notes/References/Bibliography

Ali, Agha Shahid, 1998, *The Country Without a Post Office*, New York: W.W. Norton.

Hall, Stuart and Martin Jacques, 1983, *The Politics of Thatcherism*, London: Lawrence and Wishart.

Hindu, The, 'Hardik Patel charge-sheeted for sedition', 9 January 2016 (http://www.thehindu.com/news/national/other-states/hardik-patel-chargesheeted-for-sedition/article8082842.ece; accessed on 6 August 2016).

Kaul, Suvir, 2015, *Of Gardens and Graves: Essays in Kashmir, Poems in Translation*, New Delhi: Three Essays Collective.

Notes on Editors and Contributors

Editors

Janaki Nair is professor of modern history at the Centre for Historical Studies, JNU.

Mallarika Sinha Roy is assistant professor at the Centre for Women's Studies, JNU.

Mohinder Singh is assistant professor at the Centre for Comparative Politics and Political Theory, School of International Studies, JNU.

Rohit Azad is assistant professor at the Centre for Economic Studies and Planning, JNU.

Contributors

A. Mangai is the pseudonym of Dr V. Padma, who teaches English at Stella Maris College, Chennai. She is a translator and writes in Tamil and English. She has been actively engaged in the field of Tamil theatre for over three decades now. She was a visiting fellow at the Centre for Study of Law and Governance, JNU.

Achin Vanaik is a retired professor of International Relations and Global Politics, University of Delhi, and currently a fellow of the Transnational Institute, Amsterdam. He is a founding member of the Coalition for Nuclear Disarmament and Peace (CNDP), India, and has also authored, co-authored and edited several books on subjects ranging from contemporary Indian politics and economics to matters of religion, secularism, communalism and nationalism to issues of globalization, Indian foreign policy, regional and global nuclear disarmament. He is active on civil liberties issues and was a co-recipient of the Sean MacBride International Peace Prize for the year 2000.

Anand Kumar is a sociologist with special interest in political sociology. Born in 1950 in a family of freedom fighters and socialist mobilizers, Anand Kumar studied sociology at Banaras Hindu University, JNU and University of Chicago. He began his academic career at BHU as a lecturer in sociology in 1979 and retired from JNU as professor in 2015. He has been president of the Indian Sociological Society and the Federation of Central University Teachers Associations. He has also taught as India chair in Germany at Albert Ludwigs University (Freiburg), as Fulbright fellow at Tuft University (Medford), as Global Studies Program international scholar at Humboldt University (Berlin), as GSP visiting faculty at FlASCO (Buenos Aires), as visiting international faculty at Johannes Keppler University (Linz) and Innsbruck University (Innsbruck). His authored, co-authored and edited books include *Understanding Globalization and Emerging India*, *India Chronic Poverty Report*, *Globalization of the Gandhian Way*, *Quest for Participatory Democracy*, *Nation-building in India*, *State and Society in India*, *Tibet Resource Book*, *गाँधी –लोहिया–जयप्रकाश और हमारा समय*, *लोहिया के सौ बरस*, *परिवर्तन की राजनीति और राजनीति का परिवर्तन*, *तिब्बत मुक्ति आन्दोलन और भारत का कर्त्तव्य* and *हिमालय, तिब्बत, चीन, भारत और लोहिया*। Currently, he is national president of Swaraj Abhiyan, a citizens' initiative for alternative politics.

Apoorvanand teaches Hindi at the University of Delhi. A literary and cultural critic, he is presently editing *Alochana*, a journal of criticism.

Ari Sitas is a sociologist and a writer. He joined the University of Cape Town in 2009 as a professor in sociology after a long career as a professor of sociology and industrial and labour studies at Natal University (later the University of KwaZulu–Natal). He chairs the National Institute for the Humanities and Social Sciences. His latest academic books are *The Mandela Decade: Labour, Culture and Society in Post-Apartheid South Africa, 1990–2000* (Pretoria: University of South Africa Press, 2010) and the co-authored volume *Gauging and Engaging Deviance, 1600–2000* (Delhi: Tulika Press, 2013). His latest creative book is *From Around the World in 80 Days: The India Section* (Pretoria: University of South Africa Press, 2014).

Ayesha Kidwai is professor of linguistics at Jawaharlal Nehru University, New Delhi.

B.S. Butola completed his schooling from Uttarakhand and master's and PhD from the Centre for the Study of Regional Development, Jawaharlal Nehru University. He was appointed assistant professor in the North Eastern Hill University, Shillong, in 1985 and joined Jawaharlal Nehru University in 1998 as associate professor. He became professor in 2001. Currently, he is the chairperson of the Centre for the Study of Regional Development. He has published more than fifty research papers on biopolitics, bioeconomics, regional development and political economy. He has been a visiting fellow at King's College, London.

Badri Narayan is a social historian and cultural anthropologist and currently professor at the Centre for the Study of Discrimination and Exclusion (CSDE), Jawaharlal Nehru University. His wide-ranging interests cover culture, memory and politics, contemporary histories, ethnography of marginalized politics, social and anthropological history, Dalit and subaltern issues and identity formation, language and the question of power. Besides having written a number of articles both in English and Hindi, he has authored *Kanshiram: Leader of the Dalits* (Penguin, 2014), *The Making of the Dalit Public in North India: Uttar Pradesh 1950-present* (Oxford, 2011), *Fascinating Hindutva – Saffron Politics and Dalit Mobilisation* (Sage, 2009), *Women Heroes and Dalit Assertion in North India* (Sage, 2006), *Documenting Dissent* (IIAS Shimla, 2001). He has recently edited a volume on languages of Uttar Pradesh: *Uttar Pradesh ki Bhashayien* (Orient BlackSwan, 2016). He is also the coordinator of Dalit Resource Centre, a centre established by his active efforts, funded by the Ford Foundation. He has been the recipient of many prestigious literary awards.

G. Arunima is professor at the Centre for Women's Studies, Jawaharlal Nehru University. Her work engages both the historical and the contemporary contexts of India, focusing particularly on cultural, visual and material texts, and rethinking the politics of the contemporary.

Gopal Guru is professor at the Centre for Political Studies, Jawaharlal Nehru University, New Delhi.

Harbans Mukhia was professor of medieval history at JNU and its rector. Some of his publications are *Historians and Historiography During the Reign of Akbar*,

The Mughals of India; *Exploring India's Medieval Centuries*; among his edited volumes are *Feudalism and Non-European Societies* (with T.J. Byres) centred on his essay 'Was There Feudalism in Indian History?'; *French Studies in History*, 2 vols (with Maurice Aymard); *Religion, Religiosity and Communalism* (with Praful Bidwai and Achin Vanaik); *History of Technology in India*, Vol. II. He is the founder-editor of *The Medieval History Journal*.

Jairus Banaji is research professor at the School of Oriental and African Studies in London, and is actively associated with the journals *Historical Materialism* and *Journal of Agrarian Change*. He grew up in Bombay in the 1950s till his parents left for the UK. In 1965 he won a scholarship to Oxford to study classics, ancient history and modern philosophy, after which he did a diploma and then a B.Litt in social anthropology. In 1972 he decided to come back to India and joined the Centre for Historical Studies in JNU, where he worked with Professor Bipan Chandra. In the mid-1970s he moved to Bombay and became increasingly active with workers there, along with Praful Bidwai, Javed Anand and others. Banaji returned to Oxford in 1986 to start doctoral work in late Roman economic history. This thesis was published as *Agrarian Change in Late Antiquity* (Oxford University Press, 2001; 2007). He was active in Insaaniyat following the Gujarat violence of 2002, working with Anjum Rajabali and others. His latest books include *Fascism: Essays on Europe* and *Exploring the Economy of Late Antiquity: Selected Essays*. Banaji works in several languages, has published widely, and is currently writing a book called *A Brief History of Commercial Capitalism*.

Jayati Ghosh is professor of economics at the Centre for Economic Studies and Planning, School of Social Sciences, Jawaharlal Nehru University, New Delhi. She was educated at Delhi University, Jawaharlal Nehru University and the University of Cambridge, England, where she obtained her PhD in 1983. She has a wide range of research interests, including globalization, international trade and finance, employment patterns in developing countries, macroeconomic policy, issues related to gender and development, and the implications of recent growth in China and India. Her recent books include the edited volume *India and the International Economy* (Oxford University Press, 2015), *Industrialization of China and India: The Impacts on the World Economy* (volume co-edited with Nobuharu Yokokawa and Robert E. Rowthorn, Routledge, 2013), *After Crisis: Adjustment, Recovery and Fragility in East Asia* (co-edited with C.P. Chandrasekhar, Tulika Books, New Delhi, 2009), *Never Done and Poorly Paid: Women's Work in Globalising India* (Women Unlimited, New Delhi, 2008), *Work and Well-being in the Age of Finance* (Tulika Books, New Delhi), *The Market that*

Failed: Neoliberal Economic Reforms in India (Leftword Books, New Delhi). Forthcoming books include the volume co-edited with Erik Reinert and Rainer Kattel, *Elgar Handbook of Alternative Theories of Economic Development* (Edward Elgar, 2016).

Lawrence Liang is a lawyer based in Bangalore. A co-founder of the Alternative Law Forum, Liang has worked on the constitutional dimensions of free speech for many years.

Makarand R. Paranjape has been professor of English at JNU from 1999. His latest work includes *The Death and Afterlife of Mahatma Gandhi* (Penguin Random House, 2015), *Cultural Politics in Modern India* (Routledge, 2016), and an Indo-Brazilian volume of poems, *Transit Passenger/Passageiro em Transito* (University of Sao Paolo Press, 2016).

Mridula Mukherjee taught modern Indian history at JNU for over four decades. Her research interests are in the study of the history of India's struggle for freedom, peasant protest, agrarian economy, social movements and politics after independence, and communalism. She was dean of the School of Social Sciences, JNU, and director, Nehru Memorial Museum and Library. She co-authored with Bipan Chandra and others the bestselling books, *India's Struggle for Independence* and *India Since Independence*, published by Penguin. She is also co-editor of the Sage series in modern Indian history, in which seventeen monographs have been published.

Nivedita Menon, professor at the Centre for Comparative Politics and Political Theory, Jawaharlal Nehru University, Delhi, is the author of *Seeing like a Feminist* (2012). Apart from research papers in Indian and international journals, her previous books are *Recovering Subversion: Feminist Politics Beyond the Law* (2004); and a book co-written with Aditya Nigam, *Power and Contestation: India after 1989* (2007). She also has two edited volumes, *Gender and Politics in India* (1999) and *Sexualities* (2007); and co-edited a book with Aditya Nigam and Sanjay Palshikar, *Critical Studies in Politics. Exploring Sites, Selves, Power* (2013).

Prabhat Patnaik joined the Centre for Economic Studies and Planning of the Jawaharlal Nehru University in 1974 from the University of Cambridge where he was teaching earlier. He retired from the Sukhamoy Chakravarty Chair at the Centre in 2010 and is currently professor emeritus there. His books include *Whatever Happened to Imperialism and Other Essays, Accumulation and*

Stability Under Capitalism, *The Retreat to Unfreedom*, *The Value of Money* and *Re-Envisioning Socialism*. His work *A Theory of Imperialism*, jointly authored with Utsa Patnaik, is forthcoming. He is the editor of the journal *Social Scientist*.

Ranabir Chakravarti, professor of ancient history, Centre for Historical Studies, Jawaharlal Nehru University, New Delhi, specializes in the economic and social history of early India with a particular interest in the maritime trade in the Indian Ocean. In addition to contributing regularly to peer-reviewed journals and edited volumes, Chakravarti has authored/edited ten books, including *A Sourcebook of Indian Civilization* (Hyderabad: Orient Longman, 2000), *Trade in Early India* (New Delhi: Oxford University Press, 2005), *Trade and Traders in Early Indian Society* (New Delhi: Manohar, 2007) and *Exploring Early India* (New Delhi: Primus, 2016). He has recently added annotations to a fourteenth-century Latin Crusade text, *How to Defeat the Saracens* (Washington DC: Dumberton Oaks, 2012).

Romila Thapar is professor emerita at the Centre for Historical Studies, Jawaharlal Nehru University.

Satish Deshpande studied economics at JNU and currently teaches sociology at Delhi University. His most recent books are the edited volumes *Beyond Inclusion: The Practice of Equal Access in Indian Higher Education* (Routledge, 2013) and *The Problem of Caste* (Orient BlackSwan 2014). The Kerala Sasthra Sahithya Parishath (KSSP) published *Samakalika India: Oru Samoohasasthra Veekshanam*, J. Devika's Malayalam translation of his *Contemporary India: A Sociological View* (Penguin, 2003), in 2014.

Satyajit Rath was trained as a physician and a pathologist in Pune and Mumbai, and has worked on mechanisms involved in the development and functioning of the immune system for the past thirty-five years. He has been a faculty member at the National Institute of Immunology in New Delhi since 1991. He is interested in issues related to science policy and works with the government on them. He also works on science and society issues with civil society groups such as the Delhi Science Forum and the Coalition for Nuclear Disarmament and Peace, as well as with groups involved in science education such as Eklavya.

Suvir Kaul is A.M. Rosenthal professor of English at the University of Pennsylvania. He has written *Of Gardens and Graves: Essays on Kashmir, Poems in Translation* (New Delhi: Three Essays Collective, 2015; Durham: Duke

University Press, 2016); *Eighteenth-Century British Literature and Postcolonial Studies* (Edinburgh: Edinburgh University Press, 2009); *Poems of Nation, Anthems of Empire: English Verse in the Long Eighteenth Century* (Charlottesville: The University Press of Virginia, 2000; Delhi: Oxford University Press, 2001), and *Thomas Gray and Literary Authority: Ideology and Poetics in Eighteenth-Century England* (New Delhi: Oxford University Press, 1992; Stanford: Stanford University Press, 1992). He has edited *The Partitions of Memory: The Afterlife of the Division of India* (New Delhi: Permanent Black, 2001; London: C. Hurst, 2001; Bloomington: Indiana University Press, 2002), and co-edited (with Ania Loomba, Antoinette Burton, Matti Bunzl and Jed Esty), *Postcolonial Studies and Beyond* (Durham, Duke University Press, 2005; New Delhi: Permanent Black, 2005). He teaches and writes on eighteenth-century British literature and culture, South Asian writing in English, and critical theory, including postcolonial studies.

Tanika Sarkar retired as professor of modern history from the Centre for Historical Studies, JNU.